Communications in Computer and Information Science 1762

More information about this series at https://link.springer.com/bookseries/7899

Nilay Khare · Deepak Singh Tomar ·
Mitul Kumar Ahirwal · Vijay Bhaskar Semwal ·
Vaibhav Soni (Eds.)

Machine Learning, Image Processing, Network Security and Data Sciences

4th International Conference, MIND 2022
Virtual Event, January 19–20, 2023
Proceedings, Part I

Springer

Editors
Nilay Khare ⓘ
Maulana Azad National Institute
of Technology
Bhopal, India

Deepak Singh Tomar ⓘ
Maulana Azad National Institute
of Technology
Bhopal, India

Mitul Kumar Ahirwal ⓘ
Maulana Azad National Institute
of Technology
Bhopal, India

Vijay Bhaskar Semwal ⓘ
Maulana Azad National Institute
of Technology
Bhopal, India

Vaibhav Soni ⓘ
Maulana Azad National Institute
of Technology
Bhopal, India

ISSN 1865-0929   ISSN 1865-0937 (electronic)
Communications in Computer and Information Science
ISBN 978-3-031-24351-6   ISBN 978-3-031-24352-3 (eBook)
https://doi.org/10.1007/978-3-031-24352-3

This Springer imprint is published by the registered company Springer Nature Switzerland AG
The registered company address is: Gewerbestrasse 11, 6330 Cham, Switzerland

Preface

On behalf of the department of Computer Science and Engineering, Maulana Azad National Institute of Technology, Bhopal, India, we are pleased to present the proceedings of the 4th International Conference on Machine Learning, Image Processing, Network Security and Data Sciences (MIND 2022). First, we would like to express our appreciation to the organizing committee for their constant efforts in managing this conference. The first edition in the MIND conference series (MIND 2019) was organized at NIT Kurukshetra, with the second and third editions (MIND 2020 and 2021) organized by NIT Silchar and NIT Raipur, respectively.

This conference was planned to highlight the wide range of engineering research work carried out in different industries and academic institutions, focusing on machine learning and computational intelligence, data sciences, image processing and computer vision, and network and cyber security. The MIND 2022 conference tracks represented distinct platforms for the discussion and exchange of ideas amongst national and international research scholars and professionals, successfully disseminating interdisciplinary knowledge in each track.

The MIND 2022 conference provided a wide-ranging view of the current state of the art, along with inspiration and motivation to attendees which we hope will help them to develop suggestions and strong recommendations to understand and further recent research topics and their challenges.

In response to the call for papers, MIND 2022 received 399 submissions from which only 119 papers were selected by the Program Committee (PC) for presentation. Out of these, only 64 papers were selected for publication in the proceedings (Springer CCIS Volumes 1762 and 1763). Each submission was reviewed (single blind) by at least three PC members or invited reviewers, experts in their fields, in order to supply detailed and helpful comments.

The conference featured three invited lectures:

- Genci Capi (Assistive Robotics Laboratory, HOSEI University, Japan) addressed "Machine Learning and Computational Intelligence",
- Akhtar Kalam (Victoria University, Melbourne, Australia) covered "Data Science & Engineering", and
- Youngshik Kim (Department of Mechanical Engineering, Hanbat National University, South Korea) spoke about "Neural Network-based state estimation for robotic systems".

We would like to thank the keynote speakers and all members of all the conference committees, especially the reviewers who worked very hard in reviewing papers and suggesting valuable comments to the authors for improvement of their work. We also would like to express our gratitude to the authors for contributing their research work to the conference. Special thanks go to the CCIS team at Springer for publishing the conference proceedings.

January 2023

Nilay Khare
Deepak Singh Tomar
Mitul Kumar Ahirwal
Vijay Bhaskar Semwal
Vaibhav Soni

Organization

Program Chairs

Nilay Khare (Chair)   MANIT Bhopal, India
Deepak Singh Tomar (Co-chair)   MANIT Bhopal, India

General Chairs

Meenu Chawla   MANIT Bhopal, India
Rajesh Kumar Pateriya   MANIT Bhopal, India

Publication Chairs

Mitul Kumar Ahirwal   MANIT Bhopal, India
Vijay Bhaskar Semwal   MANIT Bhopal, India
Vaibhav Soni   MANIT Bhopal, India

Founding Chairs

Gyanendra Verma   NIT Raipur, India
Rajesh Doriya   NIT Raipur, India

Advisory Board

Meenu Chawla (Chair)   MANIT Bhopal, India
Jyoti Singhai (Convenor)   MANIT Bhopal, India
Ram Bilas Pachori   IIT Indore, India
G. K. Singh   IIT Roorkee, India
Daniel Thalmann   EPFL, Switzerland
Zoran Bojkovic   University of Belgrade, Serbia
Salah Bourennane   École Centrale de Marseille, France
Pasanta K. Jana   IIT Dhanbad, India
G. C. Nandi   IIIT Allahabad, India
O. P. Vyas   IIIT Allahabad, India
Shekhar Verma   IIIT Allahabad, India
Anupam Shukla   IIIT Pune, India
Durga Prasad Mahapatra   NIT Rourkela, India
Harnath Kar   MNNIT Allahabad, India

Dheeresh K. Mallick	BIT Mesra, India
N. D. Londhe	NIT Raipur, India
Anil Kumar	IIIT Jabalpur, India
Pabitra Mohan Khilar	NIT Rourkela, India
Pavan Chakraborty	IIIT Allahabad, India
Satish Kumar Singh	IIIT Allahabad, India
Dilip Singh Sisodia	NIT Raipur, India
Bui Thanh Hung	Ton Duc Thang University, Vietnam
Balas Valentina Emilia	Aurel Vlaicu University of Arad, Romania
Ruben Gonzalez Crespo	UNIR, Spain
Zheng Xu	Shanghai University, China

Program Committee

Rajesh Kumar Pateriya (Chair)	MANIT Bhopal, India
Sanyam Shukla (Convenor)	MANIT Bhopal, India
Vasudev Dehalwar	MANIT Bhopal, India
Manish Pandey	MANIT Bhopal, India
Jyoti Bharti	MANIT Bhopal, India
Manasi Gyanchandani	MANIT Bhopal, India
Sweta Jain	MANIT Bhopal, India
Sri Khetwat Saritha	MANIT Bhopal, India
B. N. Roy	MANIT Bhopal, India
Ghanapriya Singh	NIT Uttarakhand, India
Shivram Dubey	IIIT Allahabad, India
Somesh Kumar	IIITM Gwalior, India
Debanjan Sadhya	IIITM Gwalior, India
Santosh Singh Rathore	IIITM Gwalior, India
Rajesh Wadhvani	MANIT Bhopal, India
Sanyam Shukla	MANIT Bhopal, India
Akhtar Rasool	MANIT Bhopal, India
Jaytrilok Choudhary	MANIT Bhopal, India
Dhirendra Pratap Singh	MANIT Bhopal, India
Namita Tiwari	MANIT Bhopal, India
Pragati Agrawal	MANIT Bhopal, India
Rajesh Doriya	NIT Raipur, India
Rahul Semwal	IIIT Nagpur, India
Jay Prakash	NIT Calicut, India
Basudeb Behra	NIT Jamshedpur, India
Kukil Khanikar	IIIT Guwahati, India
Badal Soni	NIT Silchar, India
Tirath Prasad Sahu	NIT Raipur, India
Sanjay Kumar	NIT Raipur, India

Rekh Ram Janghel	NIT Raipur, India
Deepak K. T.	IIIT Dharwad, India
Rajendra Hegadi	IIIT Dharwad, India
Urmila Shrawankar	G. H. Raisoni College of Engineering, Nagpur, India
Rajesh Wadvani	MANIT Bhopal, India
Pooja Jain	IIIT Nagpur, India
Anupam Biswas	NIT Silchar, India
Somendu Chakraborty	IIIT Lucknow, India

Additional Reviewers

Daniel Thalmann	Swiss Federal Institute of Technology Lausanne, Switzerland
Zoran Bojkovic	University of Belgrade, Serbia
Salah Bourennane	École Centrale de Marseille, France
Ram Bilas Pachori	IIT Indore, India
José Mario De Martino	University of Campinas, Brazil
Félix J. García Clemente	Universidad de Murcia, Spain
Marcelo Sampaio de Alencar	Universidade Federal de Campina Grande, Brazil
Wei-Chiang Hong	Asia Eastern University of Science and Technology, Taiwan
Dimitrios Alexios Karras	National and Kapodistrian University of Athens, Greece
Alexandre Carlos Brandao Ramos	Universidade Federal de Itajubá, Brazil
Kamran Arshad	Ajman University, UAE
Pradip K. Das	IIT Guwahati, India
Pascal Lorenz	University of Haute-Alsace, France
Zhao Yang	Pacific Northwest National Laboratory, USA
Tomasz Rak	Rzeszow University of Technology, Poland
Uttam Ghosh	Vanderbilt University, USA
Pradip Sharma	Aberdeen University, UK
Arpad Gellert	Lucian Blaga University of Sibiu, Romania
José Antonio Marmolejo Saucedo	Universidad Panamericana, Mexico
Raffaele Pizzolante	University of Salerno, Italy
Georgia Garani	University of Thessaly, Larissa, Greece
Adem Alpaslan Altun	Selçuk Üniversitesi, Turkey
Rajeev Shrivastava	IIT BHU, India
Viranjay M. Srivastava	University of KwaZulu-Natal, Durban, South Africa
Ashutosh Kumar Singh	NIT Kurukshetra, India
Sabe Abd-Allah	Beni-Suef University, Egypt
Eugénia Moreira Bernardino	Polytechnic of Leiria, Portugal

Rajiv Misra	IIT Patna, India
Carlos Becker Westphall	Federal University of Santa Catarina, Brazil
Dinesh K. Vishwakarma	Delhi Technological University, India
Miroslav Škorić	University of Novi Sad, Serbia
H. K. Sardana	CSIR Chandigarh, India
K. K. Shukla	IIT BHU, India
Shuai Zhao	Amazon Alexa AI, USA
Manoj Kumar Singh	Banaras Hindu University, India
S. M. Warusia Yassin	Universiti Teknikal Malaysia Melaka, Malaysia
Annappa	NIT Surathkal, India
Madhusudan Singh	Yonsei University, South Korea
Pabitra Mitra	IIT Kharagpur, India
Abdul Jalil M. Khalaf	Ministry of Higher Education and Scientific Research, Iraq
Subhrakanta Panda	BITS Pilani, Hyderabad, India
Ajay Kumar Lal	Nepal Engineering College, Bhaktapur, Nepal
Reham R. Mostafa	Mansoura University, Egypt
Dimitrios A. Karras	National Technical University of Athens, Greece
Korhan Cengiz	Trakya University Edirne, Turkey
Sherif S. Rashad	Morehead State University, USA
Vishal Passricha	Central University of Haryana, India
Reeta Sony	JNU New Delhi, India
Satish Kumar Singh	IIIT Allahabad, India
Syed Taqi Ali	VNIT Nagpur, India
A. C. S. Rao	IIT Dhanbad, India
Tarachand Amgoth	IIT Dhanbad, India
Pilli Emmanuel Shubhakar	MNIT Jaipur, India
G. R. Gangadharan	NIT Trichy, India
Pratik Chattopadhyay	IIT BHU, India
Veenu Mangat	UIET Panjab University, India
Bhupesh Kumar Singh	GBPUAT Pantnagar, India
Shyam Lal	NIT Karnataka, India
Ravi Panwar	IIITDM, Jabalpur, India
Poonam Saini	PEC Chandigarh, India
M. P. S. Chawla	SGSITS Indore, India
Anshul Verma	Banaras Hindu University, India
Vibha Vyas	College of Engineering Pune, India
S. Sridevi	Thiagarajar College of Engineering, India
K. Anitha Kumari	PSG College of Technology, India
Narendra Kohli	HBTU Kanpur, India
Ashish Khare	Allahabad University, India
Pankaj Pratap Singh	CIT Kokrajhar, India

Koushlendra Kumar Singh	NIT Jamshedpur, India
Aakanksha Sharaff	NIT Raipur, India
Vijay Bhaskar Semwal	MANIT Bhopal, India
Srinivas Koppu	VIT Vellore, India
Debajyoti Choudhuri	NIT Rourkela, India
Jayapandian N.	Christ University, India
Veena Anand	NIT Raipur, India
D. Jude Hemanth	Karunya Institute of Technology and Sciences, India
Vinutha D. C.	Vidyavardhaka College of Engineering, India
A. Muthumari	University College of Engineering, Ramanathapuram, India
Sravani Devi Y.	G Narayanamma Institute of Technology and Science, India
Dhanaraj	SMS College of Arts and Science, India
Akhilesh Tiwari	MITS Gwalior, India
Naresh Babu Muppalaneni	NIT Silchar, India
Tripti Goel	NIT Silchar, India
Sachin K. Jai	IIITDM Jabalpur, India
Deepak Gupta	NIT Arunachal Pradesh, India

Publicity and Website Committee

Saritha Khetawat (Chair)	MANIT Bhopal, India
Vijay Bhaskar Semwal (Convenor)	MANIT Bhopal, India
Mitul Kumar Ahirwal	MANIT Bhopal, India
Vishwanath Bijalwan	Institute of Technology Gopeshwar, India
Koshlendra Kumar	NIT Jamshedpur, India
Arun Kumar	NIT Rourkela, India
Lakshman Mahato	IIIT Dharwad, India
Jagadish Devagoda	IIIT Dharwad, India
Arun Kumar	IIITM Gwalior, India
Raul Kumar Chaurasiya	MANIT Bhopal, India

Organizing Committee

Narendra Singh Raghuwanshi	MANIT Bhopal, India
Manisha Dubey	MANIT Bhopal, India
Nilay Khare	MANIT Bhopal, India
Deepak Singh Tomar	MANIT Bhopal, India
Vijay B. Semwal	MANIT Bhopal, India
Mitul K. Ahirwal	MANIT Bhopal, India
Vaibhav Soni	MANIT Bhopal, India

Organizing Institution

Computer Science and Engineering Department, Maulana Azad National Institute of Technology, Bhopal, India

Contents – Part I

Data Sciences

Contents – Part II

Network and Cyber Security

Machine Learning and Computational Intelligence

Cardiac Arrhythmia Classification Using Cascaded Deep Learning Approach (LSTM & RNN)

Jay Prakash Maurya[1]([⊠]) [iD], Manish Manoria[2] [iD], and Sunil Joshi[1] [iD]

[1] Samrat Ashok Technological Institute, Vidisha, India
jpeemaurya@gmail.com
[2] Technocrats Group of Institution, Bhopal, India

Abstract. Diseases related to human cardiac system are very common now-days. Activities within the patient's cardiac system can be captured using an electrical conduction system and mapped on a waveform named an electrocardiogram (ECG). The abnormal heartbeats, or arrhythmias, can be seen in the ECG data. ECG signal data is vast and calls for many qualified medical professionals and resources. Machine learning has become a vast field of study to uncover the properties of ECG signals. Traditional approaches need additional efforts in feature extraction to support designing a more optimal system. Patients' acute and chronic heart problems must be accurately diagnosed using deep machine learning. A deep learning model can be evaluated on the MIT-BIH dataset, it has available ECG data for medical research and practices. In spite of the fact that CNN accomplishes well enough to improve computer-based diagnosis. Computer automatic diagnosis in the medical field along with present-day ML techniques may be accurate and efficient in this area. An optimal deep model design & procedures for classification of electrocardiogram waveform would be helpful to bring off medical resources and brush-up research trials. In this paper, a cascade model of LSTM and RNN is proposed and compared with the existing single model on the necessary parameters to judge. Experimental evaluation is to classify irregularities in ECG signal 12 lead data collected from MIT-BIH and classified through a proposed cascading model. The proposed cascaded model archived 89.9% accuracy with 93.46% sensitivity and 84.36% specificity. The comparison results show that LSTM with RNN suits real-time generated data sequences like ECG.

Keywords: Deep learning · Cardiac disease · Arrhythmia · ECG · CNN · LSTM · RNN

1 Introduction

In the whole world, 31% of deaths in human beings were reported due to cardiovascular issues, and among these, 85% were caused by heart attacks in human beings in the year 2016 [1]. ECG (electrocardiogram) is a time series signal in real time that is generated for each cardiac cycle of the human heart with the help of electrical signal modulation.

N. Khare et al. (Eds.): MIND 2022, CCIS 1762, pp. 3–13, 2022.
https://doi.org/10.1007/978-3-031-24352-3_1

Manual and automatic ECG signal analysis by medical resources is a way to examine the heart. The clinical assessments and medical histories of each individual patient are at the core of the traditional cardiovascular diagnosis concept. In order to categorize people according to the taxonomy of medical diseases, these findings are examined using a set of quantitative medical features. Manual identification of heart diseases is time-consuming and needs more experience to be accurate. It may cause false results also. Quick and accurate analysis of ECG signals and classification is a new area. Moreover, diagnosis results may be unsteady due to ECG's random nature, susceptibility, and low frequency.

ECG signal has some essential indication in record, shows electrophysiological incident that collides with a series of depolarization and re-polarization in the heart's atria and ventricles [10]. Heart beat signals are generally represented by three main events: P wave, T wave, and QRS complex [10], shown in Fig. 1. To detect cardiac arrhythmias, each event has its own unique peak, making it critical to examine their form, amplitude, and duration. Their analysis can also be useful for detecting breathing abnormalities like obstructive sleep apnea syndrome [4], in addition to researching the autonomic regulation of the cardiovascular mechanism for humans with hypertension.

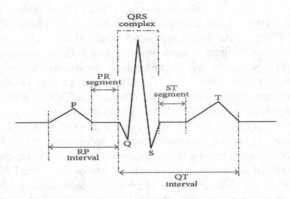

Fig. 1. ECG normal signal waves

The ECG signal structure depicts the heart's status by mentioning two primary sources of information. One is to examine the time interval, and second is to measure the robustness of the electric signal. A cardiologist can assess the timeframe and amplitude required for an electrical pulse that travel through heart. The ECG signal's regularity and rapidity help cardiologists diagnose and foretell disease. Figure 2 depicts an explanation of the various irregularities based on the three key waves: P, QRS complex, and T. Types of arrhythmia disorder can be explained using the given waves and the below sequence of terms. The flow process is to identify the cardiac arrhythmia is shown in Fig. 3, and categorical impacts on ECG signals are categorized into different conditions of ECG signal shape [3].

In review of articles related to the work given in reference section, different techniques of classification on image dataset and numerical dataset have been studied. Last article worked on SVM, decision tree, CNN, LSTM and GRU for their experiment. Last articles show good results but from time-to-time improvements in results on referenced parameters to evaluate experiments must be needed. This paper presents a proposed computer-based diagnosis system (CADS) for the diagnosis of arrhythmia. The proposed work used a publicly available ECG dataset, MIT-BIH. Experimental work employee deep learning method on MIT-BIH and results was compared for CNN, RNN, LSTM and proposed model. This work is structured so that Sect. 2 gives a quick overview of DL approaches [3, 9] and Sect. (3) is related to the proposed work & methodology. Section 4 relates to the experimental setup. The last Sect. (5) concludes and shows the results of the experiment.

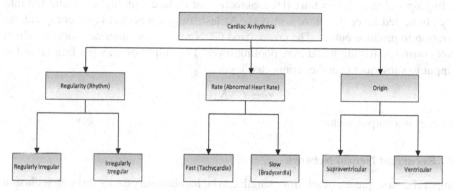

Fig. 2. Cardiac disorder classification attribute

2 Deep Learning Techniques

Deep learning (DL) techniques majorly involved in classification and prediction in different healthcare domain. DL approaches have recently been discovered to be fast developing; having an appreciable impact on classification accuracy is extensive for medical applications [7]. Modern CADS systems use arrhythmia detection in collected ECG signals, lowering the cost of continuous heart monitoring and boosting prediction quality. In medical image analysis, deep learning algorithms are widely used and basic neural network is called deep neural network. A deep neural network (DNN) is set up similarly to the way the human brain is. Neuron is a smallest unit in DNN. Neurons can learn by reiteration in activities and experience gain, same as human brain learned [29]. Some DL methods are discussed in this section.

2.1 Convolutional Neural Network (CNN)

This artificial neural network has a connected architecture as INPUT-CONV-POOL-FC where INPUT- Input, CONV- Convolutional layer, POOL- Pooling layer, FC- fully connected layer. CNN may feed time series, one dimensional (1-D) input in sequential time instant [43]. 1-D input vector can be shown as $y = (y_1, y_2, ..., y_{n-1}, y_n, CL,)$ where

$y_n \in R^d$, R represents class label. Feature map (FM) can be evaluated using following equation

$$HL_i^{FM} = tanh\left(w^{FM}y_{i+f-1} + bias\right) \qquad (1)$$

HL is a filter applied on features set (**f**) in input, feature map is mapped as **HL** = (**hl**$_1$, **hl**$_2$..............**hl**$_{n-f+1}$). In CNN model transfer convoluted output to pooling layer. Pooling completes the down sampling process while the convolutional layer utilizes activation functions like ReLU or Softtmax (X). Each operation map receives the max-pooling operation as HL = max (HL). Selection of feature with highest value fed into fully connected layer that have soft-max. At last, fully connected layer complete the operation to produce output. The customized CNN may use another network, in which CNN consist convolution and max pooling layer. The output of max pooling layer fed as input to subsequent another connected layers.

$$z_i = CNN(y_i) \qquad (2)$$

where, z_i is a output vector.

2.2 Recurrent Neural Network

Temporal data sequence of arbitrary length can be handled very easily through inclusion of feed forward network and feedback loop in simple perceptron known as RNN. Loops in network work as short memory element over time scale, to hold and extract data. RNN has the ability to swap out its attribute between time-stamp to keep away from specific nature when processing random sequences of any length. RNNs are basically models that can learn behaviors like dynamic and temporal for variable, inconsistent sequences of input-output [44]. RNN is mostly used in AI, mainly in time-consuming jobs like speech recognition, language modelling, and machine translation.

$$H(y, h) = f\left(w_{yh}\, y + w_{hh}h + bias\right) \qquad (3)$$

$$H = R^d X R^h \rightarrow R^k \qquad (4)$$

w$_{yh}$, w$_{hh}$, w$_{ho}$ - weight matrices, input layer (**y**), hidden layer (**h**), nonlinear activation function (**f**), **H** represents small memory created by feedback loop from h into k.

2.3 Long Short-Term Memory (LSTM)

To manage problem gradients, **LSTM** works with memory cells in place of traditional simple RNN block. Long-term dependencies are handled far well by LSTM compared to typical RNNs, because LSTMs can seek prior information that is far back in instance with present [17]. The data sequence is **y** = (y$_1$, y$_{2....}$, y$_{t-1}$, y$_t$) as input and **o** = (o$_1$, o$_2$, ... o$_t$) as output having read, write and reset operation with multiplication on (*in:* **input**), (*ot:* **output**), and (*fr:* **forget gate**)) and (*CL:* memory cell). Operation on LSTM is defined on time stamp T with (y$_t$, h$_{t-1}$, CL$_{t-1}$ -> h$_t$, CL$_t$)

$$in_t = \sigma(w_{yin}y_t + w_{hin}h_{t-1} + w_{CLin}cl_{t-1} + bias_{in}) \qquad (5)$$

$$fr_t = \sigma(w_{yfr}y_t + w_{hfr}h_{t-1} + w_{CLfr}CL_{t-1} + bias_{fr} \tag{6}$$

$$CL_t = fr_t.CL_{t-1} + in_t \odot \tanh(w_{yCL}y_t + w_{hCL}h_{t-1} + bias_{CL}) \tag{7}$$

$$ot_t = \sigma(w_{yot}x_t + w_{hot}h_{t-1} + w_{CLot}CL_{t-1} + bias_{ot}) \tag{8}$$

$$h_t = ot_t \odot \tan h(CL_t) \tag{9}$$

The memory cell stores data over numerous steps for assisting three adaptive gated components that functions for multiplication. The I/O gate manages memory cell's activation and input-output flow. In the case of self-recurrence where weight values are irrelevant, forget gate reset values.

2.4 Gated Recurrent Unit (GRU)

This is the advancement in LSTM with a smaller number of parameters [14]. GRU gives less computational cost and takes less memory consumption, compared to LSTM. Mathematical equation for computation in GRU is given

$$i - f_t = \sigma(w_{FMi-f}FM_t + w_{h-f}h_{t-1} + bias_{i-f})(\textbf{updated gate}) \tag{10}$$

$$f_t = \sigma(w_{FMf}FM_t + w_{fh}h_{t-1} + bias_f) \tag{11}$$

$$CL_t = \tanh(w_{FMc}FM_t + w_{hc}(f \odot h_{t-1}) + bias_c \tag{12}$$

$$h_t = (f \odot \mathbf{h}_{t-1} + (1 - \mathbf{f}) \odot \mathbf{CL}) \,(\textbf{Updated Memory}) \tag{13}$$

where **FM** is a new feature vector computed from model like **CNN**, construct a hybrid network.

3 Proposed Work and Methodology

The overview of proposed of work is shown in Fig. 3. Due to inter-patient variability in ECG data, traditional machine learning approaches may not produce effective results. Additionally, the quality and effectiveness of current systems may suffer from the growing volume of data. Previous work in this area focused on smaller datasets; nevertheless, the performance needs be tested on bigger datasets for generalization. Therefore, proposed work was involved for finding out optimized configuration of DL model in terms of performance parameter shown in Table 2. Experimental setup of DL model has been discussed in next section. A typical flow process has been shown in Fig. 4 and step incorporated are also mention below. It is also noticed here from reviewed article that the performance of 1-D ECG signal techniques can be improved further. This proposed work focuses towards cascaded model using RNN and bidirectional LSTM to on 12 lead ECG.

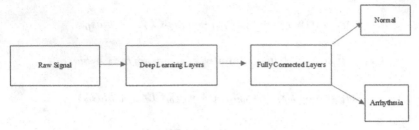

Fig. 3. Proposed Deep Learning architecture

Proposed Methodology Steps:

Step 1. Reading Input ECG data: ECG Data is collected from MIT Database.

Step 2. Data Cleaning: Removing irrelevant structures not appropriate for Work.

Step 3. Segmenting and Feature Extraction: Extracting exact area and information present in ECG waveform for signal peak.

Step 4. Feature Selection: Selecting appropriate features information.

Step 5. Data Augmentation: Creating Synthetic data for the increasing amount of learning.

Step 6. Creating Training & Test Sample: Partitioning the full dataset

Step 7. Create Cascaded model (RNN + LSTM): Creating a cascade model for learning and tested on sample

Step 8. To calculate and compare the performance: Performance is measured and compared with previous models.

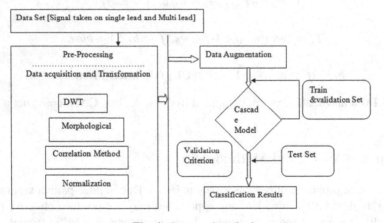

Fig. 4. Proposed method

In preprocessing data acquisition system (also known as a DAS) translates physical properties into digital form, which can then be stored and analyzed. Signals from sensors are typically sampled, transformed to digital, and stored by a computer or a separate device (often with the help of sensor). Here, in this case of ECG signal, the captured image has been taken for data acquisition and Transformation. The next step is to discrete wavelet transformation operation; an image can be analyzed by combining analysis filter bank and decimation operation. Signal decomposition in several set having time series of co-efficient is completed through DWT. Morphological procedures manipulate image data according to shapes. The actual operation in morphological procedure is that each pixel correlates with the pixels in its immediate surroundings. Finally, normalization and correlation have been set up for creating datasets ready for the learning process. Normalization is a technique for reducing the range of a dataset's attributes to a narrower range. Normalization converts all of the features of a dataset into a preset criterion so that redundant or noisy items can be removed and legitimate and reliable data can be used, which can both effect and increase the correctness of the output. Min-max, Z-score, and decimal scaling are some typical types of data normalization.

4 Experimental Setup

The MIT-BIH dataset has 47 records of 30 min each and in which 40% records are cardiac patients. This dataset contained different signal based on leads. Collected MIT data was divided 70–30 ratio for Training and Testing. Dataset signal record was divided into chunks 720 each. The core beat would be classed against arrhythmic labels since the sampling rate was 360, before and after R wave. It ensures the possibility of three beats per waveform cycle. Three primary measurements accuracy, specificity, and sensitivity were utilized to appraise performance of the proposed model. These measurements are characterized using a confusion matrix. As a result, the proportion of True Positive finding should be more in comparison to other finding for the algorithm to function properly and accurately. Classification accuracy is the total number of heartbeats correctly identified as either a normal beat or an arrhythmia.

Table 1. Confusion matrix

Total Population		Predicted Condition	
		Positive (P)	Negative (N)
Actual Condition	Positive (P)	15820	1298
	Negative (N)	1835	9188

As per the model implementation is concerned with proposed cascaded LSTM and RNN model was trained, tested and shows the results based on mentioned parameters in Tables 1 and 2.

Table 2. Classification results

Model	Accuracy	Sensitivity	Specificity
CNN	88.87	89.16	87.62
LSTM	89.06	89.15	88.14
RNN	85.1	80.13	82.25
LSTM + RNN	89.89	93.46	84.36

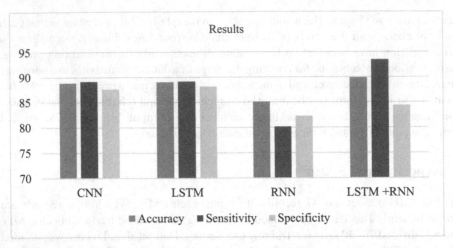

Fig. 5. Results comparison

5   Result and Future Scope

The results of worked carried are shown in Fig. 5. The background work already done in this field are compared on parameters accuracy, specificity and sensitivity. Results after experiments are found batter in the proposed method. The proposed method results in greater sensitivity, accuracy, and less specificity compared to previous works. The above results have been taken on 5 iteration of 3 hidden layer CNN with 64, 256, neurons per hidden layer and 2 pooling layers. LSTM model performs better in the entire above model implemented these models are implemented with augmentation. The cascaded model of RNN and LSTM does well as compared to the individual model. LSTM works well on time series data sequence of ECG while CNN can be worked well where direct work is executed on images. It is a future work that we are proposing to include the implementation of CNN, LSTM cascade model with reconfiguration of attributed to achieve good result compare to another existing model shown in Fig. 5 and Table 2. Next level in future work is to performs multiclass classification on mutlilead data. More accuracy may be resulted by increase in epochs or reconfiguring the structure. The experiment result expresses that the binary classification of ECG arrhythmias performs best with long-term memory with RNN and that future work on the classification can be done using Faster R-CNN on the MIT BIH dataset. The hidden layer's epoch and neuron counts may be increased even more during the classification process.

Acknowledgement. I am very thankful to Dr. Pankaj Manoria, (Cardiologist), who provide me a direct support to align deep learning area with health care domain and better understanding of ECG equipment and signal analysis for arrhythmia.

References

1. Acharya, U.R., Fujita, H., Lih, O.S., Hagiwara, Y., Tan, J.H., Adam, M.: Automated detection of arrhythmias using different intervals of tachycardia ECG segments with convolutional neural network. Inf. Sci. **405**, 81–90 (2017)
2. Acharya, U.R., Fujita, H., Oh, S.L., Hagiwara, Y., Tan, J.H., Adam, M.: Application of deep convolutional neural network for automated detection of myocardial infarction using ECG signals. Inf. Sci. **415**, 190–198 (2017)
3. Acharya, U.R., et al.: Deep convolutional neural network for the automated diagnosis of congestive heart failure using ECG signals. Appl. Intell. **49**(1), 16–27 (2019)
4. Acharya, U.R., et al.: Automated identification of shockable and non-shockable life-threatening ventricular arrhythmias using convolutional neural network. Futur. Gener. Comput. Syst. **79**, 952–959 (2018)
5. Acharya, U.R., et al.: A deep convolutional neural network model to classify heartbeats. Comput. Biol. Med. **89**, 389–396 (2017)
6. Al Rahhal, M.M., Bazi, Y., Al Zuair, M., Othman, E., BenJdira, B.: Convolutional neural networks for electrocardiogram classification. J. Med. Biol. Eng. **38**(6), 1014–1025 (2018)
7. Andersen, R.S., Peimankar, A., Puthusserypady, S.: A deep learning approach for real-time detection of atrial fibrillation. Expert Syst. Appl. **115**, 465–473 (2019)
8. Andreotti, F., Carr, O., Pimentel, M.A., Mahdi, A., De Vos, M.: Comparing feature-based classifiers and convolutional neural networks to detect arrhythmia from short segments of ECG. In: Proceeding of IEEE Computing in Cardiology (CINC), pp. 1–4. IEEE (2017)
9. Benjamin, E.J., et al.: Heart disease and stroke statistics-2018 update: a report from the American heart association. Circulation **137** (12), e67 (2018)
10. Bizopoulos, P., Koutsouris, D.: Deep learning in cardiology. IEEE Rev. Biomed. Eng. **12**, 168–193 (2018)
11. Chamatidis, I., Katsika, A., Spathoulas, G.: Using deep learning neural networks for ECG based authentication. In: 2017 International Carnahan Conference on Security Technology (iccst), pp. 1–6. IEEE (2017)
12. Chandra, B., Sastry, C.S., Jana, S., Patidar, S.: Atrial fibrillation detection using convolutional neural networks. In: 2017 Computing in Cardiology (CINC), pp. 1–4. IEEE (2017)
13. Chen, M., et al.: Region aggregation network: Improving convolutional neural network for ECG characteristic detection. In: 2018 40th Annual International Conference of the IEEE Engineering in Medicine and Biology Society (EMBC), pp. 2559–2562. IEEE (2018)
14. Can, T., et al.: Gating creates slow modes and controls phase-space complexity In: GRUs and LSTMs. PMLR, Proceedings. Mlr .press, 16 August 2020 (2020). http://proceedings.mlr.press/v107/can20a
15. Dewangan, N.K., Shukla, S.: A survey on ECG signal feature extraction and analysis techniques. Int. J. Innov. Res. Electr. Electron. Instrum. Control Eng. **3**(6) (2015)
16. Dinakarrao, S.M.P., Jantsch, A., Shafique, M.: Computer-aided arrhythmia diagnosis with bio-signal processing: a survey of trends and techniques. ACM Comput. Surv. (CSUR) **52**(2), 23 (2019)
17. Dua, D., Graff, C.: UCI machine learning repository (2017). http://archive.ics.uci.edu/ml
18. Fan, X., Yao, Q., Cai, Y., Miao, F., Sun, F., Li, Y.: Multiscaled fusion of deep convolutional neural networks for screening atrial fibrillation from single lead short ECG recordings. IEEE J. Biomed. Health Inform. **22**(6), 1744–1753 (2018)
19. Faust, O., Shenfield, A., Kareem, M., San, T.R., Fujita, H., Acharya, U.R.: Automated detection of atrial fibrillation using long short-term memory network with RR interval signals. Comput. Biol. Med. **102**, 327–335 (2018)

20. Gharehbaghi, A., Babic, A.: Structural risk evaluation of a deep neural network and a Markov model in extracting medical information from phonocardiography. Stud. Health Technol. Inform. **251**, 157–160 (2018)
21. Gharehbaghi, A., Babic, A., Sepehri, A.A.: Extraction of diagnostic information from phono-cardiographic signal using time-growing neural network. In: Lhotska, L., Sukupova, L., Lack-ović, I., Ibbott, G. (eds.) World Congress on Medical Physics and Biomedical Engineering 2018. IFMBE Proceedings, vol. 68/3, pp. 849–853. Springer, Singapore (2019). https://doi.org/10.1007/978-981-10-9023-3_153
22. Gharehbaghi, A., Lindén, M., Babic, A.: An artificial intelligent-based model for detecting systolic pathological patterns of phonocardiogram based on time-growing neural network. Appl. Soft Comput. **83**, 105615 (2019). https://doi.org/10.1016/j.asoc.2019.105615
23. Gharehbaghi, A., Lindn, M.: A deep machine learning method for classifying cyclic time series of biological signals using time-growing neural network. IEEE Trans. Neural Netw. Learn. Syst. **29**(9), 4102–4115 (2018). https://doi.org/10.1109/TNNLS.2017.2754294
24. Ghiasi, S., Abdollahpur, M., Madani, N., Kiani, K., Ghaffari, A.: Atrial fibrillation detection using feature based algorithm and deep convolutional neural network. In: 2017 Computing in Cardiology (CINC), pp. 1–4. IEEE (2017)
25. Goodfellow, I., Bengio, Y., Courville, A.: Deep Learning. MIT press, Cambridge (2016)
26. He, K., Zhang, X., Ren, S., Sun, J.: Spatial pyramid pooling in deep convolutional networks for visual recognition. IEEE Trans. Pattern Anal. Mach. Intell. (2015).https://doi.org/10.1109/TPAMI.2015.2389824
27. Hinton, G.E., Sejnowski, T.J., et al.: Learning and relearning in Boltzmann machines. Parallel Distrib. Process. Explor. Microstruct. Cognit. **1**(282–317), 2 (1986)
28. Huff, J.: ECG Workout: Exercises in Arrhythmia Interpretation. Lippincott Williams & Wilkins, Philadelphia (2006)
29. Jambukia, S.H., Dabhi, V.K., Prajapati: Cardiac arrhythmia detection using deep learning. Procedia Comput. Sci. **120**, 268–275 (2019)
30. Ji, J., Chen, X., Luo, C., Li, P.: A deep multi-task learning approach for ECG data analysis. In: 2018 IEEE EMBS International Conference on Biomedical & Health Informatics (BHI), pp. 124–127. IEEE (2018)
31. Joshi, A.J., Chandran, S., Jayaraman, V.K., Kulkarni, B.D.: Hybrid SVM for multiclass arrhythmia classification. In: 2009 IEEE International Conference on Bioinformatics and Biomedicine, pp. 287–290. IEEE (2018)
32. Jun, T.J., Nguyen, H.M., Kang, D., Kim, D., Kim, D., Kim, Y.-H.: ECG arrhythmia classification using a 2-d convolutional neural network. arXiv:1804.06812 (2018)
33. Kamaleswaran, R., Mahajan, R., Akbilgic, O.: A robust deep convolutional neural network for the classification of abnormal cardiac rhythm using single lead electrocardiograms of variable length. Physiol. Meas. **39**(3), 035006 (2018)
34. Kasper, D.L., Fauci, A.S., Hauser, S.L., Longo, D.L., Jameson, J.L., Loscalzo, J.: Harrison's Principles of Internal Medicine, (Vol. 1 & Vol. 2). Mc-Graw Hill Professional, New York City (2018)
35. Khan, A.H., et al.: Arrhythmia classification techniques using deep neural network, 20 April 2021. https://www.hindawi.com/
36. Keyvanrad, M.A., Homayounpour, M.M.: Deep belief network training improvement using elite samples minimizing free energy. Int. J. Pattern Recognit. Artif. Intell. **29**(05), 1551006 (2015)
37. Krizhevsky, A., Sutskever, I., Hinton, G.E.: ImageNet classification with deep convolutional neural networks. Adv. Neural Inf. Process. Syst. (2012)
38. Labati, R.D., Muñoz, E., Piuri, V., Sassi, R., Scotti, F.: Deep-ECG: convolutional neural networks for ECG biometric recognition. Pattern Recognit. Lett. (2018)

39. Liang, Y., et al.: Deep Learning Algorithm Classifies Heartbeat Events Based On Electro-cardiogram Signals. Frontiers (2020), https://www.frontiersin.org/, 1 January. 2020. https://www.frontiersin.org/articles/10.3389/fphys.2020.569050/full
40. LeCun, Y., Bottou, L., Bengio, Y., Haffner, P.: Gradient-based learning applied to document recognition. Proc. IEEE (1998). https://doi.org/10.1109/5.726791.Li,D
41. Zhang, J., Zhang, Q., Wei, X.: Classification of ECG signals based on 1d convolution neural network. In: 2017 IEEE 19th International Conference on e-health Networking, Applications and Services (healthcom), pp. 1–6. IEEE (2018)
42. Li, K., Pan, W., Li, Y., Jiang, Q., Liu, G.: A method to detect sleep apnea based on deep neural network and hidden Markov model using single-lead ECG signal. Neurocomputing **294**, 94–101 (2018)
43. Li, Y., Pang, Y., Wang, J., Li, X.: Patient-specific ECG classification by deeper CNN from generic to dedicated. Neurocomputing **314**, 336–346 (2018)
44. Limam, M., Precioso, F.: Atrial fibrillation detection and ECG classification based on convolutional recurrent neural network. In: 2017 Computing in Cardiology (CINC), pp. 1–4. IEEE (2017)
45. Liu, M., Kim, Y.: Classification of heart diseases based on ECG signals using long short-term memory. In: 2018 40th Annual International Conference of the IEEE Engineering in Medicine and Biology Society (EMBC), pp. 2707–2710. IEEE (2018)
46. Liu, W., Huang, Q., Chang, S., Wang, H., He, J.: Multiple-feature-branch convolutional neural network for myocardial infarction diagnosis using electrocar- diogram. Biomed. Signal Process. Control **45**, 22–32 (2018)
47. Loni, M., Sinaei, S., Zoljodi, A., Daneshtalab, M., Sjödin, M.: Deepmaker: a multi-objective optimization framework for deep neural networks in embedded systems. Microprocess. Microsyst, 102989 (2020)
48. Loni, M., Zoljodi, A., Sinaei, S., Daneshtalab, M., Sjödin, M.: NeuroPower: designing energy efficient convolutional neural network architecture for embedded systems. In: Tetko, I., Kůrková, V., Karpov, P., Theis, F. (eds.) Artificial Neural Networks and Machine Learning – ICANN 2019: Theoretical Neural Computation. ICANN 2019. LNCS, vol. 11727, pp. 208–222. Springer, Cham (2019). https://doi.org/10.1007/978-3-030-30487-4_17

A Computational Approach to Identify Normal and Abnormal Persons Gait Using Various Machine Learning and Deep Learning Classifier

Ram Kumar Yadav[1]([✉]) [iD], Subhrendu Guha Neogi[1] [iD], and Vijay Bhaskar Semwal[2] [iD]

[1] Amity University, Gwalior, India
Yadav20072@gmail.com, sgneogi@gwa.amity.edu
[2] MANIT, Bhopal, India

Abstract. Walking based human identification is a looming method. Maximum biometric structure needs more high resolution and a variety of sensors. Walking base human recognition can be classifying abnormal or normal walks. In recent times by utilizing a computer vision-oriented approach to recognize abnormal and normal walk cycles. Nowadays Machine Learning procedures have beaten and supplemented the utilization of conventional techniques in bio-clinical frameworks. In this exploration, kinetic and wearable sensors are introduced. This research paper examines the walking cycle of humans after background extraction of the image; features are extracted with gait analysis of human motion using machine learning and neural network models. These models are able to classify abnormal and normal with extending accuracy from 70 to 93% using various machine learning, deep learning algorithms and CNN classifier. The novelty of this paper is to increase the classification accuracy with fast processing and reduce the time complexity of the dataset.

Keywords: Biometric · Abnormal · Normal · Gait analysis · Machine learning · Neural network

1 Introduction

A consistently expanding crime percentage, there is consistently an interest for insightful intelligent framework. Biometric assumes a crucial part in distinguishing the person since the actual qualities are consistently with the person [1]. The new biometrics incorporates iris, finger impression and face recognition. This biometrics doesn't recognize if the subject wears a head protector, gloves and masks. Additionally biometrics requires high resolution sensors to identify face or iris or unique biometric finger impression. Moreover these subject based systems are easily breakable and detectable by unauthorized persons but now recent time supporting biometrics as an elective gait based framework to overcome this type of problem. Walk framework requires low cast and not high resolution sensors. Walk acknowledgment basically considers the stride cycle. Walk cycle begins from initial contact and ends with terminal swing, such that the walk cycle has covered seven sub phases of the walk cycle. Walk cycle is novel for each

N. Khare et al. (Eds.): MIND 2022, CCIS 1762, pp. 14–26, 2022.
https://doi.org/10.1007/978-3-031-24352-3_2

person to categorize of normal walk and abnormal walk [2, 3]. Various gait datasets are accessible, such as CASIA (China), USF step Challenge informational index, CMU Mo Bo dataset, and OU-ISIR (Japan) data set and so on.

Gait or walking is a manner or walking style of humans which depends on the limbs motion of the human body [4]. Gait is varying when a human moves naturally or in a certain training conditions. Based on human walking gait patterns can be classified into following categories which is shown in Fig. 1.

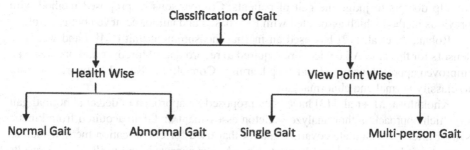

Fig. 1. Classification of Gait

Normal Gait is a rhythmic and portrayed rotating propulsive and retropulsive movement of lower furthest points. There are 5 to 15% of people who do not walk as a normal walk due to medication misuse or drug addiction and clinical restoration. So it is required to identify normal or unusual walking action [5].

Abnormal Gait or Walking Abnormality is the point at which an individual can't walk in the typical manner. This might be because of injuries, hidden conditions of the body or issues with the legs and feet. Moreover, at the point when at least one of these connecting frameworks of the human body isn't working easily, it can bring about irregularity in walking. This may occur because of any of the accompanying reasons such as accident injury, irregularity in feet or legs, Parkinson and paralysis, hereditary components and neurological factors [6]. Walking abnormality is a challenging problem of single person gait and multi-person gait pattern, single person walking patterns on the various surfaces that is called single gait and many people walk together that is called multi-gait which is extension research area of single gait recognition [7, 8]. This research paper examines the issue of categorization of the person who's having abnormal walk or normal walk. Help of this approach to minimize the classification time to recognize an individual from a big dataset and consequently decreases the processing time.

2 Related Work

Patluri, S. et al. [9] has proposed a gait abnormality system which uses sensors for data collection, in which combine inertial measurement unit (IMU) and plantar pressure measurement (PPM) and to detect gait abnormality using stacked LSTM. Author involved three Hemiplegic, Sensory ataxic and Parkinsonians gait abnormality for simulation and validates its proposed method.

Duhaylungsod, C.R.E. et.al. [10] has designed a model to recognized human gait abnormality using inter co-relationship in the middle of shanks and thighs of right and left legs of the volunteers and compared its temporary parameters of gait by utilizing Meta Motion R. Authors have been achieved extreme result which is close to 1.

Han, Y.C. et al. [11] has examined the walk cycle to recognize phases of Normal and Abnormal gait using an inertial measurement unit (IMU). The Authors approach can provide a comprehensive perception in the shanks acceleration and angular velocity to help doctors to judge the gait of patients. Comparisons of proposed method with previous method which associated with FSR based and author achieved better result.

Rohan, A. et al. [12] has used an inertial measurement unit (IMU) and wearable sensors for this aim. All devices are required to record data. Moreover authors create an improved approach using AI and deep learning, Convolution Neural Network classifier to classify normal and abnormal gait.

Khokhlova, M. et al. [13] have been proposed an approach to detect abnormal gait in which approach author analyze skeleton assessment and data acquired from kinetic sensor after that calculate covariant matrix that used for classification method such as normal gait based model and K-nearest neighbour approach and evaluation of results based on exist pathological datasets.

Hemmatpour, M. et al. [14] has been proposed non-linear predictive model with threshold based abnormal gait patterns classification with lower complication and higher accuracy. In order to dataset recorded with the help of sensors (accelerometer and gyrometer) available in Smartphone. Authors are able to speculate irregular walks and achieve good accuracy (93.5%).

Zou, Q. et al. [15] has developed a unique method for gait identification which is used a Smartphone device with accelerometer and gyrometer sensors that record the data in unconstraint path not in an ideal defined path. In this article 118 subjects have been considered and two datasets collected by the Smartphone Authors have proposed hybrid deep neural networks to achieve higher accuracy than 93.7% and 93.5% in human gait identification, respectively. Authors have developed a method which identified person and gait abnormalities with the utilization of accelerometer, gyrometer and Bluetooth device [16].

Pawin, J. et al. [17] has developed a method to recognize abnormal gait using FSR (Force Sensitive Registers). Four FSR have been installed in the shoes worn by the subject at the time of data recording and evaluate the result using ANN.

Apart from above studies, in recent years various deep learning, ELM and hybrid deep learning models are evolved for HAR recognition [27–39].

3   Data Acquisition

In the course of data acquisition, subjects are queried about distinct clothes and shoes. After they were said to walk one by one on the path and Fig. 2 shows the experimental setup devices and volunteer walk.

Fig. 2. Experimental setup and volunteer walk

The data set was recorded in motion capturing laboratory CSE department MANIT, Bhopal by calculating the gait parameter of 410 various volunteers with normal (190) and abnormal (220) volunteers. The age of volunteers was between 25 to 35 years old and their weight ranged from 45 to 90 kg. Accumulate a sample in 2.58 s. While frequency of data acquisition is 50Hz and the length of one sample is 128. An absolute 1206750 samples are accumulated, in which 96,283 are utilized for training and remaining for testing. Moreover, find out the walking parameters of normal and abnormal people. Every volunteer represents six biomechanical dimensions such as pelvis incidence angle, pelvis tilt, lumber angle, sacral incline, pelvis semi diameter and degree of spondylolisthesis derived from shape and orientation of lumbar spine and pelvis.

4 Proposed Method

The method to recognize abnormal [9] walk by using the collected own DNAA dataset that is presented 410 people who were divided into two unique categories such as abnormal and normal and the whole process given in Fig. 3. Moreover, we explore complete process from data recording to classification of normal and abnormal gait which have shown in Fig. 4.

Sensory Dataset of various objects

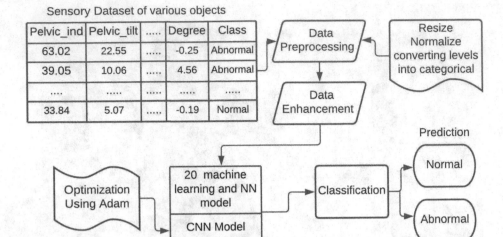

Pelvic_ind	Pelvic_tilt	.....	Degree	Class
63.02	22.55	.....	-0.25	Abnormal
39.05	10.06	.....	4.56	Abnormal
....	.....	.....	.....	.....
33.84	5.07	.....	-0.19	Normal

Fig. 3. Proposed Architecture of method

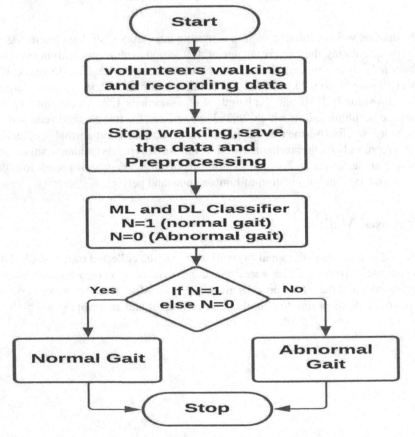

Fig. 4. Flow chart of classification method

5   Result Evaluation

The execution of the proposed approach, which is the ideal normal human motion, has a sinusoidal curve while abnormal walk does not produce proper sinusoidal curve. Figure 5 represents the normality with sinusoidal waves.

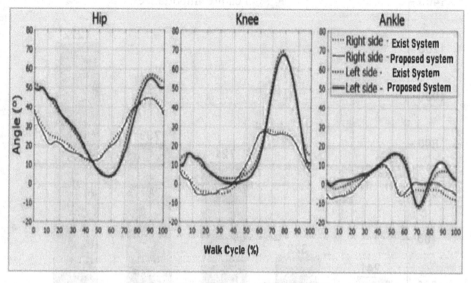

Fig. 5. Sinusoidal curve of normal walk

Analysis of sinusoidal waves to recognize normal and abnormal gait with six gait attributes such as Pelvic incidence angle, Pelvic tilt, Lumber angle, Sacral incline, Pelvic semi-diameter, Degree of spondylolisthesis etc. Table 1 represents the own DNAA dataset with attributes.

Table 1. DNAA dataset with six attributes

pelvic_incidence_angle	lumbar_angle	sacral_incline	pelvic_semidiameter	degree_spondylolisthesis	Class
52.419	35.872	33.407	116.559	1.694	Abnormal
35.492	15.590	23.790	106.938	-3.460	Abnormal
53.854	32.779	34.624	121.670	5.329	Abnormal
......	....	....	....	....	....
63.929	40.177	43.958	113.065	-11.058	Normal
61.821	63.999	48.224	121.779	1.296	Normal
69.004	55.570	55.713	126.611	10.832	Normal

Analysis of own recorded DNAA dataset which have various features such as Lumber angle, Pelvic incidence angle, Pelvis semi diameter, Sacral incline and Degree spondylolisthesis etc. furthermore based on features and its number of incidence draw a histogram which have shown in Fig. 6.

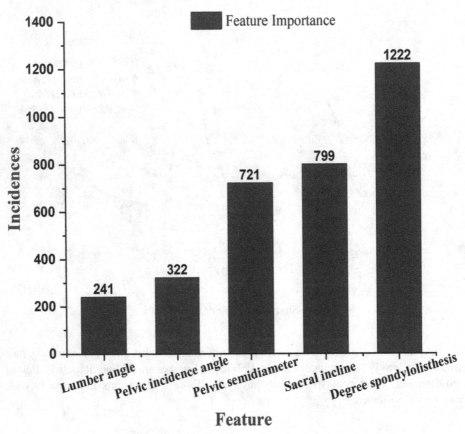

Fig. 6. Bar curve of incidences and features of normal and abnormal gait

This research paper reviews the various classification approaches. Here we calculated classification utilizing the various machine learning and neural network approaches all methods are represented in Table 2 and Fig. 7 shows various models training and testing score.

Table 2. Model with Accuracy Score in Percentage

Model/Algorithm	Accuracy%	
	Score_Train	Score_Test
Extra Tree classifier	84.15	84.15
S V M	85.67	85.37
Logistic Regression	84.76	84.15
Linear SVC	85.67	84.15
S G Decent	81.71	84.15
KNN	91.77	89.02
Ridge Classifier	83.54	86.59
Ada Boost Classifier	82.32	85.37
NN1	82.93	79.27
XGB Classifier	92.07	87.8
NN2	80.79	86.59
Perceptron	77.44	84.15
Naïve Bayes	79.88	86.59
Bagging Classifier	99.39	91.46
LGBM Classifier	89.02	80.49
Random Forest	100	91.46
Hard voting	100	91.46
Soft voting	100	90.24
CNN Classifier	100	93.00
D T Classifier	100	90.24
G B Classifier	100	90.24

Here we have to evaluate the accuracy of each model in terms of training and testing score which is represented in Fig. 8.

In Table 3 we analyze the performance of accuracy of various classifiers are evaluated and the overall best performance is evaluated by CNN classifier with reduced testing time among all.

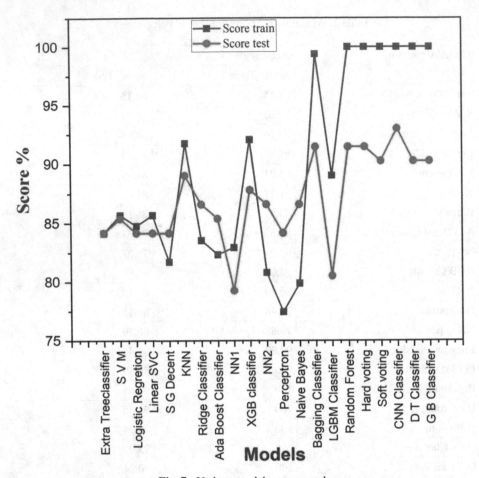

Fig. 7. Various models score graph

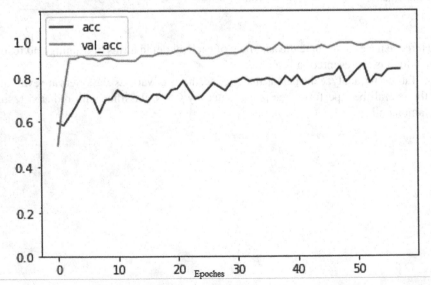

Fig. 8. Accuracy line graph of training and testing score

Table 3. Models with Accuracy Score in Percentage

Model/Algorithm [25, 26]	Accuracy%	
	Own results (Test Score in %)	Existing Results in %
Extra Tree classifier	84.15	
S V M [23, 24]	85.37	75.00
Logistic Regression	84.15	
Linear SVC	84.15	
S G Decent	84.15	
KNN [19, 21]	89.02	
Ridge Classifier	86.59	
Ada Boost Classifier	85.37	
NN1 [18]	79.27	
XGB Classifier [18]	87.80	
NN2 [20]	86.59	90.00
Perceptron [18, 20]	84.15	
Naïve Bayes	86.59	74.00
Bagging Classifier	91.46	
LGBM Classifier	80.49	
Random Forest [18]	91.46	88.00
Hard voting	91.46	
Soft voting	90.24	
CNN Classifier [22]	93.00	90.50
D T Classifier [18]	90.24	75.00
G B Classifier	90.24	

6 Conclusion and Future Work

By using various approaches to classify and recognize abnormal and normal gait using various ML (Machine Learning) and NN (Neural Network) models to improve the classification accuracy and its provide novel ideas for abnormal and normal gait pattern. Extract the required features from extraction of background of image and then apply various methods on own recorded DNAA dataset which include abnormal and normal action. These methods are easy, fast and more effective with previous methods and achieved 93% good accuracy with reduced testing time.

Future dimensions to plan more experiments with adding more human activities on remote and zigzag surface to recognize human gait abnormality and accuracy rate will be increased with large dataset. In the future perspective also used hybrid deep learning models to easily handle the large dataset of normal and abnormal gait.

References

1. Fathima, S.S.S., Banu, W.R.: Abnormal walk identification for systems using gait patterns. Biomed. Res. India **27**, S112–S117 (2016)
2. SMH, S.S.F., RSD, W.B.: Abnormal walk identification for systems using gait patterns (2016)
3. Luo, J., Tjahjadi, T.: Multi-set canonical correlation analysis for 3d abnormal gait behaviour recognition based on virtual sample generation. IEEE Access **8**, 32485–32501 (2020)
4. Chen, X., Liu, J., Sun, X.: Abnormal gait recognition based on RBF neural network. In: 2019 Chinese Control and Decision Conference (CCDC), pp. 2722–2726. IEEE, June 2019
5. Elkholy, A., Hussein, M.E., Gomaa, W., Damen, D., Saba, E.: A general descriptor for detecting abnormal action performance from skeletal data. In: 2017 39th Annual International Conference of the IEEE Engineering in Medicine and Biology Society (EMBC), pp. 1401–1404. IEEE, July 2017
6. Zhang, Y., et al.: Genetic analysis of LRRK2 R1628P in Parkinson's disease in Asian populations. Parkinson's Disease 2017 (2017)
7. Chen, X., Weng, J., Lu, W., Xu, J.: Multi-gait recognition based on attribute discovery. IEEE Trans. Pattern Anal. Mach. Intell. **40**(7), 1697–1710 (2017)
8. Zheng, Z., Zheng, L., Yang, Y.: A discriminatively learned cnn embedding for person reidentification. ACM Trans. Multimedia Comput. Commun. Appl. (TOMM) **14**(1), 1–20 (2017)
9. Potluri, S., Ravuri, S., Diedrich, C., Schega, L.: Deep learning based gait abnormality detection using wearable sensor system. In: 2019 41st Annual International Conference of the IEEE Engineering in Medicine and Biology Society (EMBC), pp. 3613–3619. IEEE, July 2019
10. Duhaylungsod, C.R.E., Magbitang, C.E.B., Mercado, J.F.I.R., Osido, G.E.D., Pecho, S.A.C., dela Cruz, A.R.: Detection of gait abnormality through leg symmetry and temporal parameters. In: 2017IEEE 9th International Conference on Humanoid, Nanotechnology, Information Technology, Communication and Control, Environment and Management (HNICEM), pp. 1–4. IEEE, December 2017
11. Han, Y.C., Wong, K.I., Murray, I.: Gait phase detection for normal and abnormal gaits using IMU. IEEE Sens. J. **19**(9), 3439–3448 (2019)
12. Rohan, A., Rabah, M., Hosny, T., Kim, S.H.: Human pose estimation-based real-time gait analysis using convolutional neural network. IEEE Access **8**, 191542–191550 (2020)
13. Khokhlova, M., Migniot, C., Dipanda, A.: Kinematic covariance based abnormal gait detection. In: 2018 14th International Conference on Signal-Image Technology & Internet-Based Systems (SITIS), pp. 691–696. IEEE, November 2018
14. Hemmatpour, M., Ferrero, R., Gandino, F., Montrucchio, B., Rebaudengo, M.: Nonlinear predictive threshold model for real-time abnormal gait detection. J. Healthc. Eng. (2018)
15. Zou, Q., Wang, Y., Wang, Q., Zhao, Y., Li, Q.: Deep learning-based gait recognition using smartphones in the wild. IEEE Trans. Inf. Forensics Secur. **15**, 3197–3212 (2020)
16. Guan-Wei, H., Min-Hsuan, L., Yu-Tai, C.: Methods for person recognition and abnormal gait detection using tri-axial accelerometer and gyroscope. In: 2017 International Conference on Computational Science and Computational Intelligence (CSCI), pp. 1691–1694. IEEE, December 2017
17. Pawin, J., Khaorapapong, T., Chawalit, S.: Neural-based human's abnormal gait detection using force sensitive resistors. In: The Fourth International Workshop on Advanced Computational Intelligence, pp. 224–229. IEEE, October 2011
18. Aziz, W., Hussain, L., Khan, I.R., Alowibdi, J.S., Alkinani, M.H.: Machine learning based classification of normal, slow and fast walking by extracting multimodal features from stride interval time series. Math. Biosci. Eng. **18**(1), 495–517 (2021)

19. Pratama, F.I., Budianita, A.: Optimization of K-Nn classification in human gait recognition. In: 2020 Fifth International Conference on Informatics and Computing (ICIC), pp. 1–5. IEEE, November 2020

20. Pourpanah, F., Zhang, B., Ma, R., Hao, Q.: Non-intrusive human motion recognition using distributed sparse sensors and the genetic algorithm based neural network. In: 2018 IEEE SENSORS, pp. 1–4. IEEE, October 2018

21. Derlatka, M., Bogdan, M.: Ensemble kNN classifiers for human gait recognition based on ground reaction forces. In: 2015 8th International Conference on Human System Interaction (HSI), pp. 88–93. IEEE, June 2015

22. Yadav, R.K., Neogi, S.G., Semwal, V.B.: Special session on recent advances in computational intelligence & technologys (SS_10_RACIT). In: Singh, P.K., Wierzchoń, S.T., Tanwar, S., Rodrigues, J.J.P.C., Ganzha, M. (eds.) Proceedings of Third International Conference on Computing, Communications, and Cyber-Security. LNNS, vol. 421, pp. 595–608. Springer, Singapore (2023). https://doi.org/10.1007/978-981-19-1142-2_47

23. Raut, A.R., Khandait, S.P., Dongre, S.S.: A machine learning based mission critical data transmission protocol in wireless sensor networks. In: 2021 6th International Conference on Communication and Electronics Systems (ICCES), pp. 846–852. IEEE, July 2021

24. Raut, A.R., Khandait, S.P.: Machine learning algorithms in WSNs and its applications. In: 2021 International Conference on Computational Intelligence and Computing Applications (ICCICA), pp. 1–5. IEEE, November 2021

25. Raut, A.R., Khandait, S.P., Chavhan, N.: QoS aware machine learning algorithms for real-time applications in wireless sensor networks. In: Komanapalli, V.L.N., Sivakumaran, N., Hampannavar, S. (eds.) Advances in Automation, Signal Processing, Instrumentation, and Control. i-CASIC 2020. LNEE, vol. 700, pp. 2665–2673. Springer, Singapore (2021). https://doi.org/10.1007/978-981-15-8221-9_249

26. Patil, S., Vairagade, S., Theng, D.: Machine learning techniques for the classification of fake news. In: 2021 International Conference on Computational Intelligence and Computing Applications (ICCICA) (pp. 1–5). IEEE, November 2021

27. Semwal, V.B., Gupta, A., Lalwani, P.: An optimized hybrid deep learning model using ensemble learning approach for human walking activities recognition. J. Supercomput. 77(11), 12256–12279 (2021). https://doi.org/10.1007/s11227-021-03768-7

28. Dua, N., et al.: Inception inspired CNN-GRU hybrid network for human activity recognition. Multimedia Tools Appl. (2022)

29. Bijalwan, V., et al.: Wearable sensor-based pattern mining for human activity recognition: deep learning approach. Ind. Robot Int. J. Robot. Res. Appl. (2021)

30. Dua, N., Singh, S.N., Semwal, V.B.: Multi-input CNN-GRU based human activity recognition using wearable sensors. Computing 103(7), 1461–1478 (2021). https://doi.org/10.1007/s00607-021-00928-8

31. Bijalwan, V., Semwal, V.B., Singh, G., Mandal, T.K.: HDL-PSR: modelling spatio-temporal features using hybrid deep learning approach for post-stroke rehabilitation. Neural Process. Lett. 1–20 (2022). https://doi.org/10.1007/s11063-022-10744-6

32. Challa, S.K., Kumar, A., Semwal, V.B.: A multibranch CNN-BiLSTM model for human activity recognition using wearable sensor data. Vis. Comput. 1–15 (2021).https://doi.org/10.1007/s00371-021-02283-3

33. Bijalwan, V., Semwal, V.B., Mandal, T.K.: Fusion of multi-sensor-based biomechanical gait analysis using vision and wearable sensor. IEEE Sens. J. 21(13), 14213–14220 (2021)

34. Raj, M., et al.: Bidirectional association of joint angle trajectories for humanoid locomotion: the restricted Boltzmann machine approach. Neural Comput. Appl. 30(6), 1747–1755 (2018)

35. Semwal, V.B., et al.: Speed, cloth and pose invariant gait recognition-based person identification. In: Pandey, M., Rautaray, S.S. (eds.) Machine Learning: Theoretical Foundations and

Practical Applications. Studies in Big Data, vol. 87, pp. 39–56. Springer, Singapore (2021). https://doi.org/10.1007/978-981-33-6518-6_3

36. Gupta, A., Semwal, V.B.: Occluded Gait reconstruction in multi person Gait environment using different numerical methods. Multimedia Tools Appl. 1–28 (2022). https://doi.org/10.1007/s11042-022-12218-2

37. Semwal, V.B., et al.: Pattern identification of different human joints for different human walking styles using inertial measurement unit (IMU) sensor. Artif. Intell. Rev. 1–21 (2021).https://doi.org/10.1007/s10462-021-09979-x

38. Semwal, V.B., et al.: Human gait state prediction using cellular automata and classification using ELM. In: Tanveer, M., Pachori, R. (eds.) Machine Intelligence and Signal Analysis. AISC, vol. 748, pp. 135–145. Springer, Singapore (2019). https://doi.org/10.1007/978-981-13-0923-6_12

39. Patil, P., et al.: Clinical human gait classification: extreme learning machine approach. In: 2019 1st international conference on advances in science, engineering and robotics technology (ICASERT). IEEE (2019)

Hierarchical-Based Binary Moth Flame Optimization for Feature Extraction in Biomedical Application

S. Jayachitra[1]($\boxtimes$) (iD), A. Prasanth[2] (iD), Shaik Mohammad Rafi[3], and S. Zulaikha Beevi[4]

[1] Department of Electronics and Communication Engineering, PSNA College of Engineering and Technology, Dindigul, India
jayachitra0804@gmail.com

[2] Department of Electronics and Communication Engineering, Sri Venkateswara College of Engineering, Sriperumbudur, India

[3] Department of Computer Science and Engineering, Sri Mittapalli College of Engineering, Guntur, Andhra Pradesh, India

[4] Department of Computer Science and Engineering, V.S.B Engineering College, Karur, India

Abstract. Feature extraction is a key challenging task to find the optimal features by alleviating irrelevant features to improve the classification accuracy. The brute force methods yield complete feature space and employ exhaustive search that makes the feature selection a non-deterministic polynomial problem. The meta-heuristic algorithm offers a better optimal solution through random search rather than a complete search. However, the MFO falls with local optima and poor convergence. In this paper, a novel methodology based on the Hierarchical Binary Moth Flame Optimization (HBMFO) with a K-Nearest Neighbor (KNN) classifier is proposed for feature extraction. The motive of this work is to reduce high dimensionality for large datasets through feature extraction. Here, the adaptive hierarchical method has been proposed to update the moth position towards the optimal solution pertaining to searching the space. The simulation results are accomplished on UCI Repository datasets to validate the superiority of the suggested optimization algorithm over existing techniques and feature selection can be carried out with respect to improving stability and accuracy.

Keywords: Feature extraction · Moth Flame Optimization · Classification

1 Introduction

In recent decades, machine learning algorithm has been extensively utilized in numerous research domains including image classification, feature selection, disease classification, and pattern recognition [1]. The research areas involved with large datasets are due to the advancement in data collection tools and techniques. This cause dimensionality problem and hence data reduction becomes an essential phase for processing them. The feature extraction is a major dimensionality reduction approach that helps to manipulate the significant subset of attributes from the dataset [2]. It can be carried out through evicting

N. Khare et al. (Eds.): MIND 2022, CCIS 1762, pp. 27–38, 2022.
https://doi.org/10.1007/978-3-031-24352-3_3

noisy features and sustaining the significant features which are greatly associated with the target class and poorly connected with non-redundant features. The motive of employing the feature selection process in pre-processing is to condense the count of attributes and enlarge the efficacy of the algorithm.

The searching and evaluation criteria are the two processes carried out in feature selection. Every candidate feature is estimated based on its capability of solution as a feature selection problem in evaluation criteria. The methods such as filter and wrapper technique are utilized to determine the feature subset. The filtering technique is the easiest evaluation method involved without underlying any learning process [3]. On contrarily, the wrapper technique is entangled with the learning process in feature selection that possesses high computational cost but results in a good performance. The searching technique is employed to choose the finest features from the dataset. It can be classified as a random, complete, and heuristic search. In random search, the features are selected randomly whereas the complete search finds the optimal features from all feature subsets, and the heuristic search is easy to implement and is extensively used in large datasets.

The meta-heuristic algorithm is a swarm intelligence model that simulates the natural movement of creatures. The technique of transforming information among groups is to hunt the prey is transferred into numerical models such as Grey Wolf Optimization [4], Binary Bat Algorithm (BBA), and Binary Cuckoo Search (BCS) [5, 6]. The feature selection in swarm intelligence has been broadly employed to enhance the classification process by pre-processing the dataset without modifying the original features. Researchers in many studies have proposed various strategies to improve swarm intelligence in feature selection problems through incorporating Transfer functions, chaotic tent map, levy flight, mutation, and hybridizing with an optimization model [7].

The Moth Flame Optimization (MFO) is excited through the natural behavior of the moth which follows a population-based mechanism that yields the initialization of the moth during the optimization process. Every moth depicts the optimal solution for an optimization problem. The position of moth can be updated using the spiral updating strategy by employing MFO optimization. The position of moths is updated and computed iteratively until the stopping criteria are reached. The optimization can be carried out in two stages namely exploitation and exploration [8]. The moth search can be done locally within a particular space. The moths are globally explored in various regions during the exploration process. The transition among exploitation and exploration during optimization enriches the performance analysis of the algorithm.

In this paper, a novel Hierarchical Binary Moth Flame Optimization (HBMFO) model is developed to forecast the optimum attributes. However, the conventional updating strategy updates every moth in a similar manner where it neglects their closeness towards a global optimal solution. Hence, every moth in the search space would be given a hierarchy which entirely relies on how farthest the position of the moth is from the global solution. The poor-quality moths have a high rank with low fitness and acquire major changes in their position. The high-quality moth has a low rank with high fitness value and incurs a tiny change in its position. The performance of HBMFO is examined for 10 benchmark medical datasets and hence the simulation outcomes are analyzed and competed with other optimization algorithms. The key contribution of research work is outlined as

- A new efficient HBMFO optimization is adopted to choose the finest features. This optimization technique is robust and affirmed as a prominent mathematical technique which yields superior results than the computational techniques.
- The vital responsibility of the proposed technique is to choose the optimum features and generates classification accuracy. The proposed hierarchy model reinforces the population diversity and alleviates the falling of local optima.
- The experimental simulations have been realized to determine the potential of the proposed method. It manipulates 10 datasets to examine the performing analysis of the HBMFO optimization technique with other existing optimization models.

2   Related Work

The following section epitomizes the existing technique related to the feature extraction process through various meta-heuristic optimizations. In [9], the MFO model has been presented to resolve engineering difficulties through moth movement mechanisms. MFO makes the movement spirally to modify the position of the moth in the flame. It has been analyzed and compared with several swarm intelligence mechanisms like Flower Pollination Optimization, Bat Algorithm, and Particle Swarm Optimization (PSO). By comparing with other meta-heuristic algorithms, the MFO generates better results for resolving engineering problems.

A correlation-based ensemble feature extraction has been proposed to compass feature selection by utilizing Differential Evolution (DE), and Glowworm Swarm Optimization. Every optimization algorithm utilized a wrapper technique where the accuracy of the AdaBoost algorithm has been utilized to choose the desired optimal features [10]. In [11], a computer-aided diagnosis has been proposed to diagnose pulmonary tuberculosis through a BCS optimization algorithm for feature selection. From this, 44 run-length features and 42 texture features were extracted and hence the lung tissues are segmented. Here, the wrapper-based feature selection technique with BCS is incorporated with the support vector machine model to examine the performance of extracted attributes.

The wrapper-based MFO optimization algorithm has been introduced for the attribute mining process. Here, the KNN is assisted as the fitness function to compute the accuracy [12]. The MFO was compared with other existing models like Genetic Algorithm (GA) and PSO. It evaluates the proposed technique using 18 distinct datasets from the UCI repository. The MFO model produces better accuracy and precision due to the execution of proper fitness functions.

In [13], an Enhanced MFO (EMFO) has been proposed to enrich the exploration stage of the MFO method. The exploration stage undergoes a global search which finds an optimistic solution in the searching space whereas the exploitation stage performs a local search for locating the finest solutions among the possible solution. The Cauchy distribution function was incorporated with EMFO to enhance exploration capability that yields diverse solutions and hence the optimal flame was infused to enrich the exploitation stage. In addition, the EMFO outperforms MFO in 16 datasets out of 20 benchmark medical datasets with distinct population sizes. In addition, E-MFO was correlated with other swarm intelligence algorithms namely PSO, GA, DE, and Bat Algorithm. However, the optimization algorithms meet the concerns of poor convergence and computation complexity amidst the attribute mining process.

Attribute mining is the mechanism of identifying the finest features from the original features to obtain the correct classification rate [14]. The techniques namely wrapper, filter, embedded, and hybrid techniques existed for analyzing the feature selection. Firstly, the wrapper technique examines the relevant features according to predictive analysis that is acquired through the intended learning approach which utilizes the classifier analysis as the unique objective function [15].

The filter technique selects features based on feature relevance score by ranking the features and neglects the less secured feature through the appropriate threshold. The feature relevance score such as Pearson's coefficient, chi-square, and Gini Index is generally adapted features [16]. The embedded technique is identical to the wrapper technique in which the parameters of the classifier are tuned and feature selections were examined concurrently. Finally, the hybrid technique incorporates both filter and wrapper technique and perform the function in a similar way [17].

According to the aforesaid analysis, MFO implements a competition mechanism to choose promising flames and sustain the flame with a low fitness function which results in rapid convergence with the optimal solution. MFO has better exploitation capability. However, MFOs have several constraints such as falling of local optima and poor exploration ability. To alleviate this problem, an enhanced variant of HBMFO is proposed. The efficacy of the anticipated optimization model has been evaluated and compared with various conventional meta-heuristic techniques. The simulation results illustrate that the HBMFO significantly outperforms the conventional MFO and other wrapper-based techniques. The practical realization of the proposed HBMFO technique provides a higher convergence speed.

3   Proposed HBMFO Model

3.1   Moth Flame Optimization (MFO)

The conventional MFO is a meta-heuristic model which corresponds to the natural action of the moth. The moth travels linearly by employing a transfer arrangement mechanism. The congruent angle is sustained while the source of light is too far from moonlight. Nevertheless, the moth attains spiral movement while the source of light is nearer to the light of a candle [18]. The natural spiral movement of the moth around the flame is demonstrated in Eq. 1, where F_l illustrates the l_{th} moth, M_k denotes the k_{th} flame, and s_p symbolize the spiral function.

Algorithm 1 – MFO Algorithm

Input: Maximum Iteration, d- dimension size, n-number of moths
Output: Best optimal solution
Begin

1　　Initialize moth position;
2　　**while** $I \leq$ *maximum iteration* **do**
3　　　　Update *the flame* using Eq. (4);
4　　FV=Fitness value(M);
5　　**if** $I==I$ **then**
6　　　　S = Sort (M);
7　　OS = Sort (FV);
8　　**else**
9　　　　S = Sort (F_{i-1}, F_i);
10　　　OS = Sort (OF_{i-1}, OF_i);
11　　**end if**
12　　**for** l = 1:q
13　　　　　　**for** k = 1:p
14　　Apprise r and t;
15　　Manipulate D_i based on linked search agent;
16　　　　　　Update M(k,l) spiral movement using Eq. (1 & 2);
17　　**end for**
18　　**end for**
19　　i=i+1
20　　**end while**
21　　**end**

The spiral movement using logarithmic function is formulated in Eq. 2, where b intends the temporary constant terminology to compute the texture of the logarithmic function and t generates the random value [−1, 1]. The function D_l symbolizes the distance between the l_{th} moth and the k_{th} flame which is depicted in Eq. 3. The number $[t = -1]$ denotes the nearest moth location to the flame and $[t = 1]$ determines the farthermost position among flame and moth. Henceforth, to acquire maximum manipulation, the function t is assumed in the interval $[r, 1]$ where r is gradually reduced over the iteration in the range -1 to -2.

$$F_l = s_p(F_l, M_k) \tag{1}$$

$$s_p(F_l, M_k) = D_l.e^{bt}.cos\ cos(2\pi) + M_k \tag{2}$$

$$D_l = |F_l - M_k| \tag{3}$$

Initially, the inevitable number of flames N is computed in the MFO algorithm. The number of flames consistently diminished with maximum iteration due to the virtue of updating the mechanism of the moth. The process of diminishing has a better ratio among exploitation and exploration. The number of flames inside MFO is represented in Eq. 4, where N depicts the inevitable number that illustrates the beginning number of flames during the initial iteration, M denotes the maximal repetitions and I symbolizes the actual repetitions. The MFO pseudocode is exposed in Algorithm 1.

$$Flame\ Number = round\,(N - I.\frac{N-1}{M})\qquad(4)$$

3.2 Hierarchical Binary MFO (HBMFO)

The traditional MFO has the phenomenon of rapid convergence speed but lags with the poor searching ability and it falls with the local optimum value which degrades the performance of classification. In order to overcome this, the Hierarchical Binary coding is combined with MFO (HBMFO) has been proposed to improve the exploitation and searching process. The feature selection can be achieved through Hierarchy-based Binary MFO (HBMFO).

MFO is based on a continuous nature algorithm which is converted into discrete space using Transfer Functions (T_rF). In discrete space, the finest solution consists of Boolean values as '0' and '1'. The operators in MFO can be modified by utilizing T_rF without affecting the original nature of the algorithm. The T_rF is the sigmoid function that has been formulated to estimate the probability value [0, 1] for every element. The Eq. (4) indicates the step vector in MFO is modified as,

$$\Delta F = |F_l - M_k|.e^{bt}.cos\ cos(2\pi)\qquad(5)$$

The sigmoid function is expressed as

$$T_rF(\Delta F_t) = \frac{1}{\left(1 + e^{\Delta F_t}\right)}\qquad(6)$$

The moth position is modified using the following equation,

$$F_l^d(t + 1) = \{1, if\ rand \geq T_rF(\Delta F_{t+1})0,\ if\ rand < T_rF(\Delta F_{t+1})\qquad(7)$$

In BMFO, the moth position is updated similar to MFO i.e., the capability function of a moth cannot be considered in moth location upgradation. This depicts that poor quality moth will relocate their position as a higher quality solution in searching space. Hence, it depraves the classification performance of the algorithm. To overcome these constraints, HBMFO is formulated to perform more exploitation and to achieve global optimum. The hierarchy of a moth is combined with MFO during the updating process. In this scenario, every moth attains a hierarchy based on the ability value. The adaptive hierarchy updating strategy term $\frac{H_l}{S}$ is incorporated with Eq. 4 and is illustrated as follows:

$$Q(F_l, M_k) = \left(|F_l - M_k|.e^{bt}.cos\ cos(2\pi) + M_k\right).\frac{H_l}{S}\qquad(8)$$

In this scenario, every moth attains a hierarchy according to the fitness value. Initially, the high fitness value obtains from high-quality moths has a lower position that causes a tiny change in their position. This leads the optimizer to perform more exploitation in the particular region and search locally. While the moth position is nearer to the finest solution, then it increases the ability to achieve global optimum. On the contrary, the poor fitness value achieved from low-quality moth has a higher position which enforces to changes their position and performs the global search.

3.3 Evaluation

The proposed feature selection method employs the wrapper technique to compute the contender attribute subset which outlines the probable resolution for the feature selection constraints. Here, two significant maxims are implicated in fitness function while delineating wrapper technique feature selection: (i) Optimize the performance of learning methodology, (ii) Minimize the number of features. Equation 10 articulates the feature selection problem where $\alpha\vartheta_{ER}D$ illustrates the error classification rate, RF symbolizes the reduced number of extracted features from the dataset, and OF denotes features from the original dataset, $\alpha \ \varepsilon \ [0, 1]$ and $\beta = (1\text{-}\alpha)$ are the major significant parameters illustrated the analysis of features and classification.

$$fitness = \alpha\vartheta_{ER}D + \beta\frac{RF}{OF} \qquad (9)$$

4 Results and Discussions

In this work, 10 different medical datasets from the UCI repository were utilized to analyze the enhanced wrapper technique. Table 1 illustrates the feature description of utilized datasets. The MATLAB 2019b is employed to execute the proposed method and the experimental results were generated. The wrapper technique based on KNN neural classifier is adapted to determine the performance of every solution in the wrapper feature selection technique.

Table 1. Attribute details of dataset

S. No	Dataset	Number of attributes	Number of instance	Class categorizes
1	Breast Cancer	9	699	2
2	Lung Cancer	23	226	2
3	Lympography	18	148	4
4	HeartEW	13	270	2
5	Dermatology	34	366	6
6	BreastEW	30	596	2
7	WineEW	13	178	3
8	ILPD	10	583	2
9	Parkinson	22	195	2
10	Diabetes	8	768	2

To acquire reliable results, the procedure was repeated with 30 independent and the obtained result demonstrates the average runs. The parameters such as α and β have the potential value of 0.99 and 0.01 in the fitness equation. The parameter value of the suggested model is illustrated in Table 2. The results are examined in two stages: (i) Comparison of MFO, BMFO, and HBMFO are carried out collectively to analyze the outcome of hierarchy-based strategy on optimization technique. The efficacy of the suggested scheme is computed based on the number of extracted features, accuracy, average fitness, and running time. (ii) The proposed HBMFO is compared with wrapper techniques such as BGWO, BBA, and BCS by simulating the same environment as like the first stage. The average classification accuracy of MFO, BMFO, and HBMFO are compared which is demonstrated in Fig. 1. The HBMFO attains seven best results among 10 different datasets where BMFO acquires the best results for 2 datasets and MFO attains the best result for 1 dataset. On the other hand, the standard deviation of accuracy results over 25 runs shows that HBMFO outperforms than other MFOs.

Table 2. Parameter Settings

Model	Parameters	Value
HBMFO	Population Size	20
	Iteration	200
	Dimension	No. of attributes
	Runs	25
	α in fitness	0.99
	β in fitness	0.01
GWO	b	[2:0]
BA	P_{min} Freq. Mmnimum	0.7
	P_{max} Freq. maximum	0.5
	B Loudness	0.2
	S Pulse rate	0.1
BCS	ka	0.25
	β	3/2

The suggested models are computed with the average (AG) and standard deviation (STA). From Table 3, it is clearly depicted that HBMFO outperforms when compared with BMFO and MFO by diminishing the number of features in the stated features. The HBMFO exhibited a lower number of extracted features across 75% of datasets. It would be helpful for large data medical datasets where the motive of attribute extraction is to a minimum the extent of the attribute with the relevant features. In addition, the HBMFO demonstrates higher stability in results while the experimental results were reiterated 25 times.

The average running time of different techniques is illustrated in Fig. 2. It clearly depicts that HBMFO imposes minimum running time to congregate towards a global solution. HBMFO acquires minimum running time for seven of 10 different datasets whereas BMFO attains minimum running time for 3 datasets. Furthermore, HBMFO

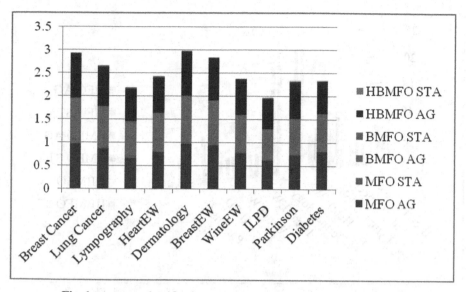

Fig. 1. Average classification accuracy of MFO, BMFO, and HBMFO

demonstrates higher stability in running time while the experiment is iterated for 25 times.

Table 3. Average number of extracted features of different optimization

S. No	Dataset	MFO		BMFO		Proposed HBMFO	
		AG	STA	AG	STA	AG	STA
1	Breast Cancer	4.103	0.352	4.001	0.256	4.065	0.001
2	Lung Cancer	4.116	0.398	4.098	0.296	4.102	0.176
3	Lympography	9.978	1.642	9.367	1.591	7.233	0.718
4	HeartEW	7.967	1.589	7.767	1.569	6.467	1.040
5	Dermatology	22.177	2.943	22.167	2.849	17.196	1.869
6	BreastEW	19.968	1.984	19.433	1.888	14.198	1.778
7	WineEW	4.126	0.402	4.026	0.302	4.100	0.182
8	ILPD	3.988	0.188	3.967	0.183	3.396	0.000
9	Parkinson	8.256	0.789	8.233	0.776	6.456	1.004
10	Diabetes	4.089	0.233	4.000	0.000	4.003	0.178

In the second scenario, the comparison can be carried out among the proposed method and the renowned existing wrapper technique using the same simulation measures and datasets. It is apparent from Table 4 that the results of HBMFO attain the best accuracy results for 9 datasets from 10 different datasets.

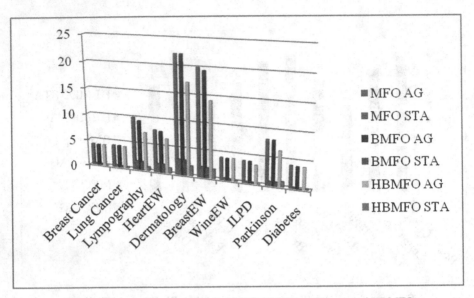

Fig. 2. Average Running Time of MFO, BMFO, and Proposed HBMFO

Table 4. Average classification accuracy of Different Algorithm

S. No	Dataset	Proposed		BGWO		BCS		BBA	
		AG	STA	AG	STA	AG	STA	AG	STA
1	Breast Cancer	0.968	0.001	0.963	0.012	0.971	0.001	0.939	0.022
2	Lung Cancer	0.743	0.028	0.723	0.018	0.714	0.019	0.693	0.044
3	Lympography	0.693	0.029	0.956	0.044	0.690	0.051	0.705	0.066
4	HeartEW	0.778	0.019	0.770	0.028	0.778	0.020	0.709	0.051
5	Dermatology	0.968	0.012	0.956	0.021	0.961	0.020	0.739	0.069
6	BreastEW	0.926	0.008	0.925	0.013	0.923	0.011	0.896	0.017
7	WineEW	0.664	0.018	0.654	0.034	0.653	0.019	0.624	0.052
8	ILPD	0.653	0.023	0.591	0.066	0.652	0.000	0.582	0.049
9	Parkinson	0.807	0.000	0.799	0.037	0.776	0.000	0.786	0.037
10	Diabetes	0.752	0.032	0.712	0.028	0.725	0.000	0.664	0.046

The BGWO and BCS techniques acquired higher classification accuracy for 5 different data sets whereas BBA does not obtain good results over any data sets. Besides, HBMFO depicts better stable results compared to other existing techniques. By obtaining the simulation results of accuracy classification, the spiral logarithmic movement of MFO is recorded, and improving the updation strategy movement using the hierarchical technique has greater potential on enhancing the optimization capability of the proposed technique and attain good trade-off among exploitation and exploration stages.

It is completely performed by accenting good exploitation for the high-quality solution and exerting continuous exploration in search space for low-quality solution.

Table 5. Average Running Time (seconds) of Different Algorithm

S. No	Dataset	Proposed		BGWO		BCS		BBA	
		AG	STA	AG	STA	AG	STA	AG	STA
1	Breast Cancer	22.10	0.10	24.17	0.84	45.72	0.60	23.01	0.29
2	Lung Cancer	12.14	0.06	13.14	0.14	15.74	0.14	12.25	0.10
3	Lympography	9.14	0.05	10.77	0.20	17.24	0.36	9.20	0.10
4	HeartEW	11.90	0.08	13.62	0.63	23.59	0.27	12.39	0.15
5	Dermatology	15.38	0.09	18.40	0.73	30.14	0.55	15.60	0.22
6	BreastEW	21.73	0.09	24.95	1.06	43.11	1.02	22.14	0.41
7	WineEW	10.20	0.08	13.15	0.75	17.24	0.34	10.34	0.18
8	ILPD	13.34	0.05	14.22	0.71	27.13	0.40	14.00	0.17
9	Parkinson	10.33	0.07	13.05	0.74	20.18	0.30	10.62	0.14
10	Diabetes	23.84	0.12	25.04	0.87	49.31	0.77	24.96	0.38

The optimization time for different algorithms is examined and the run time for various algorithms is illustrated in Table 5. It is noticed that the proposed algorithm attains a lower run time to attain a convergence rate in 90% of datasets. In contrast, the BBA has a minimum run time for 1 dataset whereas BCS and BGWO did not have a better run time for the dataset.

5 Conclusion

The traditional MFO is employed as a searching space optimization in feature extraction and KNN functioning as an examiner to analyze the aspect of the prompted dataset. In this work, a new wrapper technique-based feature extraction is used to enhance the classification mechanism in medical datasets. The proposed algorithm implements the hierarchical-based updating strategy which utilizes the fitness function of every individual moth to dynamically modify its moth position. The simulation result shows that the hierarchical-based updating strategy attains superior value rather than the traditional updating strategy.

References

1. Beheshti, M., Ganaie, A., Paliwal, V.: Predicting brain age using machine learning algorithms: a comprehensive evaluation. IEEE J. Biomed. Health Inform. **26**, 1432–1440 (2022)
2. Kumar, N., Sharma, M., PalSingh, V.: An empirical study of handcrafted and dense feature extraction techniques for lung and colon cancer classification from histopathological images. Biomed. Signal Process. Control **75**, 445–464 (2022)

3. Faris, H., Aljarah, I., Mirjalili, S.: EvoloPy: an open-source nature-inspired optimization framework in python. In: Proceedings in 8th International Conference on Evolutionary Computation Theory and Applications, pp. 171–177 (2016)

4. Liu, J., Wei, X., Huang, H.: An improved grey wolf optimization algorithm and its application in path planning. IEEE Access **9**, 121944–121956 (2021)

5. Ghanem, W., Ghaleb, S.A., Jantan, A.: Cyber intrusion detection system based on a multi-objective binary bat algorithm for feature selection and enhanced bat algorithm for parameter optimization in neural networks. IEEE Access **10**, 76318–76339 (2022)

6. Aljorani, B., Hasan, A.: An enhanced binary cuckoo search algorithm using crossover operators for features selection. In: Proceedings in IEEE International Conference on Advanced Computer Applications, pp. 1–6 (2021)

7. Jayachitra, S., Prasanth, A.: Multi-feature analysis for automated brain stroke classification using weighted gaussian naive bayes classifier. J. Circuits Syst. Comput **30**(2150178), 1–22 (2021)

8. Sekar, J., Aruchamy, P.: An efficient clinical support system for heart disease prediction using TANFIS classifier. Comput. Intell. **38**, 610–640 (2022)

9. Semwal, V.B., Gupta, A., Lalwani, P.: An optimized hybrid deep learning model using ensemble learning approach for human walking activities recognition. J. Supercomput. **77**(11), 12256–12279 (2021). https://doi.org/10.1007/s11227-021-03768-7

10. Semwal, V.B., Lalwani, P., Mishra, M.K., Bijalwan, V., Chadha, J.S.: An optimized feature selection using bio-geography optimization technique for human walking activities recognition. Computing **103**(12), 2893–2914 (2021). https://doi.org/10.1007/s00607-021-01008-7

11. Sweetlin, J.D., Nehemiah, H.K., Kannan, A.: Computer aided diagnosis of drug sensitive pulmonary tuberculosis with cavities, consolidations and nodular manifestations on lung CT images. Int. J. Bio-Inspired Comput. **13**, 71–85 (2019)

12. Zawbaa, H.M., Emary, E., Parv, B., Sharawi, M.: Feature selection approach based on moth-flame optimization algorithm. In: Institute of Electrical and Electronics Engineers (Ed.), 2016 IEEE Congress on Evolutionary Computation (CEC), pp. 4612–4617 (2016)

13. Kaur, K., Singh, U., Salgotra, R.: An enhanced moth flame optimization. Neural Comput. Appl. **32**(7), 2315–2349 (2018). https://doi.org/10.1007/s00521-018-3821-6

14. Saeys, Y., Inza, I., Larranaga, P.: A review of feature selection techniques in bioinformatics. Bioinformatics **23**, 2507–2517 (2007)

15. Chandrashekar, G., Sahin, F.: A survey on feature selection methods. Comput. Electr. Eng. **6**, 16–28 (2014)

16. Sebban, M., Nock, R.: A hybrid filter/wrapper approach of feature selection using information theory. Pattern Recogn. **35**, 835–846 (2002)

17. Pathak, Y., Arya, K.V., Tiwari, S.: Feature selection for image steganalysis using levy flight-based grey wolf optimization. Multimedia Tools Appl. **78**(2), 1473–1494 (2018). https://doi.org/10.1007/s11042-018-6155-6

18. Lavanya, S., Prasanth, A., Jayachitra, S.: A Tuned classification approach for efficient heterogeneous fault diagnosis in IoT-enabled WSN applications. Measurement **183**(109771), 1–28 (2021)

Distinctive Approach for Speech Emotion Recognition Using Machine Learning

Yogyata Singh[✉], Neetu, and Shikha Rani

Department of Computer Science, Rajkiya Engineering College, Bijnor, Uttar Pradesh, India
yogyatas29@gmail.com

Abstract. Emotions have an important role in human-computer interaction. It improves the efficiency of Human-Computer Interaction (HCI) applications. Speech Emotions Recognition (SER) modules are critical in helping robots in interpreting data through the use of emotions. With precision, vigorousness, and dormancy taken into account, this is a difficult assignment. The proposed methodology in this experiment is to implement two approaches on the same dataset and compare the efficiency. The classification strategy employed is to classify data by implementing four different machine learning algorithms. The Support Vector Method (SVM) model has a 99.57% accuracy on the Tess Dataset and a 63.73% accuracy on the Ravdess Dataset. According to the overall analysis, the model performs better without augmentation, and the model that produced the best possible performance is the Support Vector Machine Algorithm (SVM). Two more potential additions to the model's capabilities are mood swings and depression. Psychologist may implement these techniques to monitor their patients' anxiety attacks. These additions can be made for analyzing emotions of depressed person. It can be advantageous when dealing with a person's mental state.

Keywords: Feature extraction · Visualization · Support Vector Machine · Decision Tree · Random Forest

1 Introduction

Communication between Humans with Machines is the most important aspect of artificial intelligence. Human-Computer Interaction deals with the communication of machines with humans in many forms. Speech is the most natural and effective way to have a better interaction between machines with humans. Many researchers are working in the field of Speech recognition and also working on various modifications to improve the interaction of humans and machines. Recognition of the emotional state of humans is also a modification in speech recognition as it introduces an understanding of the emotional state of the Speaker. Recognition of the emotional state of the speaker is a laborious project in the context of varying ascent, pitch, and other factors too. According to "Rene Descartes", the founder of modern philosophy. Six primitive emotions were identified named wonder, love, hatred, desire, joy, and sadness. To understand the pattern in the speech of any particular emotion, there are many observations like when a person

N. Khare et al. (Eds.): MIND 2022, CCIS 1762, pp. 39–51, 2022.
https://doi.org/10.1007/978-3-031-24352-3_4

got angry, the tone raises. In another scenario when a person is happy, the tone must be musical and satisfying. Based on the patterns of those features the model will be able to classify the emotions without any human interruptions. In this paper we are classifying the emotions into seven different classses. The procedure is divided into following steps: data collection, visualization & Augmentation, modelling, and result analysis. We conducted a comparative analysis of the results of both datasets using two different approaches. The result of two different approaches produces a dataset with varying input values. This paper focuses to survey and analyse the results of various applied methodologies on the same dataset. It looks at different extracted features, a dataset of emotional speech, classification methods, and more. Signal acquisition, feature extraction, and classification approaches are the standard divisions for speech emotion recognition. The architecture of this experiment is shown in Fig. 1.

Machine learning algorithms can provide a good result with a good accuracy score, but while moving towards advancement, Deep learning is in flow. Various deep learning models are used to give a valuable and better result depending on the current requirement of the system. In this paper, we deploy machine learning models and conduct a comparison analysis of the results. We can move on to investigate deep learning models for continuous improvements.

2 Related Work

The classification of various emotions from voice signals will become easier in the future as artificial intelligence advances. The researcher is currently employing several feature extraction approaches to imbue emotion into speech samples. The auditory sound encodes actors' emotions, which can later be interpreted or viewed as different patterns. Several acoustic aspects of speech are examined as part of the investigation into more advanced techniques for emotion recognition, various classifier methods are evaluated, as well as a few thoughts on discourse feeling recognition are surveyed. It should be noted that investigations in SER are given below.

The effectiveness of a feed-forward Deep Neural Network (DNN) and the recently developed Recurrent Neural Network (RNN) known as Gated Recurrent Unit (GRU) for emotion recognition from voice was compared by V.M. Praseetha et al. [5] in two deep learning models for emotion detection from speech. This model was created using TensorFlow, a second-generation interface for deploying machine learning algorithms. The accuracy of the GRU model is 95.82%, compared to 89.96% for the DNN model. Our tests show that when it comes to categorizing emotions, the GRU model performs better than the DNN model.

To identify a person's emotional state, Neethu Sundar prasad [3] extracted their features and used the three methods. 1. Extract each of the 34 features 2. MFCC strategies 3. Implementation of PCA. To train the SER model, it makes use of a variety of algorithms that are implemented differently with each approach, including the classifiers SVM, KNN, Gradient Boosting Tree, Gaussian Nave Bayes, Random Forest, Logistic Regression, and Decision Tree. The test results for the various approaches have all increased overall. With a score of 83% using the SVM classifier, the first strategy has a passably good result. The second method fared well with a score of 80% utilizing the

KNN algorithm. And the third strategy fared well with a score of 90% utilizing the SVM algorithm.

A Deep Neural Network (DNN)-based multi-task model has been proposed by Yuni Zeng et al. [7] that makes use of these connections and handles many audio categorization tasks at once. Because it combines Deep Residual Networks (ResNets) with a gate mechanism to extract superior representations between tasks than Convolutional Neural Networks, this model is known as the gated Residual Networks (GResNets) model (CNNs).To identification of speaker and accent tasks, once the speaker is identified, the accent of that individual is also identified. To concurrently learn accent and speaker identification tasks, our approach makes use of this link. These findings from the experiment also support this. The statistics show that the multi-task model improves speaker identification accuracy from 83.05% to 88.52% and accent recognition accuracy from 89.67% to 92.44%. Thus, MTL can be utilized to enhance the two distinct but related audio classification tasks of accent recognition and speaker identification.

Adib Ashfaq A. Zamil et al. [2] retrieved MFCC features from voice signals to discern the basic emotions of the speech. With the use of the Logistic Model Tree (LMT) classifier, extracted features have been employed to categorize various emotions. The top accuracy for identifying 7 different emotions across the trained models was 70%. One of the key goals of the suggested study, according to Manoj Kaushik et al. [8], is to use spectrograms instead of the customary MFCC feature-based technique. To distinguish voices from four vocalist classes, writers used a deep learning CNN model architecture. Total test set accuracy for the CNN model was 60.656%, while validation accuracy was 57.205%.

Babak Joze Abbaschian et al. [16] In this study, various approaches to applying practical neural network techniques to speech emotion recognition are contrasted. The goal of this study is to provide a survey on discrete speech emotion recognition. LSTM, GAN, and VAE are examples of complex networks that can be tuned. The accompanying speech datasets, several emotive SER techniques, and comparisons between them from various angles. The author tried to cover all of the major deep learning techniques used for the SER problem, including DNNs, LSTMs, and attention mechanisms.

In addition to CNN [9–11], LSTMs [12], DNNs [13, 14], and CNN-LSTM hybrids have also demonstrated promising outcomes in the field of emotion recognition. LSTMs are more sophisticated Recurrent Neural Networks (RNN) that have been gate-optimized to govern the flow of information. For the experiments, Pandey et al. [15] used this methodology. They took the magnitude, log-mel, and MFCC spectrograms out of the data and used a CNN-LSTM hybrid to train and evaluate it. The authors used MFCCs as their input and obtained an accuracy of 82.35%. Only four emotions were assessed in this study, though (Table 1).

Although images and text can be used to understand emotions, voice is the most effective technique to develop the best machine learning model. By reviewing the above research papers, the researchers have used various algorithms and extracted various features to get the most fruitful result. Mel-Frequency Cepstrum Coefficients (MFCC) from audio signals, Zero Crossing Rate (ZCR), Square Root of Mean of Square (RMS), and Short-Term Fourier Transform (STFT) can all be utilized to assess a person's emotional state. This study used two alternative SER techniques, one without augmentation and

Table 1. Earlier studies on audio datasets

References	Title	Types of classifiers	Accuracy
[5]	Deep learning models for speech emotion recognition	Gated Recurrent Unit, a combination of a Deep Neural Network (DNN) and Recurrent Neural Network (RNN)	95.8%
[3]	Speech emotion detection using machine learning techniques on TESS	SVM, KNN, Gradient Boosting Tree, Gaussian Naïve Bayes, Random Forest, Logistic Regression, Decision Tree	83%
[1]	Speech Emotion Based Sentiment Recognition using Deep Neural Networks	CNN, Random Forest Classsifier, And Support Vector Machine	86.15%
[7]	Spectrogram based multi-task audio classification	Support Vector Machine	54.63%

one with augmentation, on both datasets (RAVDESS and TESS), and compared the results of both approaches. The first approach's implementation performs well, with a high score of 63.73% (RAVDESS Dataset) and 99.76% (TESS Dataset) using the SVM method.

3 Proposed Scheme

The recommended approaches for applying different classification methodologies contain four steps: Data Collection, Visualization & Augmentation, Modelling, and Result Analysis.

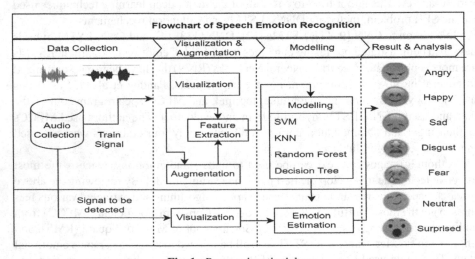

Fig. 1. Proposed methodology

3.1 Data Collection

Data Description
To address any machine learning issue, it's mandatory to have a dataset on which the result must be generated. The Dataset consists of a training sample to train the model. Simulated, semi-natural, and natural speaking speech collections make up the data sets. The same text was read aloud by trained speakers with a variety of moods using a synthetic dataset. By asking actors to recount an event with a range of emotions, semi-natural collections are created. The emotions in the datasets are categorized by human listeners using natural datasets that have been collected from television shows, YouTube videos, service providers, and many more sources.

RAVDESS
The proposed approaches for speech emotion identification were validated in this work using two separate audio datasets. For this experiment, the datasets Tess [4] and Ravdess [6] are employed. S. R., & Russo, F. A. et al. [6] was recorded by actors in the English language. This dataset was collected by the Department of Psychology at Ryerson University in Toronto, Ontario, Canada. By reading selected sentences, 12 male and 12 female actors aided in the compilation of this dataset. The dataset incorporates emotions such as anger, surprise, calm, fear, happiness, neutral sadness, and disgust. Every recording consists of two degrees of emotional intensity with the addition of neutral expression.

TESS
Kate Dupuis et al. [4] recorded by two actors in the English language. The University of Toronto's Department of Psychology in Toronto, Ontario, Canada, assembled this data set. By reading selected words, two female actors contributed to the compilation of this dataset. This aids in analyzing the speech patterns of younger and older females. It includes a range of feelings, including neutral, disgust, fear, happiness, pleasant surprise, sad, and rage.

3.2 Visualization

Visualizing the data helps to better comprehend the issue and the kind of solution that should be developed. A few techniques for visualizing the data include the distribution of classes, the number of examples under each category, the spread of the data, the correlation between the features, and clustering.

Using Librosa load and matplotlib, we import the audio data for the various genres. When using Librosa. Load, an audio time series that details the amplitude of the audio at various timesteps is returned. The graph shows the amplitude on the vertical (Y) axis and the time on the horizontal (X) axis, but it doesn't show us what's happening to the frequencies (Fig. 2).

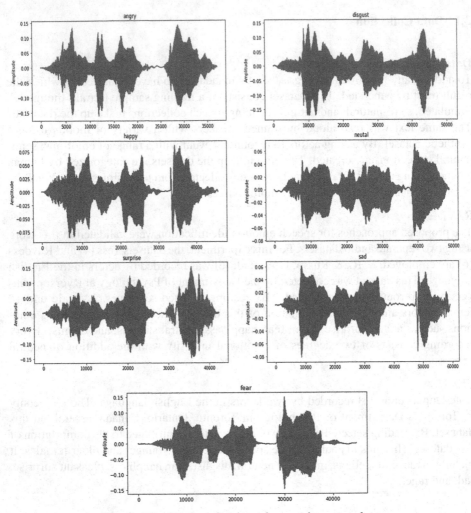

Fig. 2. Visualization of various classes using wave-plot

3.3 Augmentation

When we don't have enough data or need to add it to our dataset, we often use data augmentation to provide variations. Minor changes to the current data samples are all that is required to achieve the goal. Speech recognition enhancement entails modifying the sound waveform used in training in some way, such as accelerating or slowing spoken audio and adding background noises. The dataset grows when numerous enhanced copies of the same input are fed into the network during training. The following are methods for enhancing data-

1. **Time Stretching**: In this technique, the sound is sped up or slowed down without altering samples and a factor for stretching as inputs to the Time stretch function.

2. **Pitch Shifting**: The pitch of the sound is altered without influencing the speed of the sound. Wave samples, sampling rate, and the number of pitch steps are all considered.
3. **Time Shift**: It just shift audio to the left or the right by a random amount.

3.4 Feature Extraction

Extraction of features and the creation of parameters from the speech signal is one of the key phases in speech processing. The implementation of feature extraction focuses on the signal's information, enhances the degree of similarity and dissimilarity across different classes, and reduces the size of the data and calculations. While the features that can be recovered from each pattern are useful for classification, the goal of this study is to enhance the effectiveness of speech emotion identification using the suggested feature extraction method. The process of extracting the desirable elements to identify human emotions in speech is known as feature extraction. Humans are capable of altering the sound signal by articulating the phoneme with the help of their vocal tract, teeth, and tongue. The study and comparison of various emotional characteristic parameters was the foundation for traditional emotional feature extraction, which selected emotional characteristics with a high emotional resolution. Traditional Emotional feature extraction frequently focuses on the study of the emotional components of speech employing amplitude construction, time construction, signal feature, and fundamental frequency construction. Generally speaking, Spectral features and prosodic features are the two types of features used by SER.

- **Prosodic feature:** Prosodic qualities are those that have to do with our speaking patterns, such as how loudly, sharply, energetically, and stress-wise we talk.
- **Spectral Features:** Spectral Features are based on frequency. These features include things like MFCC, LPC, PLP, etc.

In this work, the proposed methodology contains two alternative ways to detect emotions: the first is to extract the features of the originally acceptable audio signals, and the second is to extract the spectral features of the data with the application of augmentation techniques. Spectral properties include Mel Frequency Cepstrum Coefficients (MFCC), the zero-crossing rate (ZCR), the square root of the mean of the square (RMS), and the short-term Fourier transform (STFT). The outcomes of both procedures were analyzed to attain the best possible result. Both approaches were applied to both datasets using a variety of modeling strategies.

1. **Root Mean Square (RMS):** It can be calculated by taking the root average of the square of the amplitude.

$$\sqrt{\frac{1}{n}xi^2} = \sqrt{\frac{x1^2 + x2^2 + \ldots + xn^2}{n}} \tag{1}$$

2. **Zero Crossing Rate (ZCR):** Determine the rate of change for the signal's sign change. Calculating how frequently a signal changes its sign from positive to zero to negative and vice versa axis can be stated in simpler terms. ZCR changes as a

result of variations in human genetic and psychosomatic activity as well as changes in emotion, which cause the rate of change.

3. **Mel Frequency Cepstrum Coefficients (MFCC):** An MFCC is made up of these coefficients. They are derived from an audio clip's cepstral representation (a nonlinear spectrum of a spectrum). It includes the Cepstrum Coefficients and is connected to the vocal tract. The major processes in the MFCC feature extraction method include windowing the signal, applying the DFT, computing the magnitude's log, warping the frequencies on a Mel scale, and employing the inverse DCT.

4. **Short-Term Fourier Transform (STFT):** The Short-Time Fourier Transform (STFT), sometimes known as Short-Term Fourier Transform (STFT), is a logical extension of the Fourier Transform that addresses signal non-stationarity. Using the short-time Fourier transform, we may carry out a time-frequency analysis (STFT). It is employed to create signal representations that incorporate the local time and frequency content. In audio feature extraction for time-frequency decomposition, STFT is frequently utilized.

3.5 Classification Approaches

The automatic emotion detection problem is a supervised learning problem as supervised learning employs a known set of input data and known reactions to the data and seeks to construct a predictor model that delivers good predictions for the response to incoming data. There are numerous classifiers available for supervised learning, including HMM (Hidden Markov Model), SVM (Support Vector Machine), linear classifiers, Decision tree, k-nearest neighbors, and random forest, among others. In this research, we used SVM, Decision Tree, k-nearest neighbors, and random forest.

Decision Tree

It is a visual representation of every alternative that could be used to solve a problem or make a choice. The generated conclusion is based on the dataset's characteristic properties. It offers a method for predicting the outcome by utilizing a labeled dataset for training to compute optimal estimations.

K-Nearest Neighbors

The technique aims to classify unlabelled samples based on how closely they resemble samples from the training set. It is a lazy learning technique that locates the test data's closest match in feature space using the distance function. In this study, the Euclidean metric is used. The K-NN method, which groups new data based on similarities, stores all of the data. The K-NN technique can thus be used to swiftly classify newly generated data into the appropriate category.

$$\text{Euclidean Distance between two points} = \sqrt{(x2 - x1)^2 + (y2 - y1)^2} \tag{2}$$

Support Vector Machine

An optimal margin classifier in machine learning is called a Support Vector Machine

(SVM). Each spoken emotion is given a label by the SVM classifier. Use the signal to denote the spoken emotional signal's emotional categories before training and recognition. Input the feature vector into each SVM in the emotion recognition process, after which the output of each SVM is passed via logic judgment to choose the most likely emotion. And finally, the most weight is given to the emotional nature of speech signals (most votes).

Classification is accomplished by locating an outer-space hyperplane that clearly delineates the various categories. To select the appropriate hyperplane, two conditions must be met.

- In classifying the classes, the hyperplane should be the most accurate.
- The margin distance between the hyperplane and the nearest data point must be increased.

Random Forest Classifier

A Random Forest is a randomized prediction method that employs the use of averaging to boost predicted accuracy and prevent over-fitting by fitting several decision tree classification models on different segments of the dataset. The max samples option controls the sub-sample size if bootstrap = True (the default), otherwise the complete dataset is used to analyze each tree. The model was developed with a count of 100 estimators. The following are the stages involved in developing a random forest classifier:

1. To work with, select a subset of the dataset's features and choose a node from the subsets using the best split.
2. Continue making child nodes out of subsets.
3. Continue until all nodes have been used as splits.
4. Make a forest by assembling several trees in iterative manner using 1–3.

4 Experimental Analysis

This research is separated into two parts: before and after using augmentation techniques. Augmentation procedures are the process of updating, or "augmenting," a dataset with additional data. This additional input might range from photos to text, and its inclusion in machine learning algorithms affects their performance. Two separate datasets with the same number of emotions were used for this study to compare the results and obtain an optimized analysis. The results of both methodologies were analyzed in this study on distinct datasets. This identifies the optimal classifier for the given issue statement to achieve optimized prediction and a higher prediction rate.

The first step of this study involves data gathering. Both datasets are simulated datasets that have been pre-recorded and are publicly available. Data visualization was performed to visualize the data and gain a better knowledge of the data. Two approaches were utilized following the visualizing step. The first technique in this study was labeled "Before Augmentation" and the second approach was termed "After Augmentation".

Now, let's look at the first approach: In before the augmentation phase, the original data is utilized for training the model with no augmentation procedures performed. However, in the second approach, various data augmentation techniques were used to modify the dataset. The model is trained using the changed dataset. This paper used 7:3 of data as training for testing. Modeling is the next phase, and various supervised learning algorithms were employed for training and testing. Based on the input file, such methods were employed to estimate the emotion.

Table 2. Comparison of result of both the approaches using SVM algorithm

Dataset	Tess		Ravdess	
Approaches	Without	With	Without	With
Angry	1.00	1.00	0.76	0.68
Happy	0.98	0.99	0.70	0.62
Sad	1.00	0.99	0.54	0.61
Neutral	1.00	0.98	0.51	0.54
Fear	1.00	0.99	0.63	0.58
Surprise	0.99	0.94	0.62	0.56
Disgust	1.00	1.00	0.65	0.58
Rate (%)	99.5	98.3	63.7	60.0

Table 3. Result of accuracy rate of Ravdess dataset

Classifiers	Before augmentation	After augmentation
SVM	63.73%	60.0%
KNN	44%	42.9%
Random Forest	54.40%	57.86%
Decision Tree	37.06%	35.19%

This reveals the Ravdess Dataset outcomes, as indicated in Table 3. The "Before Augmentation" method produces greater results than the "After Augmentation" method. SVM is the most effective of the four algorithms. The Before Augmentation strategy has a recognition rate of SVM of 63.73%, whereas the After Augmentation approach has a recognition rate of 60.8%.

This exhibits the Tess dataset results, as mentioned in Table 4. The "Before Augmentation" technique yields greater results than the "After Augmentation" method. SVM is the most productive of the four algorithms. Using the Before Augmentation strategy, the SVM's recognition rate is 99.76%, while using the After Augmentation approach, it is 96.43%.

Table 4. Result of accuracy rate of Tess dataset

Classifiers	Before augmentation	After augmentation
SVM	99.57%	98.3%
KNN	99.85%	90.1%
Random Forest	99.57%	96.79%
Decision Tree	92.30%	85.91%

Table 5. Classification report of various algorithms applied

Dataset	Algorithm	Without augmentation			With augmentation		
		Precision	Recall	F1 Score	Precision	Recall	F1 Score
TESS	SVM	1.0	1.0	1.0	0.98	0.98	0.98
	KNN	1.0	1.0	1.0	0.90	0.90	0.90
	Random Forest	1.0	1.0	1.0	0.97	0.97	0.97
	Decision Tree	0.92	0.92	0.92	0.86	0.86	0.86
RAVDESS	SVM	0.64	0.64	0.64	0.60	0.60	0.60
	KNN	0.47	0.44	0.43	0.43	0.43	0.41
	Random Forest	0.55	0.54	0.54	0.59	0.58	0.58
	Decision Tree	0.37	0.37	0.37	0.35	0.35	0.35

There are still many unknown factors when it comes to the optimum algorithm for classifying emotions. Emotion recognition rates vary depending on the combination of emotional features used. The experts are currently arguing which characteristics influence emotion perception in speech. Table 2 provides an in-depth explanation of the accuracy with which emotions can be predicted using SVM algorithms. Using several techniques, it demonstrates accuracy values for each emotion. The analysis of all the applied methodologies on the used dataset is briefly described in Table 5. It demonstrates a thorough overview of the complete study's results.

5 Conclusion

The notion executed in this research was recognition of the emotional state of the speaker based on numerous speech parameters. This study includes a survey to discover novel methods for extracting emotional context from speech with amazing precision. We can see a pattern where diverse Deep Learning techniques are far more effective than predictive modeling algorithms. We can improve efficiency even further by implementing deep learning models and collecting a large number of datasets. When there is an enormous amount of information for training and testing, deep learning models perform well. In this study, Various machine learning methodologies were used to determine the ideal parameters for attaining an accuracy rate. This paper is an attempt to analyze the contribution of several speech signal features, namely root mean square, zero crossing rate, and MFCC features. The proposed approaches used two schemes using the same classifiers to better comprehend the study. After comparing the two approaches, we can conclude that the Support Vector Machine (SVM) classifier produces the best results on our chosen data before introducing additional augmentation strategies.

References

1. Choudhary, R.R., Meena, G., Mohbey, K.K.: Speech emotion based sentiment recognition using deep neural networks. J. Phys. Conf. Ser. **2236**, 012003 (2022)
2. Zamil, A.A.A., et al.: Emotion detection from speech signals using voting mechanism on classified frames. In: 2019 International Conference on Robotics, Electrical and Signal Processing Techniques (ICREST). IEEE (2019)
3. Sundarprasad, N.: San Jose State University (Spring 2018) Speech Emotion Detection Using Using Machine Learning Techniques (2018)
4. Dupuis, K., Pichora-Fuller, M.K.: Recognition of emotional speech for younger and older talkers: behavioural findings from the Toronto emotional speech set. Can. Acoust. **39**(3), 182–183 (2011)
5. Praseetha, V.M., Vadivel, S.: Deep learning models for speech emotion recognition. J. Comput. Sci. **14**(11), 1577–1587 (2018)
6. Livingstone, S.R., Russo, F.A.: The Ryerson Audio-Visual Database of Emotional Speech and Song (RAVDESS): A dynamic, multimodal set of facial and vocal expressions in North American English. PLoS ONE **13**, e0196391 (2018)
7. Zeng, Y., Mao, H., Peng, D., Yi, Z.: Spectrogram based multi-task audio classification. Multimedia Tools Appl. **78**(3), 3705–3722 (2017). https://doi.org/10.1007/s11042-017-5539-3
8. Kaushik, M., Rani, S., Yadav, V.: Vocalist identification in audio songs using convolutional neural network. In: Department of Computer Science and Engineering Centre for Advanced Studies. https://doi.org/10.1007/978-981-33-6881-1_9
9. Shukla, P.K., et al.: Efficient prediction of drug-drug interaction using deep learning models. IET Syst. Biol. **14**, 211–216 (2020)
10. Liu, J., Liu, Z., Sun, C., Zhuang, J.: A data transmission approach based on ant colony optimization and threshold proxy re-encryption in WSNs. J. Artif. Intell. Technol. **2**, 23–31 (2022)
11. De Luca, G.: A survey of NISQ cra hybrid quantum-classical machine learning research. J. Artif. Intell. Technol. **2**, 9–15 (2022)
12. Sultana, S., Iqbal, M.Z., Selim, M.R., Rashid, M.M., Rahman, M.S.: Bangla speech emotion recognition and cross-lingual study using deep CNN and BLSTM networks. IEEE Access **10**, 564–578 (2021)
13. Lee, K.H., Choi, H.K., Jang, B.T.: A study on speech emotion recognition using a deep neural network. In: Proceedings of the 2019 International Conference on Information and Communication Technology Convergence (ICTC), pp. 1162–1165, Jeju, Korea, 16–18 October 2019
14. Kaur, M., Kumar, V.: Parallel non-dominated sorting genetic algorithm-II-based image encryption technique. Imaging Sci. J. **66**, 453–462 (2018)

15. Pandey, S., Shekhawat, H., Prasanna, S.: Deep learning techniques for speech emotion recognition: a review. In: Proceedings of the 2019 29th International Conference Radioelektronika (RADIOELEKTRONIKA), Pardubice, Czech Republic, 16–18 April 2019
16. Abbaschian, B.J., Sierra-Sosa, D., Elmaghraby, A.: Deep learning techniques for speech emotion recognition, from databases to models. Sensors **21**, 1249 (2021). Computer Science and Engineering Department, University of Louisville, Louisville, KY 40292, USA

A Survey on Human Activity Recognition Using Deep Learning Techniques and Wearable Sensor Data

Nidhi Dua[1]([✉]) , Shiva Nand Singh[1] , Sravan Kumar Challa[1] ,
Vijay Bhaskar Semwal[2] , and M. L. S. Sai Kumar[3]

[1] National Institute of Technology, Jamshedpur, Jharkhand, India
dua.nidhi2022@gmail.com
[2] MANIT Bhopal, Bhopal, M.P., India
[3] Vignan's Institute of Information Technology, Visakhapatnam, India

Abstract. HAR has attained major attention because of its significant use in real-life scenarios like activity and fitness monitoring, rehabilitation, gaming, prosthetic limbs, healthcare, smart surveillance systems, etc. HAR systems provide ways for monitoring human behaviors and detecting body movements and various activities by using sensor data. The collection of sensors available in the mobile and other wearable devices has made most of these HAR applications easily possible. Moreover, Deep Learning (DL) has further accelerated the research on HAR using the data obtained via wearable devices. In this paper, we have discussed the overview of HAR, its applications, and popular benchmark datasets available publicly. Further, we discussed various DL techniques applied for HAR applications. We have also presented the challenges associated with the field and the future directions for performing more vital research in HAR.

Keywords: Wearable sensors · Pattern recognition · HAR · Deep Learning

1 Introduction

In the recent past, HAR is attracting much focus from researchers and academia due to its significant role in healthcare, activity monitoring, intelligent surveillance, gaming, rehabilitation, etc. [1]. HAR systems provide a means to monitor and recognize human activities using data collected via various wearable and vision-based sensors [2]. Due to improvements in wireless communication networks and sensor technology in terms of capacity, affordability, and power efficiency over the past ten years, sensors can now be used to recognize human activities. These sensors and devices are necessary to continuously monitor the activities of people (mainly elders, dependents, etc.). The main goal of these tools is usually to support active and healthy aging and to detect possible health issues early to enable a long and independent life [3, 4]. Especially dietary risks, poor physical activities, and a lack of needed assistance can lead to difficult-to-treat long-term problems. The smart environments that interact with people based on their unique requirements are gradually becoming an inseparable part of daily life.

N. Khare et al. (Eds.): MIND 2022, CCIS 1762, pp. 52–71, 2022.
https://doi.org/10.1007/978-3-031-24352-3_5

HAR is basically a pattern recognition task. Various conventional ML approaches like Support Vector Machine (SVM), Decision Trees (DT), etc., have been widely applied for HAR and achieved decent performance. Yet, there are some drawbacks of using ML techniques. Firstly, they involve handcrafted feature extraction and thus demand high domain knowledge. Moreover, such features are heuristic driven and make the solution application specific. Furthermore, these conventional approaches could learn only shallow features using human expertise. These features generally include frequency and time domain features like variance, mean, frequency, etc. They could detect simple activities like running and walking but were not capable of detecting context-aware and complex activities [5] like drinking coffee. Owing to these limitations, the performance of these conventional approaches is restricted in terms of generalization and detection accuracy.

In the recent decade, with advancements in technology, DL algorithms have achieved huge success in the fields of image classification, object detection, natural language processing, etc. DL has accelerated the acceptance and use of HAR to various applications based on wearable sensors by improving its robustness and performance. This is because it overcomes the limitations of conventional ML approaches. DL algorithms can learn features automatically from the data; hence there is no need for manual feature engineering. These algorithms can learn hierarchical abstractions with the aid of multiple layers of deep neural networks (DNN). Thus, DNN can efficiently extract features from the raw sensor data without the need of expert domain knowledge.

Although DL has shown encouraging results, there are still numerous obstacles to be solved, which opens up new possibilities for research. We outline current difficulties, roadblocks, and potential future paths in this subject as we give a review on DL-based HAR using wearable sensors. The main contributions of our work are summarized as follows.

1. We have presented a brief overview of the HAR framework and the steps involved in recognition of human activities. The most widely used wearable sensors for activity data acquisition and publicly available commonly used activity datasets are also briefly discussed. Additionally, we mentioned various application areas where HAR researchers are putting their focus on.
2. We reviewed various research papers that applied DL-based techniques for the recognition of human activities using wearable sensor data. We have categorized the papers based on the algorithms used viz. CNN, RNN, Autoencoders, DBM, etc.
3. Various challenges associated with HAR using wearables are discussed in this work. Also, we made our humble efforts to provide possible future directions to benefit the researchers associated with this field.

To give the reader a clearer view of the contents discussed in this work, Fig. 1 presents the nomenclature of DL-based HAR using wearable sensor data. Section 2 provides a brief overview of the various steps involved in HAR. Various mainstream wearable sensors used for human activity data acquisition are discussed in Sect. 3, while Sect. 4 presents various application areas of HAR. Section 5 provides a review of various DL algorithms applied for activity recognition in literature, and challenges associated with the field and the future scope are provided in Sect. 6. Section 7 concludes the paper.

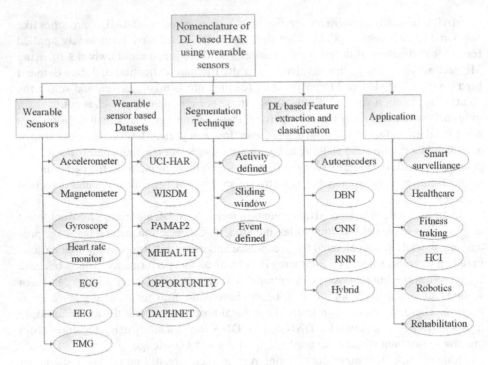

Fig. 1. Nomenclature of DL-based HAR using wearable sensors.

2 Overview of Human Activity Recognition

HAR is detecting different body movements and identifying various human actions using the data obtained via different sensors. HAR comprises four stages: acquisition of data, data preprocessing, data segmentation, feature extraction, and finally, activity classification.

2.1 Data Acquisition

Activity data is acquired via various vision-based and non-vision based sensors. Vision-based sensors involve the use of the camera. There are certain problems with vision-based sensors: occlusions, privacy issues, difficult installation, such sensors can't be mounted everywhere, and require proper illumination and other environmental conditions [6]. Wearable sensors are applied largely in Activity Recognition (AR) because of their ubiquity, low cost, installation, availability, and ease of use.

2.2 Data Segmentation

The next stage in HAR is the segmentation of sensor data. One of HAR's most significant data preprocessing steps is selecting an activity window to segment data acquired from different sensors. There are different techniques prevalent in the literature for the selection of window, namely: activity defined [7], sliding window [8], and event defined [9].

Utilizing a sliding window of fixed-length and dividing the sequence data, acquired using wearables, into equal-length segments, with or without overlap between the subsequent segments, is the most popular method for doing this.

2.3 Feature Extraction and Classification

The data segments obtained from the last step are used for the extraction of features. It is the most critical stage in the HAR framework, and it can be done in two ways: either manually or automatically. HAR framework using conventional ML-based approaches is depicted in Fig. 2. Conventional ML-based approaches involve manual feature engineering and hence demand expert knowledge. These approaches comprise data acquisition, data preprocessing and segmentation, handcrafted feature extraction followed by feature selection [10–12] techniques, and classification. Manual feature extraction requires domain knowledge to extract relevant frequency domain features, time domain features, etc. to capture signal details. Several traditional Machine Learning (ML) based techniques using classifiers like Naïve Bayes (NB), Random Forest (RF), SVM, etc. [13, 14], achieved decent performance in recognizing human activities. These traditional methods of pattern recognition, however, necessitate domain knowledge and rely heavily on handcrafted features. Furthermore, the features so obtained are application specific and lack scalability [15].

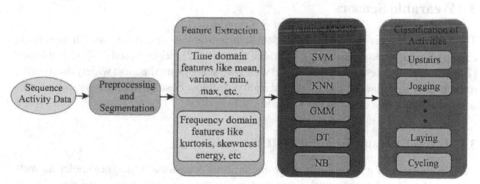

Fig. 2. Human Activity Recognition using conventional ML-based techniques

Utilizing Deep Learning (DL) methods can make the HAR pipeline simpler. Figure 3 presents the overview of HAR framework utilizing DL techniques for feature extraction and classification. In several areas, including image synthesis, image segmentation, image classification, object detection, activity recognition, human gait analysis, etc., DL has demonstrated remarkable empirical performance [16–20]. The structure of DL algorithms consists of many layers of neurons that extract hierarchical abstractions. A non-linear function is utilized by every individual layer to create new feature maps using the input feature maps from the preceding layer. With the aid of this hierarchical abstraction, DL algorithms can extract features automatically that best characterize a certain application area. Deep learning (DL) uses a DNN architecture which minimizes a certain loss function to extract features and classification boundaries. DL-based approaches may automatically learn the features and don't require any manual feature engineering. Deep Learning (DL) algorithms that are widely used for HAR include Deep Belief Networks, CNN, autoencoders, and RNN.

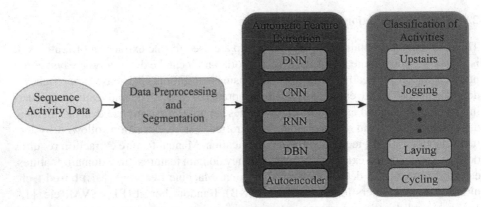

Fig. 3. HAR using Deep learning techniques

3 Wearable Sensors

The first step in activity recognition is data acquisition via various sensors. These sensors can be – smartphone sensors [21], wearable sensors [22], depth-based [23], vision-based [24], etc. Among these, smartphone and wearable sensors are the most widely used owing to their easy installation, ease of use, ubiquity, and low cost. Different wearable sensors used are briefly discussed in the following subsections.

3.1 Inertial Measurement Unit (IMU)

IMU comprises of gyroscope, accelerometer, and occasionally magnetometer as well. The accelerometer measures the acceleration in the x, y, and z axes and thus detects gravitational forces and linear motion. In contrast, the rotation rate is measured by the gyroscope [25], and the magnetometer senses and measures the magnetic fields of the earth [26]. IMU sensors are usually embedded in smart devices, wearables, and smartphones. With the extensive use of mobile phones and other smart devices, the IMU data are more easily and ubiquitously available for detecting motion and recognizing human activities [27].

3.2 Electromyography (EMG)

EMG sensors are capable of measuring the electrical activity produced by muscular movements [28]. It is used in medical examinations to diagnose and study the functionality of nerves and muscles and thus is of significant use in - the area of rehabilitation and detection of neuromuscular disorders. Additionally, these biosignals are also useful for mechanical actuators (used in human-machine interaction), controlling robot devices, gaming, etc. EMG sensors are of two types, viz. Intramuscular EMG (iEMG) and Surface EMG (sEMG). Many wearable non-invasive HAR systems use sEMG to detect and recognize various human actions [29]. The authors in [30] developed a CNN-based system using sEMG that could recognize ten different hand gestures.

3.3 Electrocardiography (ECG)

Electrocardiography is a process that records the heart's electrical activity and generates an electrocardiogram. It is a non-invasive test that makes use of electrodes that are placed on the surface of the skin on the chest and limbs. ECG is commonly used to diagnose and detect heart-related conditions. Several works in HAR have used a combination of ECG and other wearable motion sensors. For example, in [31], the authors used an accelerometer and multi-lead ECG to recognize daily human activities. Authors in [32] used heart activity data generated by ECG and photoplethysmography (PPG). They used pre-trained CNN models, namely Xception, MobileNetV2, and Resnet50V2, to classify the PPG and ECG data to recognize different human activities.

3.4 Electroencephalography (EEG)

In EEG, small metal discs with thin wires form the electrodes. Such electrodes track the electrical impulses produced by the activity of brain cells when they are pasted onto the scalp. The present-day EEG tool consists of electrodes containing an array of 128, 256, and 512 electrodes. Clinically, EEG is mainly used to detect and diagnose cognitive abnormalities that may lead to disorders like epileptic seizures, Alzheimer's, etc. In HAR, EEG data is used to recognize the cognitive activity of the user. Using EEG data for activity recognition is challenging due to low SNR, transient nature, etc. EEG can be applied to assisted living applications and long-term activity monitoring. In literature, some recent works have used EEG data to detect and classify different activities. Authors in [33] used wearable EEG headset data collected from volunteers in an unconstrained environment and classified the activities into intense ambulatory, light ambulatory, and stationary using SVM. In [34], the authors used EEG data to classify activities like watching TV, reading, and speaking loudly. These activities include eye and head movements and jaw clasping.

4 Applications of HAR Using Wearable Sensor Data

HAR using wearables is gaining huge popularity due to the abundance of wearable sensors being made available with advancements in technology. Moreover, as smartphones and other smart devices (having different types of sensors embedded in them) are being used by the majority of the population, the sensors are almost ubiquitously available to capture motion and activity data. HAR using wearable sensor data has significant applications in physical activity and fitness monitoring, human-computer interface (HCI), and health and rehabilitation. HAR has drawn an ample amount of attention from researchers in HCI. It is vital for determining how a user interacts with its surroundings and can be applied as assistive technology for robotics, health care, rehabilitation, and the development of smart systems with adaptive user interfaces.

Recognizing daily physical activity is crucial in lifestyle and fitness tracking to determine a person's risk of heart-related conditions, diabetes, and musculoskeletal disorders. [35]. Researchers discovered that physical activity and the development of cancers, type 2 diabetes, pulmonary diseases, cardiovascular diseases [36, 37], etc. are inversely related. Physical activities like sitting, standing, running, walking, etc., are monitored using data obtained by wearable devices. The data recorded by various wearable sensors while performing these activities carry important information about the individual's daily activity intensity and duration, and energy expenditure. This, in turn, may help reveal the health condition and habits of the individual [38]. Being aware of daily activity and energy expenditure may help the doctor to better diagnose the condition of patient and may inspire users to lifestyle modification by engaging in more exercise and physical activity [39].

Wearables sensors play an instrumental role in healthcare by making data capturing easy and almost ubiquitous. Data of patients and individuals captured via wearables help physicians to monitor and assess subjects' health. Several works have introduced techniques to assess and monitor symptoms of Parkinson's Disease (PD) patients [40]. Some other works have developed methods to sense cough activity (a key sign of pulmonary illnesses) using wearable sensors [41].

HAR using wearable sensor data has also made considerable advancements in robotics and prosthesis. The huge amount of data collected via wearables helps scientists design and develop more advanced robots [42] and prostheses. The hand motion and muscular activity data collected via EMG sensor aid researchers in developing better prosthetic limbs [43].

Wearable devices in HCI have provided us with a more flexible approach to interacting with the computer and other electronic devices. For instance, a wrist-worn device having IMU sensors embedded in it helps to detect wrist movements and various other hand gestures to control smart electronics devices [44].

5 Datasets

Benchmark datasets are important in the field of HAR. Researchers using DL techniques can use these datasets to evaluate their proposed HAR techniques and evaluate them against state-of-the-art techniques. While some researchers collect datasets purposely for their work, others majorly rely on the public datasets available to evaluate their algorithms. Some of the popular benchmark datasets captured using wearable sensors are presented in Table 1, and are briefly discussed in this sub-section.

Table 1. Various publicly available wearable sensor-based HAR datasets.

Dataset	Modalities used *	Number of participants	Number of activities	Context $
UCI-HAR	A, G	30	6	ADL
WISDM	A	36	6	ADL
PAMAP2	A, G, M	9	18	ADL
MHEALTH	A, G, M, ECG	10	12	ADL
OPPORTUNITY	A, G, M, Localization sensors	4	17	ADL
DAPHNET	A	10	3	PD patients' Freezing of gait

* Accelerometer (A), Magnetometer (M), Gyroscope (G)
$ Activities of daily living (ADL)

5.1 UCI-HAR

The UCI-HAR dataset [13] is an activity recognition dataset released by the UCI repository. It contains the activity data of 30 participants. Each volunteer wore a smartphone (containing gyroscope and accelerometer) around his/her waist and performed six activities (including walking, standing, laying, etc.). The data were captured at 50 Hz sampling rate, and they comprise nine features, viz. Gyroscope signals, total acceleration, and body acceleration in all three axes.

5.2 PAMAP2

PAMAP2 [45] is another AR dataset released by the UCI repository. It contains the activity data of 9 volunteers performing 18 different activities. Out of the 18 activities, 12 were protocol activities (like rope jumping, ascending and descending stairs, cycling, standing, nordic walking, ironing, etc.) performed by each participant, whereas the remaining six were optional activities performed by some of the participants. Each volunteer was wearing 3 IMUs (one each at the chest, on the dominant side's ankle, and on the wrist of the dominant arm) and a Heart Rate (HR) monitor. Each IMU data consists of 17 features/ attributes, including temperature reading, orientation data, 3 dimensional accelerometer data, 3-dimensional magnetometer data, and 3-dimensional gyroscope data. The raw sensory data, in total, consists of 52 attributes/ features. The data were collected by sampling the signals from IMUs at a rate of 100Hz, and from the HR monitor at 9 Hz. This data set is publicly available and is used for action recognition and intensity estimation.

5.3 WISDM

The Wireless Sensor Data Mining lab of Fordham University released a publicly available activity recognition dataset named the WISDM dataset [46]. It contains the activity data of 36 participants carrying out various daily activities like standing, upstairs, downstairs, sitting, walking, and jogging. The data were acquired through a smartphone (containing an accelerometer sensor) and were sampled at a rate of 20 Hz.

5.4 MHEALTH

The MHEALTH dataset [47] was made public by the UCI repository. It contains activity data of ten subjects who performed 12 different daily activities. The activities include jogging, frontal elevation of arms, running, crouching, climbing stairs, walking, waist bends forwards, sitting & relaxing, jumping front and back, lying down, standing still, and cycling. The dataset contains vital signs recording and body movements of the subjects. Sensors used to acquire the activity data were gyroscope, magnetometer, and accelerometer. In addition to this, a two-lead ECG signal is also collected. Sensors were positioned at the individual's chest, left ankle, and right wrist. The dataset consists of 23 features containing ECG and accelerometer signals taken at the chest, accelerometer, magnetometer, and gyroscope signals collected at the wrist and ankle. The signals were captured at 50 Hz sampling rate.

5.5 Opportunity

The OPPORTUNITY dataset [48] consists of composite naturalistic activities performed in a sensor-rich setting. It comprises daily morning activities performed by four subjects in an environment where the sensors are placed in objects and worn by the subjects. Each subject performed five times a session of Activities of Daily Living (ADL) and a drill session, which comprised 17 activities repeated 20 times. The ADL session was recorded when subjects performed daily activities (like lying on a chair, getting up, grooming, making and eating a sandwich, etc.), in a natural environment, following a high-level script. The drill session comprises activities like opening and closing the fridge, opening and closing the dishwasher, open and close door1 and door2, etc. The wearables used include seven IMUs, twelve 3D accelerators, and four 3D localization sensors. Among the object sensors used in this dataset were twelve objects with 2D rate of turn and 3D acceleration sensor. The ambient sensors include thirteen switches and eight 3D accelerometers. The dataset was captured at a 98 Hz of sampling rate.

5.6 Daphnet

Daphnet dataset [49] is used to spot Freezing of Gait (FOG) in PD patients. It comprises activity data recorded from ten PD patients performing various activities like turning, walking, standing, and freezing. For data acquisition, each subject was made to wear acceleration sensors on the ankle, thigh, and lower back. The dataset contains a total of 237 FOG events.

6   Deep Learning Techniques Applied for HAR in Literature

In the recent past, DL methods have outperformed the conventional ML techniques in HAR related jobs. This is mainly due to the vast amount of data being made available due to the use of wearable sensors and secondly due to the advancements in processing capabilities with the advent of GPUs. DL techniques are superior compared to ML techniques because they can extract features automatically, unlike ML techniques that require expert intervention and manual feature extraction. Various DL techniques applied to HAR are discussed in following subsections. Table 2 presents a summary of some representative works using DL techniques for HAR.

6.1 Autoencoder

Autoencoders (AE) were originally proposed as an unsupervised pre-training technique for ANN [50]. Autoencoder is an unsupervised technique for feature learning. It consists of encoder and decoder modules which are made up of several dense layers. The input signals are encoded into a latent space by the encoder module, and the latent space signals are converted back into the input domain by the decoder module. Autoencoder is a powerful tool for information retrieval, denoising, and dimensionality reduction. Its dimensionality reduction and feature extraction have been applied in various HAR works using wearables [51–53]. Mean Squared Error (MSE) or MSE with KL divergence loss function is used to train AE. AE are also used in stacked architecture. Authors in [54] used three layered AE with k-means clustering and accelerometer data to classify infant and newborn activities into four classes. AE has additionally been used in the recognition of null classes [55], detection of unseen data [56], and feature extraction in domain transfer learning [57]. AE have also been used for denoising the raw sensor data [58].

6.2 CNN

CNNs are widely applied to multiple tasks like time-series forecasting, image classification, object detection [59], etc. CNNs consist of an input layer, multiple convolutional and pooling layers, dense layers, and a classification layer (like SoftMax). The convolutional layer consists of a set of kernels, where each kernel is a matrix of integers and is applied in a sliding window fashion across the input. The number of feature maps obtained through a convolution layer is equal to the number of kernels in that layer. By virtue of their local receptive field, CNN can capture local correlations. CNN has successfully been applied to the HAR applications. In [60], the authors designed a multi-layer CNN network and used data acquired via gyroscope and accelerometer for HAR. The authors applied weight sharing for CNN networks for feature learning and classification of multimodal data. Authors in [61] proposed a CNN network that used conditionally parameterized convolutions. One more CNN-based method that used accelerometer data was developed for HAR in [62]. In order to capture the time-series signal's global properties, statistical features were retrieved, whereas local features were extracted using CNN. In [63], another CNN-based technique used data acquired using smartphone sensors. Whereas the authors proposed a one-dimensional convolutional network in [64]. It was a divide and conquer based technique in which firstly, two groups were created, one of static activity and the other of dynamic activity class, from the six activity classes. A model was then utilized to categorize individual activities within each class. The proposed two-phase HAR required 3 recognition models, which raised the

Table 2. Some representative works in the literature using DL techniques for HAR.

Paper, Year	Technique	Strength	Weaknesses	Performance Metric A/F1 (Dataset)
Hammerela et al. [70], 2016	DNN, CNN and RNN models were proposed. Extensive experimentation was done.Three datasets were used for validation of the model	BiLSTM and LSTM networks outperformed convolutional models in detecting short duration activities	BiLSTM and LSTM networks performed poorly in detecting repetitive and longer duration activities	*BiLSTM model* F1 = 86.8% (PAMAP2) F1 = 92.7% (Opportunity) *LSTM model* F1 = 88.2% (PAMAP2) F1 = 91.2% (Opportunity)
Alsheikh et al. [74], 2016	A DBN-based model was proposed. Accelerometer data used	Unsupervised training, hence can be trained on unlabelled data. Better performance compared to conventional ML approaches	Extensive parameter initialization	A = 98.23% (WISDM) A = 89.38% (Skoda)
Ha et al. [60], 2016	2-Dimensional Convolutional network with weight sharing (partial and full)	Both modality-specific and common characteristics were captured	CNN could extract local spatial features but couldn't capture global dependencies in the data	A = 91.94% (mHealth)
Lingjuan et al. [71], 2017	Proposed an LSTM and CNN hybrid	User data privacy was maintained through a privacy-preserving technique	Dataset division (train, validation, test) was random as 70–15-15 respectively. Such partition of data is undesirable for HAR	A = 98% (UCI-HAR) A = 96.2% (MHEALTH)

(continued)

Table 2. (*continued*)

Paper, Year	Technique	Strength	Weaknesses	Performance Metric A/F1 (Dataset)
Gao et al. [77], 2016	5-layered DBN-DNN architecture was designed and used to recognize the eating activity. Raw audio data collected via Bluetooth headset was used	Unsupervised training thus labelled data is not required Performed better compared to SVM	Extensive parameter initialization makes the on-board network training complex computationally	A = 94% (Self collected)
Zhao et al. [66], 2018	A residual-bidirectional LSTM based model was proposed	Residual connection in the model, aid it in converging faster	Activities with static behavior were sometimes misrecognized	F1 = 93.6% (UCI-HAR) F1 = 90.5% (Opportunity)
Zeng et al. [69], 2018	LSTMs were used with continuous sensor and temporal attention networks	Able to concentrate on key sensor modalities and important signal elements. Performed better than the baseline RNN technique	Recognition performance achieved is still low	A = 89.03% (Skoda) A = 83.73% (Daphnet Gait) A = 89.96% (PAMAP2)
Jun et al. [54], 2020	A deep model using autoencoders (AE) and k-means clustering was proposed. Accelerometer data of 10 infants were captured	Use of AE makes the model robust against corrupt sensor data	High parameter tuning and computational time	A = 96% (Self-collected dataset)
Cheng et al. [61], 2020	A CNN network that used conditionally parameterized convolutions	Computation efficient and hence suitable for real-time HAR. Good at detecting simple activities like walking, running, jumping, etc	Underperformed in detecting complex activities like fall, standing up from sitting, standing up from lying, etc.	A = 94.01% (PAMAP2) A = 77.31% (UNIMIB-SHAR) A = 81.18% (Opportunity)

(*continued*)

Table 2. (*continued*)

Paper, Year	Technique	Strength	Weaknesses	Performance Metric A/F1 (Dataset)
Wan et al. [63], 2020	Proposed a deep CNN network	Attained decent performance on the two datasets used for validation	Random data split was done. Long-term dependencies extraction was not handled	A = 91% (PAMAP2) A = 92.71% (UCI-HAR)
Dua et al. [17], 2021	CNN-GRU hybrid network was proposed. Filters of multiple-sizes were used	Validated on multiple datasets and attained good detection performance	High number of parameters and complex architecture	A = 95.27% (PAMAP2) A = 97.21% (WISDM) A = 96.2% (UCI-HAR)

level of model complexity overall. The local features in sequential sensor data are well captured by the CNN-based techniques, but they fall short of capturing global temporal interdependence [65]. This means that in the case of HAR, where accurately detecting the activities requires the ability to capture time-series data's global dependencies, CNN alone designs fall short in this regard.

6.3 Recurrent Neural Network (RNN)

RNN is another class of DNN applied widely in activity recognition tasks. In [66], a residual-bi-LSTM network was developed for human activity recognition that utilized data captured via smartphone sensors. The model could converge faster by using the residual connection and attained an F1-score of 90.5% on the OPPORTUNITY dataset. In [67] a bi-dir LSTM model was designed for HAR that used the raw sensor data captured via smartphone sensors (gyroscope and accelerometer). The network attained an accuracy of 93.79% on the UCI-HAR. An LSTM-based model was proposed in [68]. A stacked LSTM network, fed with the normalized sensor data, was used followed by a softmax classifier. The network attained an accuracy of 93.13% on the UCI-HAR dataset alone. In [69], the authors designed an attention-based LSTM network for HAR. The method, however, could attain accuracy values less than 90% on the three datasets used. Deep, convolutional, and recurrent networks were proposed for HAR in [70]. Nearly 4000 experiments were conducted and benchmark results were established on 3 datasets. The Bi-LSTM and LSTM models designed could achieve an F1-score of 88.2% and 86.8% on the PAMAP2 dataset and an F1-score of 91.2% and 92.7% on the OPPORTUNITY dataset. The authors came to the conclusion that CNNs outperformed RNN networks in the detection of repeated, long-duration activities like walking and running, whereas CNNs were outperformed by RNN networks in the detection of short duration activities with natural ordering. Several works designed models for HAR that combined both CNN and RNN in the same network exploiting the strength of both [71–73]. As RNNs perform well at capturing long-term dependencies and CNNs are good at local feature extraction; hence the hybrid of both is capable of extracting diverse information from the data.

6.4 Deep Belief Network (DBN)

A DBN is comprised of multiple unsupervised networks stacked together. In DBN, the preceding network's hidden layer serves as the visible layer for the next. The simple network used in DBN is basically an RBM. It is a generative model that has a visible input layer and a hidden layer, and is trained using contrastive divergence. A DBN is formed by stacking multiple RBMs and trained using greedy layer-by-layer manner for hierarchical features extraction from raw sensor data. DBN has been applied to several real-life scenarios like fault diagnosis, drug discovery, etc. It has also been applied for HAR applications. For instance, in [74], a DBN-based model was proposed that was trained using accelerometer data. The temporal patterns in sequence data were analyzed using HMM. It showed considerable accuracy improvement in comparison to the conventional ML techniques. In [75], the authors designed two different 5-layered DBNs and applied them to 3 public datasets, and the results demonstrated that the DBNs performed better compared to the ML techniques. Authors in [76] used an RBM, trained on the Skoda dataset, and could reach an accuracy of 81%, which was 6% greater than the Random Forest technique. In [77], a 5-layered DBN-DNN architecture was designed and used to recognize the eating activity, where the raw audio data was collected using a blue-tooth headset. Their network showed higher accuracy of 94% compared to the SVM technique, which could reach only 75.6%.

7 Challenges and Future Scope

DL-based HAR techniques face challenges in different aspects like data collection and labeling, data segmentation, designing a robust model, and generalizability of the model. The DL-based HAR techniques require a massive amount of data for training. Collection of large amounts of data that too when multiple sensors are involved, is a labor-intensive task. Therefore, there is always a need for techniques that can innovatively augment data with high quality. Several works [78, 79] used DL methods to augment datasets. Authors in [79] and [80] used GAN on existing data and synthesized sensor data. Some works used cross-modal GAN in data synthesis, like the text to image in [81] and video to audio in [82]. Another direction to further explore is to apply transfer learning on highly trained models from one domain (e.g., Image classifiers) and adapt them for HAR using a lesser number of samples of sensor data.

Most of the HAR works used the static sliding window technique for forming activity segments [83]. The use of static window size may result in segments that are either too big or too small to capture the right amount of series activity data to detect the movements. So, there is a need for more experimentation to optimally segment the activity data.

The model is said to have high generalizability when it performs well, even on unseen data. The model suffers overfitting when it performs well on training data but fails to give a similar performance on unseen data. Several works have been proposed to enhance the HAR model's generalizability [84, 85]. Most of the work to improve the generalizability of the model requires a large volume of data, and also, model complexity tends to be high, so that the model generalizes to a higher population. DL-based HAR techniques generalize well and outperform in scenarios where an abundant amount of data is available in addition to a high computing facility. But when model complexity and data availability are limited, there is a need to design DL techniques that could adapt to the specific scenarios and the amount of data available.

8 Conclusions

HAR is of great significance in the domain of healthcare, intelligent surveillance, robotics, and rehabilitation. In this paper, we have discussed the application areas of HAR using wearable technology, different types of wearable sensors used to collect activity data, and popular public datasets available for HAR. We have also discussed various deep learning techniques that are used for HAR in literature and reviewed the advances made in the DL approaches for wearable HAR. We have also identified challenges and potential opportunities in this area and finally made some suggestions for possible future directions to advance the research in wearable HAR.

References

1. Yadav, S.K., Tiwari, K., Pandey, H.M., Akbar, S.A.: A review of multimodal human activity recognition with special emphasis on classification, applications, challenges and future directions. Knowl.-Based Syst. **223**, 106970 (2021)
2. Demrozi, F., Pravadelli, G., Bihorac, A., Rashidi, P.: Human activity recognition using inertial, physiological and environmental sensors: a comprehensive survey. IEEE Access **8**, 210816–210836 (2020)
3. Dawadi, P.N., Cook, D.J., Schmitter-Edgecombe, M.: Automated cognitive health assessment using smart home monitoring of complex tasks. IEEE Trans. Syst. Man Cybern. Syst. **43**(6), 1302–1313 (2013)
4. Parsey, C.M., Schmitter-Edgecombe, M.: Applications of technology in neuropsychological assessment. Clin. Neuropsychol. **27**(8), 1328–1361 (2013)
5. Yang, Q.: Activity recognition: linking low-level sensors to high-level intelligence. In: IJCAI, vol. 9, pp. 20–25, Pasadena, California (2009)
6. Chen, L., Hoey, J., Nugent, C.D., Cook, D.J., Yu, Z.: Sensor-based activity recognition. IEEE Trans. Syst. Man Cybern. Part C (Appl. Rev.) **42**(6), 790–808 (2012)
7. Bao, L., Intille, S.S.: Activity recognition from user-annotated acceleration data. In: Ferscha, A., Mattern, F. (eds.) Pervasive Computing. Pervasive 2004. LNCS, vol. 3001, pp. 1–17. Springer, Berlin, Heidelberg (2004). https://doi.org/10.1007/978-3-540-24646-6_1
8. Figo, D., Diniz, P.C., Ferreira, D.R., Cardoso, J.M.: Preprocessing techniques for context recognition from accelerometer data. Pers. Ubiquit. Comput. **14**(7), 645–662 (2010)
9. Aung, M.S., et al.: Automated detection of instantaneous gait events using time frequency analysis and manifold embedding. IEEE Trans. Neural Syst. Rehabil. Eng. **21**(6), 908–916 (2013)
10. Chaudhuri, A., Sahu, T.P.: Binary Jaya algorithm based on binary similarity measure for feature selection. J. Ambient Intell. Humaniz. Comput. 1–18 (2021)

11. Chaudhuri, A., Sahu, T.P.: Feature weighting for naïve Bayes using multi objective artificial bee colony algorithm. Int. J. Comput. Sci. Eng. **24**(1), 74–88 (2021)
12. Chaudhuri, A., Sahu, T.P.: Multi-objective feature selection based on quasi-oppositional based Jaya algorithm for microarray data. Knowl.-Based Syst. **236**, 107804 (2022)
13. Anguita, D., Ghio, A., Oneto, L., Parra, X., Reyes-Ortiz, J.L.: A public domain dataset for human activity recognition using smartphones. In: Esann, vol. 3, p. 3 (2013)
14. Feng, Z., Mo, L., Li, M.: A random forest-based ensemble method for activity recognition. In: 2015 37th Annual International Conference of the IEEE Engineering in Medicine and Biology Society (EMBC), pp. 5074–5077. IEEE (2015)
15. Nweke, H.F., Teh, Y.W., Al-Garadi, M.A., Alo, U.R.: Deep learning algorithms for human activity recognition using mobile and wearable sensor networks: state of the art and research challenges. Expert Syst. Appl. **105**, 233–261 (2018)
16. Palla, S.R., Sahu, G., Parida, P.: Human gait recognition using firefly template segmentation. Comput. Methods Biomech. Biomed. Eng. Imaging Vis. **10**(5), 565–575 (2022). https://doi.org/10.1080/21681163.2021.2012829
17. Dua, N., Singh, S.N., Semwal, V.B.: Multi-input CNN-GRU based human activity recognition using wearable sensors. Computing **103**(7), 1461–1478 (2021). https://doi.org/10.1007/s00607-021-00928-8
18. Jain, R., Semwal, V.B., Kaushik, P.: Deep ensemble learning approach for lower extremity activities recognition using wearable sensors. Expert. Syst. **39**(6), e12743 (2022)
19. Dua, N., Singh, S.N., Semwal, V.B., Challa, S.K.: Inception inspired CNN-GRU hybrid network for human activity recognition. Multimedia Tools Appl. 1–35 (2022)
20. Raj, M., Semwal, V.B., Nandi, G.C.: Bidirectional association of joint angle trajectories for humanoid locomotion: the restricted Boltzmann machine approach. Neural Comput. Appl. **30**(6), 1747–1755 (2018)
21. Saha, J., Chowdhury, C., Ghosh, D., Bandyopadhyay, S.: A detailed human activity transition recognition framework for grossly labeled data from smartphone accelerometer. Multimedia Tools Appl. **80**(7), 9895–9916 (2020). https://doi.org/10.1007/s11042-020-10046-w
22. Bijalwan, V., Semwal, V.B., Gupta, V.: Wearable sensor-based pattern mining for human activity recognition: deep learning approach. Ind. Robot. **49**(1), 21–33 (2022). https://doi.org/10.1108/IR-09-2020-0187
23. Asteriadis, S., Daras, P.: Landmark-based multimodal human action recognition. Multimedia Tools Appl. **76**(3), 4505–4521 (2016). https://doi.org/10.1007/s11042-016-3945-6
24. Singh, R., Kushwaha, A.K.S., Srivastava, R.: Multi-view recognition system for human activity based on multiple features for video surveillance system. Multimedia Tools Appl. **78**(12), 17165–17196 (2019). https://doi.org/10.1007/s11042-018-7108-9
25. Webber, M., Rojas, R.F.: Human activity recognition with accelerometer and gyroscope: a data fusion approach. IEEE Sens. J. **21**(15), 16979–16989 (2021)
26. Masum, A.K.M., Bahadur, E.H., Shan-A-Alahi, A., Chowdhury, M.A.U.Z., Uddin, M.R., Al Noman, A.: Human activity recognition using accelerometer, gyroscope and magnetometer sensors: deep neural network approaches. In: 2019 10Th International Conference on Computing, Communication and Networking Technologies (ICCCNT), pp. 1–6. IEEE, Kanpur (2019)
27. Ashry, S., Gomaa, W., Abdu-Aguye, M.G., El-borae, N.: Improved IMU-based human activity recognition using hierarchical hmm dissimilarity. In: Proceedings of the 17th International Conference on Informatics in Control, Automation and Robotics, vol. 1, pp. 702–709 (2020)
28. Nurhanim, K., Elamvazuthi, I., Izhar, L.I., Capi, G., Su, S.: EMG signals classification on human activity recognition using machine learning algorithm. In: 2021 8th NAFOSTED Conference on Information and Computer Science (NICS), pp. 369–373. IEEE, Hanoi, Vietnam (2021)

29. Ziaur Rehman, M., et al.: Multiday EMG-based classification of hand motions with deep learning techniques. Sensors 18(8), 2497 (2018)
30. Ding, Z., Yang, C., Tian, Z., Yi, C., Fu, Y., Jiang, F.: sEMG-based gesture recognition with convolution neural networks. Sustainability 10(6), 1865 (2018)
31. Jia, R., Liu, B.: Human daily activity recognition by fusing accelerometer and multi-lead ECG data. In: 2013 IEEE International Conference on Signal Processing, Communication and Computing (ICSPCC 2013), pp. 1–4. IEEE, KunMing, China (2013)
32. Almanifi, O.R.A., Khairuddin, I.M., Razman, M.A.M., Musa, R.M., Majeed, A.P.A.: Human activity recognition based on wrist PPG via the ensemble method. ICT Express (2022)
33. Zia, S., Khan, A.N., Mukhtar, M., Ali, S.E.: Human activity recognition using portable EEG sensor and support vector machine. In: 2021 International Conference on Engineering and Emerging Technologies (ICEET), pp. 1–6. IEEE, Istanbul, Turkey (2021)
34. Salehzadeh, A., Calitz, A.P., Greyling, J.: Human activity recognition using deep electroencephalography learning. Biomed. Signal Process. Control 62, 102094 (2020)
35. Dinarević, E.C., Husić, J.B., Baraković, S.: Issues of human activity recognition in healthcare. In: 2019 18th International Symposium INFOTEH-JAHORINA (INFOTEH), pp. 1–6. IEEE, East Sarajevo (2019)
36. Hu, F.B., Leitzmann, M.F., Stampfer, M.J., Colditz, G.A., Willett, W.C., Rimm, E.B.: Physical activity and television watching in relation to risk for type 2 diabetes mellitus in men. Arch. Intern. Med. 161(12), 542–1548 (2001)
37. Schnohr, P., Lange, P., Scharling, H., Jensen, J.S.: Long-term physical activity in leisure time and mortality from coronary heart disease, stroke, respiratory diseases, and cancer. The Copenhagen City heart study. Eur. J. Prev. Cardiol. 13(2), 173–179 (2006)
38. Bauman, A.E., Reis, R.S., Sallis, J.F., Wells, J.C., Loos, R.J., Martin, B.W.: Correlates of physical activity: why are some people physically active and others not? The Lancet 380(9838), 258–271 (2012). Lancet Physical Activity Series Working Group
39. Sullivan, A.N., Lachman, M.E.: Behavior change with fitness technology in sedentary adults: a review of the evidence for increasing physical activity. Front. Public Health 4, 289 (2017)
40. Eskofier, B.M., et al.: Recent machine learning advancements in sensor-based mobility analysis: deep learning for Parkinson's disease assessment. In: 2016 38th Annual International Conference of the IEEE Engineering in Medicine and Biology Society (EMBC), pp. 655–658. IEEE, Orlando, USA (2016)
41. Zhang, S., et al.: CoughTrigger: earbuds IMU based cough detection activator using an energy-efficient sensitivity-prioritized time series classifier. In: ICASSP 2022–2022 IEEE International Conference on Acoustics, Speech and Signal Processing (ICASSP), pp. 1–5. IEEE, Singapore (2022)
42. Meattini, R., Benatti, S., Scarcia, U., De Gregorio, D., Benini, L., Melchiorri, C.: An sEMG-based human–robot interface for robotic hands using machine learning and synergies. IEEE Trans. Compon. Packag. Manuf. Technol. 8(7), 1149–1158 (2018)
43. Parajuli, N., et al.: Real-time EMG based pattern recognition control for hand prostheses: a review on existing methods, challenges and future implementation. Sensors 19(20), 4596 (2019)
44. Zhao, H., Ma, Y., Wang, S., Watson, A., Zhou, G.: MobiGesture: mobility-aware hand gesture recognition for healthcare. Smart Health 9, 129–143 (2018)
45. Reiss, A., Stricker, D.: Introducing a new benchmarked dataset for activity monitoring. In: 2012 16th International Symposium on Wearable Computers, pp. 108–109. IEEE, Newcastle, UK (2012)
46. Kwapisz, J.R., Weiss, G.M., Moore, S.A.: Activity recognition using cell phone accelerometers. ACM SIGKDD Explor. Newsl. 12(2), 74–82 (2011)

47. Banos, O., et al.: mHealthDroid: a novel framework for agile development of mobile health applications. In: Pecchia, L., Chen, L.L., Nugent, C., Bravo, J. (eds.) Ambient Assisted Living and Daily Activities. IWAAL 2014. LNCS, vol. 8868, pp. 91–98. Springer, Cham (2014). https://doi.org/10.1007/978-3-319-13105-4_14

48. Chavarriaga, R., et al.: The opportunity challenge: a benchmark database for on-body sensor-based activity recognition. Pattern Recogn. Lett. 34(15), 2033–2042 (2013)

49. Bachlin, M., et al.: Wearable assistant for Parkinson's disease patients with the freezing of gait symptom. IEEE Trans. Inf. Technol. Biomed. 14(2), 436–446 (2009)

50. Ballard, D.H.: Modular learning in neural networks. In: AAAI, vol. 647, pp. 279–284, Washington, DC, USA (1987)

51. Li, Y., Shi, D., Ding, B., Liu, D.: Unsupervised Feature Learning for Human Activity Recognition Using Smartphone Sensors. In: Prasath, R., O'Reilly, P., Kathirvalavakumar, T. (eds.) Mining Intelligence and Knowledge Exploration. LNCS, vol. 8891, pp. 99–107. Springer, Cham (2014). https://doi.org/10.1007/978-3-319-13817-6_11

52. Mohammadian Rad, N., Van Laarhoven, T., Furlanello, C., Marchiori, E.: Novelty detection using deep normative modeling for imu-based abnormal movement monitoring in parkinson's disease and autism spectrum disorders. Sensors 18(10), 3533 (2018)

53. Malekzadeh, M., Clegg, R.G., Haddadi, H.: Replacement autoencoder: a privacy-preserving algorithm for sensory data analysis. In: 2018 IEEE/ACM Third International Conference on Internet-of-Things Design and Implementation (IoTDI), pp. 165–176. IEEE, Orlando, FL, USA (2018)

54. Jun, K., Choi, S.: Unsupervised end-to-end deep model for newborn and infant activity recognition. Sensors 20(22), 6467 (2020)

55. Akbari, A., Jafari, R.: An autoencoder-based approach for recognizing null class in activities of daily living in-the-wild via wearable motion sensors. In: ICASSP 2019–2019 IEEE International Conference on Acoustics, Speech and Signal Processing (ICASSP), pp. 3392–3396. IEEE, Brighton, UK (2019)

56. Khan, M.A.A.H., Roy, N.: Untran: recognizing unseen activities with unlabeled data using transfer learning. In: 2018 IEEE/ACM Third International Conference on Internet-of-Things Design and Implementation (IoTDI), pp. 37–47. IEEE, Orlando, FL, USA (2018)

57. Akbari, A., Jafari, R.: Transferring activity recognition models for new wearable sensors with deep generative domain adaptation. In: Proceedings of the 18th International Conference on Information Processing in Sensor Networks, pp. 85–96. ACM (2019)

58. Gao, X., Luo, H., Wang, Q., Zhao, F., Ye, L., Zhang, Y.: A human activity recognition algorithm based on stacking denoising autoencoder and lightGBM. Sensors 19(4), 947 (2019)

59. Hung, B.T., Semwal, V.B., Gaud, N., Bijalwan, V.: Hybrid deep learning approach for aspect detection on reviews. In: Singh Mer, K.K., Semwal, V.B., Bijalwan, V., Crespo, R.G. (eds.) Proceedings of Integrated Intelligence Enable Networks and Computing. Algorithms for Intelligent Systems. Springer, Singapore (2021). https://doi.org/10.1007/978-981-33-6307-6_100

60. Ha, S., Choi, S.: Convolutional neural networks for human activity recognition using multiple accelerometer and gyroscope sensors. In: 2016 International Joint Conference on Neural Networks (IJCNN), pp. 381–388. IEEE, Vancouver (2016)

61. Cheng, X., Zhang, L., Tang, Y., Liu, Y., Wu, H., He, J.: Real-time human activity recognition using conditionally parametrized convolutions on mobile and wearable devices. IEEE Sens. J. 22(6), 5889–5901 (2022)

62. Ignatov, A.: Real-time human activity recognition from accelerometer data using convolutional neural networks. Appl. Soft Comput. 62, 915–922 (2018)

63. Wan, S., Qi, L., Xu, X., Tong, C., Gu, Z.: Deep learning models for real-time human activity recognition with smartphones. Mob. Netw. Appl. 25(2), 743–755 (2020)

64. Cho, H., Yoon, S.M.: Divide and conquer-based 1D CNN human activity recognition using test data sharpening. Sensors **18**(4), 1055 (2018)
65. Ordóñez, F.J., Roggen, D.: Deep convolutional and LSTM recurrent neural networks for multimodal wearable activity recognition. Sensors **16**(1), 115 (2016)
66. Zhao, Y., Yang, R., Chevalier, G., Xu, X., Zhang, Z.: Deep residual bidir-LSTM for human activity recognition using wearable sensors. Math. Probl. Eng. (2018)
67. Yu, S., Qin, L.: Human activity recognition with smartphone inertial sensors using bidir-lstm networks. In: 2018 3rd International Conference on Mechanical, Control and Computer Engineering (icmcce), pp. 219–224. IEEE, Huhhot, China (2018)
68. Ullah, M., Ullah, H., Khan, S.D., Cheikh, F.A.: Stacked LSTM network for human activity recognition using smartphone data. In: 2019 8th European Workshop on Visual Information Processing (EUVIP), pp. 175–180. IEEE, Italy (2019)
69. Zeng, M., et al.: Understanding and improving recurrent networks for human activity recognition by continuous attention. In Proceedings of the 2018 ACM international symposium on wearable computers, pp. 56–63. ACM, Newyork (2018)
70. Hammerla, N.Y., Halloran, S., Plötz, T.: Deep, convolutional, and recurrent models for human activity recognition using wearables. arXiv preprint arXiv:1604.08880 (2016)
71. Lyu, L., He, X., Law, Y.W., Palaniswami, M.: Privacy-preserving collaborative deep learning with application to human activity recognition. In: Proceedings of the 2017 ACM on Conference on Information and Knowledge Management, pp. 1219–1228. ACM, Singapore (2017)
72. Challa, S.K., Kumar, A., Semwal, V.B.: A multibranch CNN-BiLSTM model for human activity recognition using wearable sensor data. Vis. Comput. 1–15 (2021).https://doi.org/10.1007/s00371-021-02283-3
73. Semwal, V.B., Gupta, A., Lalwani, P.: An optimized hybrid deep learning model using ensemble learning approach for human walking activities recognition. J. Supercomput. **77**(11), 12256–12279 (2021). https://doi.org/10.1007/s11227-021-03768-7
74. Alsheikh, M.A., Selim, A., Niyato, D., Doyle, L., Lin, S., Tan, H.P.: Deep activity recognition models with triaxial accelerometers. In: Workshops at the Thirtieth AAAI Conference on Artificial Intelligence, Phoenix, Arizona USA (2016)
75. Zhang, L., Wu, X., Luo, D.: Recognizing human activities from raw accelerometer data using deep neural networks. In: 2015 IEEE 14th International Conference on Machine Learning and Applications (ICMLA), pp. 865–870. IEEE, Miami, FL, USA (2015)
76. Radu, V., Lane, N.D., Bhattacharya, S., Mascolo, C., Marina, M.K., Kawsar, F.: Towards multimodal deep learning for activity recognition on mobile devices. In: Proceedings of the 2016 ACM International Joint Conference on Pervasive and Ubiquitous Computing: Adjunct, pp. 185–188. ACM, Germany, Heidelberg (2016)
77. Gao, Y., et al.: iHear food: eating detection using commodity bluetooth headsets. In: 2016 IEEE First International Conference on Connected Health: Applications, Systems and Engineering Technologies (CHASE), pp. 163–172. IEEE, Washington, DC, USA (2016)
78. Ramponi, G., Protopapas, P., Brambilla, M., Janssen, R.: T-CGAN: conditional generative adversarial network for data augmentation in noisy time series with irregular sampling. arXiv preprint arXiv:1811.08295 (2018)
79. Alzantot, M., Chakraborty, S., Srivastava, M.: Sensegen: a deep learning architecture for synthetic sensor data generation. In: 2017 IEEE International Conference on Pervasive Computing and Communications Workshops (PerCom Workshops), pp. 188–193. IEEE, Kona, HI, USA (2017)
80. Wang, J., Chen, Y., Gu, Y., Xiao, Y., Pan, H.: SensoryGANs: an effective generative adversarial framework for sensor-based human activity recognition. In: 2018 International Joint Conference on Neural Networks (IJCNN), pp. 1–8. IEEE, Rio de Janeiro, Brazil (2018)

81. Reed, S., Akata, Z., Yan, X., Logeswaran, L., Schiele, B., Lee, H.: Generative adversarial text to image synthesis. In: International Conference on Machine Learning, pp. 1060–1069. PMLR (2016)
82. Zhou, Y., Wang, Z., Fang, C., Bui, T., Berg, T.L.: Visual to sound: generating natural sound for videos in the wild. In: Proceedings of the IEEE Conference on Computer Vision and Pattern Recognition, pp. 3550–3558. IEEE, Salt Lake City, UT, USA (2018)
83. Plötz, T., Guan, Y.: Deep learning for human activity recognition in mobile computing. Computer **51**(5), 50–59 (2018)
84. Abdel-Basset, M., Hawash, H., Chang, V., Chakrabortty, R.K., Ryan, M.: Deep learning for heterogeneous human activity recognition in complex iot applications. IEEE Internet Things J. **9**(8), 5653–5665 (2020)
85. Qin, Z., Zhang, Y., Meng, S., Qin, Z., Choo, K.K.R.: Imaging and fusing time series for wearable sensor-based human activity recognition. Inf. Fusion **53**, 80–87 (2020)

Refined-Para Forming Question Generation System Using Lamma

Khushbu Khandait[1(✉)], S. A. Bhura[2], and S. S. Asole[1]

[1] Babasaheb Naik College of Engineering, Department of Computer Science and Engineering, SGBAU University, Pusad, Amravati, India
Khushbukhandait1991@gmail.com
[2] Jhulelal Institute of Technology, Department of Computer Science and Engineering, RTMNU University, Nagpur, India

Abstract. The task of producing questions from a given material is known as Question Generation (QG). Its goal is to produce natural and meaningful queries. Existing QG techniques, on the other hand, frequently overlook the complex text structure that may complement the simple word sequence. Meanwhile, exposure bias and inconsistency between train and test measurement are well-known drawbacks of cross-entropy-based training. To solve the concerns, we offer a unique approach that integrates a Semantics classification discriminator into the informative para-formation process, allowing for better exploitation of passage information and a better comprehension of the passage's internal structure. We put our QGWVSL model to the test on a well-known QG Dataset to see how it performs. Extensive experimental results showed that when compared to existing models based on the public Dataset, the proposed QGWVSL may achieve a large increase in BLEU score, and it consistently outperformed all evaluated baseline models, including state-of-the-art (SOTA) approaches.

Keywords: Question generation · NLP · Dataset · SQuAD

1 Introduction

While exam-style questions are an important instructional tool that may be used for several purposes, manual question development is a time-consuming process that requires knowledge, experience, and resources. Automatic query producing (QG) techniques can be used to reduce the charges related to guide question creation and to fulfill the call for a constant supply of the latest questions. However, as compared to automated query answering (QA), QG is a more difficult challenge. Question Generation (QG) is critical but tough trouble in Machines. From numerous input forms, inclusive of a based database, textual content, or an understanding base, the goal is to syntactically construct valid, semantically sound, and appropriate queries. Transformer-based approaches, such as BART, T5, and T5 with SQuAD learning, have lately shown considerable promise in a variety of NLP tasks, including Question Generation. Denoising seq2seq for comprehension [1] recently proposed a Seq2Seq model with a transformer for text-based question

N. Khare et al. (Eds.): MIND 2022, CCIS 1762, pp. 72–85, 2022.
https://doi.org/10.1007/978-3-031-24352-3_6

generating. [2] recorded better performance when fine-tuned the T5 model on BrWac corpus to original T5, [3, 4] used a Turkish QA Dataset to fine-tune a multilingual T5 transformer in a multi-task scenario for QA, QG, and answer extraction tasks, in order to capture interactions between the passage's context and the given ground-truth. These models, on the other hand, do not leverage the rich text structure, which might lead to the development of occasionally irrelevant questions. The figure below shows the relevant question generated from the input, and collectively shows the Question Generation Scenario from text input. The case in point below entirely hinges on whatever portion of the statement you want to be answered in the negative. The example below could lead to an additional inquiry with oxygen as the response (Figs. 1, 2, 3, 4 and 5).

Sample Input- Oxygen is used in cellular respiration and re-leased by photosynthesis, which uses the energy of sunlight to produce oxygen from water.

Sample Question- What life process produces oxygen in the presence of light?

Fig. 1. Simple Example showing Machine- Generated Automatic Questions

The answer information was taken into account in many prior neural QG techniques. However, the approaches ignored the answer word feature, which is also a difficult and rapidly evolving topic. Recent publications [5] have examined several strategies to use the input just to highlight the difficulties, but there is still a gap and the topic is of great interest in the field of study. The linkages between the resultant and passage length, on the other hand, are ignored, and the global interactions between them fail to achieve that degree of precision directly. To overcome all of the aforementioned issues, we propose a sentimental-based evaluation with word vector synchronization using Lamma.

A variety of methods for question Generation had been supplied due to their extensive appeal. Traditional strategies [6–8] frequently consolidate feature engineering, layout extraction, and ordinary semantic parsing-based methods. Many neural network-primarily based techniques have currently been established to be beneficial for autonomously generating questions. Simple neural embedding-based models [9, 10], attention-primarily based recurrent fashions [11], and memory-augmented neural controller architectures [12–17] are all examples of these procedures.

In Sect. 2, we take a quick look at the current state of the question generation system. Section 3 covers the proposed methodology and gives a detailed description of our system, including training and inference methods, as well as obstacles unique to each paradigm and common solutions. The discussions and some future directions for our work are provided in the following parts.

2 Related Work

Syntax-based, semantic-based, template-based, and neural network-based Question Generation Processes are the most common. Syntax-based approaches generate questions depending on the syntax of the input like a syntactic tree of textual content.

Semantic-based techniques work on a more fundamental level like is-a or other semantic relations. Template-based techniques make use of templates with fixed text and place-holders that are filled in with data from the user. This is because we believe that the existing categorization of different generation approaches fails to reflect two important features: The generation strategy requires 1) a certain amount of knowledge of the input, and 2) a procedure for transforming the data into questions. The researchers then developed a new categorization, detailed each category, and provided examples of features that they used to classify methods into these groups. These methods typically use heuristics to produce questions and rely on rules and templates of a sentence's linguistic structures. [7, 18–21]. Scaling the approach is tough since it involves human effort and professional expertise and one of the most difficult aspects of template-oriented methodology is that the templates are usually topical or area-precise. Neural techniques, however, outperform and generalize better than conventional processes considering that they are these days' technology. Many neural sequence-to-sequence models have been developed for question-generating problems [22, 23]. In many benchmarks, these models outperform the above-mentioned rule-based methods by being trained end-to-end and exploiting the corpus of the datasets for answering questions. However, no extra attention layer or areas of the document that the decoder should focus on to generate the question are indicated in these early techniques. To ease this restriction on the reasoning depth, authors have provided ReasoNets, which offers a termination state. ReasoNets [24, 25] can dynamically decide whether to continue the comprehension process after taking in intermediate findings or to stop reading when it determines that the information already present is sufficient to give an answer using reinforcement learning [26]. Proposes three neural architectures for question generation technology demanding circumstances, all of which are built on top of BERT. The first is a genuine BERT application that highlights the drawbacks of using BERT directly for text generation. And other two such styles by reorganizing our BERT job into a sequential order for extracting information from previously decoded outcomes. They claimed that utilizing the SQuAD Dataset, they were able to improve the bleu score by six points. The neural question technology version with sentence-stage semantic matching, answer role inferring, and gated fusion is recommended by the authors [27] to address two issues: avoiding query semantics and failing to consider solution role-conscious capabilities. [28, 29] studied encoding sentences with sum and convolution operations to identify query-worth sentences and suggested a hierarchical neural sentence-level sequence tagging model. To meet the opinion query technology assignment, whereas [30] suggested using syntactic tree kernels to automatically determine whether the questions were syntactically accurate. The relevance of the questions (in the context of the sample texts) and the syntactic correctness of the questions are taken into account while ranking them [31]. Suggested a sequence-to-sequence studying methodology. They validated the educational process through the use of global attention, used the policy mechanism to improve the model, and benefited from community-based question-answering structures that include informal speech and sentences that do not always follow grammatical rules. Declarative sentences can be transformed into questions via a series of general-purpose syntactic transformations (such subject-auxiliary inversion). A logistic regression model that was trained on a tiny, customized dataset made up of labelled output from our system then ranks these questions [32, 33].

3   Problem Definition

This section outlines the automatic question generating task. We are interested in creating the question Q that achieves our main goal of creating given only paragraph P that is multi-meaning Question Generation which will solve the issue of vocabulary. It will again cover the problem of repetition of question words or question parts. For that Algorithm have to check the length of the input, if the input is a valid paragraph, then only object information will be collected & algorithm will derive one re-synchronized paragraph. Then Tokenization is performed on objects, phrases and paragraphs, and every single word. Then word vector is calculated using Lammatisation to further pass it to the Question Generation This section outlines the automatic question generating task which returns a list of Questions.

Algorithm 1 QG through word vector synchronization using Lamma

```
1:    Input=Inputted_Statements
2:    len_input =get_len(input)
3:    If len_input <=1 then :
4:    Word=Word_Symetry ()
5:    SyncWord=Word.Information()
6:    Sync_Para= SyncWord
7:    else:
8:    state_token=StatementTokenisation(Input)
9:    Sync_Para=" "
10:   for a statement in state_token:
11:   Sync_Statement=""
12:   word_token=Word_Tokenisation(statement)
13:   for singular_word in word_token:
14:   Sync_Word=" "
15:   if singular_word.isStopWord():
16:   Sync_Word= singular_word
17:   Else:
18:   Try:
19:   Sync_Word_Vector=Word_Lammatisation(singular_word)
20:   Sync_Word= Sync_Word_Vector
21:   Except:
22:   Sync_Word= singular_word
23:   Sync_Statement= Sync_Statement+ Sync_Word
24:   Sync_Para= Sync_Para+ Sync_Statement
25:   QG= InitializeQuestionGenrationModel()
26:   List_Question=QG.getQuestions()
```

Above given is our proposed Algorithm Word-Vector Synchronization using Lamma Automatic Question Generation (AQG) Algorithm. After execution of these above 26 steps, the next very important step comes that is called the manual user evaluation method used to reward questions formed. In the section below, we outline our suggested model for creating questions. The fundamental idea of our method is to foster the inquiry by focusing on the basic segments of the record utilizing a multi-stage thought technique. The figure later in this report shows the high-level architecture of the proposed model.

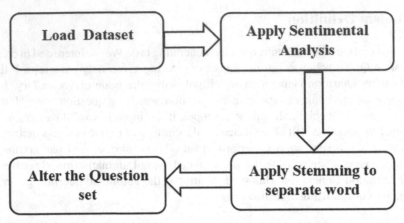

Fig. 2. Work-flow of our DistilGPT + QG System

3.1 Important Flow Steps

For moving toward our proposal and by looking toward, the problem from the existing conventional Automatic Question Generation Systems, the proposed methodology is going to be evaluated based on an evaluation of sentimental based analysis on inputted text in which the inputted data analyze and evaluate with the steaming-based evaluation in which the copy from question part will get evaluated & updated. The sentimental-based evaluation will give a new approach to the execution.

Load Unlabelled Dataset-
The SQuAD (Stanford Question Answering Dataset) dataset contains 100,000 questions, with over 50,000 of them being unanswerable. It also assesses a system's capacity to not only answer reading comprehension questions but also to avoid responding to questions that cannot be answered based on the provided text. For system training, SquAD version 2.0 is employed.

Apply Sentimental Analysis
The language that was entered is processed through Preprocessing stages, and once the data has been cleaned, the Subject, Verb, and Object parts of the Query are analyzed, and subjective vs objective differences are discovered. Later, using the seq2seq model and Named Entity Recognition (NER) and Parts of Speech tagging (POS), the WH – preference type for the aim that was evaluated in previous phases is determined.

A Search of Paste Objects
We look for the appropriate Object type in this phase of Paste Object Search when there are many object types in the same Query. The most appropriate object for the first and last preference is found first in these types of queries.

Stemming
We found the closest and related keyword to the target keyword in this step, which will later help us frame the most similar type of Questions. If we find a Paste object, we will change our current set; if we don't find a Paste object, we will find Wh word preference,

and then the Questions will be generated with the same objective found in previous stages.

In all-Natural Language Processing (NLP) projects practically, stemming is one of the most used data pre-processing processes. Simply explained, stemming is the removal of a portion of a word or the reduction of a term to its stem or root. It's possible that we're not reducing a word to its dictionary root. To decide how to cut a word off, we apply a few algorithms. Complications stemming will occur from time to time. These issues are known as over stemming, which is the process of chopping off a significantly greater portion of a word than is required, and under stemming, which is the process of incorrectly reducing two or more words to more than one root word.

4 Implementation Details

Several ways can be used to execute the loading of the squad Dataset and the generation of the question. We employed the multi-meaning para construction in the proposal, which increases the difficulty of the question. Various strategies appear to operate on the Dataset in which different delimiters are used to separate the squad paragraph and pertinent question, but it appears to be confined to the development of a single question. Many models for question generating have been presented, but none have been found to focus on multi-meaning question generation. As a result, the DistilGPT2 [34]. The transformer is recommended for the creation of necessary information, with the created statements being sent to various QG models as indicated below. The question is posed by this model. An English-language model named DistilGPT2 which is short name for Distilled-GPT2 was pre-prepared under the direction of the smallest version of Generative Pre-prepared Transformer 2 (GPT-2). Text can be created involving DistilGPT2 in a similar way as GPT-2. The GPT-2 with 124 million boundaries form was utilized to pre-train the English-language model DistilGPT2. DistilGPT2, which contained 82 million boundaries and was expected to be a faster, lighter form of GPT-2, was made through information refining. This transformer DistilGPT2 was prepared utilizing the Open Web Text Corpus, an open-source clone of OpenAI's Web Text Dataset that was utilized to prepare GPT-2 [35]. Utilizing the equivalent tokenizer as GPT-2, a byte-level Byte Pair Encoding variant, the texts were tokenized (BPE). A little model (the student) is prepared to imitate the way of behaving of a bigger model (the educator) or a bunch of models utilizing the compression strategy known as information refining.

Complete System From loading Input up to output Automatic Question Generation i.e. from semantics-Discriminator to meaningful para formation, comprises of two main steps, one is to Pre-process given Input which later undergoes very important steps like to perform statement Tokenization on document input, then to find Word tokens, which are further useful to perform Lammatisation where Using rules based on part-of-speech tags (the tag structures in the pre-trained pipelines differ by language) or lookup databases, this component assigns base forms to tokens. Language subclasses can use language-specific factories to create their Lammatisation components. The spacy-lookups-data extension package provides the default data about Lamma and calculates the word vector for every filtered word token extracted this result is passed to the Meaningful-para formation phase where the DISTILGPT2 Model is loaded and Parallel Statements are

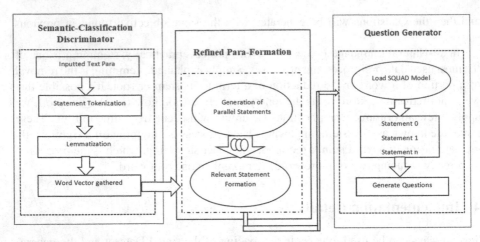

Fig. 3. Proposed Methodology of our Automatic Question Generation Approach

mapped into relevant Statements compared to the input document. Then these relevant statements are passed to the Question Generator phase where the Model is trained on the SQUAD Model and compared to where the many of the Automatic Questions are formed through 0,1,2……. N (one, two, …., N Numbers) Numbers of Statements from the para formation.

Dataset - SQuAD

The Stanford Question Answering Dataset (SQuAD) [3] is a reading comprehension Dataset derived from queries posed by crowd workers on a set of Wikipedia articles, with the response to each inquiry being a text phase, or span, from the relevant reading passage, or the question being unanswerable. SQuAD2.0 combines SQuAD1.1's 100,000 questions with over 50,000 unanswerable questions developed by crowd workers in a demeaning way to resemble answerable questions. To perform well on SQuAD2.0, structures must not only respond to inquiries when they are feasible but also recognize when the text supports no answerable is supported by the text and refrain from responding.

5   Results and Discussion

For the identical Input Paragraph, the Question Generated with several models (e.g. by T5, T5 fine-tuned on Squad, and Bart-EQG) is presented below. The multi-meaning Questions generated by our technology have been added to this representation.

Table 1. Output Generated by our system Distilgpt2 + QG

Input Paragraph	Model 1 [36]	Model 2 [37]	Proposed DistilGPT2 + QG
People often install a kitty door, only to discover that they have a problem. The problem is their cat will not use the kitty door. There are several common reasons why cats will not use kitty doors. If you read what they install a kitty door only to discover that they have a problem	Why do cats not use kitty doors?"?	What is one common reason cats will not use a kitty door?	Q-01: What they install only to discover that they have a problem? Q-02: Who install a kitty door only to discover that they have a problem? Q-03: Who have a problem?
In writing, the words point and purpose are almost synonymous. Your point is your purpose, and how you decide to make your point clear to your reader is also your purpose. Writers have a point and a purpose for every paragraph that they create	What is the meaning of the words point and purpose in writing?	What is the difference between a point and purpose?'?'?'?'?	Q-01: What is my point in writing? Q-02: Whose point is my purpose in writing? Q-03: What is my purpose in writing?
Temples typically have a main building and a larger precinct, which may contain many other buildings, or maybe a dome-shaped structure, much like an igloo. The word comes from Ancient Rome, where a templum constituted a sacred precinct as defined by a priest, or augur	What is a temple-shaped structure?"?"?'?'?	What type of structure is a dome?	Q-01: What may a temple have and a larger precinct? Q-02: Who may have a main building and a larger precinct?

5.1 Evaluation

The majority of previous studies used automatic metrics to evaluate model performance towards target questions. To make an empirical comparison, we used Bleu-1, Bleu-2, Bleu-3, Bleu-4 [38, 39], and METEOR, which shows that our approach is capable of high performance. However, because these are automatic machine-evaluated scores, there is a margin of error, so we used a feedback method to reward the outcome generated by our system.

Model 1 - The T5 version become recommended in Unified Text-to-Text Transformer for Transfer Learning: Exploring the Limits, and it changed into best-tuned the use of SQuAD for QG. Transfer getting to know is a sturdy approach in natural language processing that includes pre-training a model on a facts-rich activity earlier than fine-tuning it on a downstream venture (NLP). The fulfillment of transfer mastering has inspired a slew of techniques, strategies, and practices. It was trained with the Squad Dataset, with sample 87599 as the training sample, and 10570 as the valid data sample. Evaluation Results reflect values of the Bleu score as shown in Table 3, with Bleu_2 and Bleu_3 score as Nil & Bleu_4 as 8.89. Using the SQuAD Dataset to fine-tune the T5 model in our system, we obtain the values shown in Table 2 for Bleu 1, Bleu 4, and Meteor (Tables 1, 4 and 5).

Table 2. Evaluation Results of T5 based SQuAD [36]

Model	Bleu_1	Bleu_4	Meteor
	0.010261	8.89200	7.211

Model 2 - Bart-EQG query generator, this version is a series-to-series query generator that accepts most effective the context as enter and outputs a query. It is trained at the EQG-RACE corpus and is primarily based on a pre-educated Bart-base model. The context is used as an input sequence, and the model produces a query as an output sequence. The maximum length of a sequence is 1024 tokens. The following format should be used to organize inputs Context. The input sequence can then be encoded and supplied to the model's generate () method as the input ids argument. This model doesn't perform in terms of Bleu_2 & Bleu_3, But it performs 10.18 in terms of Meteor score which is good enough. EQG-BART model is pre-trained to our system and we get the values from Table 3 for our deployment.

Table 3. Evaluation Results of Generator Bart-EQG [40]

Model	Bleu_1	Bleu_4	Meteor
	0.023254	1.19	10.18

Below shown are the evaluation of our system with some of the state-of-the-art existing Techniques of Question Generation. That shows our Meteor score outperforms

Table 4. Previous Result with paragraph input in question generation

Method	BLEU 4	METEOR
s2s-a-at-mcp-gsa [38]	16.38	20.25
GPT2 + attention [34]	8.26	21.2
T5 with SQuAD [36]	8.89	7.21
bart-eqg-question-generator [37]	1.19	10.18
DISTIGPT2 + QG(Ours)	14.189	25.00

Table 5. Evaluation Results of Our System DistilGPT2 + QG

DistilGPT2 + QG (Ours)	Bleu_1	Bleu_2	Bleu_3	Bleu_4	Meteor
	0.191051	0.140104	0.129726	14.189	25.00

the State-of-the-art Approaches given below in the Table. Despite the fact that technique No. 1 displays a Bleu assessment score of 16.38, which is slightly greater than that of our system, our approach exceeds all of the other ways given in terms of Meteor.

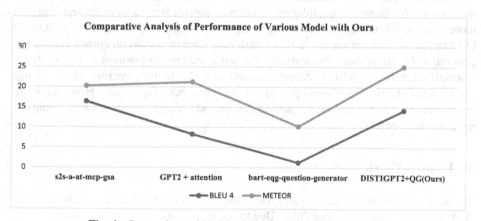

Fig. 4. Comparison of Various Models with DistilGpt2 + QG

6 Objective Evaluation

We provided a method with new training that yielded improved outcomes, and after successful training, our evaluation results are shown in the table below, which indicates a significant difference and improvement over the three state-of-the-art models. The results demonstrate an exceptional margin in Meteor score, with a difference of 6.0

when compared to other similar methodologies. Our system responds to Bleu 3 and Bleu 4 scores, whereas the three models explained above did not.

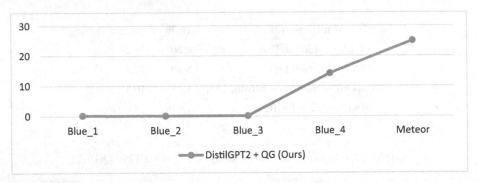

Fig. 5. Graphical representation of our Results

7   Conclusion

In this research, we offer a system for automatically creating questions by extending the relevant context with sentimental evaluation utilizing the word-vector approach to the content. We show that completing additional emotive steps aids in the learning of a more meaningful background, resulting in higher-quality generated results. On SQuAD QA Dataset, we test our method and establish new state-of-the-art outcomes in question generation for all of them. We also suggest using the answer position in the future on Datasets other than SQuAD to improve capabilities. Due to the numerous filters, we use at each level, the final result only provides a small number of questions. However, more complicated networks and deep learning can provide several questions with complete meaning and context.

8   Future Work

We suggest future direction here using the answer position in the future on Datasets other than SQuAD to improve capabilities. Due to the numerous filters, we use at each level, the final result only provides a small number of questions. However, more complicated networks and deep learning can provide several questions with complete meaning and context.

References

1. Lewis, M., Liu, Y., Goyal, N., Ghazvininejad, M., Mohamed, A., Levy, O., et al.: BART: denoising sequence-to-sequence pre-training for natural language generation, translation, and comprehension, 7871–7880 (2020)

2. Carmo, D., Piau, M., Campiotti, I., Nogueira, R., Lotufo, R.: PTT5: Pretraining and validating the T5 model on Brazilian Portuguese data, 1–12 (2020). Available from: http://arxiv.org/abs/2008.09144

3. Akyon, F.C., Cavusoglu, D., Cengiz, C., Altinuc, S.O., Temizel, A.: Automated question generation and question answering from Turkish texts using text-to-text transformers, 1–14 (2021). Available from: http://arxiv.org/abs/2111.06476

4. Madane, S., Bhura, S.: Traffic surveillance: theoretical survey of video motion detection. Int J Sci Technol Eng. **2**(08), 207–211 (2016)

5. Lopez, L.E., Cruz, D.K., Cruz, J.C.B., Cheng, C.: Simplifying paragraph-level question generation via transformer language models. Lect. Notes Comput. Sci. (including Subser. Lect. Notes Artif. Intell. Lect. Notes Bioinformat.). 13032, LNAI: 323–334 (2021)

6. Raynaud, T., Subercaze, J., Laforest, F.: Thematic question generation over knowledge bases. In: Proceedings - 2018 IEEE/WIC/ACM International Conference on Web Intelligence, WI 2018. Institute of Electrical and Electronics Engineers Inc. pp. 1–8 (2019)

7. Cao, S., Wang, L.: Controllable open-ended question generation with a new question type ontology. ACL-IJCNLP 2021 - 59th Annu. Meet Assoc. Comput. Linguist 11th Int. Jt. Conf. Nat Lang Process Proc. Conf. 6424–6439 (2021)

8. Lindberg, D., Popowich, F., Nesbit, J., Winne, P.: Generating natural language questions to support learning on-line. In: ENLG 2013 - 14th European Workshop on Natural Language Generation, Proceedings. pp. 105–114 (2013)

9. Quan, P., Shi, Y., Niu, L., Liu, Y., Zhang, T.: Automatic chinese multiple-choice question generation for human resource performance appraisal. In: Procedia Computer Science. Elsevier B.V. pp. 165–172 (2018)

10. Amdani, S.Y., Bamnote, G.R., Deshmukh, H.R., Bhura, S.A.: A novel disk scheduling algorithm in real-time database systems. Int. J. Comput. Appl. **1**(29), 1–7 (2010)

11. Yuan, W., Wang, H., Yu, X., Liu, N., Li, Z.: Attention-based context-aware sequential recommendation model. Inf. Sci. (Ny). **1**(510), 122–134 (2020)

12. Hoang, M.T., Yuen, B., Dong, X., Lu, T., Westendorp, R., Reddy, K.: Recurrent neural networks for accurate RSSI indoor localization. IEEE Internet Things J. **6**(6), 10639–10651 (2019)

13. Wang, H., Zhang, X., Wang, H.: A neural question generation system based on knowledge base. In: Zhang, M., Ng, V., Zhao, D., Li, S., Zan, H. (eds.) NLPCC 2018. LNCS (LNAI), vol. 11108, pp. 133–142. Springer, Cham (2018). https://doi.org/10.1007/978-3-319-99495-6_12

14. Sutskever, I., Vinyals, O., Le, Q.V.: Sequence to sequence learning with neural networks. Adv. Neural Inf. Process Syst. **4**(January), 3104–3112 (2014)

15. Benmalek, R.Y., Khabsa, M., Desu, S., Cardie, C., Banko, M.: Keeping notes: conditional natural language generation with a scratchpad mechanism. In: ACL 2019 - 57th Annual Meeting of the Association for Computational Linguistics, Proceedings of the Conference, pp. 4157–4167 (2019)

16. Hochreiter, S., Schmidhuber, J.: Long short-term memory. Neural Comput. **9**(8), 1735–1780 (1997)

17. Bhura, S.A., Mahamune, A., Alvi, A.S.: Limited preemptive disk scheduling for real time database system. In: Proceedings - 1st International Conference Computer Communication Control Automation ICCUBEA 2015, pp. 362–366 (2015)

18. Chali, Y., Hasan, S.A., Mojahid, M.: A reinforcement learning formulation to the complex question answering problem. Inf Process Manag. **51**(3), 252–272 (2015)

19. Heilman, M., Aleven, V., Cohen, W.W., Litman, D.J., Smith, N.A.: Automatic factual question generation from text thesis committee (2022). www.lti.cs.cmu.edu

20. Labutov, I., Basu, S., Vanderwende, L.: Deep questions without deep understanding. In: ACL-IJCNLP 2015 - 53rd Annual Meeting of the Association for Computational Linguistics and the 7th International Joint Conference on Natural Language Processing of the Asian Federation of Natural Language Processing, Proceedings of the Conference, pp. 889–898 (2015)

21. Amdani, S.Y., Bhura, S.A., Mahamune, A.A.: Real-Time disk scheduling using preemptive and non-preemptive approach: a survey (10) (2013)

22. Serban, I.V., García-Durán, A., Gulcehre, C., Ahn, S., Chandar, S., Courville, A., et al.: Generating factoid questionswith recurrent neural networks: The 30M factoid question-answer corpus. 54th Annu. Meet Assoc. Comput. Linguist ACL 2016 - Long Paper 1, pp. 588–598 (2016)

23. Du, X., Cardie, C.: Harvesting paragraph-level question-answer pairs from wikipedia. In: ACL 2018 - 56th Annual Meeting of the Association for Computational Linguistics, Proceedings of the Conference (Long Papers) [Internet]. Association for Computational Linguistics; 2018, pp. 1907–1917 (2022). https://github.com/xinyadu/

24. Shen, Y., Huang, P.S., Gao, J., Chen W.: ReasoNet: learning to stop reading in machine comprehension. In: Proceedings of the ACM SIGKDD International Conference on Knowledge Discovery and Data Mining. Association for Computing Machinery, pp. 1047–1055 (2017)

25. Bhura, S.A., Alvi, A.S., Amdani, S.Y.: Scheduling real-Time task using dynamic preemption threshold. ACM Int. Conf. Proceeding Ser. Mar 4, 04–05 March (2016)

26. Chan, Y.H., Fan, Y.C.: A recurrent BERT-based model for question generation. MRQA@EMNLP 2019 - Proc 2nd Work Mach Read Quest Answering, 154–162 (2019)

27. Ma, X., Zhu, Q., Zhou, Y., Li, X.: Improving question generation with sentence-level semantic matching and answer position inferring. In: AAAI 2020 - 34th AAAI Conference on Artificial Intelligence [Internet], pp. 8464–8471 (2020). http://arxiv.org/abs/1912.00879

28. Du, X., Cardie, C.: Identifying where to focus in reading comprehension for neural question generation. In: EMNLP 2017 - Conference Empir Methods Nat Lang Process Proc., pp. 2067–2073 (2017)

29. Sohel, A., Bhura, D.A.S.A.: Improved AED Scheduling Algorithm for Real-Time System. Int. J. Sci. Res. [Internet]. 3(9) (2014). https://www.ijsr.net/archive/v3i9/U0VQMTQyMDA=.pdf

30. Chali, Y., Hasan, S.A.: Towards Topic-to-Question Generation. undefined [Internet]. 2015 Mar 18 [cited 2022 Sep 12]; 41(1), 1–20. http://duc.nist.gov/

31. Chali, Y., Baghaee, T.: Automatic opinion question generation. INLG 2018 - 11th Int. Nat. Lang. Gener. Conf. Proc. Conf. 2018; 152–158 (2013)

32. Heilman, M., Smith, N.A.: Good question! Statistical ranking for question generation. In: NAACL HLT 2010 - Human Language Technologies: The 2010 Annual Conference of the North American Chapter of the Association for Computational Linguistics, Proceedings of the Main Conference [Internet]. [cited 2022 May 31], pp. 609–617 (2010). Available from: http://en

33. Deshmukh, P.M.V.M., Bhura, S.A., Satav, P.R., Asole, S.S., Agrawal, S.: Retrieval by color features in image databases. Int. J. Comput. Appl. 1(26), 140–142 (2010)

34. Altheneyan, A., Menai, M.E.B.: Evaluation of state-of-the-art paraphrase identification and its application to automatic plagiarism detection 34(4) (2019). https://doi.org/10.1142/S0218001420530043

35. Papineni, K., Roukos, S., Ward, T., Zhu, W.-J., Heights, Y.: IBM research report bleu : a method for automatic evaluation of machine translation. Science (80-) [Internet]. [cited 2022 Jun 4]; 22176: 1–10 (2001). http://dl.acm.org/citation.cfm?id=1073135

36. Raffel, C., Shazeer, N., Roberts, A., Lee, K., Narang, S., Matena, M., et al.: Exploring the limits of transfer learning with a unified text-to-text transformer. J. Mach. Learn. Res. 21, 1–67 (2020)

37. Du, X., Shao, J., Cardie, C.: Learning to ask: Neural question generation for reading comprehension. In: ACL 2017 - 55th Annual Meeting of the Association for Computational Linguistics, Proceedings of the Conference (Long Papers) [Internet]. [cited 2022 Jun 4], pp. 1342–1352 (2017). https://stanford-qa.com

38. Zhang, Y., Lo, D., Xia, X., Sun, J.-L.: Multi-factor duplicate question detection in stack overflow. J. Comput. Sci. Technol. **30**(5), 981–997 (2015). https://doi.org/10.1007/s11390-015-1576-4

39. Khandait, K., Bhura, S., Asole, S.S.: Automatic question generation through word vector synchronization using lamma. Indian J Comput Sci Eng. **13**(4), 1083–1095 (2022)

40. Du, X., Shao, J., Cardie, C.: Learning to ask: Neural question generation for reading comprehension. In: ACL 2017 - 55th Annual Meeting of the Association for Computational Linguistics, Proceedings of the Conference (Long Papers) [Internet]. Association for Computational Linguistics (ACL); [cited 2022 May 31], pp. 1342–1352 (2017). https://arxiv.org/abs/1705.00106v1

Estimation of Dynamic Balancing Margin of the 10-DOF Biped Robot by Using Polynomial Trajectories

Moh Shahid Khan[✉] [iD] and Ravi Kumar Mandava[iD]

Maulana Azad National Institute of Technology, Bhopal, MP 462003, India
ershahid20@gmail.com

Abstract. The dynamic balancing margin (DBM) is crucial for the locomotion of the biped robot while walking on various terrains. In the current article, the authors have attempted to estimate the DBM of the biped robot using different polynomial trajectories such as quadratic (second order), cubic (third order) and fifth-ordered polynomials. Based on forward and inverse kinematics, the 10 degrees of freedom (DOF) biped robot's gait has been generated and the DBM has been estimated by using ZMP (zero moment point) principle while walking on the flat terrain. Furthermore, after assigning several polynomial trajectories for the swing foot, the biped robot's gait generation was put to the test. The result shows that the cubic polynomial trajectory performs a more dynamically balanced gait than quadratic and fifth-order polynomials.

Keywords: Biped robot · Gait generation · Polynomial trajectory · ZMP · DBM

1 Introduction

Biped robots can assist human beings while working in various terrain conditions. The dynamically balanced walking of the biped robot over varied terrains has been reported to be a challenging issue. Many scientists around the world are focusing on the biped robot's dynamically balanced gait in different terrain situations in an effort to tackle this challenge. The DBM of the biped robot is evaluated based on the concept of ZMP i.e. zero moment point, introduced by Vukobratovic [1] in 1970. The ZMP is a hypothetical location where the sum of all the moments produced by the links of the bipedal mechanism equals zero. The resulting gait is dynamically balanced and appropriate for diverse terrain situations if the ZMP is inside the foot support polygon. It has been found that the DBM is essential for the biped robot, obtained from the foot polygon's four sides. Few researchers have developed the framework of the gait planner by using bionic kinematics [2]; inverse kinematics with ZMP [3]; human motion capture data (HMCD) with ZMP [4, 5]; LIPM (linear inverted pendulum model) [2, 6, 7]; TLIPFM (three-mass linear inverted pendulum plus flywheel model) [8]; Bezier Control Points [9], inertial measurement unit (IMU) sensor [10], design of vector fields for various joints [11], push recovery model [12, 13] hybrid automata [14] and balancing by support through hand

© The Author(s), under exclusive license to Springer Nature Switzerland AG 2022
N. Khare et al. (Eds.): MIND 2022, CCIS 1762, pp. 86–96, 2022.
https://doi.org/10.1007/978-3-031-24352-3_7

grip [15]. A biped robot's gait is generated in two stages: the SSP (single support phase) and the DSP (double support phase). Out of the two legs, one leg acts as a swing leg, and another leg acts as stand leg. The swinging leg is used to follow some specific trajectory based on mathematical equations along with boundary conditions of the terrain on which the robot has to walk. Till now, much literature has reported various kinds of foot trajectories for biped robot while walking over flat terrain as well as avoiding the obstacles, such as, Sinusoidal Fourier [16]; Cubic Polynomial [3, 17]; Fourth Order Spline [6] and Cycloidal Curve [7, 18].

In addition, a real-time walking trajectory development at constant body height in SSP was proposed by Sato et al. [12] by using ZMP and swing leg trajectory to derive an analytical model. By using a polynomial trajectory for the support leg, a Sinusoid Fourier trajectory for the swing leg, and a Sinusoid Fourier trajectory for both legs in the frontal plane, Aghaabbasloo et al. [16] created a mathematical gait generation of a biped robot. Moreover, based on central pattern generator (CPG), T-S (Takagi–Suguno) fuzzy system, and DOE (Design of Experiments) approach, Farzaneh et al. [2] suggested an effective online trajectory generating a framework for a seven-link biped model. A seamless transition between different trajectories was achieved as a consequence of the CPG model generating the necessary joint trajectories by fine-tuning its parameters with the aid of Fourier-based automatic learning central pattern generators (FAL-CPG). Also, a whole-body gait for a biped robot consisting 18-DOF was generated by Mandava and Vundavilli [3] using inverse kinematics and the ZMP concept. The biped robot's wrist and swing foot considered as cubic polynomial trajectory, for generating dynamically balanced gait. Wang et al. [4] used the aggregate data from the mathematical model of human walking, and the natural gait data gathered through HMCD to construct a gait planner for a 3D-printed customized humanoid robot. The balancing of the humanoid robot's was awkward and unsatisfactory as a result of the immediate use of HMCD. They suggested an improved trajectory generating technique to address this problem by combining the HMCD and ZMP concepts. Later on, Ayari and Knani [6] created a stable walking pattern at two distinct speeds by managing COG and ZMP to avoid the obstacles derived from LIPM modelling. The trajectory of swing foot was generated by employing a fourth ordered spline function. Similarly, Dominguez et al. [7] planned the pendulum's pivot at the ankle joint based on LIPM for determining the 12 DOF biped robot's gait. For both symmetric and asymmetric gaits, the suggested gait creates a cycloidal hip and foot trajectory. Furthermore, based on the preview control of the ZMP, Juang et al. [19] presented a method of uniform acceleration to plan the robot's foot trajectories more conveniently and succinctly. The developed method allows the robot to lift and release the legs at a fixed acceleration. Wong et al. [8] developed a natural walking trajectory generator for 23-DOF mini-sized humanoid robot named TKU-X, by using TLIPFM (three-mass linear inverted pendulum plus flywheel model). They compared it to the LIPM and DLIPM models and discovered that, by minimizing model error, the TLIPFM model outperforms the other two dynamic models in terms of accuracy of natural motion generation performance. For minimizing the velocity and acceleration of the swing leg, Chen et al. [9] created an optimization model of a rapid offline trajectory generator for the swing leg of the 16-DOF humanoid robot "BHR6". The developed model was influenced by the optimization of the Bézier control points. In addition to, probabilistic models for modelling human locomotion data were developed by Singh et al. [5] by employing Automatic relevance determination regression, Gaussian process regression, and Bayesian ridge regression to generate the reference trajectory. Later on, a centroidal online trajectory generation and stabilization control was proposed by Murooka et al. [15] for mitigating the inaccuracy of centroidal state that significantly decreased the computation cost by utilizing preview control for robustness and wrench distribution.

It is critical to obtain the dynamically balanced biped gait and to overcome its criticality the authors of this article developed a gait planner for a 10-DOF biped robot using forward and inverse kinematics analysis. Further, the quadratic, cubic and fifth-ordered polynomial trajectories are assigned to swing foot while walking on flat terrain. The biped robot's stability for walking on flat terrain has been evaluated in terms of average DBM. It will help the researchers to obtain the stable biped gait by using three different polynomial foot trajectories.

This paper has been organized into 6 sections. Section 1 contains the introduction of the problem. The mathematical model of the biped robot has been presented in Sect. 2, which contains all the fundamentals required for this study. Furthermore, Sect. 3 outlines the steps of experimentation. After which, all the results and plots have been explained in Sect. 4. Finally, Sect. 5 concludes the study and its significance. And then the future scope has been discussed in Sect. 6.

2 Mathematical Modelling of the Biped Robot

Within this section, the authors have discussed the forward and inverse kinematic analysis of the 10-DOF biped robot after assigning the various polynomial trajectories on a swing foot.

2.1 Forward Kinematics

Figure 1 shows the 10-DOF biped robot have of two legs; each leg contains 5-DOF, the hip consists of 2-DOF, Knee consists of 1-DOF and the ankle consists of 2-DOF. Every joint of the biped robot is assigned a coordinate frame to determine the D-H parameters. All the joints are revolving joints. The Table 1 provides the D-H characteristics of the right leg. The forward kinematics helps to determine the position and orientation of the swing foot concerning polynomial trajectories.

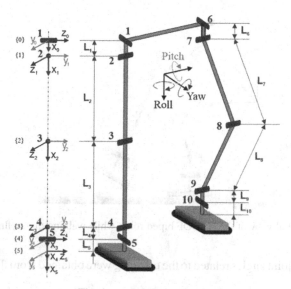

Fig. 1. 10-DOF biped robot.

Table 1. DH parameters of right leg of biped robot consisting 5 revolute joints

Frames	Link	Joint Angle (θ_i)	Twist Angle (α_i)	Link Length (a_i)	Joint Offset (b_i)
0 to 1	1	θ_1	90	L_1	0
1 to 2	2	θ_2	0	L_2	0
2 to 3	3	θ_3	0	L_3	0
3 to 4	4	θ_4	−90	L_4	0
4 to 5	5	θ_5	0	L_5	0

2.2 Inverse Kinematics

The relation between the joint angles has been derived by using the geometry of the mechanism considered for the biped robot, and this process of obtaining these expressions is called the inverse kinematics. Figure 2 is showing the various revolute joint angles of the biped robot in the sagittal view. The relations for the joint angles θ_2 and θ_3 have been derived from Eqs. 1 and 2. These angles will help to maintain the constraint of dynamic stability.

$$\theta_3 = sin^{-1}\left(\frac{H_1 L_2 sin\,sin\delta + W_1(L_3 + L_2 cos\delta)}{(L_3 + L_2 cos\delta)^2 + (L_2 sin\delta)^2}\right) \quad (1)$$

where, $H_1 = L_3 cos\theta_3 + L_2 cos\theta_2$, $W_1 = L_3 cos\theta_3 + L_2 cos\theta_2$, $\theta_2 = \theta_3 - \delta$, and

$$\delta = \theta_3 - \theta_2 = cos^{-1}\left(\frac{H_1^2 + W_1^2 - L_3^2 - L_2^2}{2L_3 L_2}\right) \quad (2)$$

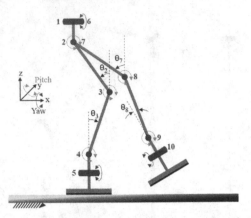

Fig. 2. Sagittal view of the 10-DOF biped robot while walking on the flat ground.

Similarly, the joint angles related to the other leg were obtained from the same inverse kinematics.

2.3 Foot Trajectory

The boundary conditions of the three different polynomial trajectories, quadratic, cubic and fifth-order, are given below.

Table 2. Polynomial equations with desired boundary conditions

	Quadratic (Second Order) Polynomial $z = \mu_1 x + \mu_2 x^2$		Cubic (Third Order) Polynomial $z = \mu_0 + \mu_1 x + \mu_2 x^2 + \mu_3 x^3$		Quintic (Fifth Order) Polynomial $z = \mu_0 + \mu_1 x + \mu_2 x^2 + \mu_3 x^3 + \mu_4 x^4 + \mu_5 x^5$	
i	xi	zi	x_i	z_i	x_i	z_i
1	x_1	0	x_1	0	x_1	0
2	$\frac{x_2-x_1}{2}$	$\frac{f_s}{2}$	$x_1 + \frac{f_s}{2}$	$\frac{f_s}{3}$	$x_1 + \frac{2f_s}{5}$	$\frac{f_s}{4}$
3	x_2	0	$x_1 + \frac{3f_s}{2}$	$\frac{f_s}{3}$	$x_1 + \frac{4f_s}{5}$	$\frac{f_s}{2}$
4			x_2	0	$x_1 + \frac{6f_s}{5}$	$\frac{f_s}{2}$
5					$x_1 + \frac{8f_s}{5}$	$\frac{f_s}{4}$
6					x_2	0

Where, the initial position of the swing leg for the first step, i.e., $x_1 = 0$, and final position $x_2 = x_1 + step\ length$, and f_s is any arbitrary variable relevant to the foot support which needs to be investigated based on its effect on the dynamic stability.

2.4 Dynamic Balance Margin (DBM)

The following equations can be used to evaluate the ZMP and DBM of the biped robot in the x-direction.

$$x_{ZMP} = \frac{\sum_{i=1}^{n}(I_i \dot{\omega}_i + m_i x_i(\ddot{z}_i - g) - m_i \ddot{x}_i z_i)}{\sum_{i=1}^{n} m_i(\ddot{z}_i - g)} \tag{3}$$

$$x_{DBM} = \frac{length\ of\ the\ foot\ support}{2} - |x_{ZMP}| \tag{4}$$

where, I_i is the moment of inertia in kg-m^2; $\dot{\omega}_i$ is the angular acceleration in rad/s^2; m_i is mass in kg; x_i, y_i and z_i are the coordinates for the lumped mass; g is the gravitational acceleration in m/s^2 and $\ddot{z}_i$ is acceleration in the z direction for i^{th} link of biped robot.

3 Experimentation

The joint angles of the biped robot have been obtained by using the inverse kinematics equations along with distinct sets of boundary conditions according to three polynomial equations used for generating the foot trajectory separately. Each foot trajectory gives unique set of joint angles, ZMP variation and DBM variation. Later, the values of ZMP and DBM were investigated for greater dynamic stability which is identified by higher value of average DBM. During the investigation, the average DBM was found more for the cubic polynomial foot trajectory than the other two trajectories used. That's why the variation of the joint parameters and also the simulated stick diagram of the biped robot have been presented only for the case of cubic polynomial foot trajectory as shown in Figs. 4 and 6 respectively. And also, the variation of the ZMP and the DBM for case of cubic polynomial trajectory can be seen in the Table 2.

Table 3. Variation of the ZMP and the DBM in case of cubic polynomial foot trajectory

Time Interval (seconds)	X_{DBM} (meter)				X_{ZMP} (meter)			
	Left Leg		Right Leg		Left Leg		Right Leg	
	SSP	DSP	SSP	DSP	SSP	DSP	SSP	DSP
1	0.0342	0.0391	0.0342	0.0391	−0.0178	0.0129	−0.0178	0.0129
2	0.0349	0.0419	0.0349	0.0419	−0.0171	0.0101	−0.0171	0.0101
3	0.0412	0.0407	0.0412	0.0407	−0.0108	0.0113	−0.0108	0.0113
4	0.0474	0.0392	0.0474	0.0392	−0.0046	0.0128	−0.0046	0.0128
5	0.051	0.0371	0.051	0.0371	0.001	0.0149	0.001	0.0149
6	0.0461	0.0355	0.0461	0.0355	0.0059	0.0165	0.0059	0.0165
7	0.0416	0.0343	0.0416	0.0343	0.0104	0.0177	0.0104	0.0177
8	0.0401	0.036	0.0401	0.036	0.0119	0.016	0.0119	0.016

4   Results and Discussion

The developed gait generation algorithm requires an initial posture consisting of joint angles of the swing leg considered as $\theta_2 = 40°$ and $\theta_3 = -30°$. The initial boundary condition $x_1 = 0$, with the step length of 0.1382 m, was taken as input for producing the swing foot trajectory. Figure 3 shows the swing foot trajectories obtained by quadratic, cubic and fifth-order polynomial equations. The initial angle of flight obtained for the swing foot trajectory is 39.08° for quadratic, 35.39° for cubic and 31.34° for fifth-order polynomial trajectories. The horizontal distance, i.e. step length and time constraint, are considered the same in all cases. It has been found that the path travelled by the fifth ordered and quadratic polynomial trajectories are minimum and maximum respectively, due to low and high velocities and accelerations of various joints of the biped robot's swinging leg. Further, it has been investigated that the cubic polynomial trajectory makes the robot's foot travel the path with moderate speed and acceleration.

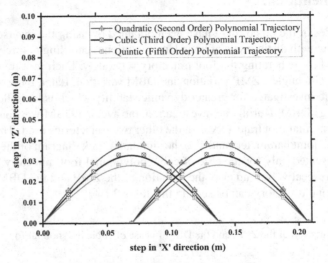

Fig. 3. All polynomial foot trajectories

Figure 3 (a) is showing the cyclic change of all the revolute joint angles of both the legs. It can be said that the generated gait is symmetric because of the similar variation of the respective joints of the biped robot. Similarly, Fig. 3 (b) is indicating the cyclic changes in values of torques at all different joints of the biped robot with respect to time intervals. It has been found that joint 1 and 6 require more torque because joint 1 carries the weight of all lower links and joints of the swing leg while generating the gait. Similarly, the stand leg of joint 6 requires more torque for holding the biped robot's other links and joints. Additionally, it has been noted that the remaining joints of the swing and stand leg require minimum torque to generate the gait systematically. In order to optimize the design of the biped robot, it is suggested to use a higher torque actuator at the hip joint than the other joints.

Equations 3 and 4 are used to obtain the ZMP and DBM to generate gait on sagittal plane. Figure 5 (a) represents the variation of ZMP with respect to the time interval

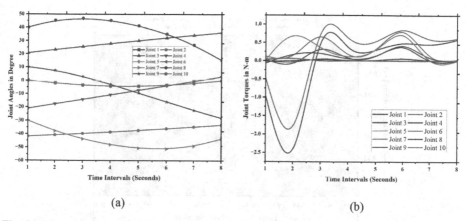

(a)   (b)

Fig. 4. The result shows the (a) various joint angles and (b) joint torques with respect to the time interval in the sagittal view.

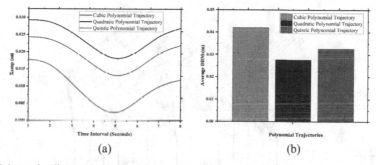

(a)   (b)

Fig. 5. Schematic diagram showing the (a) ZMP Trajectory or Cyclic change in ZMP in 'x' direction and (b) average DBM

in sagittal plane. It has been found that in cubic polynomial trajectory, the ZMP point is closer to the centre of the foot polygon in all time intervals compared to quadratic and fifth order polynomial. The average DBM of the various swing foot polynomial trajectories are shown in Fig. 5 (b). It has been observed that the DBM of the cubic polynomial is more when compared to other two trajectories. Because the height of the swing foot trajectory generated by a cubic polynomial is moderate, which is helpful to generate a more dynamically balanced gait when compared to quadratic and fifth-ordered. That's why the foot support polygon consisting the ZMP trajectory, ZMP region and DBM region for cubic polynomial trajectory has been plotted by using the results of ZMP and DBM obtained in Table 3, as shown in Fig. 6. It is to be noted that all ZMP are falling inside the polygon. The DBM region represents the stability which can be further maximized by using any evolutionary algorithms. Also shown in Fig. 7 is the stick diagram of the constructed biped robot while its swing foot following the cubic polynomial trajectory in the simulation. The produced gait on a flat surface is discovered to be more dynamically balanced.

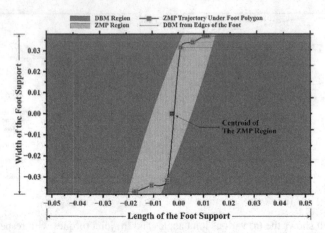

Fig. 6. Foot support polygon showing the ZMP Trajectory, ZMP Region and DBM Region

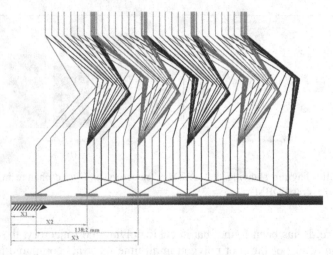

Fig. 7. Simulated stick diagram showing simulation of cubic polynomial trajectory for SSP in the sagittal view.

5   Conclusions

In the current study, the author shows how a 10-DOF biped robot generates gaits in the sagittal plane while walking on flat terrain. The biped robot's gait generation makes use of three different polynomial trajectories which are quadratic, cubic and fifth order for the swing leg with the help of the forward and inverse kinematics. The boundary conditions of all polynomial trajectories help to fall the ZMP inside the foot support polygon. It has been found that the cubic polynomial swing foot trajectory results to more DBM when compared to quadratic and fifth ordered polynomial swing foot trajectories. Therefore, cubic polynomial swing foot trajectory generates sufficient lifting height and crossing distance compared to other two polynomial trajectories similar to natural human walking.

Additionally, compared to other joints, the hip joint of the swing leg required higher torque. Finally, the simulation shows the 10-DOF biped robot's symmetric, cyclic, and dynamically balanced gait on a flat surface.

6 Future Scope

The same work can be integrated with any evolutionary optimization algorithm for minimizing the ZMP region or maximizing the DBM region. And also, various controllers' techniques can be involved for obtaining the smooth walking of the biped robot.

References

1. Vukobratovic, M., Frank, A.A., Juricic, D.: On the Stability of Biped Locomotion. IEEE Trans. Biomed. Eng. **BME-17**(1), 25–36 (1970). https://doi.org/10.1109/TBME.1970.4502681
2. Farzaneh, Y., Akbarzadeh, A., Akbari, A.A.: Online bio-inspired trajectory generation of seven-link biped robot based on T-S fuzzy system. Appl. Soft Comput. **14**, 167–180 (2014)
3. Mandava, R.K., Vundavilli, P.R.: Forward and inverse kinematic based full body gait generation of biped robot. In: 2016 International Conference on Electrical, Electronics, and Optimization Techniques (ICEEOT), pp. 3301–3305 (2016)
4. Wang, P., Wang, Y., Ru, F.: Walking trajectory generation for a 3D printing biped robot based on human natural gait and ZMP criteria. In: 2017 IEEE International Conference on Cybernetics and Intelligent Systems (CIS) and IEEE Conference on Robotics, Automation and Mechatronics (RAM), pp. 237–242 (2017)
5. Singh, B., Gupta, V., Kumar, R.: Probabilistic modeling of human locomotion for biped robot trajectory generation. In: 2021 IEEE 8th Uttar Pradesh Section International Conference on Electrical, Electronics and Computer Engineering (UPCON), pp. 1–6 (2021)
6. Ayari, A., Knani, J.: The generation of a stable walking trajectory of a biped robot based on the COG based-gait pattern and ZMP constraint. Int. J. Adv. Comput. Sci. Appl. **9**(9) (2018)
7. Domínguez, C.A.M., Sánchez, E.M., Soto, G.I.P.: Gait synthesis for a 12-degree-of-freedom biped robot by the LIPM. In: 2018 XX Congreso Mexicano de Robótica (COMRob), pp. 1–5 (2018)
8. Wong, C.-C., Xiao, S.-R., Aoyama, H.: Natural walking trajectory generator for humanoid robot based on three-mass LIPFM. IEEE Access **8**, 228151–228162 (2020)
9. Chen, H., et al.: A swing-foot trajectory generation method for biped walking. In: 2021 6th IEEE International Conference on Advanced Robotics and Mechatronics (ICARM), pp. 841–845 (2021)
10. Semwal, V.B., Gaud, N., Lalwani, P., Bijalwan, V., Alok, A.K.: Pattern identification of different human joints for different human walking styles using inertial measurement unit (IMU) sensor. Artif. Intell. Rev. **55**(2), 1149–1169 (2022)
11. Semwal, V.B., Kumar, C., Mishra, P.K., Nandi, G.C.: Design of vector field for different subphases of gait and regeneration of gait pattern. IEEE Trans. Autom. Sci. Eng. **15**(1), 104–110 (2016)
12. Semwal, V.B.: Data driven computational model for bipedal walking and push recovery. arXiv Prepr, arXiv:1710.06548 (2017)
13. Semwal, V.B., Nandi, G.C.: Toward developing a computational model for bipedal push recovery–a brief. IEEE Sens. J. **15**(4), 2021–2022 (2015)
14. Nandi, G.C., Semwal, V.B., Raj, M., Jindal, A.: Modeling bipedal locomotion trajectories using hybrid automata. In: 2016 IEEE Region 10 Conference (TENCON), pp. 1013–1018 (2016)

15. Murooka, M., Morisawa, M., Kanehiro, F.: Centroidal trajectory generation and stabilization based on preview control for humanoid multi-contact motion. IEEE Robot. Autom. Lett. (2022)
16. Aghaabbasloo, M., Azarkaman, M., Salehi, M.E.: Biped robot joint trajectory generation using PSO evolutionary algorithm. In: 2013 3rd Joint Conference of AI & Robotics and 5th RoboCup Iran Open International Symposium, pp. 1–6 (2013)
17. Sato, T., Sakaino, S., Ohnishi, K.: Real-time walking trajectory generation method at constant body height in single support phase for three-dimensional biped robot. In: 2009 IEEE International Conference on Industrial Technology, pp. 1–6 (2009)
18. Liu, Y., Heng, S., Zang, X., Lin, Z., Zhao, J.: Multiphase trajectory generation for planar biped robot using direct collocation method. Math. Probl. Eng. 2021 (2021)
19. Jiang, C., Gao, J., Shi, X., Tian, D., Huang, Q.: Foot trajectory planning of bipedal walking robot based on a uniform acceleration method. In: 2019 IEEE International Conference on Advanced Robotics and iIs Social Impacts (ARSO), pp. 251–255 (2019)

A Review on: Deep Learning and Computer Intelligent Techniques Using X-Ray Imaging for the Early Detection of Knee Osteoarthritis

Ravindra D. Kale[1]($\boxtimes$) and Sarika Khandelwal[2]

[1] Computer Science and Engineering, G H Raisoni University, Amravati, India
`ravindra.swati2012@gmail.com`

[2] Department of Computer Science and Engineering, G H Raisoni College of Engineering, Nagpur, India

Abstract. One of the most common causes of long-term impairment is knee osteoarthritis, a well-known disabling illness that lowers mobility and quality of life. It is possible for disease development to be sluggish and take many years, but it is also possible for disease progression/evolution to be rapid in some individuals. Osteoarthritis is patients are now only receiving symptomatic treatment, and standard osteoarthritis diagnosis is not very good at identifying patients who will advance rapidly. To improve treatment strategies, a thorough prediction model for individuals with early-stage osteoarthritis that stratifies them depending on how likely it is that their joint structural disease will proceed is needed. Using a deep learning system powered by computer intelligence techniques such as PSO/ACO. We anticipate it will be possible to construct a prediction model that allows as a means of early detection of patients whose knee structure will degenerate quickly due to arthritis.

Keywords: Osteoarthritis (OA) · Knee X-Ray · Deep learning · Early detection

1 Introduction

Osteoarthritis (OA), a disease that gradually develops and is characterized by structural changes in the joints, one of the most enduring constants musculoskeletal illnesses in the US. This disease is clinically quite burdensome, which includes pain, functional impairments, and multi morbidity. Despite the fact that early proactive care is critical for OA patients whose disease may develop rapidly, there is currently no validated early-stage diagnosis available [1, 2]. To do so, accurately identify the human effect of the disease, as well as to properly track and control the disease's course, it is crucial to further our understanding of the structural development of OA and to discover early predictors of the disease. The Precision medicine is being developed, which ensures that "the appropriate medication is administered at the appropriate moment," will be a crucial strategy for more tailored and efficient medicines. Currently, in clinical practice, the course of osteoarthritis is primarily determined by clinical assessment, which is

N. Khare et al. (Eds.): MIND 2022, CCIS 1762, pp. 97–113, 2022.
https://doi.org/10.1007/978-3-031-24352-3_8

frequently coupled with imaging studies (typically X-rays). However, these methods frequently decide the disparity in the middle of the patient's side effects and the amount of primary joint changes too, making early disease development prediction challenging. Therefore, it is clear and necessary that new specialized techniques be developed that reliably foresee the underlying course of the illness when it was first manifested while moreover enabling quick individualized risk evaluation for use in clinical practice.

With a better knowledge of OA mechanisms, They've started looking for chemicals or components that could be employed as biochemical indicators [3]. This disease's early progression can be tracked using biomarkers, which is a novel method of charting the disease's progression. Several biomarkers have been studied in the serum and patient's urine with various diseases throughout the last few decades, observation, with the goal of providing early detection and/or forecasting of the disease's progression. Despite this, nobody has demonstrated that any of them is sufficiently specific or sensitive.

The paper's organizational breakdown is provided below. The notion of a literature review is described in Sect. 2. Section 3 contains comparative analysis. Section 4 discusses experimental evaluation. The conclusion is found in Sect. 5.

2 Literature Review

Aamir Yousuf Bhat, A. Suhasini [1], the authors approached that osteoarthritis, the most well-known disorder that harms the knee joint's cartilage, is more prevalent in aged or obese people. Two different medical imaging procedures that may be employed in the assessment for osteoarthritis identification are X-RAY pictures and MRI scans. In terms of time efficiency and classification execution, the classifier beat the widely used iterative learning-based classifiers. It was appropriate for use in this fashion as a computer-aided tool for diagnosing OA.

Ahmed, et al. [2], review of studies presents the mid-aged and older population is disproportionately affected by knee osteoarthritis (KOA), a degenerative joint condition. Provide a thorough overview of some of the newest techniques for segmenting the knee articular bone. The assessment of the rate of articular cartilage loss, this has a clinical use practice to evaluate the morphological and illness development alteration, is made possible by segmentation techniques using deep learning (DL)-based ones instead of the traditional ones. To conclude this review, it is important to emphasize deep learning's diagnostic value for potential computer-aided diagnostic applications.

Wang Yanfei, et al. [3], it has been shown creating a prognostic algorithm to forecast how severe radiographic knee osteoarthritis will be (KOA)and the identification a list of danger signs illness progression over time for early treatment and intervention. Using the clinical data from the present visits, they precisely anticipated the KL grade of the patient's forthcoming visits 90% of the time. The primary treatment should take knee alignment into consideration, and the progression of KOA was unrelated to clinical symptoms, according the causative hypothesis.

C. Kokkotis, et al. [4], this review has been carried out to acquaint the reader with the main applications of machine learning methods for identifying and forecasting knee osteoarthritis. Based on scientific papers between the years of 2006 and 2019.Segmentation, classification, optimal post-treatment planning strategies, and predictions/regression were the four categories into which the publications were divided.

The division was made depending on each study's appropriate application domain. A summary of the findings highlights the significant outcomes of the suggested learning algorithms, the application domains, the investigated data sources, and the standard of the results.

Kokkotis, et al. [5], they followed that the steady loss of cartilage causes the inflammatory joint disease osteoarthritis the knee. Due to KOA's multifaceted personality and the lack of a thorough knowledge of its pathogenesis, Reliable methods are required to lessen medical professionals' diagnostic mistakes. To provide a powerful FS approach that can: manage the multidimensionality of the currently accessible record; as well as (ii) solve the challenges with the present element selection strategies in terms of identifying the critical risk variables that affect KOA diagnosis. The influence of the chosen characteristics on the model's output was eventually quantified through analysis, boosting our understanding of the reason for the best model's decision-making process.

Roemer, et al. [6], authors mentioned Osteoarthritis (OA) is a chronic infection that affects people's health orthe standard of living who have it and the larger community. It is quite frequent. For the detection and treatment of OA in clinical practice, radiography continues to be the primary imaging modality. We'll discuss the various developments in MRI methods that can assess the morphologic traits cartilage, as well as the strategies for figuring out its biochemical composition. The significance of artificial intelligence on the area of OA imaging will be discussed, as will various therapy theories and contemporary advancements.

Bonakdari, et al. [7], in this paper authors suggested that because the initial diagnosis of structural progresses in degenerative joint disease, automated screening technologies are necessary (OA). To determine which of the 47 factors which were assessed in relation to PVBSP were the most important, we used machine learning to classify features method. Out machine that supports vectors (SVM) exhibited the highest accuracy and efficiency among the five supervised ML approaches application for developing classifiers that account for gender. The most crucial elements in determining the structure development of OA in the-two sexes by feature selection were determined to be age Body Fat Percentage (BMI), CRP/MCP-1, and leptin/CRP, as well as combinations of these variables.

Ke Zeng, et al. [8], they have suggested that one of the most prevalent musculoskeletal illnesses is knee osteoarthritis (OA).OA is now identified by looking at plain radiographs and assessing symptoms, however this process is problematic because to the subjectivity of medical practitioners. Five mostly utilized artificial intelligence techniques, mainly the Convolutional neural network channel, were retrospectively evaluated to forecast these actual knee MRI results utilizing the Kellgren-Lawrence (K-L) grade of knee OA, from two distinct hospitals. By making the decision-making process clear to them, it fosters practitioners' faith in such automated approaches. Additionally, this decreases the workload of physicians, particularly in rural regions with a scarcity of medical professionals.

Hügle, et al. [9], authors discussed artificial intelligence, or machine learning, is increasingly used in medicine for the benefit of both patients and practitioners. Describes the principles of supervised learning, deep studying, applying what you've learned, and unsupervised learning are some of the subfields of machine learning. A review of rheumatology's existing machine learning applications is provided in this article, with a particular emphasis on managed learning strategies for sickness location, e-conclusion and picture. The patient's perspective, the rheumatologist's evidence-based experience and empirical and machine-learned evidence will all be considered moving forward while making decisions together.

Mahum, et al. [10] described numerous illnesses, especially those affecting adults, have had a powerful effect on people's lifestyles. Bone diseases, such as Knee Osteoarthritis, have the quality of life is significantly affected (KOA).The input X-ray pictures are first pre-processed, in addition the Interest Region (ROI), recovered using decomposition. Second, using pre-processed X-ray pictures comprising patella joint area width, features are employing Convolutional Neural Network's (CNN).The oriented gradient's histogram and Local Binary Patterns (LBP) are examples of hybrid feature descriptors (HOG). The findings show that for each of the four classes of KL, early identification and characterization of KOA of KL are around 97% accurate utilizing the HOG features descriptor.

XIAO, et al. [11] demonstrated to detect the knee edge from an Identify the degree of OA from an X-ray picture, create a machine learning model. The clustering approach is applied as the initial stage to perform on the dataset, unsupervised learning, and build via each individual X-ray image, clusters. A single, universal picture features are accessible. XIAO, et al. developed a CNN model in order to contrast our strategy with a deep learning technique.

Binvignat M., et al. [12] discussed in precisely and in great detail how machine learning is used to treat osteoarthritis (OA). Mesh terms and key words are found in MEDLINE and PubMed. For each selected publication, information on the patient population, machine learning algorithms employed, the types of data analyzed, data analysis techniques, and data accessibility was acquired. The study's patient population ranged from 18 to 5749. A total of 35% of the publications included deep learning applications, while 74% focused on imaging studies. In all, 85% of the papers discussed hip and 15% discussed knee OA. On hand OA, no research was conducted.

N. Bayramoglu, et al. [13] analyzed their impact on the position about the region-of-interest (ROI) when examining the subchondral bone's texture radiography of the knee, as well as 2) its capacity range of various texture descriptions to discriminate between radiography images of knee osteoarthritis (OA). They evaluated measure of our generalize ability method by educating the models using the OAI dataset and putting them to the test on the MOST dataset. They utilized region below receiver comparing the outcomes using the accuracy-recall (PR) curve and average precision (AP) from the operational characteristic curve. The adaptive ROI outperforms the mostly used standard ROI in terms of classification performance. The best LBP AUC was 0.840 [0.825, 0.852], and the corresponding AP was 0.804 [0.786, 0]. We also noted that this configuration generated the greatest performance overall.

Yun Xin Teoh, et al. [14] explained that loss of cartilage is a hallmark of the degenerative joint condition osteoarthritis (OA) of the knee, which imaging methods may identify and interpret into imaging characteristics. However, Less sensitive to transient OA changes, the imaging properties are restricted to bone changes, despite the fact to the extent that studies recognized an X-ray the most effective imaging method for identifying knee OA. Researchers advocate utilizing imaging with magnetic resonance (MRI) to look for radiomic signs of OA that are buried in soft tissues and bone structures. Continuous machine learning model improvement may aid future studies into novel OA therapies.

Abdelbasset Brahim, et al. [15] examined the creation of an operational system for computer-aided diagnosis (CAD) that uses machine learning algorithms and knee X-ray imaging to diagnose osteoarthritis (OA) in its early stages. The X-ray pictures initially pre-processed utilizing a circular Fourier filter in the Fourier domain. Then a book normalizing approach based on predictive modeling with Data are processed using multivariate linear regression (MLR) to lessen the heterogeneity between people with OA and healthy subjects. The outcomes demonstrate a high rate of prophetic categorization for OA placement in the suggested technique (82.98% for exactness, 87.15% for responsiveness and up to 80.65%t for explicitness).

An imaging biomarker known as trabecular bone surface (TBT) examination has been found to give data on alterations in trabecular cartilage welcomed on by arthritis in the knees (KOA). 683 patients from the MOST partner and 1888 individuals from the OAI companion were remembered for this review. To distinguish 16 districts of interest, radiographs were consequently fragmented. Patients with a 1–4 grade range according to Kellgren and Lawrence (KL) and a beginning phase of OA risk were picked. With a region under the bend The TBT-CNN model has (AUC) up to 0.75 in OAI and 0.81 in most had the option to foresee the JSN movement. With respect to method of securing or picture quality, the TBT-CNN model's prescient power was unaffected [16].

Early analysis of knee osteoarthritis (OA) can prompt better therapy results and lower clinical costs. The utilization of existing grouping or expectation models in clinical practice is hampered by critical limits, for example, dynamic information handling and complex dataset ascribes. The 3-level BN structure that filled in as the establishment for the proposed model's development was subsequently retrained utilizing learning via Bayesian Search (BS) calculation. The assumption expansion calculation was utilized to pick the boundaries of the model. Foundation data, the objective illness, and indicators were undeniably remembered for the dataset utilized. In light of arrangement precision, region under the bend (AUC), particularity, responsiveness, positive prescient worth (PPV), and negative predictive value (NPV), the model's exhibition was evaluated. It was likewise set facing other notable characterization models [17].

The per user will gain proficiency with the basics of manual, self-loader, and programmed knee osteoarthritis (OA) seriousness grouping from plain radiographs in this survey paper. In 2019, PubMed, Google Scholar, and RSNA radiology data sets were looked for all English-language unique examination articles on OA recognition and order utilizing X-beam pictures. The pursuit terms "knee Osteoarthritis," "seriousness," and "X-beam" were joined with the inquiry terms "AI." Only 26 of the 743 outcomes from the underlying hunt across a few distribution data sets were considered relevant to the radiographic knee OA seriousness examination [18].

To speed the development of disease-modifying medications, it is essential to recognize knee sufferers osteoarthritis Those (OA) who likely to experience rapid structural progression. They used 9280 knee magnetic resonance (MR) scans from 3268 individuals from the Osteoarthritis Initiative (OAI) database, together with clinical characteristics including body mass index, to build a deep learning algorithm to predict additional cartilage deterioration evaluated by joint space narrowing at 12 months (BMI). With a ROC AUC value of 65%, our classification algorithm correctly identified COR IW TSE pictures. The difficulty of the categorization test was demonstrated by the AUC score for ROC of 58.7% attained by radiologists with training on a task that was comparable. Additional studies performed concurrently to predict the degree of pain measured by the WOMAC pain index yielded a ROC AUC value of 72% [19].

Utilizing AI models like Karen Hernandez Abasolo's examination [20] aims to work on the recognition the full spectrum of knee osteoarthritis in view of the Kellgren-Lawrence scale using deep learning models like DenseNet201 and InceptionResNetV2 prepared with knee x-beam images. Random Forest, Gradient Boosting, and Xtreme Gradient Boosting are also used. Albeit Deep educating models had higher effectiveness as displayed in ROC bends contrasted with them, generally expectation execution for AI models was equivalent to that of those models, and the two models by and large performed better as estimated by Precision, Recall, and F1-score.

A radiologist board utilized the Kellgren-Lawrence (KL) framework to organize the Osteoarthritis Initiative's radiography. The pictures were consequently normalized and upgraded prior to being utilized as contribution to a convolutional brain network model. The model was prepared utilizing 32 116 pictures, tuned utilizing 4074 pictures, assessed utilizing a test set of 4090 pictures, and afterward contrasted with two radiologists utilizing a test subset of 50 pictures. To uncover the elements that the model used to ascertain KL grades, saliency maps were made. When council scores were used as the ground truth, it featured a typical F1 score of 0.70 and an exactness of 0.71 for the whole test set. The top one radiology specialist had a typical an F1 ranking of 0.60 and an exactness of 0.60, compared to the model's 0.64 and 0.66 for the 50 image subset [21].

This concentrate by Lucas C. Ribas presents a clever strategy for separating surface highlights related with OA from radiographic knee X-beam pictures that depends on ideas of perplexing organization hypothesis. Current various conventional surface descriptors and learning models (VGG, AlexNet, GoogleNet, InceptionV3, ResNet, DenseNet, and EfficientNet) are contrasted with our proposed approach. Results indicate that the suggested strategy is valid and could provide a guarantee in order to find knee OA early [22]. These research planned to find out: 1) the impact of the area that was designated as the region of interest (ROI) for the surface inspection on radiographs of the knee's subchondral bone, as well as 2) if different surface descriptors could be utilized to differentiate between knees with radiographic osteoarthritis and those without (OA). When it comes to order execution (OA versus non-OA), we discovered that the flexible ROI outperforms the usually applicable conventional ROI (up to 9% increment in AUC). They likewise noticed that Binary Pattern Locally (LBP), which had the best AP of 0.804 and AUC of 0.840 [23], created the greatest execution across all settings.

This capacity to unveil hidden objects designs in a volumetric view is a component of clinical processes is usually clarified by creating three layers (3D) pictures like MRI. While of late, CNN in 3D has been utilized into examine these joint issue for additional exact conclusion, recognizing that adjustments of a knee joint are a 3D intricacy. In this survey, we give an overall outline of the 2D and 3D CNN approaches right now being utilized in the field of OA research. They analyzed 74 investigations from the Web of Science data set that managed arranging and dividing knee osteoarthritis, and we examined the different cutting-edge, deep learning put forward. They underscored the potential and probability of the 3D CNN by field of knee osteoarthritis. They closed next to examining the potential hardships and headways in involving 3D CNNs in this field [24].

Despite the fact that joint inflammation can't be relieved at any stage, it tends to be made do with a right conclusion. Clinical determination and imaging methods are essential for the ongoing assessment system for osteoarthritis and rheumatoid joint inflammation. This study analyzed the different imaging techniques utilized in medication to assess joint pain. They incorporate X-beam imaging, warm imaging, ultrasound imaging, as well as pleasing reverberation imaging for the exceptionally illustrative and relative identification and characterization of osteoarthritis and rheumatoid joint pain. The different picture handling strategies, including division, highlight extraction, characterization, and AI techniques like counterfeit brain organizations and convolutional brain organizations, are consequently intricately talked about and completely overviewed [25].

This research by Shinjini Kundu et al. shows that OA identification might be conceivable at a phase where switching it might be conceivable. Since our procedure is generative, a critical commitment of our work is the immediate representation of the ligament aggregate characterizing prescient capacity. We spot the early biochemical indications of ligament fissuring that signal the approaching of OA. The future result of an illness that right now costs the American medical care framework $16.5 billion yearly could be modified by joining the location of presymptomatic OA with developing clinical treatments. Furthermore, a ton of sicknesses that are right now analyzed at cutting edge stages can be recognized before utilizing our technique utilizing pictures [26].

The standard practice in picture handling is to remove critical data from mathematically mutilated or changed pictures. At the point when the pictures are twisted mathematically, it becomes testing to recover the relevant region. Because of their extraordinary invariance property, Hu's minutes are valuable in getting data from such mutilated pictures. Using the invariant of Hu minutes to comprehend these mathematical changes of these ligament areas in patella X-beam pictures, this examination centers around the early recognition and degree of Knee Osteoarthritis. For the turned rendition of the test picture, the seven in variation minutes are processed. Muscular specialists and rheumatologists have supported the outcomes as being more serious and empowering [27].

This study looked at the biological data buried in knee MR pictures osteoarthritis risk prediction (OA). After calculating the Index of Cartilage Damage (CDI) data among 36 important places tibiofemoral cartilage compartment on these using MR 3D imaging, we employed PCA analysis to analyze the feature set. It may be thought to choose extra details from the medial pocket and fewer observations from the lateral compartment in order to enhance clinical CDI architecture because experiment results show that Compared to informative places on the lateral compartment, the medial compartment has more differentiating characteristics [28].

Creating a computerized copy to assess the degree of osteoarthritis in the knee using radiographs and to evaluate the model's performance in comparison to musculoskeletal radiologists. The model was tested within a test set of 4090 pictures after being tweaked on 4074 photos, appraised on 32 116 images during training, and compared to two radiologists on 50 images during testing. Saliency maps were made to show the factors that the model used while determining KL grades. The model's overall accuracy was 0.71 with an average F1 score of 0.70 when Committee results served as the actual data. These model's accuracy for the 50-image subset was 0.66 and its average F1 score was 0.64, whereas the best individual [21].

A device because detecting together with evaluating knee osteoarthritis (OA) in automated X-ray pictures that also demonstrates the potential of deep learning methods for predicting OA in line with the Kellgren-Lawrence (KL) grading system. Patients with post-surgical trauma, assessment, or infection were not included in the study by medical professionals. The front and posterior surfaces of the knee joint were imaged with 3172 digital X-rays. The suggested model's maximum accuracy for locating the minimum knee JSW region was 98.516%, and its accuracy for determining the overall severity of knee OA was 98.90% [29].

3 Comparative Analysis

We expect to be able to construct a prediction model that will allow for the early identification of patients whose arthritic knee structure will deteriorate rapidly using a deep learning system driven by computer intelligence techniques such as PSO/ACO. Evaluation of the suggested FLFS approach be measured against all six individually deployed FS methods. A final current illustration additionally, the published FS approach was used as a benchmark to generate the final feature ranking. Through a majority vote system [30, 31].

Table 1. Comparative analysis of FS methods

	FSFL	VoteFS	RF EmbFS	LGBMEmb FS	SVMRFEFS	LR RFEFS	FilterMI FS	Filter f-ANOVAFS
Maximum accuracy(%)	73.55	72.99	73.36	73.51	70.53	73.50	72.75	73.44
Number of selected features	21	76	43	87	96	60	91	53
DR (%)	–	+72%	+51%	+76%	+78%	+65%	+77%	+60%

Table 1 display the number of characteristics with these highest precision for each experimental feature selection strategy assessed using the top-performing model, together with the maximum precision achieved in the first 100 characteristics of the OAI dataset (RF). The suggested FS methodology is compared to other competing approaches in the last row of Table 1 in terms of dimensionality reduction.

The measure DR was designed specifically to express the percentage difference in dimensionality reduction from FSFL:

$$DR = 1 - \frac{Max\ number\ of\ features(FSFL)}{Max\ number\ of\ features(Compared\ method)} \qquad (1)$$

These best performance-dimensionality trade off was attained by the suggested FSFL method, capable of offering considerably better or equivalent prediction performance to the other competing approaches while drastically decreasing feature set dimensionality. In particular, these suggested FSFL method obtains the selected 21 items had the highest accuracy (73.55%) characteristics, although LBGM Emb gets the next-best precision (73.51%) as to 87 attributes. Which demonstrates that the suggested FSFL strategy delivers 76% little collection of chosen characteristics than the approach that performs second-best. In terms of dimensionality reduction, RF Emb was the second-best performer, 73.36% accuracy gained on a substantially in comparison to FSFL, a bigger feature subset with 43 features more than doubles the number 21.

3.1 Region of Interest (ROI) and Segmentation

In this context this review has been carried out that the proposed algorithm presents Hybrid DWT-DCT Digital image fusion algorithm. They proposed method exploits strength of two combined transform domain techniques DCT & DWT to obtain better image quality of fused image. Then they concluded that Hybrid DCT-DWT gives better result as compared to DCT, PCA and HDWT Technique [32].

The algorithm's primary strength is its capacity to recognize the knee joint's early KOA illness space width. With ageing, the gap between the knee joints expands and this condition advances. The tibiofemoral joint is the area of interest (ROI). Through the use of a database of knee pictures, the ROI is determined. The database image is applied pixel by pixel to the input image, and the similarity between the blocks of the histogram of the image is used to compute the image characteristics of the gradients. The block selected for similarity is the one with the greatest ROI. This similarity-based approach outperforms conventional methods. Assume that a single input picture The system is given an I of size that includes J, D, and I depicts a database illustration of measure $d_r \times d_c$, where v d is this HOG measure vector $1 \times h$ the picture from the database D. and $s_{m,n}$ is the building block of $d_r \times d_c$. It is found in picture I at (m,n). The HOG function of $s_{m,n}$ is shown as $V_{m,n}^s$. The Using mean absolute difference (MAD), calculate the resemblance between picture block and database row D. $s_{m,n}$.

$$U_{m,v} = \frac{1}{h} \sum_{I=1}^{h} \left[V_{m,n}^s(I) - V^d \right] \qquad (2)$$

3.2 Deep Learning

Nonlinear transformations are carried out hierarchically using deep learning. Learning may be applied to CNN because of its deep architecture and feed-forward design. The characteristics and large variance are shown every layer of CNN [34]. These deep convolutional network operates in forward direction while testing, allowing for the differentiation of all layers. Deep CNN's primary feature is its ability to find every potential match between pictures. While pooling layers collapse manifolds, convolutional layers linearize them. Layer size at the output is influenced by stride. The image will be sharpened by the filter. K size of the kernel and S is source size, and stride is 1.

$$F = FLoFL - 1o.........F1 \qquad (3)$$

where F L is the layer, as shown in the equation below, that computes the output L based on the L for each individual layer by using o output from input from the layer before it, symbolised by L −1:

$$xL = FL(xL - 1; \omega L) for L = 2, 3, ...L \qquad (4)$$

3.3 As a Feature Descriptor, Convolutional Neural Network

Following it is the max-pooling layer has a size of 2 2 and a stride of 1. A convolutional layer with is added as the next layer a filter measure of 32 or a stride measure of 1. These convolutional and max-pooling layers are alternately positioned on each of the initial six layers. The 7th layer, contains a Rectified Linear Unit (ReLU), the activation, these eighth layer, that convolutional layer, has a 40-micron filter size (4 4 32). These uppermost layers are a layers of softmax function. The convolutional layer load and operator values in the max-pooling layer must be stable for effective computations. s. The picture size in our datasets is 50 50 1, which transforms to 1 1 2 using the assistance of all levels' forwarding propagation [35].

$$(1 * f)x, y = \sum_{s=1}^{1} \sum_{t=1}^{w} f_{st} \times I_{x+s-1,+1-1} + b \qquad (5)$$

3.4 Oriented Gradient Histogram

The photographs are organised into continuous blocks that range in size from 28 by 28 to 6 by 6 with a stride of size 4 between each block. Nine containers are created altogether. 1296 low-level characteristics in total are calculated. As pulmonary pictures exhibit improved intensity and shadow normalisation, normalisation may be carried out for enhanced feature extraction. The blocks of a larger picture size take intensity into account. Given that they are categorised in the same bin, the opposing directions of the picture component are calculated with a comparable orientation. The angle's range is still 0 to 180°. The following equation gives the M-scale magnitude gradient considering its intended use for the pixel (x, y):

$$M(x, y) = \sqrt[2]{I_x^2 + I_y^2} \tag{6}$$

$$\vartheta = \frac{I_y}{I_x} \tag{7}$$

where the gradients in this equation are Iy and Ix directions the x and y, and where the angle changes from 0 to 2.

3.5 Pattern of Local Binary

The extraction of texture features makes use of an LBP description. Based on the idea that each pixel evaluates itself in relation to its neighbours, it encrypts the nearby pixels making use of the threshold function [36]. The worth of the centre pixel is set to 1 if neighbours' values that are grey are more than or equal to centre pixel. Since there are more double feature vectors produced by LBP as the size of the nearby pixels rises, let k indicate the total number of neighbouring pixels. For example, 2 16 = 65,536 feature vectors are produced. The LBP equation is shown below.

$$LBP = \sum_{i=0}^{1} k(p_i - c_i) \times 2^i \tag{8}$$

$$k(x) = \begin{cases} 1 \\ 0 \end{cases} if \; x \geq 0, otherwise \tag{9}$$

4   Experimental Evaluation

4.1 Dataset

The Mendeley dataset IV [33], known as the Knee Osteoarthritis Severity Grading dataset, it is. The investigation was carried out on a 4-core, 4.2 GHz Core-i7-7700K system with 32 GB RAM (Santa Clara, USA, CA-based Intel Corporation) or an Titan V by NVIDIA with 12 GB RAM (USA, San Jose, Nvidia Corporation) (USA, Santa Clara, Nvidia Corporation, CA). The data was gathered from several hospitals. The PRO-TECT PRS 500EX-ray machine was used to acquire X-ray images. All of the pictures were in grayscale and were hand labelled using KL's evaluation approach. 500 photos altogether were utilised to train the classifier, with 100 photos indicating wholesome knees free of KOA. KL claims that 100 photographs were used for instruction for each grade. A five-fold validation was used, such as (25, 75), (40, 60), (50, 50), (30, 70), (20, 80); Each Grade's training and testing data is represented in a separate set, and the final set is for the healthy class. The technique achieves 98% accuracy the combined feature vector of CNN, HOG, and SVM with CNN feature vector, and five-fold validation using the KNN method achieves 97.6% accuracy. Figure 1 shows examples of images from several classes.

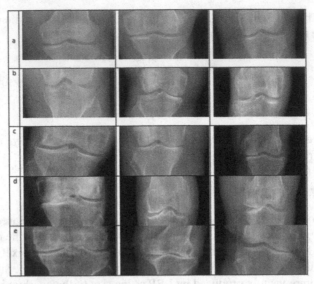

Fig. 1. Various photos row taken from the dataset typical photos; inconclusive images; mild, moderate, and strong pictures Brutal pictures [37].

4.2 State of Art Comparisons

Tables 2, 3 and 4 show the overall the speed of this hybrid's execution recommended an all-classifier system, including RF, SVM, and KNN. 4.2 s are needed to finish the SVM classifier using LBP, compared to 3.84 s for the SVM CNN. However, SVM CNN's lowest time, which is 2.3 s, is likewise longer than KNN- LBP's.

Table 2. SVM classifier execution time using LBP, CNN, and HOG

Classifier name	Time in second
Local binary pattern SVM	4.2 s
SVM using oriented gradient histogram	4.3 s
SVM combined with a convolutional neural network	3.84 s
SVM + HOG + CNN	4.8 s
SVM with CNN + LBP	3.98 s
SVM combined with HOG + CNN + LBP	10.5 s

Table 3. Time to execution by RF classifier using LBP, CNN, and HOG

Classifier name	Time in second
RF with oriented gradient histogram	3.5 s
Convolutional neural network RF	4.2 s
RF with HOG + CNN	7.8 s
CNN + RF + LBP	2.8 s
HOG with RF + CNN + LBP	3.9 s
Local binary pattern RF	2.23 s

Table 4. KNN classifier execution time using LBP, CNN, and HOG

Classifier name	Time in second
KNN with oriented gradient histogram	3.3 s
KNN combined with a convolutional neural network	4.2 s
KNN + HOG + CNN	7.3 s
KNN + CNN + LBP	2.4 s
KNN combined with HOG + CNN + LBP	3.8 s
Local binary pattern KNN	2.3 s

CNN gathered in-depth characteristics including scale, translate, or rotation, whilst Low-level features were retrieved via HOG and LBP. These goal of combining these hybrid qualities is to give form features. The CNN + HOG and CNN + LBP hybridized features are used, which are then categorized use the RF, SVM, and KNN algorithms. These following equal represents the interaction between local binary pattern and the convolutional neural network:

$$NN_{LBP} = \sum_{s=1}^{l} \sum_{t=1}^{w} fst.I_{x+s-1,y+t-1} + LBP_{p,r} \qquad (9)$$

$$LBP_{p,r} = \frac{(I \times fst)_{x,y} - (I \times fst)_{x,y}}{fst_{xc-x+1,yc-y+1}} \qquad (10)$$

$$LBP_{p,r} = \sum_{i=0}^{1} k(p_i - c_i) \cdot 2^i = I(xc, yc) \& k(x) = \begin{cases} 1, & \text{if } x \geq 0 \\ 0, & \text{otherwise} \end{cases}. \qquad (11)$$

The following is the formula for the histogram and the convolutional neural network together directional gradients:

$$\left(I_{M,\vartheta} \times K\right)_{x,y} = \sum_{s=1}^{l} \sum_{t=1}^{w} fst.I_{x+s-1,y+t-1} \cdot e^{s\vartheta\,(x+s-1,y+t-1)} \tag{12}$$

Analysis of Various Method Combinations: Twenty convolutional layers were used throughout the training phase. The pooling layer's kernel has a 2 size. Three times, convolutional and layering up were employed in alternate fashion. The ReLU layer served as the activation layer. As for the Softmax feature, utilized at the last layer to retrieve these knee's characteristics. Within 1870 iterations, an average accuracy of 93% was reached. The suggested system uses KNN, SVM and RF classification algorithms for five classes, including unhealthy and healthy, and Grade I, II, III, and IV classes. First, the dataset was used to train an SVM classifier for the true negative and true positive classes.

5 Conclusion

Patients with osteoarthritis are now treated mainly for symptoms, and traditional osteoarthritis diagnosis is ineffective at identifying patients who will progress rapidly. A thorough early-stage prediction model for osteoarthritis patients is required, dividing them up based on the likelihood that a joint disease will progress. By implementing a deep learning system powered by AI methods like PSO/ACO, we anticipate that we will be able to construct a prediction model that will allow for the early identification of patients whose arthritic knee structure will rapidly deteriorate. The first phase will be to investigate various parameters for identifying KNEE OSREOARCHRITIS X- RAY picture progression and doing a comparative analysis on several datasets. Once the dataset is fixed, we will apply known machine learning algorithms for picture segmentation and classification to a variety of datasets. Then, we will develop a novel framework for predicting knee OA using deep learning and computer intelligent techniques. Finally, we will do comparative analytics to compare the proposed approach to the present technique in terms of efficiency, accuracy, and precision. Dataset availability can be an issue which can be resolved via contacting various hospitals. Progressive detection of OA for different people might have different effects on performance of the model in real-time conditions.

Acknowledgment. We would like to show our gratitude to Dr. Sarika Khandelwal (Associate Professor, GHRCE) to share her pearls of wisdom with us during the course of our research. Also, all the information is collected from the internet.

References

1. Bhat, A.Y., Suhasini, A.: Normal and abnormal detection for knee osteoarthritis using machine learning techniques. Int. J. Recent Technol. Eng. (IJRTE) 8(2), (2019). ISSN: 2277–3878, Retrieval Number: B3733078219/19©BEIESP. https://doi.org/10.35940/ijrte.B3733.078219 (2019)

2. Ahmed, S.M., Mstafa, R.J.: A comprehensive survey on bone segmentation techniques in knee osteoarthritis research: from conventional methods to deep learning. Diagnostics **12**, 611 (2022). https://doi.org/10.3390/diagnostics12030611

3. Yanfei, W., et al.: Causal discovery in radiographic markers of knee osteoarthritis and prediction for knee osteoarthritis severity with attention–long short-Term Memory. J. Front. Public Health, **8**, (2020). https://www.frontiersin.org/article/10.3389/fpubh.2020.604654, https://doi.org/10.3389/fpubh.2020.604654, ISSN=2296–2565 (2020)

4. Kokkotis, C., Moustakidis, S., Papageorgiou, E., Giakas, G., Tsaopoulos, D.E.: Machine learning in knee osteoarthritis: a review, Osteoarthritis and Cartilage Open, **2**(3), 100069 (2020). ISSN 2665 9131, https://doi.org/10.1016/j.ocarto.2020.100069. (https://www.sciencedirect.com/science/article/pii/S2665913120300583) (2020)

5. Kokkotis, C., Ntakolia, C., Moustakidis, S., et al.: Explainable machine learning for knee osteoarthritis diagnosis based on a novel fuzzy feature selection methodology. Phys. Eng. Sci. Med. **45**, 219–229 (2022). https://doi.org/10.1007/s13246-022-01106-6

6. Roemer, F., et al.: State of the art: imaging of osteoarthritis—revisited. Radiology **296**(192498), (2020). https://doi.org/10.1148/radiol.2020192498

7. Hossein, B., et al.: A warning machine learning algorithm for early knee osteoarthritis structural progressor patient screening. Therapeutic Advances in Musculoskeletal Disease, Jan. 2021 (2021). https://doi.org/10.1177/1759720X21993254

8. Zeng, K., et al.: Multicentre study using machine learning methods in clinical diagnosis of knee osteoarthritis. J. Healthcare Eng. **2021**, 1765404, 12 (2021). https://doi.org/10.1155/2021/1765404

9. Hügle, M., Omoumi, P., Laar, J., Boedecker, J., Hügle, T.: Applied machine learning and artificial intelligence in rheumatology. Rheumatol. Adv. Pract. **4**, (2020). https://doi.org/10.1093/rap/rkaa005

10. Mahum, R., et al.: A novel hybrid approach based on deep CNN features to detect knee osteoarthritis. Sensors **21**, 6189 (2021). https://doi.org/10.3390/s21186189 (2020)

11. Xiao, Y.: Using machine learning tools to predict the severity of osteoarthritis based on knee XRay data (2020). Master's Theses (2009 -). 582. https://epublications.marquette.edu/theses_open/582

12. Binvignat, M., Pedoia, V., Butte, A.J., et al.: Use of machine learning in osteoarthritis research: a systematic literature review. RMD Open 2022; 8:e001998. https://doi.org/10.1136/rmdopen-2021-001998 (2022)

13. Bayramoglu, N., Tiulpin, A., Hirvasniemi, J., Nieminen, M.T., Saarakkala, S.: Adaptive segmentation of knee radiographs for selecting the optimal ROI in texture analysis, Osteoarthritis Cartilage **28**(7), 941–952 (2020). ISSN10634584, https://doi.org/10.1016/j.joca.2020.03.006. (https://www.sciencedirect.com/science/article/pii/S1063458420309481) (2020)

14. Teoh, Y.X., et al.: Discovering knee osteoarthritis imaging features for diagnosis and prognosis: review of manual imaging grading and machine learning approaches. J. Healthcare Eng. **2022**, 4138666, 19 (2022). https://doi.org/10.1155/2022/4138666

15. Brahim, A., et al.: A decision support tool for early detection of knee OsteoArthritis using X-ray imaging and machine learning: data from the OsteoArthritis Initiative, Computerized Medical Imaging and Graphics, Vol. 73, (2019), pp. 11–18, ISSN 0895–6111, https://doi.org/10.1016/j.compmedimag.2019.01.07

16. Almhdie-Imjabbar, A., Nguyen, K.L., Toumi, H., et al.: Prediction of knee osteoarthritis progression using radiological descriptors obtained from bone texture analysis and Siamese neural networks: data from OAI and MOST cohorts. Arthritis Res Ther **24**, 66 (2022). https://doi.org/10.1186/s13075-022-02743-8

17. Sheng, B., et al.: Identification of knee osteoarthritis based on Bayesian network: a pilot study (Preprint). https://doi.org/10.2196/preprints.13562 (2019)

18. Saini, D., Chand, T., Chouhan, D.K., Prakash, M.: A comparative analysis of automatic classification and grading methods for knee osteoarthritis focussing on X-ray images, Biocybernetics and Biomedical Engineering, Vol. 41, Iss. 2, 2021, pp. 419–444, ISSN 0208–5216, https://doi.org/10.1016/j.bbe.2021.03.02

19. Schiratti, J.B., Dubois, R., Herent, P., et al.: A deep learning method for predicting knee osteoarthritis radiographic progression from MRI. Arthritis. Res. Ther. **23**(262), 2021 (2021). https://doi.org/10.1186/s13075-021-02634-4

20. Hernandez Abasolo, K.: Detection of knee osteoarthritis severity using a fusion of machine and deep learning models. Diss. Dublin, National College of Ireland (2021)

21. Thomas, K., et al.: Automated classification of radiographic knee osteoarthritis severity using deep neural networks. Radiol.: Artif. Intelligence. 2. e190065. https://doi.org/10.1148/ryai.2020190065 (2020)

22. Ribas, L.C., Riad, R., Jennane, R., Bruno, O.M.: A complex network based approach for knee Osteoarthritis detection: data from the osteoarthritis initiative, biomedical signal processing and control, Vol. 71, Part A, 2022, 103133, ISSN17468094, https://doi.org/10.1016/j.bspc.2021.103133. (https://www.sciencedirect.com/science/article/pii/S1746809421007308) (2022)

23. Bayramoglu, N., Tiulpin, A., Hirvasniemi, J., Nieminen, M.T., Saarakkala, S.: Adaptive segmentation of knee radiographs for selecting the optimal ROI in texture analysis, Osteoarthritis and Cartilage, Vol. 28, Iss. 7, pp. 941–952 (2020), ISSN 1063–4584, https://doi.org/10.1016/j.joca.2020.03.06

24. Yeoh, P.S.Q., et al.: Emergence of deep learning in knee osteoarthritis diagnosis. Comput. Intell. Neurosci. 2021, 4931437, 20 (2021). https://doi.org/10.1155/2021/4931437

25. Revathy, B., et al.: A review on investigation and catagorization of rheumatoid arthritis and osteoarthritis using image processing techniques. Annals of the Romanian Society for Cell Biology 25.4 (2021) 2275–2290 (2021)

26. Kundu, S., et al.: Enabling early detection of osteoarthritis from presymptomatic cartilage texture maps via transport-based learning. Proc. Natl. Acad. Sci. U.S.A. **117**, 2020 (2020). https://doi.org/10.1073/pnas.1917405117

27. Gornale, S.S.: Automatic detection and classification of knee osteoarthritis using Hu's invariant moments. Front. Robot. AI **7**, 591827 (2020). https://doi.org/10.3389/frobt.2020.591827

28. Du, Y., Almajalid, R., Shan, J., Zhang, M.: A novel method to predict knee osteoarthritis progression on MRI using machine learning methods. IEEE Transactions on NanoBioscience p. 1 (2019). https://doi.org/10.1109/TNB.2018.2840082

29. Abdullah, S.S., Rajasekaran, M.P.: Automatic detection and classification of knee osteoarthritis using deep learning approach. Radiol. Med. (Torino) **127**(4), 398–406 (2022). https://doi.org/10.1007/s11547-022-01476-7

30. Ntakolia, C., Kokkotis, C., Moustakidis, S., Tsaopoulos, D.: Prediction of joint space narrowing progression in knee osteoarthritis patients. Diagnostics **11**, 285 (2021). https://doi.org/10.3390/diagnostics11020285

31. Kokkotis, C., Moustakidis, S., Giakas, G., Tsaopoulos, D.: Identifcation of risk factors and machine learning-based predictionmodels for knee osteoarthritis patients. Appl. Sci. **10**, 6797 (2020). https://doi.org/10.3390/app10196797

32. Sharma, M., Khandelwal, S.: Image fusion on coloured and gray scale multi focus images by using hybrid DWT-DCT. Int. J. Comput. Appl. (0975 – 8887) 152, 9 (2016)

33. Gornale, S.S., Patravali, P.U., Hiremath, P.S.: Automatic detection and classification of knee osteoarthritis using Hu's invariant moments. Front. Robot. AI 2020, 7, 591827 (2020)

34. Sainath, T.N., Mohamed, A.R., Kingsbury, B., Ramabhadran, B.: Deep convolutional neural networks for LVCSR. In: Proceedings of the 2013 IEEE International Conference on Acoustics, Speech and Signal Processing, Vancouver, BC, Canada, 26–31 May 2013, pp. 8614–8618 (2013)
35. Song, Q., Zhao, L., Luo, X., Dou, X.: Using deep learning for classification of lung nodules on computed tomography images. J. Healthc. Eng. 2017, 9314740 (2017)
36. Mary, N.A.B., Dharma, D.: Coral reef image classification employing improved LDP for feature extraction. J. Vis. Commun. Image Represent. **2017**(49), 225–242 (2017)
37. Shivanand Gornale, P.P.: Digital Knee X-ray Images. https://doi.org/10.17632/t9ndx37v5h.1#folder-18a3659a-1fa2-4340-b7bb-526fb81006f6, 23 June 2020

Effective Real Time Disaster Management Using Optimized Scheduling

Girish Talmale$^{(\boxtimes)}$ (iD) and Urmila Shrawankar (iD)

G H Raisoni College of Engineering, Nagpur, MH, India
girishtalmale@gmail.com, urmila@ieee.org

Abstract. In recent years we face many types of natural and man-created disasters such as tsunamis, earthquakes, hurricanes, Covid-19 pandemic, terrorist attacks, floods, etc. which cause diverse and worse effects on our daily lives and economy. In order to mitigate the impact of such disasters and reduce the causality, economic loss during disaster response cycle, the different disaster management resources such as rescue teams, transportation, healthcare and related services must be schedule and allocated efficiently. In this research, we proposed the Cluster-Based Real–Time Disaster Resource Management Framework which used edge and computing-based real-time scheduling of various resources and emergency services in disaster management. The edge computing resources are grouped into the cluster and a set of tasks is assigned to the cluster and scheduled on the edge computing cluster to increase resource utilization and acceptance rate which is the problem of existing partitioned scheduling and reduces response time, and overhead due to communication and migration which is the issue in exiting scheduling.

Keywords: Real-time scheduling · Disaster management · Emergency response system · Cluster scheduling · Edge computing

1 Introduction

1.1 Real Time Scheduling for Disaster Management

Real-time resources allocation and scheduling in disaster management is important to save life of people and economic loss during the disaster response and recovery cycle. The different emergency management tasks are computed and time sensitive such as real time alert, vision processing, scheduling of rescue units, transportation, healthcare, and other related services. The real time scheduling of theses disaster management tasks is a complex problem. The existing scheduling techniques require improvement in terms of resource sharing and acceptance rate and reduction in migration, preemption overhead and response time. So to solve this problem this paper propose the cluster based resource scheduling on edge computing platform for emergency crisis management.

N. Khare et al. (Eds.): MIND 2022, CCIS 1762, pp. 114–123, 2022.
https://doi.org/10.1007/978-3-031-24352-3_9

2   Background Work

The different resource scheduling for edge computing platform is developed in past. The Steiner tree based resource scheduling using resource caching scheme is presented [1]. Dynamic resource scheduling for fog computing is presented [2] which enhance the resource utilization by dynamically assigned the resources. The edge computing with network centric approach is used to integrate machine to machine standard system [3, 4]. The various challenges, issues and activities involve in disaster management is presented as preparedness, response, recovery and prediction phase as shown in Fig. 1 [5]. The response and recovery phase requirement is that the response must be real time so that the quick action must be take place in order to reduce loss of lives and damage of resources [6]. The prediction phase is responsible to predict the occurrence of disaster for efficient preparedness [7, 8]. The research on the preparedness and response phase depend on the real time supply of rescue service and response facility, design of supply and distribution network, real time transportation service, allocation of resources and evacuation [9, 10]. The quick responder router is design for real time communication in disaster recovery phase [11]. The various optimization model presented for scheduling resources' in disaster management [12, 13].

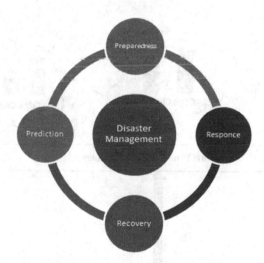

Fig. 1. Disaster management phases

3   Methodology

The architecture for resource scheduling on edge computing platform for emergency crisis management is as shown in Fig. 1. In disaster situation edge computingresources assigned to user request [14]. The system model for real time scheduling for emergency crisis management consist of set of tasks which are hard real time require to complete its execution before deadline otherwise something dangerous can be happened [15, 16]. The set of tasks represented by set t = {t1,t2,t3--------------tn}.

Each hard real time tasks is represented by attributes ti(ei,di,pi) where

ei = Execution Period of Tasks

di = Deadline of Task

pi = Period of Task

Some tasks in crises management are soft in nature means timely execution of these tasks will not result in hazards but it reduce the system performance [17, 18].

The computing resources in crisis management tasks are managed by edge computing nodes. The edge computing nodes are more close to physical sensing so real time response can be possible. The set of server are defined as

S = {S1, S2, S3,-----------------Sj}.

The edge computing servers are group into clusters S/c where each cluster consists of c number of servers. In case of high computational work load to increase resource utilization the size of cluster is tune to c = j. The size of cluster tune to c = 1 for low work load to reduce migration and preemption overhead. It also reduces the response time in emergency crisis management [19, 20]. The edge computing framework is used to allocate and scheduling services such as transportation, healthcare and rescue services as shown in Fig. 2.

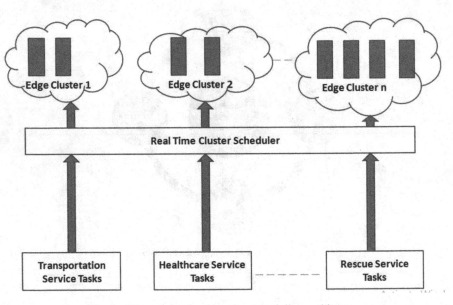

Fig. 2. Edge computing resource scheduling architecture

Table 1. Performance comparison of algorithms

Performance metrics	Proposed scheduling	Global and partitioned scheduling
Resource utilization	High	Low
Acceptance rate	High	Low
Migration cost	Low	High
Preemption cost	Low	High
Response time	Low	High

4 Implementation

4.1 Case Study of Flash Flood Crisis Management

Flash flood is the occurrence of frequent floods. The flash floods crisis management involves various real-time tasks related to with supply chain of food and essential services, healthcare tasks, transportation, and other rescue tasks [21]. The response time plays important tasks in crisis management [22]. The cluster-based resource scheduling for the edge computing platform is shown in Fig. 3 [23]. The user applications tasks are assigned to the edge computing data center and a resource monitor is used to monitor the status of resource utilization. Cluster-based resource scheduling algorithm organizes the application request and assigned it to a cluster edge computing server [24, 24].

The real time allocation and scheduling of rescue teams in the disaster affected area is handled using proposed cluster oriented scheduling framework [26].

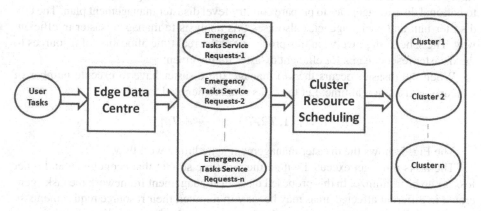

Fig. 3. Cluster resource scheduling for edge data centre

4.2 Disaster Management System Model

Figure 4 shows the disaster management system model which consist of different edge devices maps to the place of disaster and networked with edge computing cluster. The edge computing cluster consists of set of edge computing server responsible to schedule and perform real time computation. The edge devices responsible to alert rescue unit, take real time actions in case of emergency situation. The edge computing servers are group into set of clusters. The computation tasks assigned to group of edge computer server called as cluster which reduce response time, increase success ration, resource utilization and reduce the overhead cause due to migration of tasks from one computation server to another.

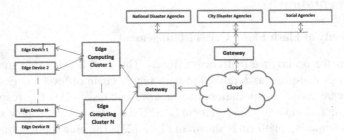

Fig. 4. Disaster management scheduling framework

The disaster information is stored on cloud for further analytics of disaster data for future prediction and performance analysis. The disaster management data is available to national disaster agencies to prepare country level disaster management plan. The city disaster unit and social agencies also uses this analysis to manage disaster in efficient way. The scheduling involve in this processes is the real time allocation of resources to the disaster rescue teams for efficient disaster management.

When the disaster occurs then to manage the disaster have to execute number of concurrent tasks in real time. Let the tasks sets are denoted as

$$T = \{T1, T2, T3 ----- Tn\}$$

The Fig. 5 shows the disaster management scheduling workflow.

The tasks must get executed within the deadline so that that economical and other losses can be minimize. In this proposed disaster management framework the tasks generated in different affected areas may be vary in number, their resource requirements so depending upon the computation requirement of the tasks the computing cluster formation done. The cluster formation depend upon the tasks computational requirements, the area of disaster affect area and the tasks resource requirements.

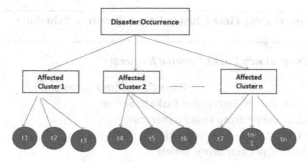

Fig. 5. Disaster management scheduling workflow

4.3   Cluster Based Scheduling Algorithm

The real time cluster based resource scheduling algorithm consists of three stages. First stage edge computing resources are group into cluster as mention in Algorithm 1, the second stage assigned emergency tasks service requests to the edge computing cluster and third stage schedules these emergency requests to edge computing server. The set of computing tasks are first allocate to the edge computing server using tasks allocation techniques and the sequence of execution of tasks is decided based on the priority of tasks. High priority tasks scheduled in real time to provide the an immediate response. The scheduling and allocation require effective data gathering and analysis for scheduling the resources on time. The edge computing servers are group into various clusters from C1 to the ratio of size of edge computing server to the cluster computing constant c.

The tasks utilization is computed as the ratio of tasks utilization verses the maximum time by which the tasks should complete the execution that is also called as the period of the tasks. The tasks assigned to edge computing cluster based on the tasks utilization. The sequence of execution of tasks is decided based on the emergency of the tasks which is decided based on the priority assign to the tasks. Higher priority tasks get executed first than the low priority tasks.

Algorithm 1: Real Time Cluster Based Resource Scheduler

Input: *Emergency Tasks Service Requests*

Edge Computing Servers

Output: Schedule of Emergency Tasks to Server

1. *Initialise tasks using tasks genetator*
2. $t = \{t1, t2, t3 - - - - - - - tn\}$
3. *Intialize Edge Computing Server*
4. $S = \{S1, S2, S3 - - - - - Sj\}$

//*Create Edge Computing cluster*

5. $C = \{C1, C2, C3 - - - - -C\left(\frac{j}{c}\right)$

   //*Where $Ci = \{S1, S2 - - - -S(c)\}$ for $i = 1$ to j/c*

6. *for all tasks $i = 1$ to n do*
7.   *Calculate $ui = \frac{ei}{pi}$*
8. $U = \sum_{i=1}^{n} ui$

9.   *for each $C = 1$ to j*

10. *while task utilization less than c*
11.   *Assigned tasks to cluster server*

                    end while

12. *Schedule Tasks with higher priority*
       to Cluster Server
13. *end for*
14. *end*

---

5 Result and Discussion

The extensive simulation was performed with a different workload. In an emergency crisis situation, the different emergency tasks related to transportation, healthcare, and rescue management are generated and must be scheduled in such a way that they should complete their execution within the deadline. The proposed real-time cluster-based resource scheduler creates the edge computing cluster and assigned these tasks to the cluster server as per its priority. The Table 1 gives the performance analysis of the proposed algorithm with benchmarking. Resource utilization and the tasks acceptance rate are high and migration cost, preemption cost, and response time is low in proposed real-time cluster scheduling as compared to a traditional scheduling algorithm. The cluster-based approach gives the real-time supply and delivery of resources in efficient disaster management. The resource utilization increases with the proposed optimized scheduling techniques by grouping the computing resource into clusters. The response time in an emergency disaster situation is reduced with the proposed optimized schedul-ing framework which ensures the real-time response by scheduling the tasks based on the dynamic priority. The percentage of tasks handled by this scheduler increases by using dynamic load balancing techniques. The communication and migration overhead is reduced with this efficient scheduling technique.

Figure 6 shows the comparative analysis of proposing the scheduler with the traditional scheduling approach. The proposed real-time cluster-based resource scheduling group the edge computing resources into clusters to increase resource utilization and reduce migration and preemption overhead and response time.

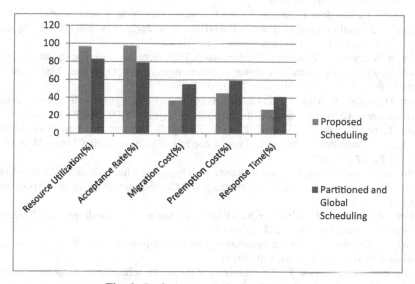

Fig. 6. Performance analysis of algorithm

6 Conclusions

Resource allocation and scheduling in disaster management is a complex and important problem and need to be addressed in order to reduce the loss of human lives and the economy. The traditional resource scheduling methods are not sufficient in terms of resource utilization and acceptance rate and incur high migration and preemption overheads. The proposed resource allocation and scheduling framework for disaster management groups the edge computing recourse into clusters which helps to improve the resource utilization and acceptance rate by 17% and 24% respectively. Migration cost, preemption cost, and response time are by 48%, 31%, and 51% respectively compared to existing scheduling frameworks.

References

1. Su, J., Lin, F., Zhou, X., Lu, X.: Steiner tree based optimal resource caching scheme in fog computing. China Commun. **12**(8), 7224698, 161–168 (2015)

2. Aazamand, M., Huh, E.-N.: Dynamic resource provisioning through Fog micro datacenter. In: Proceedings of the 2015 IEEE International Conference on Pervasive Computing and Communication Workshops (PerCom Workshops), St. Louis, MO, March, pp. 105–110 (2015)
3. Datta, S.K., Bonnet, C., Haerri, J.: Fog Computing architecture to enable consumer centric Internet of Things services. In: Proceedings of the IEEE International Symposium on Consumer Electronics, ISCE 2015, Spain, June (2015)
4. Syed, A., Fohler, G.: Efficient offline scheduling of task-sets with complex constraints on large distributed time-triggered systems. Real-Time Syst. **55**(2), 209–247 (2018). https://doi.org/10.1007/s11241-018-9320-0
5. Hebbache, F., Brandner, F., Jan, M., Pautet, L.: Work-conserving dynamic time-division multiplexing for multi-criticality systems. Real-Time Syst. **56**(2), 124–170 (2019). https://doi.org/10.1007/s11241-019-09336-w
6. Wex, F., Schryen, G., Feuerriegel, S., Neumann, D.: Emergency response in natural disaster management: allocation and scheduling of rescue units. Eur. J. Oper. Res. **235**(3), 697–708 (2014). https://doi.org/10.1016/j.ejor.2013.10.029
7. Shiri, D., Akbari, V., Salman, F.S.: Online routing and scheduling of search-and-rescue teams. OR Spectrum **42**(3), 755–784 (2020). https://doi.org/10.1007/s00291-020-00594-w
8. Tang, J., Zhu, K., Guo, H., Gong, C., Liao, C., Zhang, S.: Using auction-based task allocation scheme for simulation optimization of search and rescue in disaster relief. Simul. Model Pract. Theory **82**, 132–146 (2018)
9. Talmale, G., Shrawankar, U.: Cluster formation techniques for hierarchical real time tasks allocation on multiprocessor system. Concurrency and Computation: Practice and Experience 33 (2021)
10. Ajam, M., Akbari, V., Salman, F.S.: Minimizing latency in post-disaster road clearance operations. Eur. J. Oper. Res. **277**, 1098–1112 (2019)
11. Shiri, D., Salman, F.S.: Online optimization of first-responder routes in disaster response logistics. IBM J. Res. Dev. **64**, 1–9 (2019)
12. Bodaghi, B., Ekambaram, P.: An optimization model for scheduling emergency operations with multiple teams. In: International conference on industrial engineering and operations management at: Detroit. Michigan, USA, pp. 436–442 (2016)
13. Ferrer, J.M., Martín-Campo, F.J., Ortuno, M.T., Pedraza-Martinez, A.J., Tirado, G., Vitoriano, B.: Multicriteria optimization for last mile distribution of disaster relief aid: test cases and applications. Eur. J. Oper. Res. **269**, 501–515 (2018)
14. Ganz, A., Schafer, J.M., Tang, J., Yang, Z., Yi, J., Ciottone, G.: Urban search and rescue situational awareness using diorama disaster management system. Procedia Eng. **107**, 349–356 (2015). Humanitarian technology: science, systems and global impact 2015, HumTech (2015)
15. Hoyos, M.C., Morales, R.S., Akhavan-Tabatabaei, R.: OR models with stochastic components in disaster operations management: a literature survey. Comput. Ind. Eng. **82**, 183–197 (2015)
16. Lu, C.-C., Ying, K.-C., Chen, H.-J.: Real-time relief distribution in the aftermath of disasters—a rolling horizon approach. Transp. Res. Part E Logist. Transp. Rev. **93**, 1–20 (2016)
17. Talmale, G., Shrawankar, U.: Cluster formation techniques for hierarchical real time tasks allocation on multiprocessor system in concurrency and computation: practice and experience (2021). https://doi.org/10.1002/cpe.6438
18. Poteyeva, M., Denver, M., Barsky, L.E., Aguirre, B.E.: Search and rescue activities in disasters. In: Rodríguez, H., Quarantelli, E.L., Dynes, R.R. (eds.) Handbook of Disaster Research, pp. 200–216. Springer, New York (2007)
19. Rauchecker, G., Schryen, G.: An exact branch-and-price algorithm for scheduling rescue units during disaster response. Eur. J. Oper. Res. **272**, 352–363 (2019)
20. Schryen, G., Rauchecker, G., Comes, T.: Resource planning in disaster response: decision support models and methodologies. Bus. Inf. Syst. Eng. **57**, 243–259 (2015)

21. Talmale, G., Shrawankar, U.: Real time on bed medical services: a technological gift to the society. Biosci. Biotechnol. Res. Commun. J. 13 (2020). https://doi.org/10.21786/bbrc/13.14/32
22. Patil, P., Kumar, K.S., Gaud, N., Semwal, V.B.: Clinical human gait classification: extreme learning machine approach. In: 2019 1st International Conference on Advances in Science, Engineering and Robotics Technology (ICASERT), pp. 1–6 (2019). https://doi.org/10.1109/ICASERT.2019.8934463
23. Jain, R., et al.: Deep ensemble learning approach for lower extremity activities recognition using wearable sensors. Expert Systems **39** (2022)
24. Talmale, G., Shrawankar, U.: Tasks scheduling using dynamic cluster-based hierarchical real-time scheduler for autonomous car. Ambient Science (2021)
25. Talmale, G., Shrawankar, U.: Cluster based real time scheduling for distributed system (2021)
26. Talmale, G., Shrawankar, U.: Real-time cyber-physical system for healthcare monitoring in COVID-19. Int. J. Web Based Learn. Teach. Technol. **17**, 1–10 (2022)

Design System of Urban Residential Environment Based on Interactive Genetic Algorithm

Dandan Fan[1(✉)] and Haomiao Qin[2]

[1] College of Art and Design, Anyang Institute of Technology, Anyang 455000, Henan, China
fandandan5641@126.com
[2] Faculty of Business, City University of Macau, Macau 999078, China

Abstract. Genetic interaction algorithm transforms the cognitive evaluation of the subject into scientific quantitative factors, and quantitative evaluation of the subject users by using the genetic function based on genetic algorithm. The aim of this work is to study the optimal design of the urban residential environment based on genetic interaction algorithms. This paper first uses OpenGL to create an urban residential environment model in order to evaluate the effect of the conceptual design of urban residential environment optimization using paired comparison methods. Then, we optimize the design of greening, infrastructure, air quality and sanitation in the creation of urban living environment. The experiment proved that the questionnaire survey results of 600 people showed that the residents' satisfaction with the interactive genetic algorithm scheme was much greater than the traditional scheme.

Keywords: Interactive genetic algorithm · Living environment · Environmental optimization · Infrastructure

1 Introduction

With the increasing interest in living environment, the research of living environment evaluation is becoming more and more popular with professionals. At present, there are more research in this field in China. Community is the most basic part of social organization, and the design and construction of community should be the starting point of small and medium-sized cities. With the rapid development of China's economic system and the pace of urban expansion is accelerated, the human demand for urban landscape, people, economy, construction, transportation, region and quality of life is also constantly increasing. The design and construction of modern cities should not only reflect the progress of modern science and technology, but also pay attention to people-oriented, create a better living environment for people, and meet the natural needs and social needs of urban population. And is subject to the sustainable development of the community. The interactive genetic algorithm can very well order the influencing factors by weight [1, 2].

In the study of urban living environment optimization design system based on inter-active genetic algorithm, many scholars have studied it and achieved good results. For example, Asef P has proposed a multi-factor optimization model based on the economy and reliability of pipe network [3]. Hiekata K developed a three-objective optimization model, which includes economy, reliability, and traffic ratio objectives. The same model does not consider the operation and management cost of the later stage of the pipe net-work, which is relatively unreasonable, and the multi-objective research lacks scientific nature [4].

This paper mainly studies the necessity of optimizing the design system of urban residential environment based on the interactive genetic algorithm, and the multipur-pose estimation method is the best design of traffic area definition. Starting with the actual design optimization project of the living environment, based on the multivari-able optimization process, interactive genetic algorithm and computer technology, the multi-living environment optimization model is studied and the total living cost system is established. A multi-objective optimization model with the residential comfort as the reliability goal and the residential safety goal. The main way adopted is through the questionnaire survey.

2   Research on the Optimal Design System of Urban Living Environment Based on Interactive Genetic Algorithm

2.1   The Role of Interactive Genetic Algorithm in the Optimization of Urban Living Environment

Given the increased automation, scientists have found that traditional genetic algorithms can only solve the problems represented by signal functions during design. As more and more users find it difficult to intervene, traditional genetic algorithms may not perform well in the face of the optimal problem with incorrect performance metrics, such as data mining and knowledge acquisition performance metrics are difficult to identify performance metrics with obvious functions. Considering the weaknesses of traditional genetic algorithms themselves, scientists have proposed genetic interaction algorithms to extend the applicability of traditional genetic algorithms, that is, to improve the evaluation of the evolutionary ability of human subjects as a person. Integrated into the quality system, as a key factor in optimizing regeneration. Because the living environment should ultimately be applied to the reality, for the residents to live, so the use of interactive genetic algorithm can better optimize the living environment more in line with the residents' wishes [5, 6].

2.2   Problems Existing in the Urban Living Environment

(1) Ignoring people's needs

According to the Code, a national standard for Planning and Urban Planning, pub-lished in 1993, green space in residential areas must include public green space, green space next to houses, green space supporting public buildings and a green road. The greening and restoration amount of the old area shall not be less than

25%. In order to meet the requirements of green rate in most residential areas, the land for roads and parking lots has been reduced to a minimum, and the exploration land is increased and converted into green space to meet the green rate index. "Only reaching your potential can achieve business goals. In such residential areas, although the green area is very large, the plant structure and landscape design are also very interesting, but the space is insufficient to meet the needs of different people."

(2) Imitation of the wind is very popular

Imitation styles are common, and once the innovation is successful, it will be copied by many people. It can be found in many residential areas, pure green has become the lace of the house and functions as "coating" residential areas only. One cannot see the general landscape of the area, but only the flat cake. Because in high-rise residences, landscape design was not completely proposed, but only the ground between the buildings. After the "British landscape", such design was introduced by many foreign garden companies, mostly appearing in large "villa resorts", "golf courses" and so on. It emphasizes the importance of natural ecosystems, where families and people seem to be at the heart of this "physical storage" or "ecosphere" so that humans cannot integrate, but are isolated from the environment.

(3) No classification design was conducted

In most housing plans, residential areas are divided into three categories according to the number of families or population size: residential, residential and group. A residential area has a lot of communities, which have many groups. The system composition of residential area can be divided into three levels, namely: residential area and residential area group. In large cities, the residential system is generally three floors due to its wide boundary and large population. Therefore, there are some differences in the specific design and layout of residential communities in large and small cities. Design and design according to different conditions.

(4) Poor infrastructure

The supporting facilities of public buildings and municipal facilities are not perfect. For example, some communities only have residential places without shopping, leisure, medical care and other public places, and they cannot use water, heating, pipeline natural gas and so on. Lack of outdoor public activity space, activity space for children and the elderly: more simple arrangement, no special scientific and reasonable design. Greening mostly stays at the landscape level but does not pay attention to the ecological effect: small area, single variety, no three-dimensional level, more take the roadside house greening [7, 8].

2.3 Establishment of the Fitness Function

Physical activity in genetics, as the basis for calculating the merits of genetically evolved chromosomes, is a general evaluation model proposed by Ohsa K. The ultimate goal of the genetic interaction algorithm is to have users in a living environment, so take the "satisfaction" and "determination" of the design function as indicators to judge the quality of genetic chromosomes. The criteria divides users' preferences into three categories: 3 points are "satisfaction" with the program, 2 points mean their behavior is "normal", and 1 points are "dissatisfaction." The user satisfaction score is the cumulative result of each user score. Assuming that the user is to calculate, then the center of the satisfaction score is [n, 3n]. If the satisfaction scores were equal, the scores were calculated and the fitness function was determined together [9].

Satisfaction formula:

$$\overline{S}(Fi) = \sum_{i=1}^{n} \frac{S(Fi)}{n} \tag{1}$$

$\overline{S}(Fi)$ Where: is the average satisfaction value; Fi $\overline{S}(Fi)$ Evaluation score for each user; satisfaction for each user; i, n are positive integer and 1 i n.

$\overline{S}(Fi)$ Assuming that u and v are the degree of consensus T and satisfaction, respectively, and the proportion of adaptation values (u + v = 1), the consensus satisfaction as a function of fitness [10]:

$$F_{itness} = u\overline{S}(Fi) \tag{2}$$

2.4 Algorithm Process

Based on the above analysis, the application process of interactive genetic algorithm in the design of urban residential environment is as follows. Step 1 sets all the parameters of each scheme to initialize the population. Step 2 The fitness values of each chromosome are obtained by the interaction of the user with the design scheme. Users can modify the adaptive values of the chromosome by scoring for genetic selection for the next generation. Step 3 generates a new population based on the fitness values obtained in step 2. Step 4 uses a crossover, variation operation for the genes in the new population. Step 5 passes several rounds of repeated assessment and elimination, and ends when the user gets satisfactory results, otherwise turn back and proceed to Step 2 [11, 12].

3 System Design Experiment of Optimization Design of Urban Living Environment Based on Interactive Genetic Algorithm

3.1 Residential Environment Survey

Urban living environment is closely related to the life of urban people, so the personal wishes of local residents must be taken into account in the optimization design of urban living environment. Therefore, this paper designs the questionnaire, hoping to collect the residents 'wishes through the questionnaire, provide the construction direction for the design of urban residents' environment optimization, and apply the interactive genetic algorithm in the construction. This paper mainly conducts a questionnaire survey on the residents of different ages under the viaduct to be built in a certain place, mainly evaluating the three environmental optimization construction schemes.

3.2 Simulation System Operation

The two schemes of urban living environment optimization system design adopt the traditional way and the opportunity interactive genetic algorithm respectively. Six questionnaires were conducted on 180 local residents to explore their satisfaction with the design scheme.

4   Experimental Analysis of the Systematic Optimization Design of Urban Living Environment Based on Interactive Genetic Algorithm

4.1   Factors and Analysis of Resident Satisfaction

In this paper, a sample survey of the urban living environment under construction was conducted, and 100 residents of 6 age groups were selected for a questionnaire survey to investigate their views on the importance of elements in the living environment. The data are recorded in Table 1.

Table 1. Influencing factors of different age drama titles on living environment satisfaction

	15–20	20–30	30–40	40–50	50–60	60–70
Greening	11	9	8	9	3	4
Safety	80	73	85	84	93	92
Health	9	18	7	7	4	4

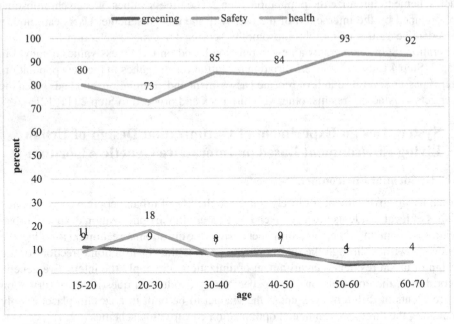

Fig. 1. Satisfaction survey of urban living environment of residents of different ages

From Fig. 1 we can clearly, no matter which age, the vast majority of residents of the living environment security requirements are clearer, so in our design living environment optimization system, the security as the main design direction, to ensure the safety of residents, is a good living environment, the basic requirements.

4.2 Program Satisfaction Analysis

This paper uses the traditional method to optimize the residential environment, and then designs a new system with the interactive genetic algorithm. Their satisfaction with the two schemes was obtained by questionnaire residents in six different localities, and data are recorded in Table 2.

Table 2. Questionnaire survey residents' satisfaction with the two schemes

	1	2	3	4	5	6
IGa	80	73	92	67	78	74
Old	20	27	8	33	22	26

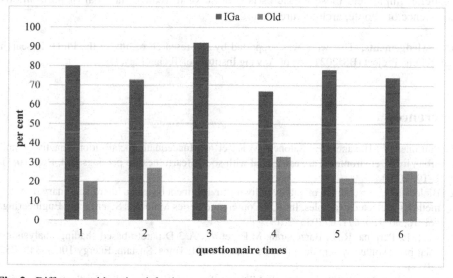

Fig. 2. Different residents' satisfaction survey on the two urban environmental design schemes

From Fig. 2, we can clearly see that the public satisfaction of the scheme involved in choosing the interactive genetic algorithm is much higher than the traditional scheme, and it is basically stable at more than 70%. It can be seen that the interactive genetic algorithm is people-oriented, and it is perfectly in line with the design system of urban living environment optimization.

5 Conclusions

In this paper, the genetic interaction algorithm is applied to the design optimization system based on urban residential environment, and uses user satisfaction as an evaluation function to maximize the evaluation device to provide design functions in response to user preferences. In the case used here, the number of atoms is reduced to easily interpret the application of the algorithm. If the number of people is large or the evolution cycle is very large, users will experience fatigue and increased cerebral pressure during the evaluation process, which will affect the overall evaluation. On the other hand, consider the integration issues. At the same time, it is also necessary to divide the living space to make the design of living space optimization more concentrated. Excellent environmental design is the premise of obtaining a pleasant environment, and occupies a dominant position in the residential environment optimization. In the future construction of urban residential areas, we should focus on optimizing the design of living environment, improve the technical level of living environment construction, so as to really improve the quality of life. Residential environment optimization design measures described in this paper, can improve the living comfort and accord with the principle of green ecology and sustainable development, to guide Xinxiang residential construction, change the current construction concept chaos situation is positive and beneficial, implement these measures is conducive to realize the goal of harmonious coexistence of people, architecture, nature.

Acknowledgements. This work was supported by the research results of the Ph.D. Research Startup Fund Project (BSJ2021025) of Anyang Institute of Technology.

References

1. Puurunen, J., Hakanen, E., Salonen, M.K., et al.: Inadequate socialisation, inactivity, and urban living environment are associated with social fearfulness in pet dogs. Sci. Rep. **10**(1), 1–10 (2020)
2. Bielecka, K.: Assessment of quality of living environment based on interdisciplinary research methods - selected examples. In: IOP Conference Series Materials Science and Engineering, vol. 10, no. 1, p. 471, 072035 (2019)
3. Asef, P., Perpina, R.B., Barzegaran, M.R., et al.: A 3-D pareto-based shading analysis on solar photovoltaic system design optimization. IEEE Trans. Sustain. Energy **10**(2), 843–852 (2018)
4. Hiekata, K., Wanaka, S., Okubo, Y.: Mining rules of decision-making for fleet composition under market uncertainty using a genetic algorithm. J. Mar. Sci. Technol. **27**(1), 730–739 (2022)
5. Kaleli, A., Akola, H.B.: The design and development of a diesel engine electromechanical EGR cooling system based on machine learning-genetic algorithm prediction models to reduce emission and fuel consumption. Proc. Inst. Mech. Eng. Part C J. Mech. Eng. Sci. **236**(3), 1888–1902 (2022)
6. Zare, S., Tavakolpour-Saleh, A.R.: Design of a traveling wave thermo-acoustic engine based on genetic algorithm. Int. J. Energy Res. **43**(14), 8790–8801 (2019)
7. Ahn, Y.J., Sohn, D.W.: The effect of neighbourhood-level urban form on residential building energy use: a GIS-based model using building energy benchmarking data in Seattle. Energy Build. **196**(Aug), 124–133 (2019)
8. Hashemi, N., Tousi, E., Chabok, N., et al.: Investigating the attachment in urban residential environments (case study: Tehran Navvab District). Int. J. Multicult. Multireligious Underst. **7**(10), 564–573 (2020)

9. Tafraout, S., Bourahla, N., Bourahla, Y., et al.: Automatic structural design of RC wall-slab buildings using a genetic algorithm with application in BIM environment. Autom. Constr. **106**(Oct), 102901.1-102901.10 (2019)
10. Amar, J., Nagase, K.: Genetic-algorithm-based global design optimization of tree-type robotic systems involving exponential coordinates. Mech. Syst. Signal Process. **156**(8), 107461 (2021)
11. Yigit, S.: A machine-learning-based method for thermal design optimization of residential buildings in highly urbanized areas of Turkey. J. Build. Eng. **38**(8), 102225 (2021)
12. Rabiei, P., Arias-Aranda, D.: Design and development of a genetic algorithm based on fuzzy inference systems for personnel assignment problem. In: WPOM - Working Papers on Operations Management, vol. 12, no. 1, p. 1 (2021)

Sensorless Control Algorithm of Permanent Magnet Synchronous Motor on Account of Neural Network

Wei Li[✉]

Beihang University, Beijing, China
by1613105@buaa.edu.cn

Abstract. Permanent magnet synchronous motor (PMSM) is widely used in the industry because of its superior performance. The feedback information of the position and speed of the PMSM is essential for high-performance vector control. The installation of conventional mechanical sensors will increase the size, cost and reliability of the system. The sensorless control algorithm extracts the position and speed information of the motor by detecting the voltage and current signals of the motor, without mechanical sensors, which is one of the development trends of the control scheme of permanent magnet synchronous motor. This paper studies the sensorless control algorithm of permanent magnet synchronous motor based on neural network, and upgrades the underlying algorithm of motor control. The test shows that the motor control model using neural network algorithm achieves more efficient accuracy in motor control.

Keywords: Neural network algorithm · Permanent magnet synchronous motor · Sensorless position · Control algorithm

1 Introduction

Permanent magnet synchronous motor has good performance in many attributes, such as high motor efficiency, high power density, and easy speed expansion in weak magnetic field. With these advantages, permanent magnet synchronous motor is widely used in aviation, trolley, devices and other motor applications. Position sensorless has the advantage of reducing cost and increasing reliability. This kind of motor control precision, speed adjustment range, strong robustness, these advantages for motor control system has great significance. The sensorless control algorithm of permanent magnet synchronous motor based on neural network is beneficial to the improvement of motor control level.

As for the research of neural network algorithm, many scholars at home and abroad have carried on the research to it. Abroad study, Skuratov V proposes a collaborative algorithm neural network model, the algorithm realizes the intelligent way to the stock price of the collection, these data include the development of the stock price data and background data and modify and adapt to the system, the research conclusion can significantly improve the precision of the transaction, It can help professionals to conduct

N. Khare et al. (Eds.): MIND 2022, CCIS 1762, pp. 132–139, 2022.
https://doi.org/10.1007/978-3-031-24352-3_11

analysis work [1]. Asrianda A proposed A neural network algorithm to detect oil palm leaves with up to 60 photos, 50 of which were of leaves with five different conditions, such as scimitaria, cerulosaccharia, ceruloplakia and nutrient deficiency. The remaining 10 are intact leaves. As a result, CNN could detect palm oil leaves with an accuracy of 99% [2]. Smys S proposed a neural network algorithm for 5G network of random neural network to simulate smart city, and 5G is expected to achieve greater transmission rate under outdoor and indoor coverage of smart city. This suggests that the introduction of 5G could lead to the replacement of Wi-Fi currently used for applications such as geolocation with continuous radio coverage by initiating iot participation in all devices in use [3].

At present, permanent magnet motor has many disadvantages, such as slow convergence of identification technology, difficult control of specific parameters of pulse by salient electrode voltage injection, and defects in second harmonic noise [1, 4]. Write the second harmonic without stopping. According to the magnetic saturation effect, the bias can be given if the current in the opposite direction is put here [5, 6]. The solution proposed in this paper can improve the convergence speed, can realize the motor rotor static or in the free state of successful position processing. The sensorless control algorithm of PMSM based on neural network accelerates the development of PMSM control technology.

2 Design and Exploration of Sensorless Control Algorithm of Permanent Magnet Synchronous Motor on Account of Neural Network

2.1 Neural Network Algorithm

The principle of artificial neural network is to simulate the process of human thinking. The calculation of this algorithm is not linear, the characteristics of which explain the distributed storage of data information, at the same time the cooperative disposal of multiple threads [7, 8]. The built-in structure and function of the algorithm model are simple and fixed, but the behaviors of all neurons composed of each other are different.

Compressed sensing depth autoencoder belongs to artificial neural network algorithm. Based on the idea of deep neural network, the original input signal X is firstly processed in a single layer for the module generated by the encoder, that is, feature transformation is carried out through the automatic encoding and decoding algorithm of compressed sensing to obtain the representation of the original input signal. Compressors for processing module object for training, after training, the results into a layer to the next entry, in this way will the basic modeling unit step by step a stacked together to form multilayer neural networks, and network parameters were obtained through the training of network initial value, the supervised algorithm model is used to adjust all the parameters for numerical modeling unit.

Handwritten data recognition is used as an example to illustrate the basic flow chart of the compression perceptron, as shown in Fig. 1:

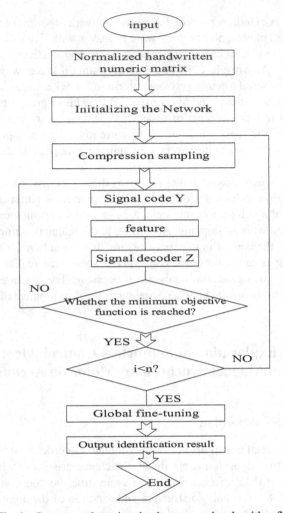

Fig. 1. Compressed sensing depth autoencoder algorithm flow

Step 1 normalized the handwritten digital image and obtained the original input X;
Step 2 initialize the training network and set the weight W and bias b;
Step 3 train the I (initial value I = 1) layer of the compressed sensing autoencoder:

(1) Use the model $\hat{x} \sim cs(x)$ to compress and sample the data;
(2) Use formula to encode the signal;
(3) Use the formula to reconstruct the input (decoding);
(4) Use the formula to calculate the minimum mutual entropy.

Step 4 take the output value of f layer as the input of f + 1 layer, and repeat Step3 until all layers are fully trained;

Step 5 use BP neural network to fine-tune the above network, and the obtained parameters are used as input of BP network to classify and recognize handwritten digits.

2.2 Sensorless Control Algorithm of Permanent Magnet Synchronous Motor Based on Neural Network

According to the requirements of the actual control system, the common motor vector control strategies are:

1) the control id = 0

The magnetization and demagnetization of the motor are related to the direct axis current component, while the electromagnetic torque of the motor is controlled by the cross axis current component [9, 10]. When id = 0 is used, the stator current will contain no direct-axis current component, only the cross-axis armature current related to the electromagnetic torque. When the torque of a given size is generated, the stator current required under the control is the smallest and the loss in the winding is also the smallest because all the current is the effective torque current, which can improve the efficiency of the system.

2) Maximum torque/current control

The application scope of current control is generally salient pole motor [11, 12]. For implicit pole motor, the control method is equivalent to id = 0 control. The specific realization of the method is to obtain the value of the means of cross - axis current control motor to complete the maximum output torque[13, 14]. This method can minimize the current of the control stator when the torque is up to standard, which can reduce power loss and improve motor performance.

3) Weak magnetic control

When the output voltage of the motor reaches the output limit of the inverter, if the actual working condition requires the motor to work at a higher speed, because the size of the permanent magnet flux is constant, the amplitude of the flux can only be controlled by changing the size of the direct axis current component [15, 16]. After entering the weak magnetic control, the motor speed increases, while the output electromagnetic torque of the motor decreases, and the motor enters the constant power operation area.

The research in this paper mainly focuses on the sensorless control level of permanent magnet synchronous motor. Through comparison, the id = 0 control scheme with good control performance and simple control mode is selected. The following is the vector control block diagram adopted in this paper. It mainly includes two closed-loop rotational speed and current, feedforward decoupling module, Clarke transform, Park transform, SVPWM, inverter and other main modules [17].

According to the equation of permanent magnet synchronous motor in synchronous rotation coordinate system, the coupling problem still exists in the voltage equation of the ac axis, so the actual control system needs to add feedforward term in the given part of ac axis voltage for cross decoupling. The current loop adopts two PI controllers, and its parameters are determined by zero-pole cancellation. The current loop is considered as a first-order system, and the open-loop frequency of the speed loop is designed accordingly.

3 Research on the Effect of Sensorless Control Algorithm of Permanent Magnet Synchronous Motor on Account of Neural Network

Compressed Sensing (Compressed Sampling, CS) processes the data of most of the signals, and the basis vectors can be characterized by sparse features. Under Nyquist frequency distribution, the actual signals are processed and samples are collected. This method reduces the amount of data that needs to be processed while storing data annotations and main information.

In the handwritten set, it is assumed that the annotation of training samples in the set is a W* H grayscale image model, and the vector is arranged in columns, where the vector is the n-dimensional sample vector signal X, $x \in R^N (R = w * h)$. The one-dimensional discrete vector $x = [x(1), x(2), ...x(N)]^T$ is transformed into the orthogonal column vector $\{\Phi\}_{i=1}^N$ of the transformed matrix $\Psi = [\Phi_1, \Phi_2, ... \Phi_N]$, which contains the sample vector $\Phi_i (i = 1, 2, 3, ...N)$ signal of N*1. Then the formula of X can be expressed as:

$$x = \Psi\alpha = \sum_{i=1}^N \alpha_i \Phi_i \tag{1}$$

where α is the coefficient of the original processing signal in the variable range, and the variation characteristics of the coefficient are sparse.

Compressed sensing model

$$\hat{x} \sim cs(x) : \hat{x} = A\alpha + e \tag{2}$$

$A = \eta\Psi$, α represents the observation matrix: M*N(M < < n).E represents an error in initialization, or is regarded as noise. η represents the observation matrix: M*N(M < < n).

Control signal entity X is captured for the motor, and all captured signals are formed into sample sets, which are generated after matrix transformation $\Psi = [\Phi_1, \Phi_2, ... \Phi_N]$. We also know that α, the x expression is formed; Determine A, and α finally form A compressed sensing model.

Through this algorithm, the accuracy of motor control is improved, and the neural network algorithm is very efficient.

4 Investigation and Research on Sensorless Control Algorithm of Permanent Magnet Synchronous Motor on Account of Neural Network

Below, Matlab/Simulink is used to model the sliding mode observer mentioned above, and it is connected to the vector control closed-loop system for simulation. The simulation parameters were set as Rs = 2.35 ω, Ldq = 6.5 mH, F = 0.062 Wb. Due to the poor observation effect of the sliding mode observer at low speed due to the problem of too small back potential, the method with sensors is used to complete the starting. When t = 0.5 s, the system runs with the sliding mode observer. When t = 1.5 s, the motor speed increases from 600 rpm to 800 rpm, and when t = 2.5 s, the motor speed increases from 800 rpm to 1000 rpm, and the load torque is 1 Nm. The observation performance of the sliding mode observer at variable speed is tested.

The observer related operating data is shown in Table 1.

Table 1. Apriori algorithm and traditional model take time

	1 (time/s)	2 (time/s)	3 (time/s)	4 (time/s)	5 (time/s)	6 (time/s)
Real speed(rpm)	0	580	910	795	1320	1145
Compression perceptron algorithm speed(rpm)	0	620	900	800	1310	1150

The first row of Table 1 is the time when the sliding mode observer is running, which respectively refers to the 1 s, 2 s... 6 s. Column 1 of the table refers to the Real speed(RPM) of the motor and the speed captured by the Compression perceptron algorithm (RPM) model. In Table 1, the actual motor speed is recorded at the moment 1 s, 2 s... The speed of 6 s is 0 rpm, 580 rpm, 910 rpm, 795 rpm, 1320 rpm, 1145 rpm respectively; The compressed sensing model captures the rotation speed record moment 1 s, 2 s... The speed of 6 s is 0 rpm, 620 rpm, 900 rpm, 800 rpm, 1310 rpm, 1150 rpm respectively. From the motor speed of the signal captured by the compressed sensing model, the actual running speed of the motor is captured very accurately.

Figure 2 shows that the Real speed (RPM) of the motor and the speed captured by Compression perceptron algorithm (RPM) are in the 1 s, 2 s... Speed of 6 s. According

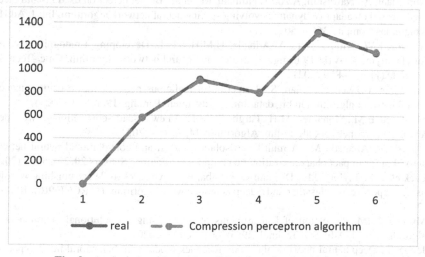

Fig. 2. Apriori algorithm and traditional mode take time to image

to the motor speed in the picture, the motor speed captured by Compression perceptron algorithm speed(RPM) is very accurate, indicating that the Compression perceptron model algorithm is very accurate in capturing signals.

The results show that the sensorless control algorithm of PMSM based on neural network has high performance in motor signal acquisition and processing.

5   Conclusions

In this paper, surface mount permanent magnet synchronous motor is taken as the control object, considering the influence of parameter change on sensorless control of permanent magnet synchronous motor, the improved sensorless control algorithm under parameter change is studied. In the research of sensorless control algorithm, two middle and high speed closed-loop sensorless algorithms, sliding mode observer and model reference adaptation, are studied. The solution proposed in this paper solves many defects of motor control. The sensorless control algorithm of permanent magnet synchronous motor based on neural network promotes the development of permanent magnet synchronous motor control technology.

References

1. Skuratov, V., Kuzmin, K., Nelin, I., et al.: Creation of a neural network algorithm for automated collection and analysis of statistics of exchange quotes graphics. Eureka Phys. Eng. 3(3), 22–29 (2020)
2. Asrianda, A., Aidilof, H., Pangestu, Y.: Machine learning for detection of palm oil leaf disease visually using convolutional neural network algorithm. J. Inform. Telecommun. Eng. 4(2), 286–293 (2021)
3. Smys, S., Wang, H., Basar, A.: 5G network simulation in smart cities using neural network algorithm. J. Artif. Intell. Capsule Netw. 3(1), 43–52 (2021)
4. Almomani, A., Nawasrah, A.A., Alauthman, M., et al.: Botnet detection used fast-flux technique, based on adaptive dynamic evolving spiking neural network algorithm. Int. J. Ad Hoc Ubiquitous Comput. 36(1), 50 (2021)
5. Alsaade, F.W., Aldhyani, T., Al-Adhaile, H.M.H., et al.: Developing a recognition system for classifying COVID-19 using a convolutional neural network algorithm. Cmc -Tech Sci. Press- 68(1), 805–819 (2021)
6. Rajendran, B., Venkataraman, S.: Detection of malicious network traffic using enhanced neural network algorithm in big data. Int. J. Adv. Intell. Paradig. 19(1/2), 1 (2021)
7. Mohamed, E.M., Mohamed, M.H., Farghally, M.F.: A new cascade-correlation growing deep learning neural network algorithm. Algorithms 14(5), 158 (2021)
8. Nobari, A., Aliabadi, M.: A multilevel isolation forrest and convolutional neural network algorithm for impact characterization on composite structures. Sensors 20(20), 5896 (2020)
9. Ezekiel, P.S., Taylor, O.E., Deedam-Okuchaba, F.B.: A model to detect phishing websites using support vector classifier and a deep neural network algorithm. IJARCCE 9(6), 188–194 (2020)
10. Mustafa, M.M.: Detection of leaf ailments of plants using convolutional neural network algorithm. Int. J. Adv. Sci. Technol. 29(6), 6069–6075 (2020)
11. Jeong, T.: Deep neural network algorithm feedback model with behavioral intelligence and forecast accuracy. Symmetry 12(9), 1465 (2020)

12. Osman, A.H., Mohamed, A.A., Motwakel, A., et al.: Nominate of significant features for unknown internet traffic applications filtering based on a neural network algorithm. Int. J. Adv. Appl. Sci. **8**(2), 106–116 (2020)
13. Yassein, M.B., Aljawarneh, S.A., Alodibat, S., et al.: An improvement of neural network algorithm for anomaly intrusion detection system. Int. J. Commun. Antenna Propag. **10**(2), 84–93 (2020)
14. Tao, T., Zhao, W., Du, Y., et al.: Simplified fault-tolerant model predictive control for a five-phase permanent-magnet motor with reduced computation burden. IEEE Trans. Power Electron. **35**(4), 3850–3858 (2020)
15. Lutonin A S, Shklyarskiy J E. Topology and control algorithms for a permanent magnet synchronous motor as a part of a vehicle with in-wheel motors. E3S Web of Conferences, 2021, 266(3):04001–04001
16. Odo, K., Ohanu, C., Chinaeke-Ogbuka, I., et al.: A novel direct torque and flux control of permanent magnet synchronous motor with analytically-tuned PI controllers. Int. J. Power Electron. Drive Syst. **12**(4), 2103–2112 (2021)
17. Mousavi, M.H., Karami, M.E., Ahmadi, M., Sharafi, P., Veysi, F.: Robust speed controller design for permanent magnet synchronous motor based on gain-scheduled control method via LMI approach. SN Appl. Sci. **2**(10), 1–15 (2020). https://doi.org/10.1007/s42452-020-03453-z

A Techno Aid to Ease in e-Rehabilitation

Urmila Shrawankar[1]([✉]) [iD], Chaitreya Shrawankar[2] [iD], and Girish Talmale[1] [iD]

[1] G H Raisoni College of Engineering, Nagpur, Maharashtra, India
urmillaa@gmail.com
[2] RTM Nagpur University, Nagpur, Maharashtra, India

Abstract. Whenever any health related physical/psychological problems or accidents happen in life, well equipped hospitals, physicians or surgeons, para medical staff, nurses, technicians, and other health care workers are available to help a person. After discharged from the hospital when person comes to home real challenges start to get back to the original health conditions to survive daily life. Rehabilitation plays a major role to recover from the losses because of disease or injury. Some person may not able to get medical services due to unavailability of services at local places or mobility issues. Technology is the only solution to help such persons. If technology helps during rehabilitation, person may get better medical, psychological and social services to improve his/her quality of life. This work focus on connectivity of a patient with hospitals, family, friends and society during rehabilitation phase.

An interactive, distributed person monitoring, computer assistive rehabilitative cloud based, IoT framework system is developed to help patient in every step of his/her rehabilitation from long distance and keep connecting to health care services, family, friends and society. This system is very helpful to the persons those are under rehabilitation, aged persons as well as disables.

Keywords: Assistive Technology (AT) · Rehabilitative Technology (RT) · Robotic technology · Wearable technology · Virtual reality technology · IoT framework · Cloud technology · Tele-rehabilitation · Patient monitoring system

1 Introduction

When patients partially recover from the health problem and stable in medical condition, generally he/she gets discharge from the hospital. Now the next step starts for his/her full recovery. In this phase, person requires help from everyone like physicians, therapist, other medical professions, family, friends and society. The main difference is that the person is at home that means far away from everyone therefore the technology is the solution to connect all them together and each other. Technology will also boost the self-confidence of a patient as he/she will get the daily feedback for their recovery and gradually dependency will get finished. To achieve this goal a computer software based system has been developed.

To develop an assistive system for self-operated rehabilitation [1] many related technologies are involved mainly Assistive Technology & Rehabilitative Technology. The role of these technologies are explain in further sections of the paper.

N. Khare et al. (Eds.): MIND 2022, CCIS 1762, pp. 140–152, 2022.
https://doi.org/10.1007/978-3-031-24352-3_12

This system not only monitor the patient but also take care of his room conditions like monitoring and controlling temperature and humidity, light, fan, air quality etc. System records and send the parameters data to the related user and admin can control these values of patient's room through IoT devices from remote location.

Besides that family members and related users are able to watch the video streaming remotely with the help of Amazon Web Services (AWS). All these feature and parameters reading along with graphs are access through website. An additional feature, the face reorganization is implemented through video streaming with the help of AWS services to provide the security when patient is alone at home.

Motivation of this research comes from the requirement of remote healthcare services in COVID-19. The importance of remote healthcare services plays an important role in rural areas with limited availability of healthcare resources.

2 Role of Assistive Technology (AT) and Rehabilitative Technology (RT) in Rehabilitation

Rehabilitative (RT) and Assistive Technology (AT) are the computer tools, software applications or Apps that are helpful to the people those are under rehabilitation phase at home, and outside of home.

Rehabilitative Technology (RT) helps people to come out from post illness to original physical or mental health state to perform day-to-day life.

Assistive Technologies (AT) offers the aides for supporting to recover from the illness as well as post illness state through computer based devices and applications as shown in Fig. 1.

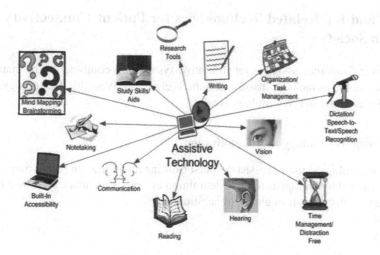

Fig. 1. Assistive technology

The multidisciplinary engineering approaches support to develop assistive tools for such people such as computer based controlled wheelchairs, Motion trackers, Voice

Recognition Systems, eye trackers, Hearing aids, communication aids, spectacles, Text to Speech, Reading Pens,, Word Prediction Software, Visual Search Engines, Head pointers and many more as shown in Fig. 2.

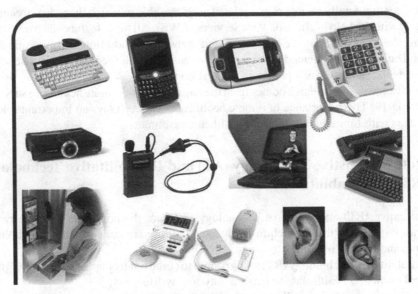

Fig. 2. Assistive technology devices

3   AT and RT Related Technologies for Patient Connectivity with Society

A proposed Computer assistive rehabilitative system is a combination of many other related technologies includes mainly, Robotic Technology, Wearable Technology, Virtual reality Technology, IoT Technology etc.

3.1   Robotic Technology in Rehabilitation

Robotic technology is used to assist the person during rehabilitation [2] for doing various therapy assisted by therapists to provide training as well as feedback as shown in Fig. 3 from the long distance through tele-rehabilitation.

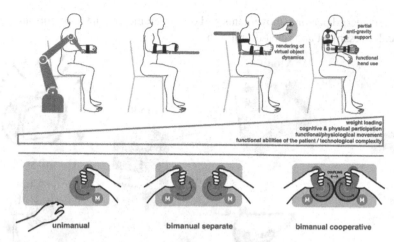

Fig. 3. Robotic technology in rehabilitation

3.2 Wearable Technology in Rehabilitation

Wearable technology is very comfortable for gathering patient's information as shown in Fig. 4 with the help of very tiny sensors and instruments [3]. Through the wearable sensors, person can connect to their physicians. Physicians can monitor patient from the data they get from these wearable sensors and help in rehabilitation from long distance also.

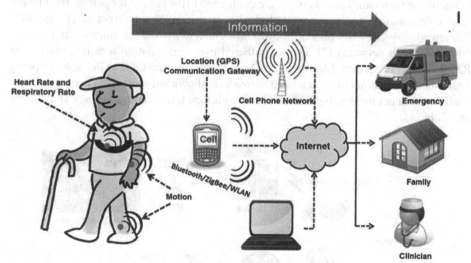

Fig. 4. Wearable technology in rehabilitation

3.3 Virtual Reality Technology in Rehabilitation

Virtual reality (VR) is developing technology [4] with many benefits that can help during rehabilitation process. It can stimulate 3D environments as shown in Fig. 5 which observes and record person's movements and other parameters, theses inputs are helpful for clinical assessment and rehabilitation [5].

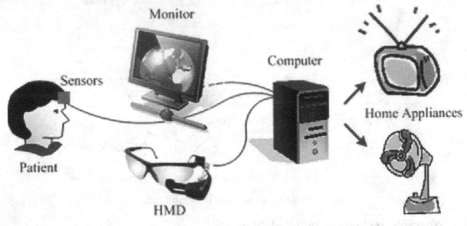

Fig. 5. Virtual reality technology

3.4   Internet of Things (IoT) Technology in Rehabilitation

Now a day's automated computerized controlled systems have been gained popularity in health care domain. These systems are connected to the patient for getting their health related information which is directly linked to hospitals. This Internet of Things (IoT) framework [6] gives the patient-to-hospital connectivity via the Internet and mobile communication networks [7]. Data is gathered using information sensing devices like RFID - Radio Frequency Identification Devices, sensors and GPS - Global Positioning Systems using Internet to from a huge network as shown in Fig. 6. This network is very useful to connect patient, hospitals, other health care industries, pharmacy and society [8] (Table 1).

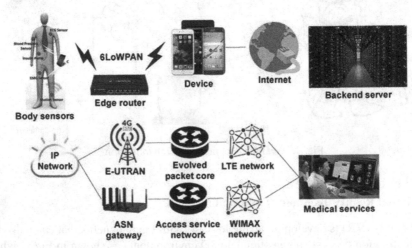

Fig. 6. IoT technology in rehabilitation

Table 1. Sensors used in rehabilitation

Sr. no	Sensor	Role in rehabilitation
01	Force-based sensors	To measure the body movement
02	Gyroscopes	To track motion
03	Accelerometers	To measure body movement
04	Magnetometers	To measure body orientation
05	ECG	To help diagnose and monitor conditions affecting the heart
06	Blood Pressure Sensor	To measure blood pressure
07	Blood Glucose	To measure blood glucose level
08	Body Temperature,	To measure temperature
09	Oxymeter	To measure breathing activity

4 System Model for Patient Monitoring System

Proposed system as shown in Fig. 7 has been come up with monitoring virtually 24/7 and controlling activities from anywhere around the globe with following features.

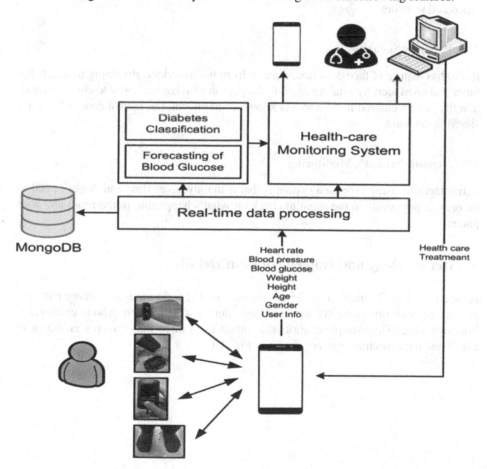

Fig. 7. System Model for patient monitoring system

4.1 Keeping Track of Patient Conditions

It keeps track of real time room conditions like temperature, humidity, brightness etc. A person can also switch on/off room devices like fan and light etc. According to temperature, brightness and humidity a person can change the controlling activities from the website i.e. switch fan on/off. It shows weekly graph of room conditions parameters.

4.2 Collection of Patient's Heath Parameters

All collected patient's heath parameters like heart rate, respiratory rate, and oxygen saturation and all required related data and all other movements along with exercises activities are stored in website which is directly available to clinical personnel (hospitals), family and related persons.

4.3 Interact with Patient

Further, Hospitals and family members can directly interact with patient through audio, video and website.

4.4 Patient's Security

It also has feature of face detection, directly from the live video streaming it detects the faces and gives alert by sending email to the person who has authority to check in room that the person entered in the room is known or unknown, the known people faces are stored in database.

4.5 Remote Patient's Monitoring

Advantages of using proposed system is that it mainly saves time and doesn't need to be present physically in the room to check on what's happening in the room and with patient.

5 Methodology and Implementation Details

A cloud based, IoT (Internet of Things) framework [9] is developed to record patient's parameters, monitor moments, activities and interact with a patient who is under rehabilitation state. This complete work is designed in to three major stages as shown in Fig. 8 and the flowchart is as per shown in Fig. 10.

Fig. 8. Patient monitoring system

5.1 Design an IoT Framework

Devices are installed as shown in Fig. 9 in rooms for monitoring room conditions parameters and activities happening in the room Raspberry Pi 3B+, PCB, FAN, LED, DHT 22, LDR Diode, Memory card are connected to each other in desired circuit [10]. The led and fan is controlled remotely through website's button/slider called ON and OFF. Other devices can be added to different pins and ports given in Pi. A USB camera is connected through cable and the important thing is to connect the raspberry Pi with internet connectivity or hotspot to make it work and voltage supply of 5 V. Devices connected to Raspberry pi model B 3+ via PCB module as:

i.   Led is connected to device on pin number 21 which is GPIO 9 (MISO)
ii.   DHT sensor is connected through GPIO 11 (SCLK) pin number 23
iii. LDR diode is connected on pin 17 which is a 3V3 pin
iv.   Fan is connected via pin 16 (GPIO pin 23)
v.   Camera is connected to device via USB port located on the motherboard of Raspberry pi.
vi.   Raspberry Pi 3 b+ require a 5.1 V micro USB power connector.

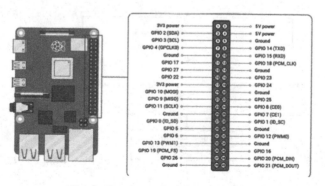

Fig. 9. Raspberry device connectivity

This is how device connectivity is implemented. Once devices are connected, Room activities are capture directly on the Raspberry Pi camera with live streaming.

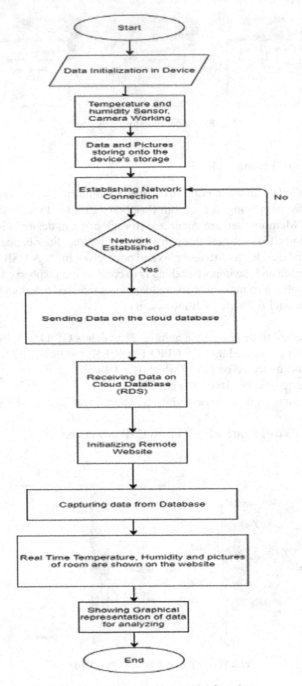

Fig. 10. System working model flowchart

5.2 Connecting and Storing Data on Cloud

Cloud formation and device implementation, AWS services like EC2, Amazon kinesis, Lambda, Recognition are used for various features to be covered in the system [11]. Also computation is done by python language and database is created using MySQL.

The sensors and embedded devices are connect with each other through cloud which are deployed at the AWS EC2 services. Once the devices are connected to the cloud [12], the sensors detect the current room conditions and camera will start capturing the activities in room and that data will be stored in the form of database in the cloud. Now audio, video and image streaming is started.

5.3 Website Application

After all the connectivity of the devices and creation of database, website ready to display results (patients parameters, movements and all activities). Website includes the login page of the user where their individual monitoring systems is working. In the website application, PHP, HTML, JavaScript programming languages are used in the front end and its back end. All previous data is stored in cloud database as well as in website [13]. User can see the live streaming video of the room where camera is installed. Whatever movements or actions carried they are captured and can be seen on website [14]. If user is not watching live streaming and any actions like patient is trying to do any movements or someone else is also present in room unusually then it will immediately send the notification to the user to their mail.

6 System Working Model Flowchart

7 Results and Analysis

After successful implementation of an interactive Cloud based IoT framework [15] for Room equipment control and person's movements and activity monitoring system [16], as shown in Fig. 11 objective and subjective analysis is done and following are the observations:

i. Under the objective analysis, room parameters like temperature, humidity are checked by apparatus as well as readings recorded by sensors deployed in the room randomly 4–5 times per day. It is found that both the values are almost same only 5% difference is observed.
ii. A nurse is appointed to check Patient's temperature, heart rate, respiratory rate, oxygen saturation etc. and also noted by body sensors. In both readings only 5–10% difference is recorded and shared successfully with hospital [16].
iii. Room has been connected to physiotherapist through video streaming and asked patient to do his regular exercises suggested by his physiotherapist, therapist could see patient's all movement and do interactive session to share the feedback [17].
iv. System was trained with 10 family members and friends faces and tested with all 10 known and 4 unknown faces, accuracy was 100%. Alert were generated and sent to identified user for unknown faces [18].

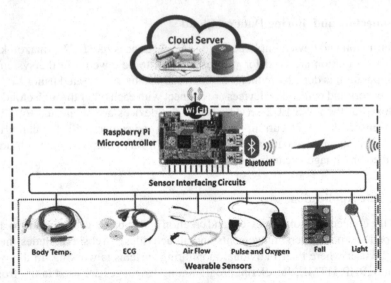

Fig. 11. Cloud based IoT framework

v.   All the reading were successfully stored in the database and available at website under authentic login.

vi. The main and very important observation is patient could do interaction with his family members and friends though audio-video streaming facility. He was very happy and confident for doing all activities required during rehabilitation independently suggested by his physician and therapist [19] (Table 2).

Table 2. Comparative analysis of IoT based rehabilitation system

Sr no	Performance metric	IoT based system	Traditional system
01	Automatic	Fully automatic	Semi-automatic
02	Remote monitoring	Remote monitor	Not applicable
03	Real time monitoring	Real time monitoring	Non-real time
04	Maintenance	Low maintenance	High maintenance
05	Cost	Cheaper	More expensive
06	Operator requirement	Not required	Need skilled operator
07	Error	Less error	More error

8   Conclusion

This is an interactive, user friendly system which is very helpful during rehabilitation of any patient. This is not only useful to the patient but also useful to family members, physicians, therapists and all heath workers those can offer their services form long distance. Web-based feature helps to store the patient's history and current readings and observations.

User does not require any additional physical connection, just mobile phones with internet connection is sufficient. Room can be monitored anywhere and has an additional feature like it can send the notification mail to the user if any malpractice noticed on camera. Additionally, it is location independent and secured system with video streaming facility, the mail will pop-up as soon as the unexpected activity is noticed in the room.

A single system gives the multiple facilities includes room conditions control, patient body parameters reading recording and sharing, feedback oriented movement and activities capturing, interactive sessions using live video streaming, face detection facility for safety, alert email notifications etc.

This handy, user friendly and cost effective system further can be tuned for monitoring disabled person, baby, aged persons as well as regular home and offices monitoring in day-to-day life.

With the help of Assistive Technology (AT) and Rehabilitative Technology (RT) this is the gift from my side to the person who are alone and struggle during rehabilitation. I wish to donate the system to the society through this publication.

Acknowledgment. Thanks to RGSTC: Rajiv Gandhi Science and Technology Commission, Government of Maharashtra, Science and Technology Scheme "Assistance for S&T applications through University System" at RTMNU – Rashtrasant Tukadoji Maharaj Nagpur University, Nagpur (MS), India. For Research Grant Support for "Real Time Patient Monitoring System" Letter No.: RTMNU/IIL/RGSTC/P/2021/795, Dt. 12 February 2021.

References

1. Benitez, L.M.V., Tabie, M., Will, N., Schmidt, S., Jordan, M., Kirchner, E.A.: Exoskeleton technology in rehabilitation: towards an EMG-based Orthosis system for upper limb neuro-motor rehabilitation. J. Robot. **2013**, 13 (2013). Article ID 610589, https://doi.org/10.1155/2013/610589
2. Laut, J., Porfiri, M., Raghavan, P.: The present and future of robotic technology in rehabilitation. Curr. Phys. Med. Rehabil. Rep. **4**, 312–319 (2016)
3. Bonato, P.: Advances in wearable technology for rehabilitation. In: Series Studies in Health Technology and Informatics, Ebook: Advanced Technologies in Rehabilitation, vol. 145, pp. 145–159 (2009). https://doi.org/10.3233/978-1-60750-018-6-145
4. Yang, T.: Application of virtual reality technology in rehabilitation training by rehabilitation medical students in universities. In: Sugumaran, V., Xu, Z., Zhou, H. (eds.) MMIA 2021. AISC, vol. 1384, pp. 543–549. Springer, Cham (2021). https://doi.org/10.1007/978-3-030-74811-1_79
5. Schultheis, M.T., Rizzo, A.A.: The application of virtual reality technology in rehabilitation. Rehabil. Psychol. **46**(3), 296–311 (2001)
6. Xiang, G., et al.: Clinical guidelines on the application of Internet of Things (IOT) medical technology in the rehabilitation of chronic obstructive pulmonary disease. J. Thoracic Dis. **13**(8), 4629–4637 (2021). https://doi.org/10.21037/jtd-21-670

7. Talmale, G., Shrawankar, U.: Dynamic clustered hierarchical real time task assignment & resource management for IoT based smart human organ transplantation system. In: 2017 Conference on Emerging Devices and Smart Systems (ICEDSS), pp. 103–109. IEEE (2017)
8. Talmale, G., Shrawankar, U.: Real time on bed medical services: a technological gift to the society. Biosci. Biotechnol. Res. Commun. **13**(14), 133–137 (2020)
9. Shrawankar, U., Talmale, G.: Cloud model for real-time healthcare services. In: Cloud Computing Technologies for Smart Agriculture and Healthcare, pp. 139–149. Chapman and Hall/CRC (2021)
10. Tebje, K.S.D., Suryadevara, N.K., Mukhopadhyay, C.S.: Towards the implementation of IoT for environmental condition monitoring in homes. Sens. J. IEEE **13**(10), 3846–3853 (2013)
11. Lai, C.-F., Chao, H.-C., Lai, Y.-X., Wan, J.: Cloud-assisted real-time transrating for http live streaming. IEEE Wirel. Commun. **20**(3), 62–70 (2013)
12. Wazalwar, S., Shrawankar, U.: Community cloud service model for people with special needs. In: Cloud Computing Technologies for Smart Agriculture and Healthcare, pp. 47–55. Chapman and Hall/CRC (2021)
13. Wazalwar, S., Shrawankar, U.: Online healthcare consultation system for deaf & dumb during pandemic situation. Biosci. Biotechnol. Res. Commun. **13**(14), 213–216 (2020)
14. Balpande, M., Shrawankar, U.: Medical image fusion techniques for remote surgery. In: 2013 Annual IEEE India Conference (INDICON), pp. 1–6. IEEE (2013)
15. Talmale, G., Shrawankar, U.: Dynamic clustered hierarchical real time scheduling for IoT based human organ transplantation. Int. J. Control Theory Appl. **10**(14), 239–249 (2017). ISSN: 0974-5572
16. Talmale, G., Shrawankar, U.: Real-time cyber-physical system for healthcare monitoring in COVID-19. Int. J. Web-Based Learn. Teach. Technol. (IJWLTT) **17**(5), 1–10 (2022). https://doi.org/10.4018/IJWLTT.297622
17. Talmale, G., Shrawankar, U.: Tasks scheduling using dynamic cluster-based hierarchical realtime scheduler for autonomous car. Ambient Sci. **8**(2), 01–06 (2021). https://doi.org/10.21276/ambi.2021.08.2.ga01
18. Talmale, G., Shrawankar, U.: Cluster formation techniques for hierarchical real time tasks allocation on multiprocessor system. Concurr. Comput. Pract. Experience **33**, e6438 (2021)
19. Talmale, G., Shrawankar, U.: Cluster based real time scheduling for distributed system (2021)

A Novel Approach to Analyse Lung Cancer Progression and Metastasis Using Page Rank Technique

Hema Dubey[1]([✉]), Nilay Khare[2], and Prabhat Kumar[1]

[1] Department of Accessory Design, National Institute of Fashion Technology, Bhopal, India
hema.dubey@nift.ac.in
[2] Department of Computer Science and Engineering, Maulana Azad National Institute of
Technology, Bhopal, India

Abstract. Lung cancer is the most prevalent cause of cancer mortality worldwide, accountable for about 1 in 5 cancer-related deaths, or an estimated 1.6 million people. It is generally assumed that metastasis is the principal cause of high mortality rate of lung cancer. It is widely accepted that cancer metastasis is a dreadful hindrance for effective treatment of lung cancer. To address this problem, in this paper, PageRank technique is proposed to analyse the metastatic progression of primary lung cancer. We perform experiments on dataset obtain from post-mortem tissue examination of 3827 autopsies, performed between 1914 and 1943 on untreated patients from 5 affiliated medical centres, reporting all primary tumour locations and metastatic sites from this populace. We analyse that primary lung cancers tend to metastasize with different frequencies to different metastatic sites. Generally, regional lymph nodes are the most frequent metastatic target whereas uterus is the least common.

Keywords: Lung cancer · Metastasis · PageRank

1 Introduction

Lung cancer is the most widespread cancer in the world and accounts for 12.3% of all new cancer cases with millions of deaths per year [1]. According to reports by the American Lung Association, the huge majority of patients newly diagnosed with lung cancer (nearly 85%) have metastases to other parts of the body [2, 7]. In the Human body, normal cells grow, divide, and die in a controlled way and with an estimated lifespan. Most of the cells divide only to replace old cells or to repair the damage [10, 19, 20]. Malignancy cells have been destroyed in such a manner that they have lost their normal control mechanisms. They grow and divide abnormally at a rapid rate, and live longer than their normal lifespan [21]. Most of the cancer types lead to the formation of tumours that is abnormal clusters of cells [22–24]. However, not all tumours are cancerous. Tumours that cannot invade nearby tissues or spread to other body parts are known as benign tumours. With rare exclusions, benign tumours do not cause severe

N. Khare et al. (Eds.): MIND 2022, CCIS 1762, pp. 153–161, 2022.
https://doi.org/10.1007/978-3-031-24352-3_13

illness and are not life threatening [25, 26]. Malignant tumours are cancerous tumours that can invade and destroy neighbouring tissues and organs, and spread to other parts of the body. This process of spreading cancer cells from one part of the body to another distant location is called metastasis [27, 28].

A schematic diagram associated with the metastatic process of cancer has shown in Fig. 1.

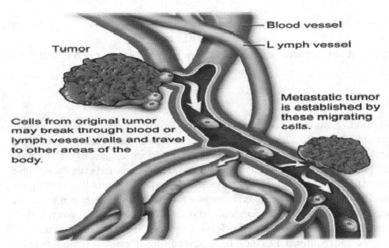

Fig. 1. Cancer metastatic process. Source: Copyright © 2005 Nucleus Medical Art (www.nucleu sinc.com). All rights reserved.

Cancer can spread when cells break off from the tumour, from where it has originally started to another part of the body through the bloodstream or the lymph system. The original cancer is called the primary tumour and cancer in another part of the body is called metastatic or secondary cancer [14, 16]. These secondary cancers are identified by their site of origin. Thus, a lung cancer that metastasizes to the brains is still known as a lung cancer. Metastasis is the most deadly characteristic of any type of cancer and results from a series of interconnected processes consisting of (i) local infiltration of tumour cells into the neighbouring tissue, (ii) trans-endothelial migration of cancer cells into blood vessels or lymph vessels termed as intravasation, (iii) survival in the circulatory system, (iv) extravasation refers to cancer cells exiting the circulatory system and entering distant organs and (v) proliferation denotes multiplication of cancer cells at the distant location to form small tumours known as micro-metastases [27, 29].

Metastatic progression represents the major reason for the death of cancer patients [11–13]. Metastasis is accountable for 90% of the deaths caused by cancer [18, 30]. Therefore, increased knowledge of metastatic patterns is vital in the treatment of cancer patients.

Hence, there is a growing interest in the field of medical science to use some mathematical models to predict the spread of cancer. In this paper, we propose a novel approach to the study of metastases. Here we introduce PageRank Prestige parameter to describe metastatic patterns of lung cancer. We applied PageRank technique on the cancer dataset described in [2] to rank the metastatic sites for primary lung cancer, which helps in finding out with how much probability tumour cells can affect which body organ. The proposed work presents a quantitative framework for charting the statistical or probabilistic description of the metastatic progression of primary lung cancer to metastatic targets.

2 Materials and Methods

2.1 Dataset Description

The dataset used in this work was obtain from the post-mortem tissue examination in [2], in which metastatic distributions in a population of 3827 died cancer patients were analysed. None of these cancer patients received chemotherapy or radiation treatment. The autopsies were performed between 1914 and 1943 at 5 different affiliated medical centres, including 41 primary tumour types, and 30 different metastatic locations. The dataset shows cancer distribution to various sites in the dead patients A great benefit to use this dataset is that we are capable to construct a network centred on the natural progression of tumour cells (in untreated cancer patients). This paper focuses on a model for primary lung cancer; therefore, we have considered only those metastatic sites, which are associated with primary lung cancer. The 27 metastatic sites for primary lung tumour as deduced from the dataset of [2] are Adrenal, Bone, Bladder, Brain, Diaphragm, Gallbladder, Heart, Kidney, Lung, Large Intestine, Liver, Lymph Nodes (reg), Lymph Nodes (dist), Omentum, Pancreas, Pericardium, Peritoneum, Pleura, Prostate, Skeletal Muscle, Skin, Small Intestine, Spleen, Stomach, Thyroid, Uterus and Vagina. Based on these 27 metastatic sites, a metastatic network-based model of lung cancer growth and metastases is constructed, on which PageRank algorithm is performed.

The 27 metastatic locations associated with lung cancer are connected in the form of a graph or network with incoming and outgoing links to other sites as shown in Fig. 2. Cancer spreads across the network from an initial site to metastatic sites. Figure 2 is created based on standard dataset taken from [2]. Nodes with red colour denote the body organs and edges (shown in blue colour) denote the cancer progression from one body organ to another. The PageRank technique is applied on this web graph to analyse with how much probability can lung cancer metastases to other metastatic sites (body organs).

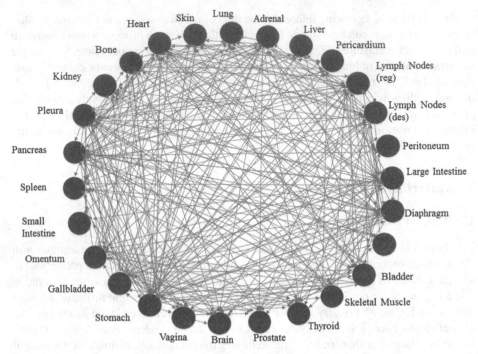

Fig. 2. Web graph consisting of 27 metastatic sites for lung cancer.

2.2 PageRank Algorithm

The main idea behind the Rank prestige [4, 5] is the propagation of importance from one node (web page) towards others, via its outgoing edges (links). Rank prestige considers the prominence of individual actors who do the voting. Votes cast by "important" web pages (nodes) are more prestigious and help to make other pages more "important". For example, in the real world, a company chief officer voting for a person is much more imperative than an employee voting for that person is. Thus, prestige of an actor is influenced by the ranks of the involved actors. For computing the rank vector for all pages of a web graph, we iteratively perform the following PageRank formula until the values stabilize within some threshold.

$$RP_{i+1}(x) = \frac{(1-\alpha)}{N} + \alpha \sum_{y \in S_x} \frac{RP_i(y)}{N_y} \tag{1}$$

In Eq. 1, N is the total number of nodes present within the web graph, $RP_{i+1}(x)$ is the Rank Prestige of node x at iteration $i + 1$, S_x denotes a set consisting of all incoming links of node x, y is node which belongs to set S_x, RP_i is Rank Prestige of node y at iteration i, N_y is total number of outgoing links from node y. α is a damping factor that connotes the probability of a user going along with hyperlinks present in the web graph and its value lies between 0 and 1. The value of α is usually set to 0.85 as suggested by google [5, 6]. 1-α identifies the probability of a user skipping to a random web page after he abandoned clicking on hyperlinks.

Rank Prestige is based on Markov chain model, in which states are represented as nodes and transitions correspond to hyperlinks between web pages [3, 4]. Cancer dataset can be depicted in the form of a web graph. Rank Prestige can be applied to cancer dataset to predict the most dangerous cancer metastatic sites. Metastatic locations with high Rank Prestige are measured to be most infected sites. Rank calculation is based on a Random Surfer model, in which a random surfer (user) starts surfing from a node (web page) and goes from one node (web page) to another node (web page) following hyperlinks on the web graph. Similar concept can be applied to cancer web graph Fig. 2 in which the cancer cells progress from one body organ (node) to another body organ (node) representing metastatic progression of primary lung cancer.

3 Results and Discussion

Not all the body organs (nodes) in a web graph are of equal importance. Based on the in links and out links connectivity in the network, some nodes are more significant than other nodes. We have computed the PageRank scores for the 27 metastatic sites (body organs) associated with lung cancer.

We have calculated rank prestige scores for various metastatic sites for primary lung cancer based on formula 1. Table 1 depicts the rank scores for 27 metastatic sites in decreasing order using damping factor $(\alpha) = 0.85$. The results show that this algorithm is taking 109 iterations to converge using $\alpha = 0.85$. Based on Rank Prestige values, we conclude that the most common metastatic targets for primary lung cancer are regional lymph nodes having highest score $= 2.45$, then distant lymph nodes $= 2.33$, Adrenal $= 2.33$, Liver $= 2.21$, lung $= 2.19$, bone $= 2.07$, kidney $= 2.02$ and the least common is uterus having rank prestige value $= 0.18$. Since Rank prestige algorithm states that if a web page (node) is having high rank value, then it means that the web page (node) is more important. So, in the case of lung cancer metastases, the metastatic site with highest rank value is highly affected.

There is a correlation between cancer metastases and rank prestige algorithm, in a way that cancerous cells transmit from primary origin to other body organs in a similar way as certain web pages have so many incoming links from other web pages.

The experimental results are illustrated in connection with a random surfer, who starts from the lung site and traverses across the web graph (network), moving from body organ (site) to another, following one of the out links available to it at the node (site) he is leaving. Table 1 shows the rank values for different metastatic locations related with lung cancer and also displays with how much percentage metastatic sites can have metastases. So, we conclude from Table 1 that regional lymph nodes have 100% possibilities to be infected, then secondly distant lymph nodes have 96.10% chances to be injured and uterus is least to be infected.

One more interesting finding we have shown in Table 2, taking 7 different damping factors (α) viz. 0.35, 0.45, 0.55, 0.65, 0.75, 0.85, and 0.95 in rank Prestige calculation. The value of (α) is always set between 0 and 1, since it is a probability of a random surfer following hyperlinks. We can analyse from Table 3 that if α is more towards zero, then Rank Prestige algorithm takes few iterations to converge and if α is more towards one, then Rank Prestige algorithm takes more iterations to converge. It can also be analysed

Table 1. Rank prestige for 27 metastatic sites (taking $\alpha = 0.85$) along with how much percentage metastatic sites can have metastases.

S. No.	Metastatic sites (body organs)	Rank prestige	Percentage
1	Lymph Nodes (reg)	2.44862747035817	100%
2	Lymph Nodes (dist)	2.33484127507637	96.1%
3	Adrenal	2.30353471157211	92.30%
4	Liver	2.21109303963487	88.40%
5	Lung	2.18974851629031	84.60%
6	Bone	2.07314720857732	80.70%
7	Kidney	2.0268511631638	76.90%
8	Pleura	1.88768479940225	73.00%
9	Pancreas	1.86118522221911	69.20%
10	Spleen	1.5343545940454	65.30%
11	Heart	1.43539349973041	61.50%
12	Brain	0.367294128100489	57.60%
13	Thyroid	0.349803931524275	53.80%
14	Pericardium	0.348438372214567	46.10%
15	Diaphragm	0.348438372214567	46.10%
16	Peritoneum	0.315031972021157	42.30%
17	Large Intestine	0.312808206824053	38.40%
18	Skin	0.310565391062234	34.60%
19	Gallbladder	0.309951495615135	30.70%
20	Small Intestine	0.309184261367464	26.90%
21	Stomach	0.283874359420954	23.00%
22	Omentum	0.281118841962247	19.20%
23	Prostate	0.268987516353644	15.30%
24	Vagina	0.262961849254599	7.60%
25	Bladder	0.243405549156841	6.3%
26	Skeletal Muscle	0.20244156989535	11.50%
27	Uterus	0.179232235172032	0.00%

Table 2. Rank prestige computation with different damping factors.

S. N	Damping factor (α)	Number of iterations taken to converge
1	0.35	19
2	0.45	24
3	0.55	32
4	0.65	43
5	0.75	63
6	0.85	109
7	0.95	322

from Table 3 that the rank prestige scores become more accurate when damping factor is closer towards 1. Therefore, that is the reason why damping factor is chosen to be 0.85.

Table 3. Rank prestige scores for 27 metastatic sites associated with primary lung cancer with seven different values of damping factor (α)

S. No	Nodes	Rank Prestige scores						
		α = 0.35	α = 0.45	α = 0.55	α = 0.65	α = 0.75	α = 0.85	α = 0.95
1	Lymph Nodes (reg)	1.39090681173547	1.53917878332575	1.71116283771943	1.91333627376392	2.154779194824	2.44862470358817	2.81462130614897
2	Lymph Nodes (dist)	1.36023413120723	1.49689778564522	1.65540642155511	1.8471354201784	2.06416710079697	2.33484127507637	2.67188347606275
3	Adrenal	1.33830841919231	1.47027489959265	1.62512941525206	1.80912539683196	2.03103351837158	2.30353471157211	2.64569112479766
4	Liver	1.31476795651925	1.43744948680351	1.58134357926851	1.752356820113	1.95824170315738	2.21109303963487	2.5234263825634
5	Lung	1.30763573866407	1.42799390141212	1.56937299909775	1.7350406508588	1.94042142434454	2.18974851629031	2.50295329471144
6	Bone	1.28333500742075	1.38909808291153	1.5157468349155	1.66041256459	1.84937441650467	2.07314720857732	2.35399005058653
7	Kidney	1.27957709988927	1.38830161204393	1.51095030490248	1.652906714195	1.82228481798087	2.0268511631638	2.28039053625554
8	Pleura	1.23122419560149	1.3211363611737	1.4265365842561	1.5516763029009	1.70251697534741	1.88768479940225	2.12014531299454
9	Pancreas	1.21539757103013	1.30183471770005	1.4043266594799	1.52721032083095	1.67656503683356	1.86118522221911	2.09428647381048
10	Spleen	1.13868159058225	1.19270354441053	1.25610969218015	1.3314933425137	1.42248918917456	1.5343545940454	1.67498917488225
11	Heart	1.11196954259969	1.15589164342593	1.2075775913885	1.26516690281432	1.34365904499377	1.43539349973041	1.5508918118846
12	Brain	0.904089429073015	0.846548334541821	0.770023280528165	0.6695657731813121	0.538694806075678	0.367294128100489	0.140731074624578
13	Thyroid	0.885851313789123	0.824717575198336	0.745891496807909	0.64505751846023	0.515930537706284	0.349803931524275	0.135282911900714
14	Pericardium	0.883254306658543	0.821995439916355	0.74318907278143	0.642558672237533	0.513931195616302	0.348438372214567	0.132765012477875
15	Diaphragm	0.883254306658543	0.821995439916355	0.74318907278143	0.642558672237533	0.513931195616302	0.348438372214567	0.132765012477875
16	Peritoneum	0.836338461782933	0.769016433679389	0.688021348047927	0.5891472481770978	0.467742309448397	0.315031972021157	0.116387288750501
17	Large Intestine	0.833760506018265	0.766008430197904	0.684770406110198	0.586473919513257	0.46476821935977	0.312808206824053	0.118455265331772
18	Skin	0.83340489657894	0.764984597236722	0.683152560825987	0.584730919513257	0.462254061908362	0.310565391062234	0.117394600056673
19	Gall-bladder	0.830827236134867	0.762279036653911	0.680670728370608	0.5820022482039835	0.461104837829999	0.309951495615135	0.117264750385853
20	Small Intestine	0.830642043455459	0.762231648038327	0.680342248737513	0.58142323598571	0.46023023693145	0.309184261367464	0.116670340127201
21	Stomach	0.801574189034287	0.7279988669597	0.643306153431731	0.544341147072317	0.426657155267911	0.283874359420954	0.106284358864788
22	Omentum	0.7974896969784802	0.723474863400168	0.638664407997229	0.539822159978331	0.42285644605322	0.281118841962247	0.105175250467974
23	Prostate	0.78518981555953	0.708658039682899	0.622187196427555	0.522887588927354	0.407144826129122	0.268987516353644	0.09993863612365775
24	Vagina	0.778599226797797	0.700841455495765	0.613633386309789	0.51431679045657	0.399231217242565	0.262961849254599	0.0971442162105251
25	Bladder	0.752681482393631	0.671335368020908	0.582571157435005	0.4846969976854	0.372581031614936	0.243405549156841	0.0894828519969948
26	Skeletal Muscle	0.707229254497703	0.617714371049896	0.524087625491952	0.425035066864372	0.318711019914059	0.202441569898535	0.0722044628477191
27	Uterus	0.683779104795665	0.589511012759561	0.492736876846598	0.392791078465382	0.288739915850929	0.179232235172032	0.0622374393554406

The experimental results describe the probabilistic model for metastatic progression of lung cancer considering all the possible pathways. We have proven experimentally that if a person is suffering from primary lung cancer, then there is possibility to spread the disease from lungs to other body organs (sites) with different degree prestige values, proximity prestige values and rank prestige values. The tumour progression is not rigorously one-dimensional from primary cancer to other metastatic sites, rather it is multi-dimensional. So, the results help in making quantitative predictions in finding out which body locations can have metastases (infected) if a patient has primary lung cancer.

4 Conclusion

The proposed research work uses social network parameters such as degree prestige, proximity prestige and rank prestige with an aim to quantitatively analyse the lung cancer progression (metastasis) to other body organs. In this paper we have presented quantitative investigation of metastatic patterns of primary lung cancer based on data obtained from post mortem tissue analysis of 3827 autopsies. From the experimental results we conclude that regional and distant lymph nodes are the most common metastatic targets. Adrenal, liver, lung, bone and kidneys are the next most frequent metastatic targets, and uterus is the least common. With the help of these results, doctors who are treating patients of primary lung cancer can easily detect the other body organs, which are at high risk.

References

1. Chen, L., Blumm, N., Christakis, N., Baraba'si, A., Deisboeck, T.: Cancer metastasis networks and the prediction of progression patterns. Br. J. Cancer **101**, 749–758 (2009)
2. DiSibio, G., French, S.: Metastatic patterns of cancers: results from a large autopsy study. Arch. Pathol. Lab. Med. **132**, 931–939 (2008)
3. Bu, Y.M., Huang, T.Z.: An adaptive reordered method for computing PageRank. J. Appl. Math. **2013**, 1–6 (2013)
4. Dubey, H., Roy, B.N.: An improved PageRank algorithm based on optimized normalization technique. IJCSIT **2**(5), 2183–2188 (2011)
5. Brin, S., Page, L., Motwani, R., Winograd, T.: The PageRank citation ranking: bringing order to the web. Technical Report 1999-0120. Computer Science Department, Stanford University, Stanford, CA, USA (1999)
6. Brin, S., Page, L.: The anatomy of a large-scale hypertextual web search engine. Comput. Netw. ISDN **30**(1–7), 107–117 (1998)
7. Alvarez, J.G.B., et al.: Advances in immunotherapy for treatment of lung cancer. Cancer Biol. Med. **12**, 209–222 (2015)
8. Dubey, H., Khare, N., Kuttan, K.K.A., Bhatia, S.: Improved parallel PageRank algorithm for spam filtering. Indian J. Sci. Technol. **9**(38), 1–7 (2016)
9. Newman, M., Watts, D., Strogatz, S.: Random graph models of social networks. Proc. Natl. Acad. Sci. **99**, 2566–2572 (2002)
10. Campbell, S., Buffalo, S.: The space between: a previously unrecognized and pervasive space in the body may hold solutions for cancer metastasis. Immunother. Fibrosis Treat. IEEE Pulse **9**(5), 12–15 (2018)

11. Gotte, M., Kovalszky, I.: Extracellular matrix functions in lung cancer. Matrix Biol. **73**, 105–121 (2018)
12. Liu, T.C., Jin, X., Wang, Y., Wan, K.: Role of epidermal growth factor receptor in lung cancer and targeted therapies. Am. J. Cancer Res. **7**(2), 187–202 (2017)
13. Julie, A., Barta, M.D., Ralph, G., Zinner, M.D., Michael, U.M.D.: Lung cancer in the older patient. Clin. Geriatr. Med. **33**(4), 563–577 (2017)
14. Florian, J., Ravi, V., McDermott, S., Matthew, D., Inga, T.: Lung cancer screening: why, when, and how? Radiol. Clin. North Am. **55**(6), 1163–1181 (2017)
15. Hogg, R.V., McKean, J.W., Craig, A.T.: Introduction to Mathematical Statistics, 7th edn. England, London (2004)
16. Hanahan, D., Weinberg, R.A.: The hallmarks of cancer. Cell **2000**(100), 57–70 (2000)
17. Tsalatsanis, A., Barnes, L., Hozo, I., Skvoretz, J., Djulbegovic, B.: A social network analysis of treatment discoveries in cancer. PLoS ONE **6**(3), 1–9 (2011)
18. Ishii, H., Tempo, R., Bai, E.: A web aggregation approach for distributed randomized PageRank algorithms. IEEE Trans. Automat. Control **57**(11), 2703–2717 (2012)
19. Agrawal, A.: Lytic Skeletal Metastasis from Lung Cancer. Indian J. Clin. Pract. **24**(6), 572–573 (2013)
20. Winter, C., et al.: Google goes cancer: improving outcome prediction for cancer patients by network-based ranking of marker genes. PLoS Comput. Biol. **8**(5), 1–16 (2012)
21. Riihimaki, M., et al.: Metastatic sites and survival in lung cancer. Lung Cancer **2014**(86), 78–84 (2014)
22. Halakou, F., Gursoy, A., Kilic, E.S., Keskin, O.: Topological, functional, and structural analyses of protein-protein interaction networks of breast cancer lung and brain metastases. In: IEEE Conference on Computational Intelligence in Bioinformatics and Computational Biology, Manchester, UK, 23–25 August 2017, pp. 1–7 (2017)
23. Sfakianakis, S., Bei, E.S., Zervakis, M., Vassou, D., Kafetzopoulos, D.: On the identification of circulating tumor cells in breast cancer. IEEE J. Biomed. Health Inform. **18**(3), 773–782 (2014)
24. Daraselia, N., et al.: Molecular signature and pathway analysis of human primary squamous and adenocarcinoma lung cancers. Am. J. Cancer Res. **2**(1), 93–103 (2012)
25. Liao, W., Jordaan, G., Srivastava, M.K., Dubinett, S., Sharma, S., Sharma, S.: Effect of epigenetic histone modifications on E-cadherin splicing and expression in lung cancer. Am. J. Cancer Res. **3**(4), 374–389 (2013)
26. Donia, M., et al.: The real-world impact of modern treatments on the survival of patients with metastatic melanoma. Eur. J. Cancer **108**, 25–32 (2018)
27. Gogichadze, G., Gogichadze, T., Mchedlishvili, E.: Assumptions about the invasion and metastatic processes of carcinogenesis. Br. J. Cancer Res. **1**(2), 153–155 (2018)
28. Wang, X., Adjei, A.A.: Lung cancer and metastasis: new opportunities and challenges. Cancer Metastasis Rev. **34**(2), 169–171 (2015). https://doi.org/10.1007/s10555-015-9562-4
29. SoneEmail, S., Yano, S.: Molecular pathogenesis and its therapeutic modalities of lung cancer metastasis to bone. Cancer Metastasis Rev. **26**, 685–689 (2007)
30. Fry, W.A., Menck, H.R., Winchester, D.P.: The National Cancer Data Base report on lung cancer. Cancer **77**(9), 1947–1955 (1996)

Homomorphic Encryption of Neural Networks

Purnendu Shekhar Pandey[1]($\boxtimes$), Vinod Kumar[2]($\boxtimes$), and Ruth Wario[3]

[1] Department of Computer Science and Engineering, KIET Group of Institutions, Ghaziabad, India
purnendu.pandey@kiet.edu
[2] Department of Computer Science and Engineering, GNIOT, Greater Noida, India
vinod242306@gmail.com
[3] Department of Computer Science and Informatics, University of the Free State, Bloemfontein, South Africa

Abstract. The modern world is moving towards an intelligent future where AI and ML will be playing an important role in improving technologies across all domains. The most basic requirement for training an ML model is data. Without the availability of data, there is no use for AI or ML. Data is freely and openly available but still, the privacy of the data is a deeper concern, which can create hurdles in developing new technologies. This paper suggests various ways which can be used to train ML models on such private data while maintaining the privacy of both the data as well as the ML model, using homomorphic encryption. This paper implemented a neural network on homomorphic encryption and proved the increase in accuracy of finding attacks over data on the fly and data at still. Thus, this paper mainly focuses on what happens when we apply Neural networks along with Homomorphic Encryption over data on still and data on the fly.

Keywords: Homomorphic Encryption · Neural Networks · Security · AI · Attack-detection

1 Introduction

In today's world, cryptography plays an important role in our lives. Virtually every communication of ours over the internet is encrypted. This all started with the development of symmetric encryptions where the two communicating parties, say Alice and Bob used a secret key to encrypt and decrypt their communications. The key was meant to be kept a secret by Alice and Bob so that an adversary, say, Eve is not able to eavesdrop on their conversation. The main problem arises when it was time to exchange these secret keys over the internet. There was no method to securely transfer it over the internet. This is when public key encryption came into the picture. It allows this paper two people to exchange secrets over the internet without using a key that needs to be shared by both of them. The key that Alice and Bob are using in this paper could now be shared using asymmetric encryption techniques. But then the researchers started to think of a technique that not only would encrypt the data to protect it from eavesdroppers but would also allow the user to keep it hidden from the person/resource which is providing the user

N. Khare et al. (Eds.): MIND 2022, CCIS 1762, pp. 162–173, 2022.
https://doi.org/10.1007/978-3-031-24352-3_14

some services using his/her data. So, researchers started finding encryption techniques that would allow computation on the encrypted data as if it is being performed on plain data. This would solve the issue of sharing private, personal, and sensitive data with third parties for the services provided by them. This is called the homomorphic encryption technique.

Homomorphic encryption enables us to perform computations over cipher texts. And when this algorithm decrypts it, gets the plain text which would reflect all those operations performed on the encrypted text. There are different kinds of homomorphic encryptions techniques such as partially homomorphic, which allows only one kind of operation to be performed or limits the number of times an operation can be performed; the second one is fully homomorphic encryption, which allows several operations any number of times.

This paper selected this encryption system because it is very efficient compared to other techniques. And efficiency is a major bottleneck for using homomorphic encryption on Neural networks. In this paper, we have shown the effect of homographic encryption over encrypting data, and then we will show how the security improves once we apply homographic encryption along with Neural Network. Thus, this paper mainly focuses on what happens when we apply Neural networks along with Homomorphic Encryption over data on still and data on the fly.

2 Literature Survey

2.1 Homomorphism

Homomorphism may be defined according to two operations, i.e. addition and multiplication. Below are the equations representing the properties of homomorphic encryption:

"*Homomorphic encryption is additive if:*

$$Enc(x + y) = Enc(x) + Enc(y) \tag{1}$$

Homomorphic encryption is multiplicative if:

$$Enc(x * y) = Enc(x) * Enc(y) \tag{2}$$

A homomorphic encryption system is made up of some building blocks which are presented below:

1. **Key generation:** This block outputs a public key and a secret key to be used by the user.
2. **Encryption algorithm:** This block takes the message and the public key as the input and outputs the cipher text.
3. **Decryption algorithm:** This block takes the secret key and the cipher text as the input and gives the message as the output.
4. **Evaluation function:** This block takes input as an evaluation key, circuit (realized using logic gates), and a group of cipher texts and outputs a single cipher text which would represent the result of the calculations performed on the cipher texts [2].

2.2 Partially Homomorphic Systems

Partially homomorphic systems have some limitations to the number and type of operations which can be performed on the cipher texts. Some techniques support only addition,
some support only multiplication, while some support both but one of the operations
can be performed a limited number of times. Based on these properties, these systems
can be divided into the following categories:

2.3 Additive Homomorphic Systems

These systems allow any number of additions to the cipher texts. Some of the techniques
include the Goldwasser-Micali system [3], and the Pallier system [4]. It allows any number of addition operations over the cipher texts. The cipher in this scheme is calculated
according to the following equation

$$C_i = g^{m_i}.r^n.modn^2 \tag{3}$$

$$C_j = g^{m_j}.r^n.modn^2 \tag{4}$$

$$C_i.C_j = g^{m_i+m_j}.(r_i.r_j)^n.modn^2 \tag{5}$$

where,
  C = cipher text
  g = number calculated from cryptographic techniques
  r = random number
  m = message/plain text
As this paper can see in the above scheme that if the cipher texts are multiplied and
the resultant cipher text is decrypted, this paper will get the addition of the plain texts
that this paper are encrypted.

2.4 Multiplicative Homomorphic Systems

These systems calculate the cipher texts in such a way that allows the performing operations on cipher text in such a way that it reflects multiplication on plain text. Some
techniques which allow such operations include RSA algorithm [5], ElGamal encryption
scheme [6]. Equations that support the above claims are listed below:

$$C_i = (m_i)^e modn \tag{6}$$

$$C_j = (m_j)^e modn$$

$$C_i.C_j = (m_i.m_j)^e modn \tag{7}$$

where,
  C = cipher text

$m = message$

$e = number\ generated\ by\ cryptographic\ methods$

As this paper can see from the above equations, this paper can perform certain operations on the cipher text so as to produce a cipher text which when decrypted would replicate the multiplication of the plain texts.

2.5 Additive and Multiplicative Homomorphic Encryption Systems

All the previously discussed techniques allothis paperd only one operation, addition or multiplication, to be reflected on plain text. But there are some other techniques as this paperll which allow one of those operations any number of times and other operation a limited number of times. One of such techniques is Boneh-Goh-Nissim cryptosystem [7]. This technique allows any number of additions but allows "at most one multiplication".

2.6 Somewhat Homomorphic Encryption

The way from partially homomorphic systems to fully homomorphic systems goes through somewhat homomorphic systems. These systems like all others have to encrypt and decrypt modules. But they also have an additional module called *evaluate* which is used to perform operations on the cipher texts. While encrypting the plain text, a noise is added to it which is removed while decrypting. Addition usually doubles this noise and multiplication squares the noise. If the noise rises above a certain level, the cipher text cannot be decrypted. So this paper cannot perform operations beyond that. Because of this, these systems are called *somewhat homomorphic encryption systems*. But this can be overcome by using *bootstrapping*. In this process, evaluating the function, which normally works on encrypted texts, is made to run the decrypting module because of which this paper gets other cipher text but with a much lesser amount of noise. So virtually because of bootstrapping, this paper can perform an unlimited number of operations. This leads the way to fully homomorphic encryption. The equations supporting the concept of this technique are listed below:

$$C_i = q_i.p + 2.r_i + m_i \tag{8}$$

$$C_j = q_j.p + 2.r_j + m_j \tag{9}$$

$$C_i + C_j = (q_i + q_j).p + 2.(r_i + r_j) + m_i + m_2 \tag{10}$$

$$C_i.C_j = (q_i.q_j).p + 2.(2.r_i.r_j + r_i.m_j + r_j.m_i) + m_i + m_2 \tag{11}$$

From the above equations, this paper can see the effect of addition and multiplication on the rise in the amount of noise. Also, they show how somewhat homomorphic encryption can be used for computations involving both additions and multiplications.

2.7 Fully Homomorphic Encryption Systems

The scheme from Brakerski and Vaikuntanathan is known as "Fully Homomorphic Encryption without Bootstrapping" where their approach is based on "Learning with Errors and Ring Learning with Errors problems" [8]. This technique is proposed over a ring which makes it support both addition and multiplication as operators over the cipher text. The algorithm doesn't need any bootstrapping, because it is optimized in such a way that any operation performed on the cipher text affects the noise only linearly, and that too to a very small amount. So the noise remains below the threshold and the final cipher text can be decrypted without any problems.

2.8 Encryption Scheme

This encryption scheme was proposed by Zhou and Wornell [1]. Before introducing the scheme, this paper will explain all the variables and notations which are used in the algorithm.

Variables that are used:

- K: This is a matrix that represents Private Key. This will be used as decryption.
- M: This is a matrix that represents the Public key. This will only be used for encryption.
- c: This is a vector representing encrypted data.
- p: This is a vector representing a message or plaintext.
- w: This scaler vector represents this paperght.
- e: This represents added Noise.
- row and col are the size of the matrix (Number of rows and Number of columns respectively).

For a Private Key matrix of row x col K, a plain text or message p, error term e, this paperight w, and Ciphertext c satisfies:

$$Kc = wp + e$$

For Decryption:

$$p = \left\lceil \frac{Kc}{w} \right\rfloor \tag{12}$$

Here, $\lceil c \rfloor$ represents the nearest integer or rounded integer value.

Key Switching

Using the key switching technique one can change the private key of the message without changing the original plaintext.Compute a new private key K' such that:

$$K'.c' = K.c \tag{13}$$

It is a four-step process.

1. First, convert K' to an intermediate private key K* and represent c in its binary form such that new ciphertext |c*|= 1. Ensure that:

$$K^*.c^* = K.c \tag{14}$$

2. Now the intermediate private key and ciphertext are converted to desired key K'. For this construct a switch key matrix M such that:

$$K'M = K^* + e \tag{15}$$

Here, e is the random noise matrix.

3. Now represent $K' = [I, T]$ and calculate M:

$$M = \begin{pmatrix} -TA + K^* + e \\ A \end{pmatrix} \tag{16}$$

4. Now solve c' such that:

$$c' = M.c^* \tag{17}$$

Linear Transformation

Calculate transformation of encrypted text c by R then

$$(RK)'c = wRp + Re \tag{18}$$

Now, the switching technique discussed above to compute switch matrix M and thus c'.

$$c' = M.c \tag{19}$$

3 Proposed Algorithm and Its Application

This paper proposes a homomorphic encrypted Neural Network. A neural network has many different types of operations and for some operations, this paper needs to apply some tricks to work with homomorphically encrypted data. Since the neural network involves gradient descent, which is represented in decimals, and the homographic encryption technique that this paper is using rounds the original message to integer, this paper scale decimals into integers. For example, this paper can scale up every number by 10000 for precision up to 4 decimal digits. But scaling can sometimes result in an overflow of the variable storing the number, so this paper needs to choose the scaling factor appropriately and uniquely for each number. This paper can perform Vector multiplication by using the key switch technique which this paper discusses above. Dot product operations can be computed using the Linear Transformation technique, which is proposed. For a neural network, this paper needs a non-linear activation function. This paper will be using the Sigmoid function:

$$y=1/(1+e^{\wedge}(-x)) \tag{20}$$

Since this homographic encryption technique does not supports exponential function so this paper proposes to use the Taylor series to do polynomial operations and thus this paper can calculate the sigmoid function approximately.

$$e^{\wedge}x=1+x/1!+x^{\wedge}2/2!+x^{\wedge}3/3!+\cdots,-\infty<x<\infty \tag{21}$$

Above, it is the Taylor series expansion of e^x.

Other basic operations such as multiplication and addition are this paper will be supported by this homographic encryption technique.

3.1 Applications

As homomorphic encryption systems become more efficient, their applications will cover very diverse industries. With homomorphic encryption, people won't need to trust 3rd parties with their data. Everything is secure and private fully end-to-end. The User uploads the encrypted data on the cloud server and then 3rd party performs computations over the cipher text and the result, which is also encrypted, can only be decrypted by the user with his key.

3.2 Medical Records

With advancements in machine learning and AI, this paper can predict and diagnose diseases with very fast speed and even better than human experts. CheXNet is a convolution neural network developed by researchers at Stanford which has achieved better results at predicting pneumonia from X-Ray than expert radiologists [9]. This solution can be easily deployed on cloud servers for the usage of doctors around the world. But people are very conscious of sharing their medical data with 3rd parties. If the medical records of a person are leaked to his employers, then he may be subject to discrimination and maybe even fired from his job. So, there's a need to protect data as this paper results.

Genome Analysis
Today with advancements in DNA analysis, this paper can recognize disease risk and create personalized medicines for people. Soon people will be able to share their DNA for analysis and get results about their health profile and disease risks [10]. But to achieve this requires people to share DNA sequences of people. DNA sequences are identity markers that can't be changed. If the DNA of a person is leaked to financial organizations then it may be possible that they reject loan applications from the person just because his DNA sequence suggests that he is at higher risk. So, protecting the privacy of DNA sequences is very important for the success of the DNA Analysis industry. With the use of homomorphic encryption, the privacy of the person and his results can be protected.

Elderly medical data protection. As they can be an easy victim for attackers. To provide them with real-time medical help and to keep their medical information secret, a complex entropy-based encryption approach can be used [12–14].

3.3 Finance and Advertising

Nowadays, banks keep records of their customers to create a risk profile using Machine Learning. But theirs is the threat of data being leaked when it is in decrypted form while being prepared for computations. There are these applications that calculate our credit score, but people don't trust the scoring company for such private information. Now, it's possible that these applications can file our tax returns without decrypting our financial data and ensuring privacy.

Recently, there was the Facebook-Cambridge Analytica Scandal where Facebook said that [11] they trusted Cambridge Analytica for using data of users only for Advertising, but Cambridge Analytica broke their trust and used data to manipulate voters in US presidential elections. If Facebook had used Homographic Encryption on its data, then the privacy of the users could have been saved.

Improvements
The following are the additions made by us to the already proposed algorithm to increase the functionality of the algorithm and to increase the domain of its applicability.

3.4 Neural Network Support

The current paper mentions the implementation of the technique in some ML algorithms like Support Vector Machines, Naïve Bayes, and Linear Regression, but it does not discuss the use in Neural Networks.

Approximation of Nonlinear Function
As this technique of Homomorphic Encryption deals with only integers, implementing a nonlinear function directly as the activation function in a neural network was not possible. To solve this problem, this paper made use of the Taylor series for the activation function and used it to get the approximation of the nonlinear activation function which was very close to the real value and made the prediction more accurate [15].

3.5 Support for Floating Point Numbers

The nonlinear activation function would give a result in floating points. The current technique only uses integers. Converting the floating points to numbers would result in drastically reduced accuracy. So, this paper needed to add support for floating points while keeping the calculations still in integers. This paper did that by scaling up all the calculations to pre-decided. The results at the end would be scaled down again.

3.6 Encrypting Neural Network

There might be some sources that would not be willing to share even the homomorphically encrypted data with us for the training of the model. This paper came up with a solution in which this paper encrypts our NN and sends it to the source for training. The network gets trained over the data and is decrypted once it comes back to us. This way, the privacy of the data of the source will increase [16, 17].

4 Result and Analysis

To compare the proposed neural network including encryption with an unencrypted neural network, this paper plotted their loss vs time graph. The graph of the unencrypted neural network converges very early (1000X) when compared with the encrypted neural network because of the obvious delay in the calculation of encrypted numbers as shown in Fig. 1 and Fig. 2. The graphs are given below:

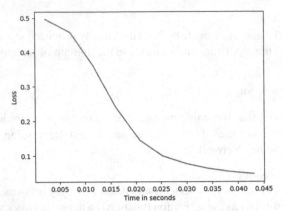

Fig. 1. Loss vs Time graph for normal Neural network

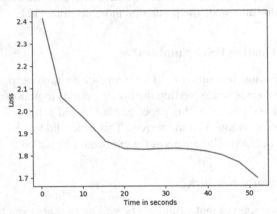

Fig. 2. Loss vs Time graph for Encrypted Neural Network

Also, it was noted that the loss for the encrypted neural network shot up unexpectedly during training when it reached a value below a point as shown in Fig. 2. This is because the loss calculated originally was encrypted which had to be decrypted for comparison. But since this technique does not use bootstrapping, when the value of the loss goes below a certain point, the error value overshadows the original value of the loss, and decryption becomes impossible hence this paper sees the unexpected rise beyond a certain point, as shown in Fig. 3.

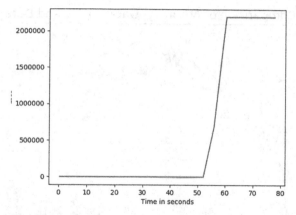

Fig. 3. Loss vs Time where loss shoots up unexpectedly

In Fig. 4, depicts the encryption loss for an increase in epochs. Data on the fly(green line) has more encryption loss as during network congestion or congestion at network interface there will be more packet drop and thus the chances of loss will be more as compared to data on still (blue line).

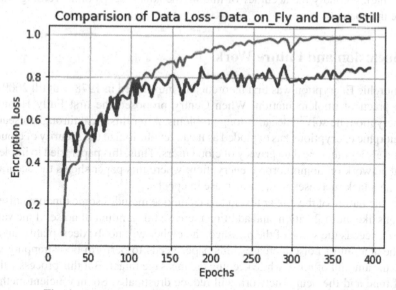

Fig. 4. Comparison of data loss for data on the fly and data still

Figure 5 shows a clear picture that losses may be high but when we need encryption (priority) for real-time applications that need to maintain confidentiality we have to apply homomorphic encryption along with a neural network. This paper clearly shows the accuracy of finding an attack during data on still (green) is more than data on the fly

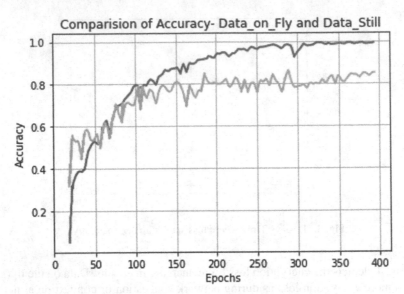

Fig. 5. Comparison of Accuracy for data on fly and data still

(yellow line), secondly the accuracy of finding the attack keeps on increasing with the increase in epochs.

5 Conclusion and Future Work

Homomorphic Encryption was first theoretically introduced in 1978. But till 2009 there was no practical implementation. When Gentry proposed the first Fully Homomorphic Encryption, he solved decades-long problems. After this breakthrough, research in Homomorphic encryptions has exploded as it can revolutionize the security of cloud services and also protect the data privacy of cloud users. Thus, this paper tried to implement a neural network on homomorphic encryption, where this paper shows the accuracy of finding an attack increases with an increase in epochs.

The calculation of the cipher text in this technique includes some random noise. The operations like multiplication, and addition increase this amount of noise. If the value of the noise exceeds the value of the message, the cipher will not be decryptable anymore. So as the amount of noise increases, this paper needs to perform bootstrapping which reduces the amount of noise while keeping the message intact. But this process will take a lot of time and the neural network will reduce drastically. So an efficient method of bootstrapping must be found to implement in the present model.

References

1. Zhou, H., Wornell, G.: Efficient homomorphic encryption on integer vectors and its applications. IEEE (2014)
2. D. H., Picek, S.: Homomorphic Encryption in the cloud. IEEE, Zagreb (2014)

3. Gentry, C.: A fully homomorphic encryption scheme. Stanford (2009)
4. Paillier, P.: Public-key cryptosystems based on composite degree residuosity classes. In: Stern, J. (ed.) Advances in Cryptology — EUROCRYPT '99. EUROCRYPT 1999. Lecture Notes in Computer Science, vol. 1592. Springer, Heidelberg (1999). https://doi.org/10.1007/3-540-48910-X_16
5. Rivest, R. L., Adleman, L., Dertouzos, M. L.: On Data Banks and Privacy Homomorphisms. Academia Press (1978)
6. ElGamal, T.: A public key cryptosystem and a signature scheme based on discrete logarithms. In: Blakley, G.R., Chaum, D. (eds.) CRYPTO 1984. LNCS, vol. 196, pp. 10–18. Springer, Heidelberg (1985). https://doi.org/10.1007/3-540-39568-7_2
7. Boneh, D., Goh, E.-J., Nissim, K.: Evaluating 2-DNF formulas on ciphertexts. In: Kilian, J. (ed.) TCC 2005. LNCS, vol. 3378, pp. 325–341. Springer, Heidelberg (2005). https://doi.org/10.1007/978-3-540-30576-7_18
8. Brakerski, Z., Vaikuntanathan, V.: Efficient fully homomorphic encryption from (standard) lthis paper. In: FOCS (2011)
9. Rajpurkar, P., Irvin, J., Zhu, K., Yang, B., Mehta, H.: CheXNet: radiologist-level pneumonia detection on chest x-rays with deep learning. arXiv preprint arXiv:1711.05225 (2017)
10. Farah, S., Sushma, M.S., Asha, T., Cauvery, B., Shivanand, K.S.: DNA based disease prediction using pathway analysis. In: 2017 IEEE 7th International Advance Computing Conference (IACC) (2017)
11. The Guardian (2018). https://www.theguardian.com/technology/2018/mar/21/mark-zuckerberg-response-facebook-cambridge-analytica
12. Kumar, V., Badal, N, Mishra, R.: Elderly fall due to drowsiness: detection and prevention using machine learning and IoT. Mod. Phys. Lett. B **35**, 2150120 (2021)
13. Kumar, V., Badal, N., Mishra, R.: Elderly fall detection using IoT and image processing. J. Discrete Math. Sci. Cryptogr. **24**, 681–695 (2021)
14. Kumar, V., Pathak, V., Badal, N., et al.: Complex entropy based encryption and decryption technique for securing medical images. Multimed Tools Appl. **81**, 37441–37459 (2022). https://doi.org/10.1007/s11042-022-13546-z
15. Harikrishnan, V.K., Deore, H., Raju, P., Agrawal, A., Sharma, M.M.: Predictive analysis using machine learning techniques for fantasy games. In: Manik, G., Kalia, S., Sahoo, S.K., Sharma, T.K., Verma, O.P. (eds.) Advances in Mechanical Engineering. LNME, pp. 683–692. Springer, Singapore (2021). https://doi.org/10.1007/978-981-16-0942-8_65
16. Vijarania, M., Agrawal, A., Sharma, M.M.: Task scheduling and load balancing techniques using genetic algorithm in cloud computing. In: Sharma, T.K., Ahn, C.W., Verma, O.P., Panigrahi, B.K. (eds.) Soft Computing: Theories and Applications. AISC, vol. 1381, pp. 97–105. Springer, Singapore (2021). https://doi.org/10.1007/978-981-16-1696-9_9
17. Chauhan, M., Joon, A., Agrawal, A., Kaushal, S., Kumari, R.: Intrusion detection system for securing computer networks using machine learning: a literature review. In: Sharma, H., Saraswat, M., Yadav, A., Kim, J.H., Bansal, J.C. (eds.) CIS 2020. AISC, vol. 1334, pp. 177–189. Springer, Singapore (2021). https://doi.org/10.1007/978-981-33-6981-8_15

An Empirical Study to Enhance the Accuracy of an Ensemble Learning Model for Crop Recommendation System by Using Bit-Fusion Algorithm

Shraban Kumar Apat[1]([✉]), Jyotirmaya Mishra[1], Neelamadhab Padhy[1], and V. Madhusudan Rao[2]

[1] Department of CSE, GIET University, Gunupur, Odisha, India
{shraban.apat,jyoti}@giet.edu
[2] School of Computer Science and Informatics, Geethanjali College of Engineering and Technology, Keesara, Hyderabad, India
madhuveldanda.cse@gcet.edu.in

Abstract. Agriculture is indispensable to the global economy. In this sense, there is a greater demand for efficient and safe food production methods for increasing food grains. Rice production is predominantly determined by climatic factors such as rainfall, temperature, humidity, fertilisers, and so on. Farmers can take appropriate steps to increase rice production if they receive timely guidance on changes in climatic conditions. This factor motivates the authors to create a computational model for farmers and, ultimately, for society. Information technology is one of the tools serves for this purpose. of late, technological advances such as the use of electronic systems, IoT, ML, DL, and data transmission have resulted in radical changes in the agricultural working environment. Through this paper we wish to present a structured review that focuses to identify the use of new precision in agriculture; India's most produced grain. The main contribution of this work is to present a fusion-based ensemble prediction model for the Rabi season using original rice yield and climatic datasets from three different districts in Odisha, namely Balasore, Kalahandi, and Rayagada, from the year 1993 to 2016. In the construction of a robust model, we have identified six different classifiers, including SVM, Ada Boost, XG-Boost, Gradient Boosting, LSTM, CNN, and one fusion-based ensemble learning, SVM + CNN. To make it possible to combine and analyse various farm data for better prediction. The Proposed Deep learning with SVM and fusion-based algorithms improved performance by 95%, 94%, and 94% for the three districts, respectively. In comparison, existing deep learning methods achieve 94%, 93%, and 90% accuracy. Among the available tools, we highlighted a fusion-based solution combined with deep learning techniques that achieves significant results in crop production.

1 Introduction

Agriculture is the foundation for many countries' social stability and national development, particularly in developing countries. Adequate production of grain and other basic

N. Khare et al. (Eds.): MIND 2022, CCIS 1762, pp. 174–189, 2022.
https://doi.org/10.1007/978-3-031-24352-3_15

agricultural products is primary foundation for ensuring a country's economic stability. As it is the chief food crop, rice is critical to agricultural production [1]. The country's demand for food is increasing in tandem with the country's rapid population growth. We have a problem with deteriorating soil quality and an unpredictability of the environment, which effects the growth status of rice because it plays such a vital role in food security. Since industrialization reduces agrarian land area, it is necessary to increase rice yield to compensate for population growth. Consequently, rice production and the cultivation of high yielding varieties have emerged as major research topics in agricultural research institutions [3]. Rice is the main diet for nearly half the world population, so rice cultivation research is critical to political, economic, and social stability [4]. The significance is laid on achieving highest crop produce through cost-effective methods. This could be made possible if the problems speculated by the crop yield indicators are detected quickly and dealt with them appropriately. This can be attained with prior discovery and dealing the issues related with crop produce pointers. Further, this prognosis can be used to increase crop produce at whichever point the potential for growing conditions exists [5]. Precise forecasting may assist stakeholders in taking relevant and timely decisions. In particular, people involved directly with rice production may avoid disagreeable situations. Reliable and punctual forecasts can provide important and key inputs for planning towards achieving food security in India. As such, the pressing priority is to build models that can precisely predict subsequent agricultural production [7].

To keep up with the country's population and income growth, food production must be doubled by 2050. Subsequently, small and peripheral farmers play a significant role in the Nation's food security and achievement of the SDGs. According to the report State of Food Security and Nutrition in the World, 2020. The Global Hunger Index 2020 ranked India 94th out of 107 countries [8]. Achieving 'zero hunger' by 2030 is a colossal challenge that requires an integrated and multi-dimensional modern approach for the country's overall sustainable agriculture and food systems change and its effect in the form of extreme weather changes is one of the most pressing challenges for a country's food security [9]. Hence, intelligence has been viewed as a further enabler. To that end, the development of deep learning with SVM has provided an effective approach to facilitating intelligent decision making in many aspects of prediction. To assist the prediction process that characterize the agricultural mission in this study, we introduce a novel domain specific dataset from Directorate of Agriculture and Food Production, Ministry of Agriculture and Farmers Empowerment, Govt. of Odisha, specific to rice crops of three districts. In this article exploration of ML, DL and Fusion based techniques in the constructions of robust methods when applied to precision agriculture is being considered.

2 Literature Review

In this section, we discuss relevant prior research pertaining to two aspects. First the application of machine learning algorithms, while the second aspect focuses on machine learning, deep learning and fusion based techniques approaches for smart agriculture and allied decision-making.

Van Kloppenburg et al. [1] used features like temp, rainfall, & type of soil, and applied ANN algorithm in the prescribed models along with this few additional analysis performed on deep learning algorithm- such as CNN, LSTM, &DNN. It was noted that LSTM, DNN & CNN, algorithms are highly preferred DL techniques. Paudel Dilli et al. [2] Along with ML used agronomic to build a ML base to forecast large-scale crop yield with consideration of the following features like crop simulation outputs weather, soil data& remote sensing and used MCYFS database. Experiment has been performed with various crops over different geographical areas. Wang, Y et al. [3] used advanced ML techniques with seasonal data collected from different sources i.e. images from satellite, climatic data, soil etc. author used OLS, LASSO along with four well-known ML Techniques such as SVM, RF, Ada Boost, and DNN in the above study it was found that ada boost method (A reliable prediction ($R2 > 0.84$)) shows better result than other techniques. Guo, Y et al. [4] In this study traditional MLR along with 03 advanced ML Methods such as BP, SVM&RF were considered with phenology, climate and geographical data to forecast rice yields. The results indicates that ML methods shown better results incontrast to MLR method and the difference between RMSE (R2) prediction and observed rice yields were 800 (0.24), 737 (0.33), and 744 (0.31) kg/ha for BP, SVM and RF, respectively.

Bali, N. et al. [5] Survey over more than 80 research paper performed and reasonably gap has been identified. So a good no. of hybrid model and DL methods were summarized as means of crop prediction, Also analysed how various factors like temp, humidity etc. has adverse effect on overall productivity of crops. ANN and ANFIS are capable to produce better result. Good accuracy has been shown by hybridized model which used fuzzy and ANN so hence we can explore more such hybridized techniques in future for better to best predictions. Khaki, et al. [6] Corrn and soybean production has been forcasted in his proposed model which used CNN-RNN techniques along with RF, DFNN, and LASSO, across the entire Corn Belt which includes13 states of USA for the three years. i.e. 2016 to 2018. The proposed model achieved a RMSE 9% and 8% of their respective average yields, and outperforming all other methods that were tested. Chu, Zheng et al. [9] Proposed a novel prediction model which combine two BPNNs with an IndRNN, named BBI-model worked with three stages. The outcome of this model indicate that BBI-model achieved the lowest MAE and RMSE for the summer and winter rice prediction (0.0044, 0.0057), and (0.0074, 0.0192) respectively, when the layers in the network was set to number six. This finding proves that the proposed model can make precise predictions for summer and winter rice yields of at least 81 countries in China. Chu, Zheng, and Jiong [11] To improve the Model's prediction effect, authors combined fractal dimension with traditional rice image features. Their model performed as, with the dry weight prediction model R2 reaching 0.8697, the fresh weight prediction model R2 reaching 0.8631, and the plant height prediction model R2 reaching 0.8631.

Kumar et al. [12] Rice yield prediction using SVM-based classification models used authors experimented with the one-against-one multi classification method, k-fold cross validation, and for SVM training were carried out. For this work, rice production data from India was obtained from the Directorate of Economics and Statistics, Ministry of Agriculture, Government of India. Using the 4-fold cross validation method, the best prediction accuracy for the 4-year relative average increase was 75.06%. The MATLAB software was used. Nishant, Potnuru Sai, et al. [13] Research forecasts the yield of nearly all types of crops grown in India. it uses simple parameters such as state, district, season, and area to predict crop yields by user choice year. The paper predicts yield using advanced regression techniques such as Kernel Ridge, Lasso, and ENet algorithms, as well as the concept of Stacking Regression to improve the algorithms. Used RMSE, ENet it was around 4%, Lasso had an error about 2%, Kernel Ridgewas about 1% and finally after stacking it was less than 1%. Qazi et al. [14] the authors used a three-stage model, with the first stage pre-processing the original area and meteorology data. In stage 2, one BPNN and one IndRNN are used in parallel to learn deep spatial and temporal features. Another BPNN in stage 3 combines two types of deep features and learns the relationships between these deep features and rice yields to make summer and winter predictions. According to the experimental results, the BBI-model had the lowest mean absolute error (MAE) and root mean square error (RMSE) for summer rice prediction (0.0044 and 0.0057, respectively) and corresponding values of 0.0074 and 0.0192 for winter rice prediction.

3 Proposed Methodology

Our proposed model work with three phases as shown in the Fig. 1.

Phase#1: In this phase pre-processing of agricultural data, feature normalization and extraction is carried out to identify the desired features.

Phase#2: Here filtered data is splitted into training set (80%) and testing set (20%).

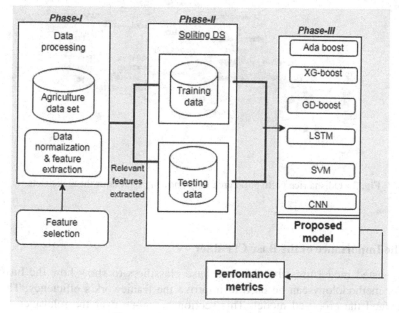

Fig. 1. Proposed three phase model

Phase#3: Our Model is trained with training data and then tested with various Ml algorithms individually as shown in the fig, then it was experimented with the combination of SVM+CNN and stacking ensemble, which shows improvement of the predicted results.

3.1 Dataset Preparation

During the literature review, we investigated various existing methods and discovered that deep learning methods produce better results in the majority of cases. The raw data collected has some missing values and is unclassified. One of the methods for dealing with missing values is to simply replace them with the most insignificant positive real number. D must be in form $D = \{d_i, y_i\}$ for classification, where di refers to features and yi refers to the class label. To forecast rice crop production, the class label must be properly defined. One approach is to use clustering and assign each feature a class label that corresponds to its cluster number.

3.2 Study Area

The proposed work focuses on the major rice-producing states of Odisha, India. Odisha is one of the states in India that contributes significantly to agriculture. Odisha has a total area of 1, 55,707 square kilometers. The total cultivation area is 61.50 lakh hectares. The total area under cultivation for rice is 87.46 lakh hectares. Finally, we have taken three districts: Rayagada, Kalahandi, and Balasore as shown in below Fig. 2

Fig. 2. Odisha rice cultivation area map showing the major three districts

3.3 The Importance of the Base Classifier

The suggested model uses five different base classifiers to show how the bit-fusion classifier methodology can be used to improve the framework's efficiency. They are used to feed the proposed model. This section has gone over the relevance of base classifiers.

SVM: SVM is a critical classifier, that has been characterized by an isolating hyper plane. In two-dimensional, a line which divides a plane in two parts – a hyper plane includes one class on either side. Non-linear class boundaries are created by SVMs.

Ada Boost: These classifiers are meta estimators start fitting a classifier on the original data set and then fit additional copies of the classifiers on the same data set, but the weights of incorrectly classified instances adjusted so that subsequent classifiers focuses more on difficult cases.

XG-Boost: Unlike other Ml algorithms, it is more like an ensemble learning approach. XG-Boost combines the outcome of many other models known to be base learners to forecast.

LSTM: This is a type of ANN used in artificial intelligence and deep learning unlike traditional feed forward neural N/Ws. LSTM includes feedback connections.

CNN: It is a deep learning technique that can take input as a image file assign important learnable weights and biases, to different aspects or objects in the image and differentiate one from other.

4 Results of Experimental Assessment and Simulation

In our study we used Ada boost Classifier Simulation, Gradient Boosting Simulation and XGB Classifier Simulation for measurement of Accuracy, Precision and Sensitivity for the predictive model by considering the confusion matrix as represented in the fig no. 3, 4 & 5.

4.1 Ada Boost Classifier Simulation Results

As represented in Confusion matrix for Ada boost Classifier Simulation in Fig. 3
Here, TP = 106, TN = 130, FP = 20, FN = 20

$$Accuracy = \frac{TP + TN}{TP + TN + FP + FN} = \frac{106 + 130}{106 + 130 + 20 + 20} = 86\%$$

$$Precision = \frac{TP}{TP + FP} = \frac{106}{106 + 20} = 86\%$$

$$Sensitivity = \frac{TP}{TP + FN} = \frac{106}{106 + 20} = 84.12\%$$

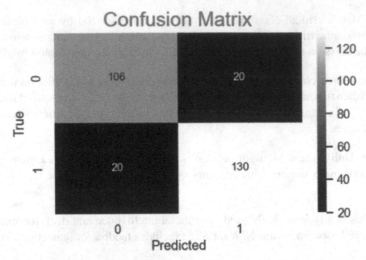

Fig. 3. Confusion matrix for Ada boost Classifier Simulation

4.2 Gradient Boosting Simulation Results

As shown Fig. 4, Confusion matrix- Gradient Boosting Simulation
Here, TP = 104, TN = 135, FP = 22, FN = 15

$$Accuracy = \frac{TP + TN}{TP + TN + FP + FN} = \frac{104 + 135}{104 + 135 + 22 + 15} = 87\%$$

$$Precision = \frac{TP}{TP + FP} = \frac{104}{104 + 22} = 87\%$$

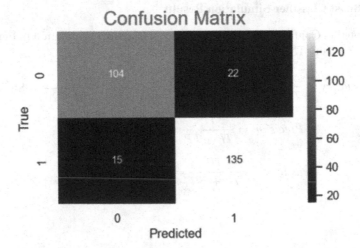

Fig. 4. Confusion matrix: Gradient Boosting Simulation

$$Sensitivity = \frac{TP}{TP + FN} = \frac{104}{104 + 15} = 87.39\%$$

4.3 XGB Classifier Simulation Results

Figure 5 shows Confusion matrix for XGB Classifier Simulation
   Here, TP = 102, TN = 128, FP = 24, FN = 22

$$Accuracy = \frac{TP + TN}{TP + TN + FP + FN} = \frac{102 + 128}{102 + 128 + 24 + 22} = 83\%$$

$$Precision = \frac{TP}{TP + FP} = \frac{102}{102 + 24} = 83\%$$

$$Sensitivity = \frac{TP}{TP + FN} = \frac{102}{102 + 22} = 82.22\%$$

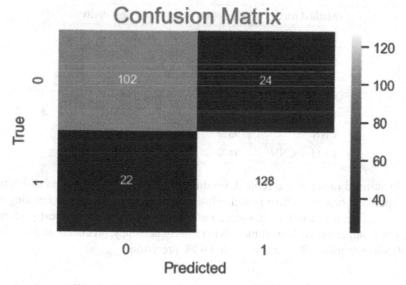

Fig. 5. Confusion matrix: XGB Classifier Simulation

Table 1. Performance measures of rice production for Rabi season in Balasore district.

Method used	Accuracy	Precision	Sensitivity
SVM	87%	86%	85%
AdaBoost	86%	86%	84.12%
XGBoost	83%	83%	82.22%
GBoosting	87%	87%	87.39%
LSTM	92%	89%	89.02%
CNN .	**94%**	**90%**	**91.25%**
SVM + CNN	**95%**	**92%**	**92.23%**

We have used six different algorithms to determine and compare the best predictive model, as shown in Table 1 above. Three Meta classifier ensemble learning models, as well as deep learning techniques, are used. If we consider the best-performing model, CNN outperforms the other models slightly. SVM+CNN outperform 95% accuracy.

Table 2. Performance measures of rice production for Rabi season in Rayagada district.

Method used	Accuracy	Precision	Sensitivity
SVM	89%	90%	89%
AdaBoost	89%	86%	86.39%
XGBoost	86%	81%	84.22%
Gradient Boosting	84%	88%	86.39%
LSTM	91%	90%	86.02%
CNN	**93%**	**90%**	**92.25%**
SVM + CNN	**94%**	**92%**	**93%**

As mentioned in the above Table 2, six different algorithms were used to determine and compare the best predictive model. Three meta classifier ensemble learning models, as well as deep learning techniques, are used. If we consider the best-performing model, CNN outperforms all other models in terms of accuracy, precision, and sensitivity. SVM+CNN outperform 95% accuracy and 92% precision.

Table 3. Performance measures of rice production for Rabi season in Kalahandi district.

Method used	Accuracy	Precision	Sensitivity
SVM	87%	86%	80.12%
AdaBoost	79%	82%	76.39%
XGBoost	76%	80%	81.20%
GBoosting	81%	84%	81.32%
LSTM	89%	79%	81.10%
CNN	**90%**	**89%**	**91.14%**
SVM + CNN	**94%**	**92%**	**93%**

Table 4. The structure of our proposed model

#inputs	SVM + CNN	Name of training rule included	#of outputs obtained	#of iteration performed
8	8	Stacking	1	60

As shown in the above Table 3, among the six different classifiers used to determine the best predictive model, three Meta classifier ensemble learning models and deep learning techniques are used. If we consider the best-performing model, CNN outperforms the other models slightly. SVM+CNN, on the other hand, outperform with 94% accuracy and 92% precision.The datasets have collected thereafter and assigned the class labels. For prediction, the main classifier is used, which contains the dataset augmented with the output of the base classifiers. After the main classifier processes the augmented dataset, the result is compared to the expected output.

5 Proposed Algorithm based on SVM and CNN

The primary goal of this study is to forecast rice crop yield in terms of production for the coming year using historical data from previous year, i.e. training set, such as season, humidity, temperature, rainfall, fertilizer use, district, and year. The research focuses on three districts in Odisha where rice crop production is higher than in other districts in the state. SVM + CNN is proposed in this work to improve prediction accuracy. The proposed work employs both a SVM algorithm and a CNN (deep neural network) to improve prediction accuracy. Many researchers use the SVM algorithm to improve prediction accuracy in general crop prediction as well as rice crop yield prediction. Many researchers use deep neural networks in the same way. In this study, we combine these two algorithms with the assistance of an advanced ensemble technique known as stacking. The main features input to the model are mainly season, humidity, and temperature, and rainfall, use of fertilizers, district, and year. In turn, it will provide the best rice prediction. The prediction for the 'nth' part is completed once a deep neural network is fitted on the 'n-1' parts. Each portion of the training set is repeated. The full train dataset is then fitted with the deep neural network. Deep neural completes the prediction on the test set. With the help of stacking ensemble learning, predictions from both the random forest method and the deep neural network were combined and utilized as features (training set) to develop a new model termed SVM +CNN (DNN). Finally, on the training set obtained from the two models, SVM + CNN (DNN) is utilized to make the final prediction. Finally, the two algorithms are combined and turned into a single dataset that will be used as a feature set for testing. Stacking, an ensemble approach can be used to accomplish this. The rice crop production for the testing set can be predicted using the stacking technique. The RF-DNN algorithm, by the way, is effective.

5.1 Ensemble Method (SVM + CNN)

As shown in the Fig. 6, The basic purpose of this research is to improve the performance of our predictive model, as described in Sect. 3. Support vector machine along with deep learning as an ensemble approach is used and found that the results has considerably improved.

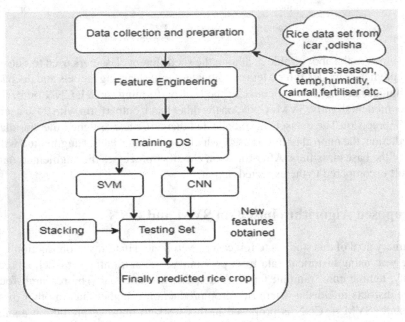

Fig. 6. Proposed architecture of SVM + CNN

The stacking method has used by the author, as shown in Fig. 4. Stacking is a common ensemble machine learning technique used to predict multiple nodes in order to build a new model and improve model performance. Stacking allows us to train multiple models to solve similar problems and then combine their output to create a new model that performs better.

5.2 Description of the Bit-Fusion Algorithm

This section describes a bit fusion algorithm, as well as its theoretical design and operation. The proposed algorithm's work is thoroughly discussed with the various parameters. The trained classifier is subjected to the bit fusion algorithm. This algorithm takes into account the classification algorithm's output to achieve the highest possible accuracy while reducing execution time.

Let Classifier = $\{C_1, C_2 \dots C_p\}$ be the set of p number of classifiers, x = $\{x_1, x_2 \dots x_n\}$ be the input features of the dataset $x_i \in Rn$ of n instances; where each feature can have m conditions and set of class labels $\omega = \omega 1, \omega 2, \dots \omega k$. For input feature X, individual classification methods are developed and tested. Each classifier takes an input x_i and predicts which class category it belongs to.

5.2.1   ALGORITHM 1 | Bit-Fusion Ensemble Algorithm

[acc] ← Bit-classify (Xtr, Xts, ωtr, ωts, M, δ).

Input: Xtr, Xts are used in training and testing data, and ωtr, ωts are the class labels used during training and testing, M is the number of maximum iterations, N is the size Threshold value for feature classification is denoted as δ.

```
Output: accuracy of the classifier is denoted as acc.
[n m] ← N(Xtr );
[x y] ← N (Xts); max_class ← max(ωtr ); wt ← rand(max_class, m);
// code for training
For iter ← 1: M
Δwt ← wt;
     for p ← 1 : n
        for q ← 1 : max_class
           f (q, :) ← Xtr (p, :). × wt(q, :);
           for r ← 1 : m
             if (f (p, r) > δ)
                  bin(p, r) ← 1;
           else
                  bin(p, r) ← 0;
        endif
     endif
endif
error(i, :) ← bin − expected;
Δwtlearnswt − 2 × μ × error
m ← mean (mean (errorneighbor)
wt ← wt + Δ wt/n
er(iter) ← ( m × m')^2/n;
endif
// testing code
for p ← 1 : x
for q ← 1 : max_class
f (q, :) ← Xts (p, :). × wt(q, :);
for r ← 1 : m
    if (f (q, r) > δ)
         bin (q, r) ← 1;
else
       bin (q, r) ← 0;
     endif
   endif
endif
  [value class (p)] ← max (sum (bin));
endif
// Accuracy computation
diff ← class − ωts;
match ← find (diff == 0);
acc ← len(match)/x × 100;
```

5.2.2   Algorithm Steps

The above-mentioned, Fig. 7 represents for bit-fusion ensemble model. The proposed model mechanism consists of three parts:

Stage#1: Min-Max normalisation as shown in Eq. (1) is used to normalise the input feature $X \in Rn$. Min-max normalisation is the traditional method for converting input features to a scale of [0, 1]. The feature's minimum value is set to 0 and its maximum value is set to 1. The remaining values are converted from 0 to 1.

$$x_{ij} = \frac{X_{ij} - Min(X_j)}{Max(X_j) - Min(X_j)} \tag{1}$$

where $x_{ij} \in X$.

Principal Component Analysis (PCA)

Principal component analysis (PCA) is used for feature extraction, which is carried out in three steps:

Use Eq. (3) to compute the covariance matrix (Z),

$$Z = \frac{1}{n} \sum_i^n x_i x_i^T, z \in R^{m \times m} \tag{2}$$

$$u^T z = \lambda u \tag{3}$$

II. Use Eqs. (4) to compute the eigenvalue and eigenvector U of Z, and

$$U = \left\{ \begin{matrix} | & | & ||| & | \\ u_1 & u_2 & \dots & u_m \\ | & | & ||| & | \end{matrix} \right\}_{u_i}, \overset{m}{\in} R \tag{4}$$

III. Use Eq. (6) to project the row data into k-dimensional subspace (5)

$$x_{new}^i = \left[u_i^T x_i u_i^T x_i \dots \dots u_k^T x_i \right] \in R^k \tag{5}$$

where m dimensions were used for row data and k dimensions were used for new features.

Stage#2: Classifier Building

According to the literature review, every ensemble technique has fixed a few base classifiers and used fusion using ensemble techniques. Similarly, we used $l = 6$ classifiers and one proposed ensemble classifier in the proposed experiment.

We get a soft class label output matrix of dimension $l \times n$ for a dataset with n features and l classifiers, as shown in (6)

$$\varepsilon = \begin{pmatrix} c_{11} & \cdots & c_{n1} \\ \vdots & \ddots & \vdots \\ c_{11} & \cdots & c_{nl} \end{pmatrix} \tag{6}$$

where C_{ij} is the predicted class level by the jth classifier for the ith feature.

Stage#3: Training of Bit-Fusion Classifier

As shown in Fig. 4, every value is categorized using the bit fusion classification technique.

Figure 3, ξ is used as an input to the fusion method, and it is trained for the supplied feature input for 100 iterations. All occurrences of the data set contribute to the model's training at each epoch. Let ξi represents each classification result from a single classifier by taking the Ith feature into account. To tune the Weight wt, a random value between [0.5, 0.5] is chosen. The wt dimension is set to |ω| × 1, where 1 denotes the number of classifiers. Each row in wtij has been tuned for ξgc.

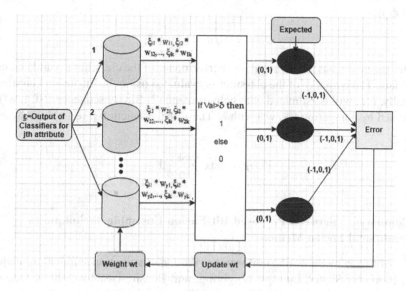

Fig. 7. Bit fusion classification process

Initially, Eq. (7) is used to calculate the cross product of the f (ξi, Wt)

$$f(\varepsilon_i, \omega mathrmt) = \varepsilon_i \times \omega t \tag{7}$$

The binary output B is now evaluated by comparing f (εi, &t) to high. a threshold parameter δ.

In the above-mentioned proposed algorithm, initially, we have set the value as 0.9. The value is close to one for better training. For all values of f (ξiWt > δ. is set to 1 otherwise 0. Set Bf (ξiWt) to the binary value 0 and 1 to represent the function that connects the value of f (ξiWt) with δ.

$$B(f(\varepsilon_i, \omega t),), \delta = \begin{cases} 1 f(\varepsilon_i, \omega t) > \delta \\ 0 Otherwise \end{cases} \tag{8}$$

To evaluate model training error, Bf (ξiWt)) is compared to the expected output. Equation (10) can be used to calculate training error.

$$E_{iter}, i = B(f(\varepsilon_i, \omega t),), \delta - \omega_i \forall i \varepsilon 1, ..., n \tag{9}$$

Model learning is accomplished by updating wt with Eq. (11)

$$\Delta wt = n \times wt \times \mu \times error \tag{10}$$

$$wt = wt + \frac{\Delta wt}{n} \tag{11}$$

where η and μ are the learning and accelerator coefficients, respectively, modified and initialized to 0.71 and 0.00001. For maximum iteration, we have used the above-mentioned Eqs. (7–10) to be repeated. The maximum number of iterations we have considered in this experiment is 100. The mean square error for the jth period is calculated and placed in (12). $\phi(j)$.

$$\varnothing(j) = (E/n \times E/n)^{2/n} \tag{12}$$

After the model has been trained, the performance of the classifier is validated using testing data. The output ξ' of the classifier is evaluated using the bit-fusion classifier.

Finally, $F(\xi, wt)'$ is estimated with help of using (7) Binary sequence $B(f(\xi, wt), \delta)'$ is evaluated by comparing $f(\xi, wt)$ with δ. Then final prediction p (ξ) is done by using (13)

$$P(\varepsilon\prime) = \max_{i \in T} \sum_{j=1}^{k} B'_{ij} \tag{13}$$

5.3 Comparison Between Proposed Bit-Fusion Ensemble Technique vs Traditional Fusion Methods

Traditional fusion methods like uniform distribution, distribution summation, majority voting, Dempster-Shafer, Entropy Weighting, and Density-based weighting take individual input from each of the (1–6) base classifiers plus the proposed method. As stated in the introduction, a variety of fusion methods operate on the classifier's outputs in an attempt to improve classification accuracy. If the majority of classifiers predict that the instance belongs to class 1, the fusion algorithm automatically assigns class 1 as its class label to that instance. However, the accuracy may be reduced in some cases if the data belongs to a different class. The time complexity of majority voting is high, but it increases the efficacy (10). Fusion methods are crucial in improving the accuracy of classification problems. Selecting the right fusion method is one of the best ways to solve any problem with pattern recognition.

The proposed bit-fusion ensemble classifier conveys the issue of traditional fusion methods by not relying on the number of classifiers or the output of the base classifiers, instead, by tuning its parameter it decides the output of a data element and making a decision based on the threshold δ value. For the training and testing of the data sets, a 10-fold cross-validation approach was utilized. We have also compared the functioning of individual classifiers using the proposed method.

6 Conclusion and Future Scope

The combined solution of these two models significantly improves crop yield prediction. The performance of the proposed model is assessed using a variety of performance indicators such as recall, accuracy, and precision. In terms of crop yield prediction, the results show that SVM + CNN (DNN) with stacking ensemble model outperform the other classifiers as mentioned. Deep learning with SVM and fusion-based algorithms improved performance by 95%, 94%, and 94% in the three districts, respectively. Existing deep learning methods, on the other hand, achieve 94%, 93%, and 90% accuracy. Thereby, we are confident that our model will be very much beneficial for modern farmers, and in the near future, this model will be competent to work with real-time data.

References

1. Van Klompenburg, T., Kassahun, A., Catal, C.: Crop yield prediction using machine learning: a systematic literature review. Comput. Electron. Agriculture **177**, 105709 (2020)
2. Paudel, D., et al.: Machine learning for large-scale crop yield, forecasting. Agricultural Syst. **187**, 103016 (2021)
3. Wang, Y., Zhang, Z., Feng, L., Du, Q., Runge, T.: Combining multi-source data and machine learning approaches to predict winter wheat yield in the conterminous United States. Remote Sens. **12**(8), 1232 (2020)
4. Yoshida, S.: Fundamentals of Rice Crop Science. Los Banos, Philippines: International Rice Research Institute (1981). http://books.irri.org/9711040522_content.pdf
5. Guo, Y., et al.: Integrated phenology and climate in rice yields prediction using machine learning methods. Ecol. Ind. **120**, 106935 (2021)
6. Bali, N., Singla, A.: Emerging trends in machine learning to predict crop yield and study its influential factors: a survey. Archives Comput. Methods Eng. **29**(1), 95–112 (2021). https://doi.org/10.1007/s11831-021-09569-8
7. Khaki, S., Wang, L., Archontoulis, S.V.: A cnn-rnn framework for crop yield prediction. Front. Plant Sci. **10**, 1750 (2020)
8. https://www.usda.gov/topics/food-and-nutrition/food-security
9. https://www.downtoearth.org.in/blog/agriculture/why-india-needs-climate-resilient-agriculture-systems-75381
10. https://www.ibef.org/industry/agricultureindia#:~:text=Agriculture%20is%20the%20primary%20source,%24%20276.37%20billion)%20in%20FY20
11. Chu, Z., Jiong, Y.: An end-to-end model for rice yield prediction using deep learning fusion. Comput. Electron. Agric. **174**, 105471 (2020)
12. Amanah, H.Z., et al.: Near-Infrared hyperspectral imaging (NIR-HSI) for nondestructive prediction of anthocyanins content in black rice seeds. Appl. Sci. **11**(11), 4841 (2021)
13. Hu, Y., Shen, J., Qi, Y.: Estimation of rice biomass at different growth stages by using fractal dimension in image processing. Appl. Sci. **11**(15), 7151 (2021)
14. Kumar, S., Kumar, V., Sharma, R.K.: Rice yield forecasting using support vector machine. Int. J. Recent Technol. Eng. **8**(4), 2588–2593 (2019)
15. Nishant, P.S., et al.: Crop yield prediction based on Indian agriculture using machine learning. In: 2020 International Conference for Emerging Technology (INCET). IEEE (2020)
16. Qazi, S., Khawaja, B.A., Farooq, Q.U.: IoT-equipped and AI-enabled next generation smart agriculture: a critical review, current challenges and future trends. IEEE Access (2022)
17. Nesarani, A., Ramar, R., Pandian, S.: An efficient approach for rice prediction from authenticated Block chain node using machine learning technique. Environ. Technol. Innov. **20**, 101064 (2020)
18. Cho, S., Lee, Y.W.: Deep learning-based analysis of the relationships between climate change and crop yield in china. The International Archives of Photogrammetry, Remote Sensing and Spatial Information Sciences **42**, 93–95 (2019)
19. Liu, L.-W., et al.: Using artificial intelligence algorithms to predict rice (Oryza sativa L.) Growth rate for precision agriculture. Comput. Electron. Agric. **187**, 106286 (2021)

Bayesian Learning Model for Predicting Stability of System with Nonlinear Characteristics

Advait Pujari[1], Harsh Singh Rajput[1], Mohit Law[1]([✉]) [ID], and Manjesh Singh[2] [ID]

[1] Machine Tool Dynamics Laboratory, Department of Mechanical Engineering, Indian Institute of Technology Kanpur, Kanpur 208016, India
mlaw@iitk.ac.in
[2] Department of Mechanical Engineering, Indian Institute of Technology Kanpur, Kanpur 208016, India

Abstract. Instabilities in machining are detrimental. Usually analytical model-predicted stability charts guide selection of cutting parameters to ensure stable processes. However, since models often fail to account for how inputs to them such as the cutting force coefficients and dynamics change with speed and/or time, and because models make several linearizing assumptions, charts often fail to guide stable cutting in industrial praxis. As an alternate way to guide stable cutting, this paper demonstrates how stability charts can be learnt from experimental data using a supervised Bayes' learning approach. We build on prior work related to learning stability for processes with linear characteristics and demonstrate herein that the model can be trained and tested on datasets for processes exhibiting nonlinear characteristics, thus showing how the prediction model is agnostic to the process or to any potential nonlinearities in it. Factors affecting the training capacity of Bayesian model like the likelihood probability distributions and the thresholds of probability necessary to decide on a stability contour, are tuned to give maximum accuracy possible. Predictions to learn the stability were accurate up to 96.5%. Since data that is used to train the model includes in it all the vagaries and uncertainties associated with the cutting process, results herein can inform further development towards self-optimizing and autonomous machining systems.

Keywords: Machining stability · Bayesian learning · Machine learning

1 Introduction

Selection of stable cutting parameters for high performance machining is often guided by knowledge of stability diagrams. These diagrams chart the boundaries between cutting parameters that might result in stable and unstable cutting and further guide selection that will likely result in higher material removal rates. Analytical models usually predict these diagrams. Quality of prediction is governed by inputs to the models. These include measured cutting force coefficients and measured dynamics. However, since inputs seldom account for the speed-dependent behaviour of the cutting process or the dynamics,

N. Khare et al. (Eds.): MIND 2022, CCIS 1762, pp. 190–200, 2022.
https://doi.org/10.1007/978-3-031-24352-3_16

and since models make several linearizing assumptions, models, though useful, often fail to guide stable cutting parameter selection in real industrial settings. Since instabilities are detrimental to the part, the tool, and to elements of the machine, there is need for better quality predictions. To address this need, this paper discusses the use of a supervised machine learning (ML) technique that can 'learn' the stability diagram from real experimentally classified stable and unstable data points without relying on an analytical model. Since the real data is expected to better capture the vagaries and uncertainties in the cutting processes and/or in the dynamics, the 'learnt' stability is expected to be accurate.

Use of ML models in the domain of machine tools and machining process related research has gained traction over the recent years, as is nicely and succinctly summarized in the review paper [1]. Since learning from real and/or simulated data has value, ML has been shown to be useful for tool wear analysis, thermal error compensation, monitoring and classifying states of machining as being stable and/or unstable, identifying dynamics, and to learn the stability diagram – which is of direct relevance to this research.

Prior research on learning stability using ML models has discussed the use of artificial neural networks (ANN) [2], support vector machines (SVM) [2, 3], the k-nearest neighbourhood (kNN) method [4], and Bayesian methods [5–8]. Given that training models requires that experiments be done to obtain unstable data points, and since those experiments can be destructive due to the nature of instabilities, an accurate model that can be trained with less data, and one that extends itself to a continual learning scheme should be preferred. The Bayes' method fits these criteria. It is hence our preferred method for implementation.

The Bayes' method to learn stability was in its original form intended to be agnostic to the process physics [5]. However, in other related work, physics-informed modifications have been reported to work well [6, 7]. Since it is desirable to develop a generalized ML model that is agnostic to the process physics and that can work with many different data sets, this study follows the approach reported in [5, 8] that was blind to the physics of the process.

For given data that is pre-classified as stable/unstable, the goal with the Bayesian approach is to calculate the posterior probability of stability at each grid point on the stability map. Though this was done in prior work [5–7], that work did not systematically characterize the influence of changing Gaussian likelihoods, or the influence of changing threshold of the stability contour on the learning accuracy. Moreover, there was no discussion on how to characterize and quantify the learning accuracy of the prediction. In our concurrent research [8], we report on the influence of changing Gaussian likelihoods, on the influence of changing threshold of the stability contour, and on the influence of data size in a continuous learning scenario.

Although, in [5–8], the Bayes' method is clearly agnostic to the physics of the system, that research was limited to learning stability for processes with linear characteristics. The use of the Bayes' method for learning stability with nonlinear characteristics remains previously unexplored and forms the focus of this paper. We train and test the Bayes' method for a process exhibiting non-linear force characteristics resulting in bistabilities and for a process exhibiting the interesting process damping phenomena. In doing so, we further show the strength of the Bayes' method for learning the machining stability behavior directly from the data, even when the data embeds nonlinearities within it. This is the main new technical contribution of this paper to the state-of-the-art in the use of ML methods for learning stability.

The remainder of the paper is organized as follows. At first, in Sect. 2, we discuss how we gather data that we feed to our learning model. We then briefly overview the Bayes' method in Sect. 3. In Sect. 4, we demonstrate the results obtained from the model which learn stability for processes with nonlinear characteristics and for those with process damping. This is followed by the main conclusions.

2   Gathering Data for the ML Model

Since the experimental pathway to gather data that is needed to train a Bayesian model is costly due to the destructive nature of unstable experiments, this paper trains and tests the ML model using data obtained from emulations on an in-house developed hardware-in-the-loop (HiL) simulator that was built to study machining instabilities [9–12]. Experiments on the HiL simulator are used to classify combinations of depths of cuts and spindle speeds that result in unstable conditions. The process is akin to procedures in real cutting experiments. When the process has nonlinear force characteristics, there exist regions of conditional stabilities that are characterized by the process being stable for small perturbations and unstable for larger ones for cutting at parameters within the conditionally stable regions. The procedure to find the global unstable limits in this case is the same as for the case of cutting with linear force characteristics. And, to find the find the global stable limits, i.e., to find the lower limits of the bistable regions, for every speed of interest, the depths of cuts were decreased in the same step size as they were increased. And the last but one depth of cut at which the finite amplitude instabilities disappear, was recorded as the lower limit of the bistable region. Experimental data characterizing the stability boundaries for cutting with a process having non-linear force characteristics is shown in Fig. 1(a) and is obtained as detailed in [11].

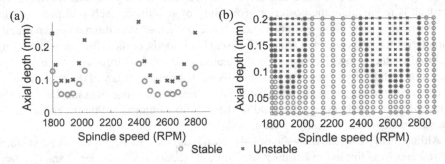

Fig. 1. (a) Experimental data corresponding to unstable cutting conditions obtained from emulations on a HiL simulator for the case of a process with nonlinear characteristics i.e., bistability, (b) synthesized data used for testing the model.

When the cutting process exhibits process damping due to interference of a worn tool's flank face with a previously cut surface, the critical chatter-free depths of cuts at low-speeds are observed to be higher than those at high-speeds. Experimental data characterizing the stability boundaries for cutting with a process having linear force characteristics and exhibiting process damping is shown in Fig. 2(a). Data shown in Fig. 2(a) is obtained as detailed in [12].

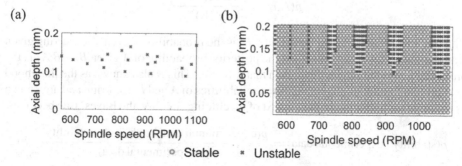

Fig. 2. (a) Experimental data corresponding to unstable cutting conditions obtained from emulations on a HiL simulator for the case of a process exhibiting process damping, (b) synthesized data used for testing the model.

Since the main idea of fitting a model to data is for the model to be agnostic to the data type, a comparison between the above two cases is not intended and/or recommended. What is however clear is that for the case with the nonlinear force characteristics there exists a clear bistable region with there being a globally stable boundary as well as a globally unstable boundary. This case will evidently need to be addressed differently due to the ternary types of classification of the data with some data being stable, some being conditionally stable, and some being unstable. Previous studies [5–8] using the Bayesian approach were limited to cases with linear force characteristics in which the classification was of the binary type with some data being stable and some being unstable.

The case of the nonlinear force characteristics has a total of 32 (16 each for global stable and global unstable case) data points (Fig. 1(a)). And the case of the process exhibiting process damping has a total of 20 data points (Fig. 2(a)). Though the Bayesian model can be adequately trained with this data, testing the model for its learning capacity needs more data than we have obtained. As such, we synthesize the emulated data with more data. Since the region below the boundary is stable and that above unstable, we add data points at depth of cut intervals of choice to pad the emulated data. In this manner, we generate additional 1227 and 434 data for the case of a process with nonlinear characteristics (Fig. 1(b)) and a process with linear characteristics exhibiting process damping (Fig. 2(b)), respectively. Synthesized data allows us to systematically quantify the learning capacity of the model, something that was missing from previous investigations [5–7]. More on how we quantify the learning accuracy is discussed in the next section.

3 Bayesian Learning for Machining Stability

This section outlines the Bayes' procedure to learn machining stability diagrams. We only provide an overview and direct the reader to the original source [5] for details. Bayes' rule updates probabilities when new information is made available. Mathematically, it can be stated as:

$$p(A|B) = \frac{p(B|A).p(A)}{p(B)} \tag{1}$$

wherein A and B are separate events. $p(A|B)$ is the probability of event A occurring given that B is true. This is also known as the posterior probability of A given B. $p(B|A)$ is the probability of event B occurring given that A is true. This is also known as the likelihood of A given a fixed B. $p(A)$ and $p(B)$ are probabilities of A and B occurring and are known as the prior probabilities. In the context of machining stability, the Bayes' rule becomes:

$$p(\text{stability} \mid \text{experimental data}) = \frac{p(\text{experimental data} \mid \text{stability}).p(\text{stability})}{p(\text{experimental data})} \tag{2}$$

wherein $p(\text{stability})$ is an assumed prior probability of stability, $p(\text{experimentaldata})$ is the known probability of a data point being stable or not, $p(\text{experimentaldata}|\text{stability})$ is the likelihood probability of a stable result at the given experimental data point, and $p(\text{stability}|\text{experimentaldata})$ is the evaluated posterior probability of a stable data point for the given experimental condition. Likewise, it is also possible to evaluate the posterior probability of an unstable data point for the given experimental condition and given an assumed prior probability of instability, $p(\text{instability})$.

For the given data points on the stability diagram (in Figs. 1 and 2) the goal with the Bayesian approach is to calculate the posterior probability of stability at each grid point on the axial depth of cut – spindle speed map. The procedure to do so is outlined in a flowchart in Fig. 3.

For every data point, we first evaluate the prior probability. This is done by assuming that as the depths of cut increase at any spindle speed, the likelihood of encountering instabilities increases. A linear distribution for the prior probability is assumed as shown in an inset in the flowchart in Fig. 3. This prior probability remains the same for all spindle speeds.

The influence of a test result along spindle speeds at the depth of cut of interest, b_T is defined as $\sigma_{N_{b_T}}$ with the mean being the test spindle speed of interest, and the influence of the test result being restricted to 3 $\sigma_{N_{b_T}}$. The subscript T refers to the test result under consideration. The likelihood probability of a stable result at T $(p(+_T)_{N_T,b_T})$ given G, another test result on the depth of cut – spindle map that is stable, is one, i.e., $p(+_T|s_G)_{N_T,b_T} = 1$. For the same depth of cut, b_T, the likelihood probability of a stable result at T given G is stable reduces for other spindle speeds N_j following a Gaussian distribution, as shown in the schematic and in the equation in the insets in the flowchart in Fig. 3.

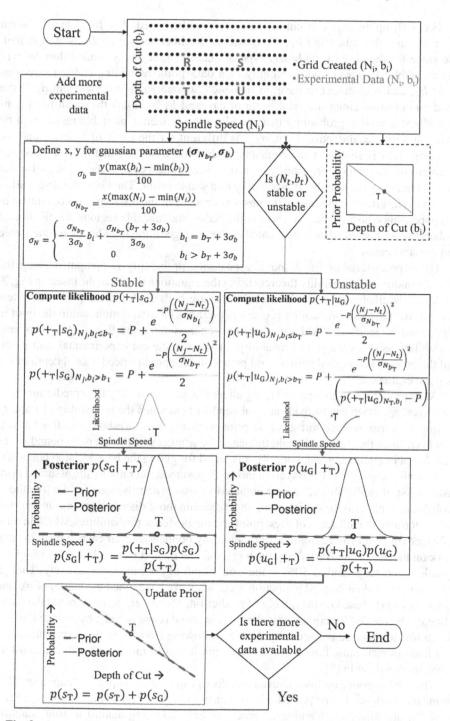

Fig. 3. An overview of our implementation of the Bayes' rule to learn stability diagrams.

For a changing depth of cut at the same spindle speed, N_T, for example, when $b_i < b_T$, and the data point b_T, N_T is stable, the likelihood probability will remain one since for the case of the binary type of classification, every point below b_T will remain stable. However, the probability of a data point remaining stable reduces as $b_i > b_T$, and is assumed to have no influence beyond $b_T + 3\sigma_b$, wherein σ_b is the standard deviation along the axial depth of cut, and $b_T + 3\sigma_b$ is the mean for a non-normalized Gaussian probability density. Since the influence of stable results will be higher at lower axial depths of cut, $\sigma_{N_{b_T}}$ is different for the cases of $b_i < b_T$ and for $b_i > b_T$. This is shown in the equations within the flowchart in Fig. 3. Procedures to obtain the likelihood probability of instabilities follows the same logic as for the case of obtaining the likelihood probability of a stable result. The Gaussian distribution however is inverted for the case of the unstable result. For the bistable cases of interest in this paper, since bistable data lies within the stable and unstable regions, the likelihood probability for bistable data is calculated as the average of the likelihoods for the stable and unstable cases.

Using procedures outlined above, a posterior probability is computed using the Bayes' conditional probability theorem using the equations shown in the insets in Fig. 3. To do so, the likelihood and prior probabilities are both used. For a representative test result T, the posterior probability is overlaid on the prior assumption within the inset in Fig. 3, and it clearly shows that probabilities change using the Bayes' rule. This new probability becomes the prior probability for the subsequent experimental data point, and the process is repeated until all grid points on the spindle speed – axial depth of cut map are evaluated.

After probabilities are updated using all test results, a stability lobe prediction from the Bayes' approach can be made at axial depths of cut when the probability of stability is equal to a user-defined threshold. In prior work [5], that threshold was fixed at 0.5. However, since the threshold could influence the accuracy of the decision boundary, as was shown in our concurrent work [8], it is tuned for giving the best decision boundary.

Learning capacity of the Bayesian model is governed not only by the assumed prior distribution of probabilities, and the assumed Gaussian distributions for the likelihood probabilities, but also the choice of σ_N and σ_b within those distributions. σ_N and σ_b will both determine the influence of a test point and the posterior probabilities, which in turn, influences the width and amplitude of the stability boundaries after each update. In prior work on the use of the Bayes' approach [5], σ_N and σ_b and were selected as 3% of the spindle speed range and as 10% of the axial depth of cut range, respectively. Though these values resulted in good prediction accuracies, we have tuned the values of σ_N and σ_b for this work, based on the quality of prediction. Moreover, the attempt to take σ_N as a linearly increasing function within the spindle speed range is made by us in [8], which was found to enhance the accuracy. Hence, following from there, we have chosen σ_N as a linearly increasing function within the spindle speed range, rather than a constant value, as was done in [5].

Though the above outlined above procedures can be used to predict/learn a stability boundary, there need to be procedures to quantify the goodness of that prediction. Prior work [5] quantified the learning accuracy by benchmarking against a 'true' stability boundary that was presumably obtained from an analytical model. Instead of relying on a model, we train using the available experimental data, and test the goodness of our predictions against the whole data set that includes the synthesized data and some experimental data using a confusion matrix. From the confusion matrix, we evaluate accuracies and F1 scores to quantify the goodness of fit.

4   Learning Stability with Non-linear Characteristics

This section first discusses learning stability for a for a process exhibiting bistable behaviour, followed by a discussion on learning stability for a machining process exhibiting process damping.

4.1   Learning Stability for a Process Exhibiting Bistable Behaviour

Processes exhibiting bistable behaviour are characterized by data points that are stable, conditionally stable, and unstable. As such, the model must be trained with representative data from each of these different classes. We hence train using nine stable, four unstable and 27 bistable data points. For testing, we use 242 stable, 106 unstable and 86 bistable data points. Training and testing data is shown in Fig. 4(a). In this case σ_N was linearly increased from 3% to 10% of spindle speed range, and σ_b was taken to be fixed at 4% of the axial depth of cut range. And, since bistable behaviour is characterized by a globally stable and a globally unstable boundary, two thresholds were used to evaluate these contours. For the globally stable contour, we used a threshold of 0.05, and for the globally unstable contour, we used a threshold of 0.95. These parameters were tuned for this data set. The predicted stability contour is shown in Fig. 4(b). The color map in Fig. 4(b) depicts the probability of stability, with blue representing a very low probability of stability and yellow indicating a high probability of stability. Although the stability boundary is determined by the threshold value, the color map gives an overview of the distribution of the evaluated posterior probabilities. And as is evident, the Bayesian approach can learn stability behaviour even with processes exhibiting bistabilities. The F1-score evaluated for correctly predicting the globally stable and unstable regions is >90%. However, for the bistable data, the F1-score falls to ~75%. This suggests that there is still room for improvement of the algorithm.

Since bistabilities are characterized by the process being stable for small perturbations and unstable for larger ones, learning this behaviour from data can guide selection of cutting parameters to lie outside these zones of conditional instabilities. Moreover, since bistabilities occur due to nonlinearities in cutting force characteristics, which can be difficult to identify and/or model, and since the data learning model used herein is shown to be agnostic to the underlying causes of the observed bistable behaviour, and since it is still able to learn that bistable behaviour, these results are useful.

Furthermore, the computational time required to train and test the model is only ~1.6 s and ~0.0433 s, respectively. These times were for calculations performed on a laptop with a i5-8250U processor running at a base speed 1.8 GHz and with 8 GB or RAM. This makes this method suitable for an in-situ real-time implementation with real data on real machines.

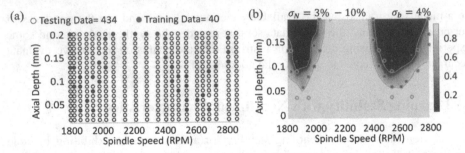

Fig. 4. (a) Data for training and testing the process with nonlinear force characteristics, (b) stability charts capturing bistable behaviour with unstable, bistable, and stable data used for training.

4.2 Learning Stability with Process Damping

Training and testing data for process damping is shown in Fig. 5(a). The model is trained with 20 unstable data points and is subsequently tested on 972 stable and 255 unstable data points. The model hyperparameters for this data set are again tuned to give maximum F1-score. σ_N was linearly increased from 1% to 2% of the spindle speed range. σ_b was taken to be fixed at 1% of the axial depth of cut range. The threshold to evaluate stability contours was taken to be 0.05. The predicted stability contour is shown in Fig. 5(b), and as is evident, the process damping phenomena is well-captured with the Bayesian approach that has no knowledge about the underlying process mechanics. The accuracy and F1-score were found to be 96.58% and 97.80%, respectively.

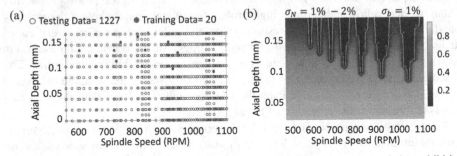

Fig. 5. (a) Data for training and testing the process with linear force characteristics exhibiting process damping, (b) stability chart capturing process damping with unstable data used for training.

Since process damping is an interesting phenomenon in which the absolute minimum stability limit improves for lower speeds while remaining unchanged for higher speeds – as is evident from Fig. 5(b), and since improvements are usually observed as the tool wear progresses, and since modelling the tool wear's influence on stability is non-trivial, the hereby demonstration of learning the stability diagram from data will aid selection of cutting parameters to stabilize a process and improve the productivity potential.

The computational cost for the case of learning process damping behavior is lower still than for the case of bistable behavior, taking ~0.48 s for training and ~0.05 s for testing, respectively.

5 Conclusion

Analytical model-predicted stability diagrams often fail to guide stable cutting parameter selection in praxis due to the assumptions the models make and due to the vagaries and uncertainties in the inputs to the model. Since machining instabilities should be avoided, this paper demonstrated successfully that the stability diagram can instead be learnt from experimental data using a supervised Bayesian learning model. We successfully quantified the learning accuracy of Bayesian model and tuned the two hyperparameters – standard deviation of Gaussian likelihood distributions, and threshold of probability indicating the stability contour. The tuned model has been shown to be consistent across two different types of datasets gathered from emulated experiments in which the cutting mechanics and dynamics involved non-linear behaviour and were different for both datasets. This suggests that the learning model is agnostic to the underlying process physics. This is the first such report in the literature of a machine learning model being blind to potential nonlinearities in the cutting process. This is also the strength of the learning model.

Since the very nature of the Bayes' rule is that the posterior probability updates with every new data point that is provided to the model, the analysis done in this paper can inform future research to help the community move closer towards self-optimizing and autonomous machining systems in which cutting parameter selection can be adapted autonomously and in real-time based on predictions from a ML model that trains itself directly from data, and captures all possible vagaries of its dynamics.

References

1. Aggogeri, F., et al.: Recent advances on machine learning applications in machining processes. Appl. Sci. **11**(18), 8764 (2021)
2. Friedrich, J., et al.: Estimation of stability lobe diagrams in milling with continuous learning algorithms. Robot. Comput. Integr. Manuf. **43**, 124–134 (2017)
3. Denkana, B., et al.: Analysis of different machine learning algorithms to learn stability lobe diagram. Procedia CIRP **88**, 282–287 (2020)
4. Friedrich, J., et al.: Online learning of stability lobe diagrams in milling. Procedia CIRP **67**, 278–283 (2019)
5. Karandikar, J., et al.: Stability boundary and optimal operating parameter identification in milling using Bayesian learning. J. Manuf. Process. **56**, 1252–1262 (2020)
6. Chen, G., et al.: Physics-informed Bayesian inference for milling stability analysis. Int. J. Mach. Tools Manuf **167**, 103767 (2021)
7. Schmitz, T., et al.: Receptance coupling substructure analysis and chatter frequency-informed machine learning for milling stability. CIRP Ann. **71**(1), 321–324 (2022)
8. Pujari, A., et al.: Learning machining stability using Bayesian model. In: Communicated for consideration of presentation and for appearing in the Proceedings of the COPEN12 (2022)

9. Sahu, G.N., et al.: Validation of a hardware-in-the-loop simulator for investigating and actively damping regenerative chatter in orthogonal cutting. CIRP J. Manuf. Sci. Technol. **29**, 115–129 (2020)
10. Sahu, G.N., Law, M.: Hardware-in-the-loop simulator for emulation and active control of chatter. HardwareX **11**, e00273 (2022)
11. Sahu, G.N., et al.: Emulating bistabilities in turning to devise gain tuning strategies to actively damp them using a hardware-in-the-loop simulator. CIRP J. Manuf. Sci. Technol. **32**, 120–131 (2021)
12. Sahu, G. N., et al.: Emulating chatter with process damping in turning using a hardware-in-the-loop simulator. In: Proceedings of the 8th International and 29th National All India Manufacturing Technology, Design and Research Conference AIMTDR, pp. 253–262. Springer, Singapore (2023). https://doi.org/10.1007/978-981-19-3866-5_22

Data Sciences

Novel ABC: Aspect Based Classification of Sentiments Using Text Mining for COVID-19 Comments

Kanchan Naithani(✉) ⓘD and Y. P. Raiwani

Department of Computer Science and Engineering, HNB Garhwal University, Srinagar Garhwal, Uttarakhand, India
kanchannaithani696@gmail.com

Abstract. Intricate text mining techniques encompass various practices like classification of text, summarization and detection of topic, extraction of concept, search and retrieval of ideal content, document clustering along with many more aspects like sentiment extraction, text conversion, natural language processing etc. These practices in turn can be used to discover some non-trivial knowledge from a pool of text-based documents. Arguments, difference in opinions and confrontations in the form of words and phrases signify the knowledge regarding an ongoing situation. Extracting sentiment from text that is gathered from online networking web-based platforms entitles the task of text mining in the field of natural language processing. This paper presents a set of steps to optimize the text mining techniques in an attempt to simplify and recognize the aspect-based sentiments behind the content obtained from social media comments.

Keywords: Text mining · Sentiment analysis · Social media comments · ABC: Aspect-Based Classification

1 Introduction

Text mining, is the process of attaining a cinched understanding of the textual content. It is applied for studying and analytically processing unstructured information which forms nearly 80% of the world's data [1]. To explore unstructured data for mining meaningful patterns and perceptions required for exploring text-based data. Organizations and institutions belonging to many different and crucial fields, gather and store enormous data in data warehouses and cloud platforms which continues growing exponentially as a result of new data approaching from various sources. The overall purpose of text mining is to derive exclusive and applied knowledge from text, allowing concerned authorities to make well-versed decisions [2]. The exponential growth of textual data available on online platforms impel researchers to accomplish their research in analyzing sentiments for various products, services and managements.

Classification of Sentiment comes under the techniques for text mining that practices ML (Machine Learning) and NLP (Natural Language Processing) for analyzing text with respect to the sentiment (positive, negative, neutral, and beyond) of the writer [3]. There

N. Khare et al. (Eds.): MIND 2022, CCIS 1762, pp. 203–219, 2022.
https://doi.org/10.1007/978-3-031-24352-3_17

is excessive information available – right down to the actual opinions and emotions of the writer. The focus is on applying the ability to automatically tap into tweets, Facebook posts, and other with almost no human interaction required [4].

This paper is organized as follows: Firstly some research work related to the text mining and aspect based classification of sentiments is reviewed. Then fundamental introduction to text mining as a process is discussed. After that basic and advanced techniques used for text mining are discussed. Later, methodology is realized in terms of novel ABC: Aspect Based Classification of Sentiments, in four major phases for optimizing text mining which in turn will help in providing better results for sentiment analysis. Finally, results are discussed that lead to decisive conclusion and future scope.

2 Related Work

A lot of research work is experienced by various scholars in the area of text mining by various researches to examine the state of affairs and to gain an insight of the emotions behind them. Navaneetha kumar and Chandrasekar reviewed a reliable "web document based text clustering" where an assessment between novel mining approaches for web documents and standard clustering processes was conducted [5]. Gharehchopogh and Abbasi Khalifehlou addressed their work on NLP and AI techniques to obtain functional statistics from unstructured documents [6].

Researchers have concentrated on algorithm practices while implementing innovative procedures to expand the productivity of Pattern-Based methods. An improved "clustering quality" has been attained by semantically discovering the sentence structures in corpus by Lincy Liptha and Wang [7]. Review on various machine learning techniques was provided by Kotsiantis to highlight that supervised machine learning approaches provide better results than unsupervised machine learning approaches. An evident domain transferable lexicon set for Twitter sentiment analysis was proposed by Ghiassi using a supervised machine learning approach [22].

Although, a wide-ranging exploration has been accompanied for sentiment analysis and classification of emotions, but much more advancement can be obtained. A detailed classification method is required that can categorize data with high accuracy. For the same reason, where *unsupervised* or *semi-supervised* approaches have shown low accuracy; *supervised* methodologies have provided better results in terms of classification [9]. The most common challenge faced with supervised approaches is that labelled data are hard to find. As a result, the need to work on semi-supervised approaches that led to high accuracy outcomes, is of prime importance [24].

3 Text Mining: The Process

The process of text mining comprises of various intermediate steps that deal with Natural Language Understanding. The process can be explained with the help of following steps:

3.1 Steps in Text Mining

Text Selection. The first step of text mining works on the gathering of textual data that may be present in structured or unstructured format. As, majority of the text can be extracted through online web portals, researches tend to work on this real time data to get effective insights. Text selection is done taking language identification and under consideration and selecting text that is relevant for further processing [9].

Text Preprocessing. The second step is to arrange the text data for the model building using text preprocessing. The fundamental preprocessing steps are:

a) *Punctuations Removal like., ! $() * % @*
b) *URLs Removal*
c) *Stop words Removal*
d) *Lower casing*
e) *Tokenization*
f) *Stemming*
g) *Lemmatization*

Text Transformation. Text is generally available in an unstructured format so it is obligatory to organize it in a structured format in the third step. The two major ways of document representation are Bag of words and Vector Space. It is done in order to identify meaningful patterns and observe new insights. Transformation of unstructured documents into a structured format is accomplished to empower the study and implementation of practical insights [10].

Feature Extraction. Text feature extraction accounts for the fourth step by directly impelling the accuracy of text classification. Feature selection methods can be divided into four categories: filter, wrapper, embed, and hybrid. The filter conducts a statistical analysis on the feature space to nominate a distinct subclass of features. Wrapper method chooses several subsets of features which are initially recognized and then evaluated using classifiers. Embedded approach embeds the feature selection process into training phase of the classification. The Hybrid approach benefits from the filter as well as wrapper methods.

Text Mining/Pattern Discovery. Text mining proves to be beneficial while generating classification from the collection of documents by realizing the content's main topic/theme. Pattern discovery techniques embrace "categorization of text," "summarization," "topic detection," "concept extraction," "search and retrieval," "document clustering," and much more. These methods can be exploited to gain a number of significant knowledge from any Text based content.

Interpretation/Evaluation. Interpretation and Evaluation generally comprise of concepts where the information accomplished in the previously discussed steps is utilized to constitute practical conclusions in order to achieve convenient decision-making ability. These concepts basically build their foundation from the multiple aspects behind the content while working on sentiments, concordance, cognition, interests, compliance and summarization [9].

Extraction of attention-grabbing patterns from the information in massive text based content is known as Text Mining. It synthesizes the information, by evaluating relations, patterns, and rules among textual data. The general process of Text mining can be viewed in the Fig. 1 where major steps can be observed [10].

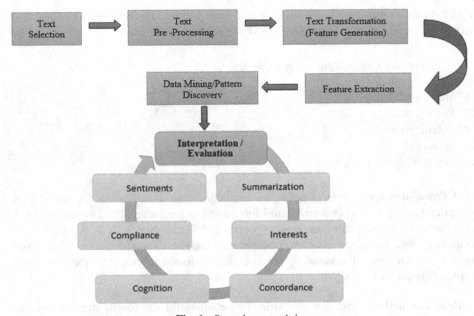

Fig. 1. Steps in text mining

Machine Learning and Text Mining methodologies have established various tools and techniques in collaboration that are well studied and examined. These techniques have been practiced on extensive research areas that comprise "eLearning, social networking, bio informatics, pattern matching, user experience, intelligent tutoring systems," and many more.

Most of the practices used for text mining are established on methods like "clustering, classification, relationship Mining and Pattern Matching [7]". Following are the most common text mining techniques that come in handy while extracting sentiments from textual content.

The text mining approach is often used to find, identify and extract relevant data and information from unstructured and unorganized data.

4   Classification of Sentiments for Text-Based Content

The sentiment classification for text based content proposes computational study of opinions, sentiments, views, emotions, polarity, subjectivity and other aspects of human feelings expressed through textual content [21, 24]. The sentiment classification often chooses one approach that utilizes machine learning model. This approach has even proven to generate improved and enhanced outcomes for the classification by topic, genre, etc. It is based on the word frequency analysis and unique words identification that represent a certain group of texts [16]. Natural Language Processing (NLP) is an important aspect that is taken under consideration while deducing sentiments from textual content. NLP comprises of many tasks that are already executable or can be reformulated as classification tasks, to determine the subjective value of a text-document [17, 20]. Figure 2 below provides insights of computational linguistics, including the complications of text classification while trying to achieve sentiment classification.

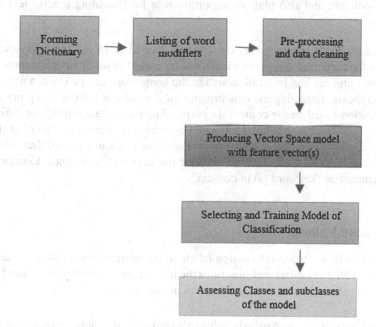

Fig. 2. Steps in Sentiment Classification

5   Frequently Used Methods and Techniques

Most of the text mining techniques are established on methods like clustering, classification, relationship Mining and Pattern Matching [7]. Following are the most common text mining techniques that come in handy while extracting sentiments from textual content.

5.1 Basic Methods

Word Frequency. This method can be used to identify the most recurrent terms or perceptions in a document. Finding the most commonly used words in unstructured text is advantageous when exploring text based content to gain detailed statistical analysis of the word distributions. It helps in developing complex linguistic analysis for classifying the contents like client reviews, social media conversations, or consumer feedback as per the subject [18].

Collocation. Collocation is a set of words that are often displayed next to each other. The most common types of collocations comprise of bigrams and trigrams. A Bigram is defined as pair of words that are generally used together, such as time saver and decision making, whereas a trigram comprises of combination of three words, such as and stay in contact and see you later. Identifying collocations and considering them as one single word helps in enhancing the granularity of the text, better understanding of its semantic structure and also play an important role for providing precise text mining results [20].

Concordance. Concordance looks out for the queried word in a text document and recognizes the particular context or idea in which a word or set of words become apparent. Human language can be ambiguous i.e. the same word can be used in a variety of different contexts. Exploring the concordance of a word can help in accepting its precise implication based on the context. In corpus linguistics, text mining, or digital text analysis, concordance is generated for each occurrence of a particular word in the corpus for the context in which that word appears in the next place. It is a list that recognizes the specific number of words before and after the keyword occurrence. Concordances are also denoted as "keyword (s) in context".

5.2 Advanced Methods

Text Classification. Its job is to assign labels to the unstructured textual content. This crucial step of NLP organizes and structures the intricate text, into meaningful and logical data. The prevalent tasks of text classification are as follows:

a) **Topic Analysis:** Topic Analysis helps in identifying the main themes or areas of a text. It is one of the principal techniques of data organization. The job of topic analysis is to unite terms with analogous meanings and differentiate between practices of terms with several meanings. A process also known as *"Topic modelling"* is used to identify patterns of word-use and how documents with similar patterns can be associated. Topic analysis is achieved over documents by observing the mixtures of topics, where a topic is recognised using probability distribution over words [10]. The various kinds of approaches used for topic modelling, such as *"Latent Semantic Analysis (LSA), Probabilistic Latent Semantic Analysis (PLSA), Latent Dirichlet Allocation (LDA), Correlated Topic Model (CTM)"* have shown upgraded accuracy for topic modeling [11].

b) **Sentiment Analysis:** Sentiment analysis studies the emotions that underlie any given text by identifying the feelings in a text. From the standpoint of text mining, sentiment analysis discovers a connection amongst the writer's emotional state, the style with which he writes and theme around which the content revolves [12], and then categorizes keywords into emotional levels i.e. positive, negative, neutral and beyond. Machine Learning algorithms like *SVM, Naives Bayes, Random Forest, J48, KNN*, along with various new ideologies like *fine-grained subjectivity* and development of a prototype for sentiment recognition system have shown outstanding results than the baseline methods for sentiment classification [11, 13].

c) **Language Detection:** Language Detection classifies a text based on its language. Text mining approaches working with natural language are generally "language-specific" and thus have need of data that is *monolingual*. For generating any project in the target language, a pre-processing scheme is required that eliminates text written in languages other than the target language. For this purpose, languages like R, python, Julia and tools like langdetect, spaCy language detector, langid, FastText etc., have shown much adequacy for detecting language [14].

d) **Intent Detection:** Intent Detection is used to discover the intentions or the purpose behind a text spontaneously. It can be viewed as a process to analyze the textual data for identifying the chief objective of the writer. Several popular text retrievals techniques are used for identifying the intent like inverted indices and signature files [18, 19].

Text Extraction. Text extraction comes under techniques used for text analysis. It is essentially used to extract explicit fragments of data from textual content. These fragments comprise of primary keywords, entity names, addresses, emails, etc [23]. With the help of text extraction, sorting the data manually to pull out key information could be avoided at times, as it can prove to be useful while combining text extraction with text classification in the corresponding analysis [14]. The main responsibilities of text extraction are displayed below:

a) **Keyword Extraction.** Keywords are the most significant entity contained by a text based content that can be used to review its content. Developing a keyword extractor supports the indexing of data, briefing the content of a text or generates *tag clouds*, amidst usual content.

b) **Named Entity Recognition.** It recognizes the key elements in the text by extracting the names of people, institutional brands, monetary values, concerns and more from a text. Mining these main sources in a text helps in sorting unstructured data and distinguishes important information, which plays a vital role in dealing with large datasets.

c) **Feature Extraction:** Features classify specific characteristics of a content or service in a corpus. The approaches like *Bag-of-Words and TF-IDF* used for extracting the features from that corpus convert textual content into a matrix (or vector) of features [8].

Various methods that are used for mining are practiced with machine learning algorithms, to provide context and design. Seven different approaches that include "*classification, clustering, regression analysis, association rule learning, anomaly detection techniques, summarization and other supervised learning approaches*" are identified for the purpose of planning and executing the data warehouses for many crucial motives and reasons [15].

6 Proposed Methodology

Machine learning algorithms are often used to recognize statements as Positive, Negative, or Neutral. Further, more granular results can be achieved using "Aspect-Based Sentiment Analysis," that focuses on the subtleties of human sentiments like joy, anger, sadness, guilt, fear, disgust and the different ways in which opinions can be expressed.

The proposed methodology makes use of Aspect-based sentiment analysis that compares subjective vs. comparative and explicit vs. implicit by organizing the text. This is achieved primarily by attaining *Feature Vectors* in the form of ten hot topics, from COVID19 dataset, comprising of 75,565 comments, tweets and replies that are manually extracted via text mining from three different platforms (Facebook, twitter and YouTube) related to COVID -19 over the social media platforms. Then effort is made to identify sentiments into six major categories that are happy, joy, sad, fear, anger, disgust with neutral tag for different time durations.

6.1 Steps for Novel ABC: Aspect Based Classification

Proposed Novel ABC provides more comprehensive and detailed classifications in comparison with other methods that deliver a generalized summary of emotions. The classification uses machine learning approach to identify and assign emotions to the aspects, features and topics categorized in the content. This approach is achieved using optimization of text mining through four major phases as shown in Fig. 3.

The novelty of the work can be observed in the following phases of proposed methodology, where features identified at phase 2 using TF-IDF Vectors are clustered in such a way that they provide initial step for the abstract classification of sub-topics at phase 3. Later at phase 4, *Classification Algorithm* is introduced in order to train the 70% data (52,890 comments from the combined corpus of three social media platforms) to be classified into six regions of sentiments, along with a neutral tag. The Testing data then classified the remaining 30% data (22,675 reaming comments) into the six emotions along with linear growth of neutral comments for four different time periods.

Phase 1: Data Gathering and Integration
This is the initial step where data from three social media platforms i.e. Facebook, YouTube and twitter is collected in two phases. First phase comprised comments from Late March 2020 to mid-September 2020 and Late September 2020 to Mid-February 2021. The second phase comprised comments from Early March 2021 to Late May 2021 and Early June 2021 to Late October 2021. A total of 39,775 comments from Facebook,

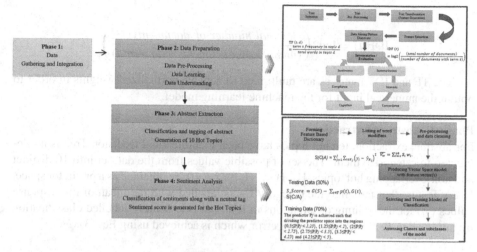

Fig. 3. Methodology

15,634 comments from YouTube and 20,156 tweets from twitter on the topics that covered almost all aspects of COVID19 are manually collected for four different time periods.

Phase 2: Data Preparation

In this phase, data that is collected and arranged in the previous step is pre-processed. *R* packages like *OpenNLP, tm, SnowballC* and text stemming library are used to perform basic Pre-Processing steps- tokenization, part-of-speech tagging, stemming, lemmatization, stop word removal, punctuation elimination and removal of extra white spaces which in turn transformed the text into a structured dataset. This data is then explored in search of patterns and deviations to learn some conclusive insights. The learnings are then utilized towards accepting the insights that are gained to understand the topic.

The frequency of words' occurrences is found using Term Frequency (TF) that is assigned for the hot topics in the dataset that comprises of the features as words.

$$\text{TF}(t, d) = \frac{term\ t\ frequency\ in\ topic\ d}{total\ words\ in\ topic\ d} \tag{1}$$

- where t is the word frequency in topic based document d.

IDF (Inverse Document Frequency) is used to retrieve the most crucial or least commonly used words in topic-based documents. IDF helps in extracting meaningful words from the document. The words with highest degree are extracted with the help of TF whereas words with the lowest using IDF by taking their logarithmic values.

$$\text{IDF}(t) = \log 2\left(\frac{(\textit{total number of documents})}{(\textit{number of documents with term t})}\right) \tag{2}$$

The TF and IDF matrices are multiplied to achieve normalized weights in order to obtain the numerical input for the machine learning model.

Phase 3: Abstract Extraction

For abstract extraction, ten hot topics have been identified and Decision Tree is implemented to categorize them. The set of possible values from the dataset into 10 distinct and non-overlapping hot topics, $H_1, H_2 \ldots H_j$ for $j = 10$ are obtained as a predictor space. Every feature that falls into the category H_j, is labelled with the mean of the response values (y_t) for the training observations in R_j. Goal is to achieve labelled classification by minimizing *Residual Sum Square* error which is achieved using Eq. (3).

$$\textit{Error}_{Rss} = \sum_{j=1}^{J} \sum_{t \in H_j} \left(y_t - \hat{y}_{H_j}\right)^2 \tag{3}$$

- where $\hat{y}_{H_j}$ is the mean response for the training observations within the *jth* topic.

The predictor Pj is achieved such that dividing the predictor space into the regions $\{0.5 \leq P|Pj < 1.25\}, \{1.25 \leq P|Pj < 2\}, \{2 \leq P|Pj < 2.75\}, \{2.75 \leq P|Pj < 3.5\}, \{3.5 \leq P|Pj < 4.25\}$ and $\{4.25 \leq P|Pj < 5\}$. Thus achieving accurate Classification and tagging of abstract by generating the Hot Topics. The ten hot topics that were derived are as follows:

- "Social distancing"
- "Distribution of Masks, Sanitizers and food entities"
- "Medical Conditions and Aid"
- "Political Agendas during Crisis"
- "Bed availability"
- "Oxygen Cylinders availability"
- "Online Educational Policies"
- "Work from home routine"
- "Financial Crisis"
- "Transportation"

Phase 4: Sentiment Analysis

Six aspects of emotions that are happy, sad, angry, disgust, joy and fear on 10 Hot Topics selected from the data are extracted using classification Algorithm. Firstly a features set is created that stored text on the basis of its frequent occurrence, in an ordered fashion to classify the comments later under hot topics. Sentiment score "S_Score" is calculated for each hot topic lying under the feature set where score for each category of sentiment "C" under aspect "A" is achieved using decision tree. The hot topic is assigned with a sentiment score for each sub category of emotion, calculated from the hot topic tagged along the aspect of the feature set. This algorithm is repeated for the entire corpus until it is organised for each sentiment in an ordered way. Finally, average percentage P(A) for each aspect of for sentiments along with a feature set under neutral tag, is obtained for the hot topics for four time periods.

Classification Algorithm

Input: Comment
Output: Sentiment Score
Procedure:

1. For every comment
2. Implement PoS Tagging
3. Create a decision tree
4. Categorise phrases containing features
5. Calculate sentiment score (out of 5) in six aspects of comments w.r.t respective hot_topic
6. End for
7. For every feature do
8.   Compute IF-IDF
9.   If freq >=0.2
10. $feature_{set} \rightarrow feature_{set} + feature$
11.   Return $feature_{set}$
12. For every $feature_{set}$ (C|A)
13.   do
14.   Approximate S_Score(C|A)
15. For every S_Score in S(C|A)
16.   do
17.   if I(C|A)==0.25 then
18.   For every A in hot_topic
19.   if P(A) ==P(A|C) +A
20.   hot_topic $\rightarrow$ hot_topic + A
21.   Else
22. $feature_{set\_neutral} \rightarrow feature_{set\_neutral} + A$
23. Return $feature_{set\_neutral}$

---

7 Results and Analysis

The proposed methodology resulted in providing sentiments for 10 different themes of COVID19 comments extracted during and after the extreme effects of the pandemic. The sentiment score (out of 5) for the six sentiments along with a neutral tag from Late March 2020 to mid-September 2020 can be observed in Table 1, from Late September 2020 to Mid-February 2021 in Table 2, from Early March 2021 to Late May 2021 in Table 3 and from Early June 2021 to Late October 2021 in Table 4. The S_Score was ranged from *0 to 5* for *0* being *lowest intensity* and *5* being *highest* for respective category of sentiments. The observation deduced from the Tables 1, 2, 3 and 4 has shown diversity of emotions during the course of four periods.

Table 1. S_Score for late march 2020 to mid-september 2020

Hot topics	Happy	Joy	Sad	Fear	Anger	Disgust	Neutral
Following social distancing	2.1	3.5	2.6	4	4.3	2.4	1.2
Distribution of masks, hand sanitizers and food entities	2.5	3.6	2.5	1	3.6	4.4	2.5
Medical conditions and aid	3.5	1.8	3.5	3	3.5	1.8	1.5
Political agendas during the crisis	2.3	2.8	4.5	1.2	4.5	2.8	1.5
Bed availability	2.6	2.4	3.6	4.3	3.9	2.4	4.6
Oxygen cylinders availability	2.5	3.5	3.6	3.9	1.3	4.4	2
Online education policies	3.5	2.8	3	2.9	3	1.8	3
Work from home routine	4.5	3.9	1.2	0.25	1.3	2.8	2.8
Financial crisis	2.8	1.3	4.5	3.9	4.6	5	2.3
Transportation	2.3	3.1	1.6	3.6	4.8	3.8	3.1

Table 2. S_Score for late september 2020 to mid-february 2021

Hot topics	Happy	Joy	Sad	Fear	Anger	Disgust	Neutral
Following social distancing	3.2	2.3	1.3	1.5	2.6	4.6	2.5
Distribution of masks, hand sanitizers and food entities	1.5	2.6	2.4	1.2	1.3	0.56	2.5
Medical conditions and aid	3.5	1.8	3.5	3	3.5	1.8	1.5
Political agendas during the crisis	2.3	2.8	4.5	1.2	4.5	2.8	1.5
Bed availability	2.6	2.4	3.6	4.3	3.9	2.4	4.6
Oxygen cylinders availability	2.5	3.5	3.6	3.9	1.3	4.4	2
Online education policies	3.5	2.8	3	2.9	3	1.8	3
Work from home routine	4.5	3.9	1.2	0.25	1.3	2.8	2.8
Financial crisis	2.8	1.6	4.5	3.9	4.6	5	2.3
Transportation	2.3	3.1	1.6	3.6	4.8	3.8	3.1

Table 3. S_Score for early march 2021 to late may 2021

Hot topics	Happy	Joy	Sad	Fear	Anger	Disgust	Neutral
Following social distancing	3.6	3.7	1.2	4.3	0.15	0.06	4
Distribution of masks, hand sanitizers and food entities	2.6	2.6	4.5	1.3	2.3	3.1	2
Medical conditions and aid	2.8	1.3	3.6	4.6	3.9	3.6	2.3
Political agendas during the crisis	2.5	2.3	2.3	2.3	4.2	4.5	0.26
Bed availability	3.8	3.3	3.6	3.89	4.6	4.6	3.9
Oxygen cylinders availability	3.4	2.6	3.9	4.12	4.8	4.8	0.12
Online education policies	3.8	3.6	1.2	0.49	2.5	0.26	2.6
Work from home routine	3.6	3.4	0.23	0.23	0.23	3.23	3.1
Financial crisis	1.2	2.1	2.89	1.56	2.6	2.0	3.5
Transportation	0.3	0.5	3.69	2.3	4.6	4.3	1.9

Table 4. S_Score for Early June 2021 to Late October 2021.

Hot topics	Happy	Joy	Sad	Fear	Anger	Disgust	Neutral
Following social distancing	3.9	2.3	0.3	1.2	1.5	0.23	4
Distribution of masks, hand sanitizers and food entities	1.5	0.23	0.6	0.36	1.3	0.13	4.1
Medical conditions and aid	3.6	3.1	2.5	3.5	3.1	1.5	2.3
Political agendas during the crisis	2.1	2.0	2.1	1.5	2.6	3.2	2.3
Bed availability	3.6	3.1	3.1	2.6	3.4	1.2	2.1
Oxygen cylinders availability	3.5	3.5	2.3	2.1	3.9	2.9	1.5
Online education policies	3.5	2.3	0.2	0.6	2.6	1.3	4.6
Work from home routine	3.1	3.5	1.6	1.5	1.6	3.6	3.5
Financial crisis	2.0	3.2	3.1	3.2	2.6	2.6	3.6
Transportation	3.9	4.1	0.3	0.9	2.8	2.8	1.6

Distinct features of Novel ABC for sentiment analysis, extract granular information from the data hence presenting a complete understanding of the sentiments. It is observed that the *happy* and *joy* aspects for COVID19 comments are maximum for the time duration from *Early June 2021 to Late October 2021*, the *sad, fear* and *anger* aspects are maximum for *duration Early March 2021 to Late May 2021*, *disgust* was maximum from *Late March 2020 to mid-September 2020*. The linear growth in trend line is the proof that with the time, the topic COVID19 neutralized and people maintained a system where they can fight and coexist with the disease. To analyse this average percentage of sentiments for four-time intervals along with the trend line of neutral tag is observed in Fig. 4.

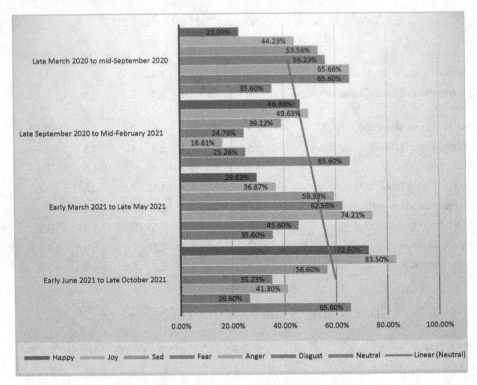

Fig. 4. Average percentage analysis of sentiments for four time intervals

7.1 Comparative Analysis

The confusion matrix is put to use for witnessing the models developed with the *Classification* Algorithm. Four statistical measures are used i.e. the Accuracy (ACC), Precision (PRE), Recall (REC) and F-measure (F) for analyzing the *Decision based Classification Algorithm*. The accuracy evaluates the probability of detecting the true class. Precision is responsible for obtaining the probability of correctly identifying the True Positive (TP) class. Recall is responsible for obtaining the probability of correctly identifying the True Negative (TN) class. Following Eqs. (4–7) present the mean of the PRE and REC, where an F provides its finest value at 1 (perfect PRE and REC) and the poorest at 0.

Equation (4) presents the Accuracy value

$$ACC = \frac{T_P + T_N}{T_P + T_N + F_P + F_N} \tag{4}$$

Equation (5) presents the Precision value

$$PRE = \frac{T_P}{T_P + F_P} \tag{5}$$

Equation (6) presents the Precision value

$$REC = \frac{T_P}{T_P + F_N} \tag{6}$$

Equation (7) presents the F-measure value

$$F = \frac{2 * Precision * Recall}{Precision + Recall} \tag{7}$$

Table 5. Comparative analysis

Ref. No	Year	Approaches	ACC	PRE	REC	F
[25]	2020	Sentiment classification using recurrent neural network	0.89	0.89	0.91	0.89
[26]	2021	Deep learning-based sentiment analysis – Recurrent Neural Network- (RNN-)oriented architecture, including Long Short-Term Memory (LSTM) and Bidirectional LSTM (Bi-LSTM)	0.90	0.92	0.91	0.91
[27]	2021	Convolutional neural network and recurrent neural network	0.84	0.82	0.86	0.83
[28]	2022	XGBoost (eXtreme gradient boosting) – tree base model for	0.96	0.89	0.86	0.88
Proposed method		Aspect based classification using decision trees	0.94	0.91	0.92	0.91

8   Conclusions and Future Work

The proposed work showed maximum accuracy than the three existing approaches for sentiment classification. Although, as observed from Table 5, the XGBoost have shown better results in terms of accuracy but lacks in aspect based classification. The proposed approach have also shown competing values of Precision, Recall and F-measure. It was observed that recently majority of work has been done using variety of Neural Networks for classifying sentiments, but decision trees could provide better results if implemented with tagged aspects.

The field of computer science dealing with *text mining*, has developed various tools and techniques using machine learning and data mining approaches. The work also describes that text mining along with Machine Learning approach to extract aspects for sentiments can aid the "infodemiology study," thus assisting researchers for observing public discussions and concluding sentiments based on those discussions during the COVID-19 pandemic.

Future work includes improving the proposed model to analyze sarcasm level also. It will also observe many more variations of text mining by discovering different weighing schemes for feature vectors and estimating the research on various other social media datasets. "Named Entity Recognition" and "Negation Problems" could be taken under consideration to advance sentiment analysis. Also, utilization of various techniques like "bootstrap aggregation," "boosting" and "stacking" could be implemented to expand and enhance the outcomes in the field of sentiment analysis.

Authors Contribution. All authors contributed to the study conception and design. Material preparation, data collection and analysis were performed by Kanchan Naithani, Y. P. Raiwani. The first draft of the manuscript was written by Kanchan Naithani and the second author commented on previous versions of the manuscript.

All authors have read and approved the final manuscript.

References

1. Patel, R., Sharma, G.: A survey on text mining techniques. Int. J. Eng. Comput. Sci. (2014)
2. Dhawan, S., Singh, K., Khanchi, V.: Emotion mining techniques in social networking sites. Int. J. Inf. Comput. Technol. **4**, 1145–1153 (2014)
3. Maca, V.M.M., et al.: Measurement of viewer sentiment to improve the quality of television and interactive content using adaptive content. In: Proceedings of the 2016 International Conference on Electrical, Electronics, and Optimization Techniques (ICEEOT). IEEE (2016)
4. Gupta, A., Semwal, V.B.: Multiple task human gait analysis and identification: ensemble learning approach. In: Mohanty, S.N. (ed.) Emotion and information processing, pp. 185–197. Springer, Cham (2020). https://doi.org/10.1007/978-3-030-48849-9_12
5. Navaneethakumar, V.M., Chandrasekar, C.: A consistent web documents based text clustering using concept based mining model. IJCSI Int. J. Comput. Sci. Issues **9**(4), 365 (2012)
6. Gharehchopogh, F.S., Abbasi Khalifehlou, Z.: Study on information extraction methods from text mining and natural language processing perspectives. In: AWER Procedia Information Technology and Computer Science, 2nd World Conference on Information Technology (2011)
7. Liptha, L., Arasu, G.T.: Enhancing text clustering using concept-based mining model (2012)
8. Naithani, K., Raiwani, Y.P., Sissodia, R.: Text-based analysis of COVID-19 comments using natural language processing. In: Artificial Intelligence and Speech Technology, AIST 2021. Communications in Computer and Information Science (2022)
9. Gupta, V.: A survey of text mining techniques and applications. J. Emerg. Technol. Web Intell. **1**(1), 60–76 (2009)
10. Rath, S.K., Jena, M.K., Nayak, T., Bisoyee, B.: Data mining: a healthy tool for your information retrieval and text mining. Int. J. Comput. Sci. Inf. Technol. **2** (2011)
11. Kotsiantis, S.B.: Supervised machine learning: a review of techniques. Informatica **31**, 249–268 (2007)
12. Hashimi, H., Hafez, A.M., Mathkour, H.: Selection criteria for text mining approaches. Comput. Hum. Behav. **51**, 729–733 (2015)
13. Alghamdi, A.: A survey of topic modeling in text mining. Int. J. Adv. Comput. Sci. Appl. **6** (2015)
14. Hofmann, T.: Unsupervised learning by probabilistic latent semantic analysis. Mach. Learn. **42**(1), 177–196 (2001)
15. Argamon, S., Bloom, K., Esuli, A., Sebastiani, F.: Automatically determining attitude type and force for sentiment analysis. In: Vetulani, Z., Uszkoreit, H. (eds.) LTC 2007. LNCS (LNAI), vol. 5603, pp. 218–231. Springer, Heidelberg (2009). https://doi.org/10.1007/978-3-642-04235-5_19
16. Whitelaw, C., Navendu, G., Argamon, S.: Using appraisal groups for sentiment analysis. In: Proceedings of the 14th ACM International Conference on Information and Knowledge Management (2005)

17. Salloum, S.A., Al-Emran, M., Monem, A.A., Shaalan, K.: Using text mining techniques for extracting information from research articles. In: Shaalan, K., Hassanien, A.E., Tolba, F. (eds.) Intelligent Natural Language Processing: Trends and Applications. SCI, vol. 740, pp. 373–397. Springer, Cham (2018). https://doi.org/10.1007/978-3-319-67056-0_18

18. Naithani, K., Raiwani, Y.P.: Realization of natural language processing and machine learning approaches for text-based sentiment analysis. Expert Syst. (2022)

19. Akhtar, M.S., Ghosal, D., et al.: A Multi-task ensemble framework for emotion, sentiment and intensity prediction, computation and language

20. Imtiaz, M.N., Ben Islam, M.K.: Identifying significance of product features on customer satisfaction recognizing public sentiment polarity: analysis of smart phone industry using machine-learning approaches. Appl. Artif. Intell. **34**(11), 832–848 (2020)

21. Kaur, H., Ahsaan, S.U., Alankar, B., Chang, V.: A proposed sentiment analysis deep learning algorithm for analyzing COVID-19 Tweets. Inf. Syst. Front. **23**(6), 1417–1429 (2021). https://doi.org/10.1007/s10796-021-10135-7

22. Ghiassi, M., & Lee, S. (2018). A domain transferable lexicon set for Twitter sentiment analysis using a supervised machine learning approach. Expert Systems with Applications

23. Hung, B.T., Semwal, V.B., Gaud, N., Bijalwan, V.: Hybrid deep learning approach for aspect detection on reviews. In: Singh Mer, K.K., Semwal, V.B., Bijalwan, V., Crespo, R.G. (eds.) Proceedings of Integrated Intelligence Enable Networks and Computing. AIS, pp. 991–999. Springer, Singapore (2021). https://doi.org/10.1007/978-981-33-6307-6_100

24. Semwal, V.B., Gupta, A., Lalwani, P.: An optimized hybrid deep learning model using ensemble learning approach for human walking activities recognition. J. Supercomput. **77**(11), 12256–12279 (2021). https://doi.org/10.1007/s11227-021-03768-7

25. Nemes, L., Kiss, A.: Social media sentiment analysis based on COVID-19. J. Inf. Telecommun. **5**(1), 1–15 (2020)

26. Khan, Mhd., Nabiul, A.K, Dhruba, A.: Deep learning-based sentiment analysis of COVID-19 vaccination responses from Twitter data. Comput. Math. Methods Med. (2021)

27. Ezhilan, A., Dheekksha, R., Anahitaa, R., Shivani, R.et al.: Sentiment analysis and classification of COVID-19 Tweets. In: Proceedings of the 2021 5th International Conference on Trends in Electronics and Informatics (ICOEI) (2021)

28. Jalil, Z., et al.: COVID-19 related sentiment analysis using state-of-the-art machine learning and deep learning techniques. Front. Pub. Health **9** (2022)

Topic Modeling, Sentiment Analysis and Text Summarization for Analyzing News Headlines and Articles

Omswroop Thakur[✉], Sri Khetwat Saritha, and Sweta Jain

Department of CSE, Maulana Azad National Institute of Technology, Bhopal 481001, India
thakuromswroop@gmail.com

Abstract. Newspapers and News Websites have become a part and a crucial medium in society. They provide information regarding the events that are happening around and how society is getting influenced by these events. For example, a pandemic like Covid-19 has raised the importance of these mediums. They have been giving detailed news to society on a variety of topics, such as how to detect the strains of the coronavirus, reasons for lockdown along with what are the other restrictions to be followed during the pandemic. They also provided information about the government policies which were built to be taken care of in case of pandemics and so on and they kept updated with the details about the development of the vaccines. Due to this lot of information on Covid-19 is generated. Examining the different topics/themes/issues and the sentiments expressed by different countries will aid in the understanding of the covid-19. This paper discusses the various models which were built to identify the topics, sentiments, and summarization of news headlines and articles regarding Covid-19. The proposed topic model has achieved a Silhouette score of 0.6407036, 0.6645274, 0.6262914, and 0.6234863 for 4 countries like South Korea, Japan, the UK, India on the news articles dataset, and it was found that the United Kingdom was the worst-hit, and it had the largest percentage of negative sentiments. The proposed XlNet sentiment classification model obtained a validation accuracy of 93.75%.

Keyword: NLP · COVID-19 · XLNet · BERTopic · Topic modeling

1 Introduction

A pneumonia outbreak with a source that was unknown was reported in the Hubei Province of Wuhan, China, in December 2019. The virus which was responsible for the outbreak was identified and it was termed severe acute respiratory syndrome coronavirus 2 later on (SARS-CoV-2). In February 2020, the World Health Organization (WHO) designated SARS-CoV-2 as "COVID-19," a disease that is triggered by the virus. As of January 18, 2021, over 456.908 million individuals have been infected by the coronavirus which resulted in the deaths of over 6.041 million individuals, according to the Johns Hopkins Coronavirus Resource Center. The News websites and newspapers started covering the information about the COVID-19 pandemic continuously around the

© The Author(s), under exclusive license to Springer Nature Switzerland AG 2022
N. Khare et al. (Eds.): MIND 2022, CCIS 1762, pp. 220–239, 2022.
https://doi.org/10.1007/978-3-031-24352-3_18

globe. These are an eminent resource for learning about the social, economic, and political realities of a society's or country's response to the fatal pandemic. Furthermore, news production is influenced by a wide range of cultural attitudes and opinionated assumptions [1]. As a result, news can be considered as a social text that figuratively incorporates as well as recirculates those assumptions and ideas, thereby recreating the reality of society. Due to the lockdown, millions of people lost their employment all across the world. The complete lockdown in India resulted in a massive migrant crisis [2], and several of the world's top nations encountered negative values of Gross Domestic Product growth [3]. In the United States, over three fifty companies were bankrupted because of the coronavirus pandemic.

To perform processing as well as analyzing massive amounts of natural language data, Natural Language Processing and its numerous methodologies have gained significance. The amalgamation of Artificial Intelligence, as well as Linguistics, takes place in the field of Natural Language Processing so that computers can comprehend human or natural language [4]. The significance of Natural Language Processing in today's world is heightened by the reason that we generate tremendous quantities of unstructured text information every day. Named Entity Recognition [5], Sentiment Analysis [6], Machine Translation [7], Topic Modeling [8], and Text Summarization [9] are some of the most established as well as eminent methodologies of Natural Language Processing. Gathering as much information as possible about the COVID-19 problem is a critical asset in the current pandemic caused by the coronavirus. The research objective presented in this paper is, firstly, to look for trends in important subjects and themes in News (considered English language) related to the coronavirus pandemic from 4 countries (South Korea, Japan, UK, India) and also, to conduct an analysis that includes a comparison of the different issues to identify the common trends. Secondly, to categorize and analyze the sentiments of news websites headlines that are related to the pandemic caused by the coronavirus.

The organization of the paper is as follows, the paper first discusses the related work, then the proposed methodology and Results and Experiments.

2 Related Work

2.1 Topic Modeling

The epidemic caused by the coronavirus is being studied by researchers all around the globe. After the disease caused by coronavirus was discovered in Dec 2019, several studies from multiple domains have been published. The research based on the concept of Natural Language processing which analyzes the contents based on coronavirus like news, scientific articles, and social media posts is one of the emerging aspects of research related to the COVID-19 pandemic. R. F. Sear et al. [10] utilized the Facebook dataset to identify the topics amongst the Pro vax community and Anti vax community using the LDA topic modeling approach. Bái et al. [11] proposed research based on topic evolution analysis of news articles that are related to COVID-19 from the news articles of Canada. Liu et al. [12] utilized an automated approach based on topic modeling for evaluating the data from news in the initial phases of the onset of the coronavirus in China. Jelodar H et al. [13] proposed a topic modeling methodology using LDA on the sub-reddits linked to coronavirus. [14] demonstrated a system that performs infoveillance for recognizing relevant topics as well as keeping traces of them. The tweets used in the system were Italian. Noor et al. [15] evaluated how people reacted to the COVID-19 epidemic caused by coronavirus on the Twitter dataset. M. Bahja et al. [16] proposed a topic modeling approach in which the tweets linking the COVID-19 pandemic to 5G were considered.

2.2 Sentiment Analysis and Emotion Detection

Samuel et al. [17] discussed the perception as well as the sentiments of the people towards the coronavirus and also discussed the classification of tweets through machine learning. Imran et al. [18] utilized an approach based on deep learning to predict the emotions as well as the polarities which were cross-cultural in nature from the tweets collected from 6 nations. A methodology was presented by Huang et al. [19] to analyze the sentiment of sentences that contained the sentiment details as well as the contextual information of sentiment terms. To discover the viewpoint of the people about the outbreak caused by coronavirus Boon-Itt and Skunkan [20] proposed the topic modeling as well as sentiment analysis approach using tweets. Das et al. [21] proposed a methodology to classify the sentiments as well as emotions of the people in the coronavirus outbreak in India. Barkur et al. [22] describe an approach based on sentiment analysis of the coronavirus outbreak in India, which resulted in a countrywide lockdown. Ali Shariq Imran et al. [23] on the Kaggle dataset and Trending hashtag # data, proposed a Deep learning LSTM technique for the classification of sentiments. To obtain the needs of individuals during the coronavirus pandemic who are in New York State, Zijian Long [24] Proposed a Platform for the analysis of tweets by utilizing the Support vector machine algorithm. R. L. Rosa et al. [25] proposed a methodology using Tree-CNN, DBN (Deep Belief Network) on Twitter, Sina Weibo dataset. A. Mourad [26] proposed a heuristic study that was conducted during the coronavirus pandemic, to provide a quantitative estimation of the infodemic caused by social media platforms. This research studied the good and bad impact of social media platforms on beating the coronavirus pandemic. They proposed a methodology that is based on mixed ontology data analytics techniques and experiments that target the tweet contexts as well as the profiles of individuals. F. Es-Sabery [27] proposed a MapReduce enhanced weighted ID3 decision tree classification strategy for the purpose of opinion mining and primarily comprised the 3 aspects. In the first step, they utilized feature extractors such as TF-IDF, word embedding (Word2Vec and Glove), along with feature extractors such as FastText as well as N-grams to identify and capture the data which is relevant efficiently. After that, they utilized various feature selectors such as Gini Index, Gain Ratio along with other feature selectors like Chi-square as well as Information in order to decrease the high feature's dimensionality. After that the work of classification using an enhanced ID3 decision tree classifier was by utilizing the collected features, the classifier seeks to evaluate the weighted information gain rather than the usual id3 information gain. T. Da and L. Yang [28] proposed a model with three steps that sequentially perform the following steps. The first step includes the task of labeling the tweets of Sina Weibo by utilizing the Sentiment Knowledge Enhanced pre-training (SKEP) which is a state-of-the-art pre-trained model. T. Wang [29] considered the social platform, Sina Weibo, in which they deal only with the posts which have sentiments with only negative polarity. They utilized 999,978 coronavirus posts which were arbitrarily chosen from the Sina Weibo platform between the time duration of 01/01/2020 and 18/02/2020. M. K. Elhadad [30] presented a methodology for detecting false information that uses data from the United Nations, WHO, as well as UNICEF. P. Gupta [31] proposed a methodology that aims to find out how the people of India feel about the government's nationwide lockdown, which was implemented to slow the spread of COVID-19. The sentiment analysis of tweets produced by the people of India was carried out utilizing Natural Language Processing as well as machine learning classifiers in this research.

2.3 Topic Modeling and Sentiment Analysis

All of the works listed from [10] to [31] utilized the coronavirus data for either topic modeling or sentiment analysis. Whereas, there are few studies that have analyzed the coronavirus data that utilize the approaches of sentiment analysis as well as topic modeling. Methodologies such as Valence Aware Dictionary for sentiment Reasoning as well as latent Dirichlet allocation were utilized by Chandrasekaran et al. [32] to examine the sentiments as well as trends. Among these topics related to coronavirus were also discussed. Xue et al. [33] proposed a methodology that utilized Latent Dirichlet Allocation for performing topic modeling and analyzed the tweets for getting insights about sentiments of people. Finally, Xie et al. [34] analyzed the people's reactions on Weibo which is a microblogging site from China, and utilized sentiment analysis as well as latent Dirichlet allocation for topic modeling. Piyush G [35] proposed a technique in which they collected the data of headlines and news articles from the news websites and for determining the topics on these datasets, they applied the model named top2vec. After that, they performed sentiment analysis by applying two steps which includes the creation of a dataset that is labeled by the method of unsupervised machine learning, and after that, this labeled dataset was trained and tested by applying the algorithm of Roberta.

2.4 Text Summarization and Other Approaches

X.Wan [36] proposed a system that filters articles from numerous digital sources using the concept of NLP and converts them into information that can be understood by the user. They also modeled the topics from various sources that are frequently debated to help the users to achieve opinions about the serious situation such as coronavirus pandemic. X. Yu [39] Proposed a methodology which is a visual analytic system that is also interactive named Senti-COVID-19 as shown in Fig. 9. The system analyses the sentiment of people and also identifies the fluctuations triggers of sentiments on social platforms. The system utilizes sentiment analysis which is based on lexicons to reveal the perceptions of coronavirus events.

3 Methodology

There are three modules in this research. In the first module BERTopic model is used to identify and analyze the topics which are most representative in the dataset of the 4 nations (South Korea, Japan, UK and India). In the second module, text summarization is being performed on news articles by using BERT model. The third module is sentiment analysis. In this module, training and testing are performed on a labeled dataset with XLNet.

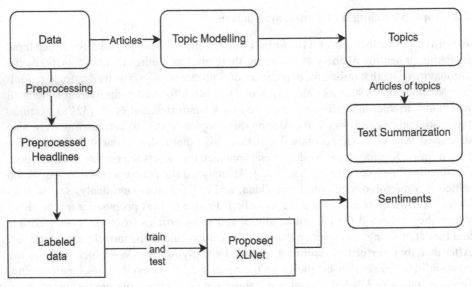

Fig. 1. Proposed architecture

Figure 1 shows the proposed model for identifying the topics, summarization of news articles and analyzing the sentiments of news headlines. The architecture is divided into 3 modules.

3.1 Module 1: Topic Modeling

In NLP, arranging, finding, and condensing a huge amount of textual data is a common issue. Topic modeling is a type of statistical modeling for identifying the abstract "topics" that exist in a set of documents. Topic modeling is an unsupervised machine learning technique that's capable of scanning a collection of documents, detecting word as well as phrase patterns within them, and it also automatically clusters word groups and similar expressions that best characterize a collection of documents as shown in Fig. 2.

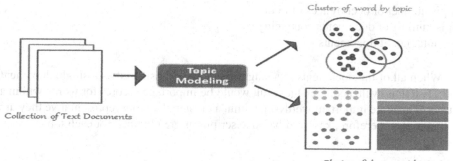

Fig. 2. Topic modeling

When a person is unable to read and sort through a vast corpus of text, topic modeling is applied. The semantic structure which is hidden or topics that exist in the corpus can be discovered using a topic model. BERTopic is a topic modeling technique that utilizes BERT embeddings along with c-TF-IDF to produce clusters of dense nature that allows a clear understanding of subjects and along with this, in the rendition of topic it keeps the keywords intact. The two most significant advantages of BERTopic are its simple out-of-the-box use and its innovative interactive visualization approaches. An internal view of the model's quality and the most noteworthy topics wrapped in the corpus can be constructed by having an overall overview of the topics that the model has learned.

Three main algorithm components of BERTopic model are:

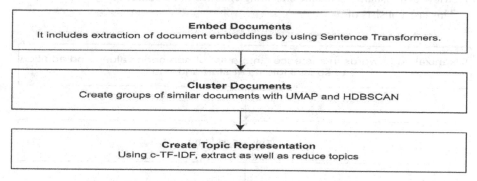

Fig. 3. Three main algorithm components of BERTopic model

The TF-IDF (term frequency-inverse document frequency) method compares importance of words between documents by calculating the frequency of a word in a given document as well as the measure of how prevalent the word is in the entire corpus it is calculated as follows (Fig. 3):

$$w_{i,j} = tf_{i,j} \times \log(\frac{N}{df_i}) \tag{1}$$

where:

$tf_{i,j}$ is number of occurrences of i in j
df_i is number of documents containing i
N is total no. of documents.

When all of the documents in a single cluster are considered as a single document and TF-IDF is evaluated, then the result would be importance scores for words within a cluster. The more important words are within a cluster, the more representative they are of that topic. Therefore, keyword-based descriptions are obtained for each topic.

3.2 Module 2: Text Summarization

Various topics were generated in the Module 1. The module considers these topics particularly the top 10 topics. Since these 10 topics obtained are the most representative topics as the relevance. They can be considered as the representatives of complete article dataset as they are representing the top topics of the news articles. The second module considers the 1000 articles containing these top 10 topics. As the topic modeling approach described in Module 1, only evaluates the topics and their related words based on c-TF-IDF scores, there is a need for more elaborate descriptions of those topics. Thus, module 2 performs the text summarization of the articles containing the top 10 topics. The methodology utilized for this purpose is described in this module. For the purpose of extractive summarization, the pre-trained BERT model has been utilized. This BERT model is being used as a sentence embedding tool. Machine learning tools, namely nearest-neighbors, k-means clustering, and dimensionality reduction have been utilized to retrieve and visualize semantic clustering encoded in the text (Fig. 4).

This task consists of:

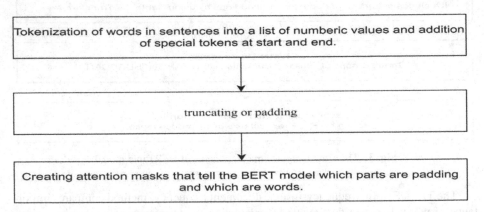

Fig. 4. Text summarization methodology

3.3 Module 3: Sentiment Classification

The traditional Natural Language Processing classifiers which are based on bag-of-words approach like Naive Bayes, LogisticRegressionCV along with LinearSVC ignore word order and thus ignore the context and this results in the ignorance of semantics which is the meaning of the words. But as far as Natural Language Processing is concerned the meaning as well as text are very vital. The XLNet [40] is a machine learning technique that is based on a transformer. It is well-known for its generalized autoregressive pretraining method, and it is amongst the remarkable transpiring models of Natural Language Processing. The XLNet contains the most recent advances in NLP, as well as solutions and alternative methods to language modeling. One more important aspect of XLNet is the auto-regressive language model. This model promotes the combined predictions across token sequences by utilizing the design of transformers. Its goal is to determine whether overall adjustments of word tokens in a sentence are possible (Fig. 5).

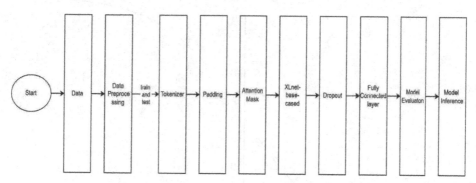

Fig. 5. Model Architecture for sentiment analysis

The language model is divided into 2 parts: pretrain and fine-tune. XLNet focuses mostly on the pre-train phase. One of the new objectives implemented in the pre-train phase is permutation language modeling. The data is first preprocessed and then the data is converted into tokens by performing tokenization and then padding is performed. Then the data is passed through the attention layer, after that the data is into the "xlnet-base-cased" layer. The data, then passes through a Dropout layer and then to a fully connected layer for fine-tuning and classification. The activation function used in the "xlnet-base-cased" is GELU Activation function. GELU stands for gaussian error linear unit. This activation can be given as (Fig. 6):

Mathematically it can be represented as-

$$GELU(x) = xP(X \leq x) = x\varphi(x) = x \times \frac{1}{2}\left[1 + erf\left(x/\sqrt{2}\right)\right] \tag{2}$$

The Dropout layer is utilized in this architecture. Dropout is implemented per-layer in a neural network. Dropout is a technique used to prevent a model from overfitting. Also, another activation function used is the sigmoid function and it is given by (Fig. 7):

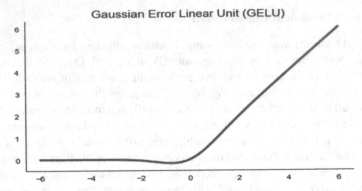

Fig. 6. GELU activation function

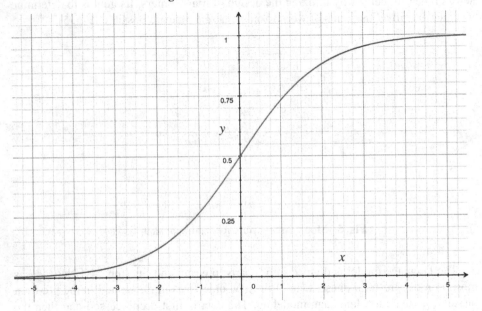

Fig. 7. Sigmoid activation function

Mathematically it can be represented as-

$$f(x) = \frac{1}{1 + e^{-x}} \tag{3}$$

Preprocessing

Text preprocessing is the process of preparing as well as cleaning text data in Natural Language Processing (NLP). Steps which were used to perform the preprocessing of news headlines are listed below.

Tokenization

Tokenization is the process of obtaining small parts of text from a text document, like single words, phrases, sentences, and paragraphs. Tokens are supposed to be the smaller units. Before feeding it to the model, all of this is broken down with the help of a tokenizer. "XLNetTokenizer" was used on our pre-trained model, because models require tokens to be placed in a specific order. As a result, word segmentation can be defined as the process of dividing a sentence into its constituent words that are to be given as input to the model.

Fine-Tuning

To categorize the text, the proposed model is employed, using an encoder subnetwork paired with a fully connected layer along with a dropout layer to perform the task of prediction (Fig. 8).

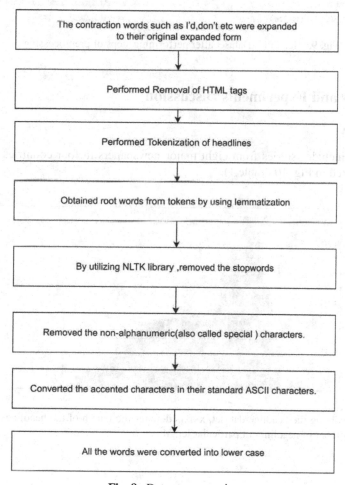

Fig. 8. Data preprocessing

Furthermore, the model weights are fine-tuned using the tokenized training data. For sequence classification, we utilized "XLNetForSequenceClassification". On the test data, our model aims to perform binary classification (Fig. 9).

index	Headline_Original	Sentiment	Headline_Clean
0	Rs 500 notes lay on Delhi street, no one touches due to coronavirus fear	0	rs note lay delhi street no one touch due coronavirus fear
1	Charu Asopa on trolls attacking her over pics with husband: If we keep thinking what will people say, we will not be able to do anything in life	0	charu asopa troll attack pics husband keep think people say not able anything life
2	People abandoning their pets are cruel and ignorant: Richa	0	people abandon pet cruel ignorant richa
3	Indian women's hockey team to raise funds for poor affected by lockdown	0	indian women hockey team raise fund poor affect lockdown
4	Real estate sector faces serious setback due to Covid-19: Report	0	real estate sector face serious setback due report
5	Himachal tea growers suffer losses due to coronavirus lockdown	0	himachal tea growers suffer losses due coronavirus lockdown
6	Coronavirus: Your risk of getting sick from Covid-19 may lie in your genes	0	coronavirus risk get sick may lie genes

Fig. 9. Headlines Dataset after performing steps of preprocessing

4 Results and Experiments Discussion

4.1 Dataset

The dataset includes stories from eight major newspapers in four countries that have been visualized in Fig. 10 (Table 1).

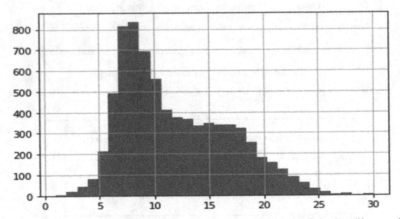

Fig. 10. Visualizing the headline dataset, x-axis denotes the length of the headlines and y-axis denotes the number of headlines of particular length

Table 1. Number of articles

Newspapers	Countries	No. of articles
Mainichi Shimbun, The Japan Times, Asahi Shimbun	Japan	21039
The Daily Mail	UK	24078
Korea Herald, Korea Times	South Korea	10076
Hindustan Times, The Indian Express	India	47350

4.2 Module 1: Topic Modeling Results

Following are the result obtained for the Module 1.

Table 2. Number of topics discovered from the BERTopic model

Country	Number of articles	Number Of topics from the BERTopic model
South Korea	10076	194
India	47,350	588
Japan	21,039	303
UK	24,078	336

Table 2 shows the number of topics discovered from the BERTopic model. From the table, it can be seen that highest number of topics were generated for Indian news articles i.e., is around 588, whereas for South Korean news articles produced the least no. of topic i.c., 194 topics.

Table 3. Four countries news article's Silhouette scores

Country	Silhouette score
South Korea	0.6407036
India	0.6234863
Japan	0.6645274
UK	0.6262914

Table 3 shows the Four countries news article's Silhouette scores. Silhouette score is used to evaluate the quality of clusters(topics) in terms of how well news articles are clustered with other news articles that are similar to each other (Fig. 11, 12, 13 and 14).

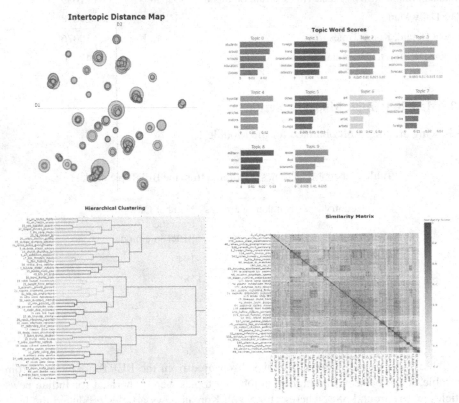

Fig. 11. South Korea's topic modeling results and visualizations

4.3 Module 2: Text Summarization Results

Euclidean distance is utilized to measure how close in semantic space are the News articles related to COVID-19 and it is visualized as heatmap. The news articles (sentences) are being depicted to visualize the semantic similarity amongst them for each countries news articles dataset. Heatmaps are colored maps that depict data in a two-dimensional format. To display diverse details, the color maps use hue, saturation, or luminance to produce color variation. This color variation provides readers with visual information as to the magnitude of numerical values. Because the human brain understands pictures better than numbers, text, or other written data, Heatmaps is about substituting numbers with colors (Fig. 15).

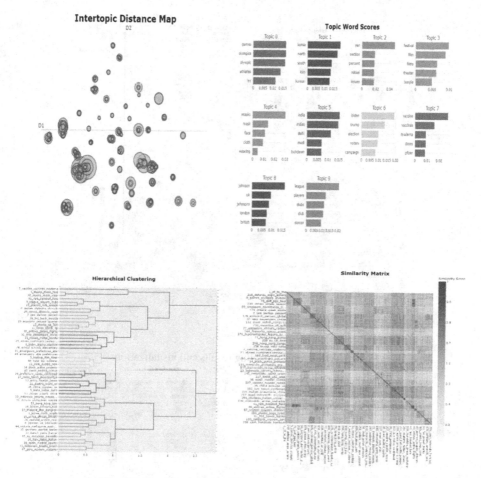

Fig. 12. Japan's topic modeling results and visualizations

4.4 Module 3: Sentiment Analysis Results and Analysis

To perform the task of sentiment classification proposed XLNet model is used, with a learning rate of 4e-5. 4 epochs, the batch size of 32, and Adam optimizer are used to predict the labels. The results were also compared with the existing models as shown in Table 4. The proposed XLNet Model has performed well with an accuracy of 93%.

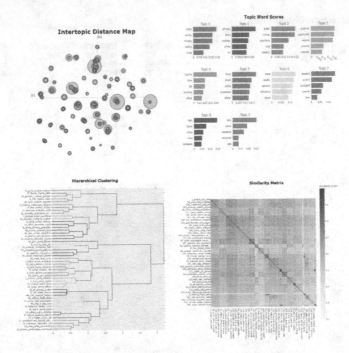

Fig. 13. UK's topic modeling results and visualizations

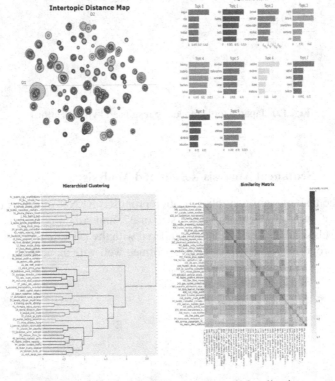

Fig. 14. India's topic modeling results and visualizations

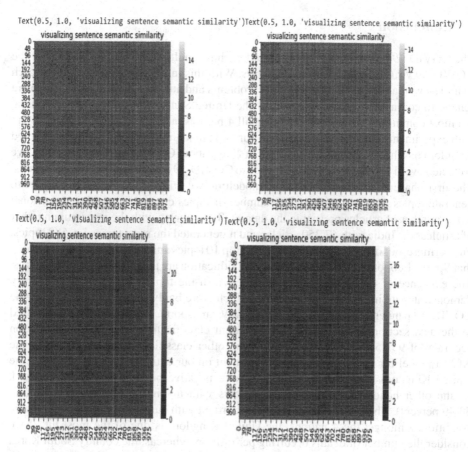

Fig. 15. Sentence semantic similarity heatmap of India, Japan, South Korea, UK respectively

Table 4. Accuracy comparison of proposed model and other classifiers

System	Accuracy (%)
RoBERTa [35]	90
LSTM	72
Bi-LSTM	70
XLNet-Base	91.89
DeBERTa	92.59
ELECTRA-Base	92.82
Proposed XLNet model	**93**

5 Conclusion

The COVID-19 pandemic still prevails and we have multiple waves and variants of the COVID-19 virus affecting various countries. With this in mind, we conducted research to find as well as apprehend the essential problems and attitudes around news which are related to coronavirus Sports, Economy, The United States, and Education, are among the most commonly reported problems in all 4 nations, according to the analysis along with experiments performed according to our topic modeling approach, while the United Kingdom has the most negative coverage of News about COVID-19. For 11 months, we collected over 1 lakh news which are related to COVID-19 or Coronavirus from 4 nations. The first phase of this study was topic modeling, we utilized the BERTopic model to generate topics for the 4 nations. The number of topics created is exactly proportional to the number of articles present in the dataset. The country with the maximum number of articles was India with 47,350 articles and it generated the most topics i.e. 588 topics. Furthermore, our detailed examination of the top 10 topics amongst the 4 nations revealed that Sports, Economy, The United States, and Education are the most prevalent concerns. The existence of the United States of America in the top 10 topics in each country demonstrates its importance. The sectors which were badly influenced because of the COVID-19 pandemic were education, economy, and sports. The XLnet model was used in the next section of this study. Our sentiment classification model had a validation accuracy of 93.75% which is better than the other classifiers. Our application of the XLNet model for the classification of sentiment on our entire dataset revealed that the United Kingdom has the news with maximum negative polarity (i.e. 73.28 percent), on the other hand, South Korea has the news with maximum positive polarity (i.e. 54.49 percent). The findings obtained are accordant with current coronavirus pandemic condition. Amongst the 4 nations, the United Kingdom is one of the most hit, if we consider the number of deaths occurring per million, whereas, the country South Korea has better statistics if we consider deaths per million with its values being just 16 deaths per million. The study could be used as a template to research news related to coronavirus around the world based on these findings, supporting us in recognizing and grasping major problems and their represented feelings in COVID-19 news in other nations. Finally, we would like to include more nations in our dataset in order to broaden the scope of this study and make it more worldwide.

References

1. Reese, S.D.: Prologue—framing public life. In: Reese, S.D., Gandy, O.H., Grant, A.H. (eds.) Framing Public Life. Perspectives on Media and our Understanding of the Social World, pp. 7–31. Lawrance Erlbaum, Mahwah (2001)
2. Chandrashekhar, V.: 1.3 billion people. A 21-day lockdown. Can India curb the coronavirus? Science **10** (2020). https://doi.org/10.1126/science.abc0030
3. Business Today. Which top Economies Have Suffered Worst GDP Fall Due to COVID-19 Pandemic? Accessed 17 Dec 2020. https://www.businesstoday.in/current/economy-politics/which-topeconomies-have-suffered-worst-gdp-fall-due-to-covid-19/story/414683.html
4. Krishnan, K., Rogers, S.P.: Social Data Analytics: Collaboration for the Enterprise. Morgan Kaufman, Walthman (2015)

5. Nadeau, D., Sekine, S.: A survey of named entity recognition and classification, Lingvistic Investigationes. Int. J. Linguistics Lang. Res. **30**(1), 3–26 (2007). https://time.mk/trajkovski/thesis/li07.pdf

6. Liu, B.: Sentiment Analysis: Mining Opinions, Sentiments, and Emotions. Cambridge Univ. Press, New York (2015)

7. Wu, Y., et al.: Google's neural machine translation system: Bridging the gap between human and machine translation (2016). arXiv:1609.08144. http://arxiv.org/abs/1609.08144

8. Blei, D.M.: Probabilistic topic models. Commun. ACM **55**(4), 77–84 (2012). https://doi.org/10.1145/2133806.2133826

9. Torres-Moreno, J.M. (ed.): Automatic Text Summarization. Wiley, Hoboken (2014)

10. Sear, R.F., et al.: Quantifying COVID-19 content in the online health opinion war using machine learning. IEEE Access **8**, 91886–91893 (2020). https://doi.org/10.1109/ACCESS.2020.2993967

11. Bai, Y., Jia, S., Chen, L.: Topic evolution analysis of COVID-19 news articles. J. Phys. Conf. Ser. **1601**, Art. no. 052009 (2020)

12. Liu, Q., et al.: Health communication through news media during the early stage of the COVID-19 outbreak in China: digital topic modeling approach. J. Med. Internet Res. **22**(4), Art. no. e19118 (2020). https://doi.org/10.2196/19118

13. Jelodar, H., Wang, Y., Orji, R., Huang, S.: Deep sentiment classification and topic discovery on novel coronavirus or COVID-19 online discussions: NLP using LSTM recurrent neural network approach. IEEE J. Biomed. Health Inf. **24**(10), 2733–2742 (2020). https://doi.org/10.1109/JBHI.2020.3001216. Epub 2020 Jun 9 PMID: 32750931

14. Santis, E.D., Martino, A., Rizzi, A.: 'An infoveillance system for detecting and tracking relevant topics from Italian tweets during the COVID- 19 event.' IEEE Access **8**, 132527–132538 (2020). https://doi.org/10.1109/ACCESS.2020.3010033

15. Noor, S., Guo, Y., Shah, S.H.H., Fournier-Viger, P., Nawaz, M.S.: Analysis of public reactions to the novel Coronavirus (COVID-19) outbreak on Twitter. Kybernetes (2020). https://doi.org/10.1108/K-05-2020-0258

16. Bahja, M., Safdar, G.A.: Unlink the link between COVID-19 and 5G networks: an NLP and SNA based approach. IEEE Access **8**, 209127–209137 (2020). https://doi.org/10.1109/ACCESS.2020.3039168

17. Samuel, J., Ali, G.G.M.N., Rahman, M.M., Esawi, E., Samuel, Y.: COVID-19 public sentiment insights and machine learning for tweets classification. Information **11**(6), 314 (2020). https://doi.org/10.3390/info11060314

18. Imran, A.S., Daudpota, S.M., Kastrati, Z., Batra, R.: Cross-cultural polarity and emotion detection using sentiment analysis and deep learning on COVID-19 related tweets. IEEE Access **8**, 181074–181090 (2020). https://doi.org/10.1109/ACCESS.2020.3027350

19. Huang, M., Xie, H., Rao, Y., Liu, Y., Poon, L.K.M., Wang, F.L.: Lexicon-based sentiment convolutional neural networks for online review analysis. IEEE Trans. Affect. Comput. (2020). https://doi.org/10.1109/TAFFC.2020.2997769

20. Boon-Itt, S., Skunkan, Y.: Public perception of the COVID-19 pandemic on Twitter: Sentiment analysis and topic modeling study. JMIR Public Health Surveill. 6(4), Art. no. e21978 (2020). https://doi.org/10.2196/21978

21. Das, S., Dutta, A.: Characterizing public emotions and sentiments in COVID-19 environment: a case study of India. J. Hum. Behav. Social Environ., 1–14 (2020). https://doi.org/10.1080/10911359.2020.1781015

22. Barkur, G. V., Kamath, G.B.: Sentiment analysis of nationwide lockdown due to COVID 19 outbreak: evidence from India. Asian J. Psychiatry 51, Art. no. 102089 (2020). https://doi.org/10.1016/j.ajp.2020.102089

23. Imran, M.A.S., Daudpota, S.M., Kastrati, Z., Batra, R.: Cross-cultural polarity and emotion detection using sentiment analysis and deep learning on COVID-19 related tweets. IEEE Access **8**, 181074–181090 (2020). https://doi.org/10.1109/ACCESS.2020.3027350

24. Long, Z., Alharthi, R., Saddik, A.E.: NeedFull – a tweet analysis platform to study human needs during the COVID-19 pandemic in New York state. IEEE Access **8**, 136046–136055 (2020). https://doi.org/10.1109/ACCESS.2020.3011123

25. Rosa, R.L., et al.: Event detection system based on user behavior changes in online social networks: case of the COVID-19 pandemic. IEEE Access **8**, 158806–158825 (2020). https://doi.org/10.1109/ACCESS.2020.3020391

26. Mourad, A., Srour, A., Harmanani, H., Jenainati, C., Arafeh, M.: Critical impact of social networks infodemic on defeating coronavirus COVID-19 pandemic: twitter-based study and research directions. IEEE Trans. Netw. Serv. Manag. **17**(4), 2145–2155 (2020). https://doi.org/10.1109/TNSM.2020.3031034

27. Es-Sabery, F., et al.: A MapReduce opinion mining for COVID-19-related tweets classification using enhanced ID3 decision tree classifier. IEEE Access **9**, 58706–58739 (2021). https://doi.org/10.1109/ACCESS.2021.3073215

28. Da, T., Yang, L.: Local COVID-19 severity and social media responses: evidence from China. IEEE Access **8**, 204684–204694 (2020). https://doi.org/10.1109/ACCESS.2020.3037248

29. Wang, T., Lu, K., Chow, K.P., Zhu, Q.: COVID-19 sensing: negative sentiment analysis on social media in China via BERT model. IEEE Access **8**, 138162–138169 (2020). https://doi.org/10.1109/ACCESS.2020.3012595

30. Elhadad, M.K., Li, K.F., Gebali, F.: Detecting misleading information on COVID-19. IEEE Access **8**, 165201–165215 (2020). https://doi.org/10.1109/ACCESS.2020.3022867

31. Gupta, P., Kumar, S., Suman, R.R., Kumar, V.: Sentiment analysis of lockdown in India during COVID-19: a case study on twitter. IEEE Trans. Comput. Social Syst. **8**(4), 992–1002 (2021). https://doi.org/10.1109/TCSS.2020.3042446

32. Chandrasekaran, R., Mehta, V., Valkunde, T., Moustakas, E.: Topics, trends, and sentiments of tweets about the COVID-19 pandemic: Temporal infoveillance study. J. Med. Internet Res. **22**(10), Art. no. e22624 (2020). https://doi.org/10.2196/22624

33. Xue, J., Chen, J., Chen, C., Zheng, C., Li, S., Zhu, T.: Public discourse and sentiment during the COVID 19 pandemic: using latent Dirichlet allocation for topic modeling on Twitter. PLoS ONE 15(9), Art. no. e0239441 (2020). https://doi.org/10.1371/journal.pone.0239441

34. Xie, R., Chu, S.K.W., Chiu, D.K.W., Wang, Y.: Exploring public response to COVID-19 on Weibo with LDA topic modeling and sentiment analysis'. Data Inf. Manag. **5**(1), 86–99 (2020). https://doi.org/10.2478/dim-2020-0023

35. Ghasiya, P., Okamura, K.: Investigating COVID-19 news across four nations: a topic modeling and sentiment analysis approach. IEEE Access **9**, 36645–36656 (2021). https://doi.org/10.1109/ACCESS.2021.3062875

36. Wan, X., Lucic, M.C., Ghazzai, H., Massoud, Y.: Topic modeling and progression of american digital news media during the onset of the COVID-19 pandemic. IEEE Trans. Technol. Soc. (2021). https://doi.org/10.1109/TTS.2021.3088800

37. Yu, X., Ferreira, M.D., Paulovich, F.V.: Senti-COVID19: an interactive visual analytics system for detecting public sentiment and insights regarding COVID-19 from social media. IEEE Access **9**, 126684–126697 (2021). https://doi.org/10.1109/ACCESS.2021.3111833

38. Lamsal, R.: Coronavirus (COVID-19) Tweets Dataset (2020). https://doi.org/10.21227/781w-ef42

39. A survey of word embeddings for clinical text - Scientific Figure on ResearchGate. https://www.researchgate.net/figure/BERT-model-10-Taking-masked-input-and-outputting-the-masked-words_fig3_332543716

40. Yang, Z., Dai, Z., Yang, Y., Carbonell, J., Salakhutdinov, R.R., Le, Q.V.: Xlnet: generalized autoregressive pretraining for language understanding. Adv. Neural Inf. Process. Syst. **32** (2019)
41. Vaidyanathan, G.: India will supply coronavirus vaccines to the world - will its people benefit? Nature **585**(7824), 167–168 (2020). https://doi.org/10.1038/D41586-020-02507-X
42. Kumar, K.S., Singh, N.P.: Retinal blood vessel segmentation using a generalized gamma probability distribution function (pdf) of matched filtered. Int. J. Fuzzy Syst. Appl. – IGI-Global Scopus indexing **11**(2), 16 (2022)
43. Kumar, K.S., Chandrashekar, S.N.P.: Segmentation of Retinal Blood Vessel using an Algorithm-based Gamma Distribution of Matched filter. In: IIENC-2020 (Integrated Intelligence Enable Networks & Computing) – Springer Conference, Algorithms for Intelligent Systems Book Springer Proceeding (2021). https://doi.org/10.1007/978-981-33-6307-6_9

BioBodyComp: A Machine Learning Approach for Estimation of Percentage Body Fat

Vishnu Pratap Singh Kirar[1]([✉]) [iD], Kavita Burse[2], and Abhishek Burse[3]

[1] School of Computer Science, University College Dublin, Dublin, Ireland
vishnupskirar@live.com
[2] Department of Electronics and Communication, Technocrats Institute of Technology, Bhopal, India
[3] Data Science Department, EURECOM, Biot, France

Abstract. Bio Body composition (BBC) analysis describes and assesses the human body in various components such as total body water, lean muscle mass, fat mass, bone skeletal mass, and bone density. Excessive fat mass in the human body is associated with ill health and related to obesity, a phenotype of body composition. Obesity is a serious medical condition in which non-essential fat is accumulated along with a decrease in lean muscle mass. Body Mass Index (BMI), an equation, has been used for a very long time as a predictor of body fatness and obesity. As a predictor of obesity and based on height and weight, BMI is unable to explain and calculate the percentage body fat (PBF). BMI, which is based on only two anthropometric measurements, also misclassified obesity in many cases because it is not age and gender specific. Two people with the same height and weight i.e., BMI can have different PBF. An athlete who has more muscle mass than fat mass can also be misclassified as obese. BMI is a *Rough Guide* it cannot be used as an assessment tool for PBF. All these facts indicate that there is a need to develop a less complex technique to predict PBF and other body composition components. In this study, we have developed a normative and data-driven prediction model for structural body composition phenotype to predict PBF. The developed predictive model is based on less expensive and simple to measure anthropometric measurements such as age, gender, height, waist, hips, and weight.

Keywords: Bio Body Composition (BBC) · Body Mass Index (BMI) · Obesity · Percentage Body Fat (PBF) · Machine learning

1 Introduction

Obesity is a metabolic health condition. Both, developed and developing nations, are facing obesity as a growing health-related issue. BMI is used as a predictor of obesity as it is easy-to-measure and inexpensive method. It is based on simple measurements of body weight and body weight and calculated when body weight is divided by the square of height. As a two-digit number, BMI and obesity have a strong co-relation but it neither calculates nor distinguishes between the fat mass and lean mass [1–3]. It is just a tool for the classification of weight distribution related to height. Thus, it is misclassified the obesity, for example, an athlete who has more muscle mass than fat mass is classified as obese. People with small body frames, females, and elder persons are also misclassified by BMI. Apart from this, BMI does not identify where this weight comes from either from lean tissue mass or from the adipose fat tissue mass. Females and males have different body fat percentages, male with > 25 and females with > 35 PBF is classified as obese [4, 5]. It also shows the different results for the young and elder populations. BMI is unable to explain the discrimination between different bio-body compositions such as lean tissue, adipose tissue, visceral fat, and body fat and their relationship with body weight [6, 7].

Over the period, the definition of obesity has changed but BMI is still used as an assessment of body fat [8]. BMI is not a perfect assessment tool for obesity and other health risks. BMI is not alone able to explain obesity, for accurate prediction of obesity other parameters should be taken into the account, for example, muscle mass, fat mass, and fat-free mass. For good health, the issue is not how much weight any individual has, but how much visceral fat is distributed around the internal organs and abdominal region. The BMI remains enshrined as the standard method for the classification of overweight and obesity. Although BMI takes height into account, which is a very good index for the relative study of the classification, still BMI is unable to describe about PBF and adiposity.

A Dual Energy X-ray Absorptiometry (DEXA) scan is used to calculate PBF. DEXA scan determines accurate measurement and generates a dedicated segmental report for fat mass, lean mass, visceral fat, and bone density. BIA also provides a similar segmental report, but it also includes the total body water in it. However, these techniques are not always convenient due to fixed equipment and need a technically skilled person. Also, a Fasting condition of four hours is one of the required conditions for participation in both BIA and DEXA scan. Which can limit the population who have a diabetic condition. Also, they are expensive and time-consuming procedures.

In the present scenario, Health data is now collected very easily and examined by various technologies. Machine learning techniques together with e-health record provides a great opportunity to find insights into body composition and its relationship with various medical that was not possible in the last decades. The idea for this research is to develop a prediction model which uses a more reliable, simple, and inexpensive method to access body fat without using sophisticated equipment. This research will introduce a data-driven prediction model, based on simple anthropocentric measurements, which can help to estimate PBF in the human body.

This paper is organized as follows: Sect. 2 describes the different assessment methods and tools for body composition, Sect. 3 presents the limitation of BMI as an assessment method for classification of obesity. Section 4 presents our experimental setup for body composition assessment using machine learning with results and comparisons. In Sect. 5, we discuss our analyzed results. Finally, in Sect. 6, we conclude our research paper.

2 Bio Body Composition Assessment Methods and Tools

The body composition of a human reflects lifetime nutrition intake, lifestyle, and other substrates acquired from the surrounding environment. The components of human body composition are ranging from the atomic level to the tissue-organ level. These components are the basic building block of the human body that provides shape and functionality to the human body. These phenotypic characteristics of the human body are the most essential aspect of modern research of chronic and nutritional diseases as they change with age and metabolic state [9]. The study of human body composition is organized into three interconnected research areas: (1) study of body composition components or compartment models and rules, (2) various body composition measurement methods, and (3) body composition variation with respect to biological alteration (see Fig. 1).

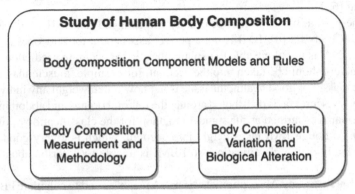

Fig. 1. Study of body composition assessments

The study of human body composition begins with the identification of various body components, their definitions, and the relationship between them. In this research area, scientists determine various characteristics of human body component and their quantitative and qualitative relationship with each other. The body composition rule area combines 30 to 40 major body components into five different levels of complexity in descending order [10].

The second research area of body composition study involves various in vitro and in vivo techniques and methods for the measurement of human body composition [11, 12].

The third research area of body composition is body composition variation and biological alteration. This area involves various changes in body composition at all five levels. These changes are related to pathological and physiological conditions. The area of investigation includes the physical appearance, height, weight, development, growth, age, nutritional effects, and hormonal changes effects. The variation and alteration in body composition also provide new insights for disease diagnosis and medication [13].

The body composition compartment model divided the whole human body into different segments and each of them containing distinct component. The human body is generally composed of water, protein, minerals, and fat. Based on these basic elements various component models are proposed as shown in Fig. 2. The component of these models can be facilitated to study various medical conditions related to body composition [14].

Body composition analysis is based on body partitioning methods and ranges from two to multi-compartment models. There are two types of analytical methods for body composition: first is the direct method based on "Cadaver Dissection Analysis" and the second is the indirect or "in vivo" method. Cadaver Dissection Analysis is a method of measuring and analyzing body composition components by dissecting a fresh, dead human body, and determining the fat and fat-free mass percentage in each body segment.

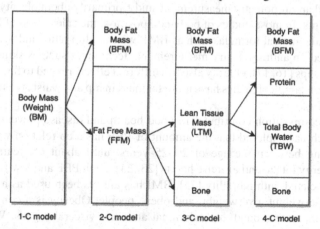

Fig. 2. Body composition component model

The indirect or in vivo methods are non-invasive, such as Densitometry, Hydrometry, Neuron activation analysis, BIA, DEXA, and MRI. These techniques use some unique biochemical properties of the human body. For example, BIA uses the human body's electric conduction. The tissues of the human body can absorb the energy particles which enables to develop the absorptiometry techniques like DEXA scan. The accuracy of body composition measurements is much higher in these non-invasive methods (Fig. 3).

Although, only one method is not enough or suitable for whole body composition, the selection of the appropriate method is dependent on the type of body composition components and depend sometimes on individuals according to their age and sex [15].

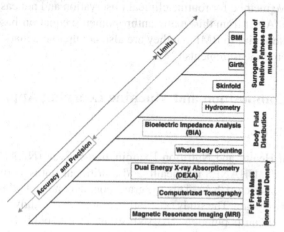

Fig. 3. Accuracy and precision of body composition assessment tools

3 Limitations of BMI

Bio body composition (BBC) has been included in the literature of human body assessment study, and anthropometry measurement study, primarily about obesity and various body components. In most studies of body composition, the calculation of body fatness is based on mathematical formulas such as BMI, waist-to-hip ratio, and waist-to-height which are based on anthropometry measurements techniques such as skinfold calipers and measuring taps [16, 17]. Obesity also has different effects related to female and male sex groups. For example, females have more fat mass in hip and waist areas as compared to males [18, 19].

The body composition contributes to good health and disease prevention [20–22]. Recent research has explored that the amount of PBF has a co-relation with age. PBF starts increasing between the age of 20–25 years, until about 65 years, even with unchanged energy intake and exercise habits [23, 24]. High PBF and low BMI are independently associated with mortality [25]. BMI has always been used as a rough guide to classify underweight, overweight, and obese people. Obesity is a condition where PBF starts to increase around the abdominal area and visceral organs. World Health Organization (WHO) already endorsed that obesity is a matter of concern and there is a need to develop more accurate estimation methods of PBF [26, 27]. The definition of obesity, based on PBF, has changed over time and with different research studies [28]. In an early research study on the treatment of obesity, it was observed that a person can be classified as normal if the person has a weight distribution of 300 g per centimeter of height, and obesity is classified if someone have 20–40% excess weight with respect to normal class [29]. The obesity can be classified for a male if PBF > 25\% and for a female if PBF > 35\% [30]. At present, if BMI is greater than 30, the person is obese [31]. BMI has an inherent problem of not having gender and age specification which leads to limited accuracy to estimate PBF and misclassification of obesity [32]. DEXA scan has the advantage of accurate estimation of PBF. But DEXA scan has some limitations as it is an expensive method for routine clinical observation and not easily accessible to a large population. Apart from this, many anthropometric equation-based formals have been used as an alternative to BMI, but they are also not up to the mark as they required many anthropometric measurements [33].

4 Bio Body Composition and Machine Learning Approach

4.1 Study Population

We used National Health and Nutrition Examination Survey (NHANES) 2005–2006 dataset for this study. NHANES is a health and nutritional status study program in the United States of America (USA). This program conducts annually, and the dataset is released in every two years. The study population of NHANES study is limited to ethnic groups of the American population. NHANES dataset is a publicly available dataset thus this study did not require ethical approval [34]. Assessment methods and tools are explained in Fig. 4.

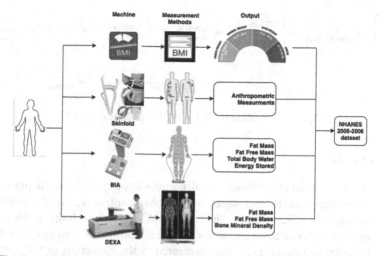

Fig. 4. NHANES 2005–2006 body composition assessment and data collection

4.2 Dataset Description

NHANES data is the largest dataset which contains the whole-body composition of the USA population. In this study, we selected DEXA, BIA, and body measurements and demographic datasets from NHANES 2005 2006 for the development of the PBF prediction model. DEXA data is used as a reference to compare and calculate the PBF for this developed model.

NHANES 2005–2006 dataset was collected from 10,348 participants. Multiple imputations were performed on the missing data. For this study, we only select the person who is eligible for a DEXA scan i.e., who is between 20 to 69 years. We also eliminate incomplete, non-imputed data and missing values. Finally, we get 3,456 observations for this study. Data preparation is explained in Fig. 5.

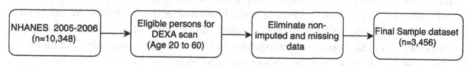

Fig. 5. NHANES 2005–2006 data preparation and processing

4.3 Body Measurements and Demographic Data

Height was measured by a stadiometer and body mass was recorded with a BIA machine. Skin thickness was measured by Harpenden calipers at ten different sites with an additional chest site measured on male participants. Corresponding girth measures were also taken at seven body sites using a Physiomed tape measure with an additional chest girth measure for male participants. International Society for the Advancement of Kinanthropometry (ISAK) standards was followed for data collection.

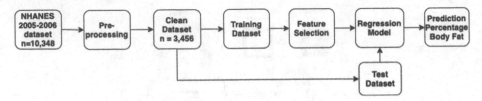

Fig. 6. Percentage Body Fat (PBF) Prediction Model

4.4 DEXA Scan

NHANES 2005–2006 data from healthy adult participants were collected using a Hologic X-ray fan beam densitometer and stored using Hologic software. The dataset was collected as full analysis which includes the full DEXA scan only. All the attribute related to body composition is collected and stored but for simplification and easily understand of the data, a redefined data set can also be created by the University of California. The body fat percent was calculated as the ratio of DEXA whole body fat mass and DEXA whole body mass multiplied by 100.

4.5 Feature Selection and Model Development

Anthropometric measurements age, height, body mass, BMI, forearm girths, upper arm girths, upper thigh girths, calf, abdomen girths, waist girths, hip girths, waist to hip ratio, forearm skinfold, bicep skinfold, triceps skinfold, subscapular skinfold, mid axilla skinfold, iliac crest skinfold, supraspinal skinfold, abdomen skinfold, anterior thigh skinfold, and medial calf skinfold were used for feature selection.

The flow diagram of the development of the prediction model is shown in Fig. 6. MXM, Boruta, and Relative importance using linear regression are performed in R Studio on combined female and male datasets. Apart from this, these feature selection methods were also applied separately to the female and male datasets for the sex-based study. Different features were identified by different feature selection methods. Three predictive models were developed based on these three feature selection methods, MXM feature selection, Boruta Feature selection, and Relative Importance LR. The fourth Model was developed by selecting common features between these three feature selection methods. The last model is developed by using a confidence level > 90% with all features.

4.6 Model Performance

For model performance evaluation we use Root Mean Square Error (RMSE). For comparison we use a combined dataset for males and females (Table 1).

For gender-specific performance evaluation and to check the generalization of the model, we separate the dataset for males and females. First, we use the male dataset as an independent dataset (Table 2) and then the female dataset as an independent dataset (Table 3).

Table 1. Model for male and female combined dataset

Models	Features	RMSE	Accuracy
Model 1 (MXM Features)	PBF ~ Tri + AbS + Age + AT + Ht + MC + Bi	3.47	90.11%
Model 2 (Boruta Features)	PBF ~ AbS + MA + Tri + Bi + Age + AT	3.79	88.97%
Model 3 (Relative Importance LR)	PBF ~ Tri + AT + MC + Bi + MA + Sup + AbS + Ht + FAS + Sub + FAG + IC	3.49	90.12%
Model 4 (Features with confidence level > 90% from model 1 + 2 + 3)	PBF ~ Age + Ht + FAG + Tri + Sub + MA + AbS + AT + MC	3.19	91.05%
Model 5 (Features with confidence level > 90% from regression model with all features)	PBF ~ Age + Ht + BM + FAG + UTG + AbG + W + FAS + Bi + MA + IC + AbS + AT + MA	2.82	91.38%

Table 2. Model for Female dataset; Male dataset as an independent dataset

Models	Features	RMSE		Accuracy	
		Female	Male	Female	Male
Model 1 (MXM Features)	PBF ~ MA + BMI + Tri + Age + MC + AbS + MC + AbS + Sub	3.24	8.19	92.22%	50.48%
Model 2 (Boruta Features)	PBF ~ BMI + Tri + Bi + Sup + MA + Sub	3.50	9.16	91.54%	46.38%
Model 3 (Relative Importance LR)	PBF ~ BMI + MA + Tri + Sup + AbG + BM + Bi + MC + Sub + AT + AbS + W	3.64	5.51	91.72%	70.47%
Model 4 (features with confidence level > 90% from model 1 + 2 + 3)	PBF ~ Age + BM + BMI + AbG + W + Tri + MA + Sup + AbS + MC	3.34	5.22	92.19%	72.05%
Model 5 (features with confidence level > 90% from regression model with all features)	PBF ~ Age + FAG + UTG + AbG + W + H + WH + FAS + MA + Sup + AT + MC	3.26	3.85	92.09%	80.96%

Table 3. Model for Male dataset; Female dataset as an independent dataset

Models	Features	RMSE		Accuracy	
		Male	Female	Male	Female
Model 1 (MXM Features)	PBF ~ AbS + Age + AbG + MC + MA	2.75	7.51	89.41%	79.31%
Model 2 (Boruta Features)	PBF ~ AbS + MA + IC + Sub + AT + AbS	3.51	7.88	87.63%	79.24%
Model 3 (Relative Importance LR)	PBF ~ AbS + AbG + W + MA + IC + Sub + WH + Age + Bi + Tri + BMI	2.77	8.70	89.83%	75.70%
Model 4 (features with confidence level > 90% from model 1 + 2 + 3)	PBF ~ Age + AbG + Tri + MA + IC + AbS + AT + MC	2.76	6.64	89.60%	82.82%
Model 5 (features with confidence level > 90% from regression model with all features)	PBF ~ Age + FAG + UTG + AbG + IC + AbS + AT + MC	2.45	5.10	90.24%	87.39%

RMSE-Root Mean Square Error; Ht-Height; BM-Body Mass; BMI-Body Mass Index; PBF-Percentage Body Fat; FAG-ForeArm Girth; UAG-Upper Arm Girth; UTG-Upper Thigh Girth; ChestG-Chest Girth; AbG-Abdomen Girth; W-waist; H-Hip; WH-Waist to Hip ratio; FAS-ForeArm Skinfold; Bi-Bicep; Tri-Tricep; Sub-Subscapular; ChestS-Chest Skinfold; MA-Mid Axilla; IC-Iliac Crest; Sup-Supraspinous; AbS-Abdomen Skinfold; AT-Anterior Thigh; MC-Medial Calf.

5 Discussion

We now report on the experimental results obtained by our developed machine learning models. Here each table has five different models so in total we have developed fifteen machine learning models. But for convenience we named them model 1, model 2, model 3, model 4, and model 5 based on linear regression methods applied to them such as MXM feature, Boruta feature, Relative Impedance LR, feature with confidence level > 90% from model 1 + 2 + 3, and feature with confidence level > 90% for all features respectively.

We evaluate these models by RMSE and to check the accuracy of these models we compared calculated PBF with PBF from the DAXA scan. Table 1 explains the results for combined datasets and indicates that model 5 performs better than all other models as it obtained the lowest value of RMSE (2.82). A lower value of RMSE indicates the best fit trained model. Also, model 5 achieved the highest accuracy (91.38%) as compared to other models. Thus, for the combined dataset model 5 is the best suitable.

Table 2 describes the model developed (trained and tested) for females and we use the male dataset as an independent dataset to validate this model. This model achieved a better RMSE value (3.24) and an accuracy of 92.22% for model 1. When we validate this model with the male dataset the performance was very low.

Table 3 explains the results for the models which are developed (trained and tested) for males and we use the female dataset as an independent dataset to validate this model. The male dataset achieved the best RMSE value (2.45) and high accuracy (90.24%). The gender-specific male dataset models achieved better RMSE values for the male dataset as compared to the female dataset also vice-vera for female dataset models. From obtained results from the gender-specific developed model, we conclude that gender-specific models are not generalized models.

6 Conclusion

In this paper we have observed that model developed by using combined dataset, it perform well for both the male and female dataset but for gender-specific developed models are not generalized. The reason behind this behaviour of gender-specific models is the PBF amount in females into abdominal, hip and thigh regions. Our developed model accurately identify the male and female participants easily and provide accurate PBF for according to their gender. Our developed model have a capacity to develop a clinical decision support system (CDSS) to calculate the PBF and classification of obesity. In our future work we will develop a explainable CDSS for healthcare system.

Bio Body Composition (BBC) can ascertain how healthy a normal human being is, which is influenced by his own lifestyle and various environmental agents. Body composition analysis reflects the states of change in human health, morbidity, and mortality. The accurate prediction of body composition is significant to identify the human nutritional status and able to diagnose chronic diseases at an early stage. This developed model of body composition will be helpful for both patient and practitioner to detect and cure the diseases which are related to body fatness. It also helps to reduce the social-economic burden.

References

1. Abramowitz, M.K., Hall, C.B., Amodu, A., Sharma, D., Androga, L., Hawkins, M.: Muscle mass, bmi, and mortality among adults in the United States: a population-based cohort study. PLoS ONE 13(4), 0194697 (2018)
2. Chatterjee, A., Gerdes, M.W., Martinez, S.G.: Identification of risk factors associated with obesity and overweight—a machine learning overview. Sensors 20(9), 2734 (2020)
3. Bosy-Westphal, A., Müller, M.J.: Diagnosis of obesity based on body composition-associated health risks—time for a change in paradigm. Obes. Rev. 22, 13190 (2021)
4. Bray, G.A., et al.: The science of obesity management: an endocrine society scientific statement. Endocrine Rev. 39(2), 79–132 (2018)
5. Wong, J.C., O'Neill, S., Beck, B.R., Forwood, M.R., Khoo, S.K.: Comparison of obesity and metabolic syndrome prevalence using fat mass index, body mass index and percentage body fat. PLoS ONE 16(1), 0245436 (2021)
6. Zemel, B.S.: Body composition during growth and development. Hum. Growth Dev., 517–545 (2022)
7. Gibson, A.L., Wagner, D., Heyward, V.: Advanced fitness assessment and exercise prescription. 8E. Human kinetics (2018)
8. Piqueras, P., Ballester, A., Durá-Gil, J.V., Martinez-Hervas, S., Redón, J., Real, J.T.: Anthropometric indicators as a tool for diagnosis of obesity and other health risk factors: a literature review. Front. Psychol. 12, 631179 (2021)
9. Müller, M.J., Heymsfield, S.B., Bosy-Westphal, A.: Are metabolic adaptations to weight changes an artefact? Am. J. Clin. Nutr. 114(4), 1386–1395 (2021)

10. Tinsley, G.M.: Five-component model validation of reference, laboratory and field methods of body composition assessment. Br. J. Nutr. **125**(11), 1246–1259 (2021)
11. Wei, D., Liao, L., Wang, H., Zhang, W., Wang, T., Xu, Z.: Canagliflozin ameliorates obesity by improving mitochondrial function and fatty acid oxidation via pparα in vivo and in vitro. Life Sci. **247**, 117414 (2020)
12. Domingos, C., Matias, C.N., Cyrino, E.S., Sardinha, L.B., Silva, A.M.: The usefulness of Tanita tbf-310 for body composition assessment in judo athletes using a four-compartment molecular model as the reference method. Rev. Assoc. Med. Bras. **65**, 1283–1289 (2019)
13. De Lorenzo, A., Romano, L., Di Renzo, L., Di Lorenzo, N., Cenname, G., Gualtieri, P.: Obesity: a preventable, treatable, but relapsing disease. Nutrition **71**, 110615 (2020)
14. Kuriyan, R.: Body composition techniques. Indian J. Med. Res. **148**(5), 648 (2018)
15. Arumäe, K., Mõttus, R., Vainik, U.: Beyond BMI: Personality traits' associations with adiposity and metabolic rate. Physiol. Behav. **246**, 113703 (2022)
16. Khader, Y., Batieha, A., Jaddou, H., El-Khateeb, M., Ajlouni, K.: The performance of anthropometric measures to predict diabetes mellitus and hypertension among adults in jordan. BMC Public Health **19**(1), 1–9 (2019)
17. Tomas, Ž, Škarić-Jurić, T., Zajc Petranović, M., Jalšovec, M., Rajić Šikanjić, P., Smolej Narančić, N.: Waist to height ratio is the anthropometric index that most appropriately mirrors the lifestyle and psychological risk factors of obesity. Nutr. Diet. **76**(5), 539–545 (2019)
18. Crafts, T.D., Tonneson, J.E., Wolfe, B.M., Stroud, A.M.: Obesity and breast cancer: preventive and therapeutic possibilities for bariatric surgery. Obesity **30**(3), 587–598 (2022)
19. Gilley, S.P., et al.: Associations between maternal obesity and offspring gut microbiome in the first year of life. Pediat. Obes., 12921 (2022)
20. Marra, M., et al.: Assessment of body composition in health and disease using bioelectrical impedance analysis (BIA) and dual energy x-ray absorptiometry (DXA): a critical overview. Contrast Media Molec. Imag. **2019** (2019)
21. Buscemi, S., Buscemi, C., Batsis, J.A.: There is a relationship between obesity and coronavirus disease 2019 but more information is needed. Obesity **28**(8), 1371–1373 (2020)
22. Wlodarczyk, M., Śliżewska, K.: Obesity as the 21st century's major disease: the role of probiotics and prebiotics in prevention and treatment. Food Biosci. **42**, 101115 (2021)
23. Cerqueira, M.S., et al.: Equations based on anthropometric measurements for adipose tissue, body fat, or body density prediction in children and adolescents: a scoping review. Eating Weight Disord.-Stud. Anorexia Bulimia Obesity, 1–18 (2022)
24. Mott, J.W., Wang, J., Thornton, J.C., Allison, D.B., Heymsfield, S.B., Pierson Jr., R.N.: Relation between body fat and age in 4 ethnic groups. Am. J. Clin. Nutr. **69**(5), 1007–1013 (1999)
25. Palaiodimos, L., et al.: Severe obesity, increasing age and male sex are independently associated with worse in-hospital outcomes, and higher in-hospital mortality, in a cohort of patients with covid-19 in the bronx, new york. Metabolism **108**, 154262 (2020)
26. Uçar, M.K., Ucar, Z., Köksal, F., Daldal, N.: Estimation of body fat percentage using hybrid machine learning algorithms. Measurement **167**, 108173 (2021)
27. Chiong, R., Fan, Z., Hu, Z., Chiong, F.: Using an improved relative error support vector machine for body fat prediction. Comput. Methods Programs Biomed. **198**, 105749 (2021)
28. Ponti, F., et al.: Aging and imaging assessment of body composition: from fat to facts. Front. Endocrinol. **10**, 861 (2020)
29. Perry, A.: Nature and treatment of obesity. California State J. Med. **1**(12), 356 (1903)
30. DeGregory, K., et al.: A review of machine learning in obesity. Obes. Rev. **19**(5), 668–685 (2018)
31. Rahmani, J., et al.: Relationship between body mass index, risk of venous thromboembolism and pulmonary embolism: a systematic review and dose-response meta analysis of cohort studies among four million participants. Thromb. Res. **192**, 64–72 (2020)

32. Akman, M., Uçar, M., Uçar, Z., Uçar, K., Baraklı, B., Bozkurt, M.: Determination of body fat percentage by gender based with photoplethysmography signal using machine learning algorithm. IRBM **43**(3), 169–186 (2022)
33. Harty, P.S., et al.: Novel body fat estimation using machine learning and 3-dimensional optical imaging. Eur. J. Clin. Nutr. **74**(5), 842–845 (2020)
34. National Health and Nutrition Examination Survey (NHANES) 2005–2006. https://wwwn.cdc.gov/nchs/nhanes/continuousnhanes/default.aspx?BeginYear=2005. Accessed 5 Aug 2022

Wearable Technology for Early Detection of Hyperthermia Using Machine Learning

Muhammad Syahin Ihsan Bin Nor'en[1](✉) and Venkatratnam Chitturi[2]

[1] JET Engineering Solutions Sdn Bhd, 47810 Kota Damansara, Malaysia
syahin.ihsan@jetengsolutions.com
[2] School of Engineering and Technology, CMR University, Bengaluru 562149, India

Abstract. In some cases of elevated body temperature, the subject might not represent it as fever but rather a condition called hyperthermia. In contrast to infections in fever, hyperthermia can be introduced as an uncontrolled elevation of body temperature that exceeds the body's ability to lose heat. In this work, a wearable device is presented for early detection of hyperthermia through the development of predictive machine learning algorithms of Logistic Regression (LR) and Random Forest (RF). The wearable device measures clinical parameters of body temperature and heart rate along with non-clinical parameters of surrounding temperature and humidity for the calculation of Heat Stroke Risk Coefficient (HSRC). Based on the results, RF has higher rates of accuracy, precision, and recall of 0.75, 0.667, and 1 respectively. In contrast, the LR has corresponding rates of 0.6875, 0.636, and 0.875 respectively for similar tests. Also, the highest obtained hyperthermia prediction probability rate is found to be 72 percent from the proposed studies.

Keywords: Hyperthermia · Internet of Things · Logistic Regression · Machine learning · Random Forest · Wearables

1 Introduction to the Study

In today's era where people are always moving around, the need of wearable devices is rising as being the fastest advancing sector in the technology industry to the point that its demand is likely to have surpassed that of smartphones. Wearable devices, otherwise called as wearables, are a type of devices that are worn on human body parts such as on wrists, forearms, ears, chest, and fingers. The most found wearables that one is expected to encounter in the market can range from a basic fitness tracker that counts typically on the number of person's steps to smartwatches that are capable in assisting individuals going through the day in numerous sorts of way imaginable. These wearables usually come with high connectivity such as Bluetooth, Wi-Fi, and in some cases a standalone 4G internet connection. Most of these wearables are incorporated with various types of sensors to enable them to achieve their specific product goals, whether it is to track fitness levels or physical and mental health condition. Wearables are believed to have high potential in its contribution to shaping our future, offering wide doors of opportunities

N. Khare et al. (Eds.): MIND 2022, CCIS 1762, pp. 252–263, 2022.
https://doi.org/10.1007/978-3-031-24352-3_20

for education and entertainment unboundedly thus possibly changing our way of life and the world around us.

Wearable biomedical devices are one branch of wearables that have also caught the attention of many, in which these devices have rapidly emerged in a particular sector of digital health under numerous medical applications which includes patients' health recording, monitoring, and tracking for vital signs for prevention of diseases and better medical treatment to improve lives of every individual. A number of these devices are now becoming part of our lives in the form of watches, glasses, and armbands. Advancement of technology in the field of fabrication has enabled microelectronic and micromechanical sensors that includes accelerometers and image sensors to exist in a small rigid substrate with high sensitivity at a low-cost. According to International Telecommunication Union (ITU), it has been estimated that 84% of the world's population, that is approximately 5.1 billion people had connectivity of at the minimum 3G or better by the end of 2016.

Access to the internet by having high connectivity is crucial as it is consistent with the emerging industrial revolution 4.0 where areas such as big data and automation are soon to overtake and transform the world we know today. This ongoing trend, particularly in the biomedical sector, helps to put in place the era of mobile health by means of improving its tracking, detection, and management. Since wearables usually are that of personal devices, biomedical wearables are aimed to personally provide continuous monitoring of vital parameters, as data captured can be used as a clinical tool in determining the patterns of a particular disease, that helps in better understanding of the disease and patient's health information at the time of diagnosis by medical professionals. This technology in biomedical wearables has enabled one to have early detection of diseases through the gathering of clinical parameters that are relevant to disease and in development of effective algorithms from its available parameters [1].

Hyperthermia is a medical term of a disease when a person has a condition of high body temperature which could potentially threaten his/her health leading to organ failures. The term of the disease can instead be considered as an umbrella term, which further refers to several other conditions that can occur when one's body heat regulation fails to handle the surrounding heat. Unlike the concept of fever, which is body's immune system reaction, hyperthermia is a result of body's response to the environment where it's natural cooling mechanism fails to overcome the surrounding heat [2].

Wearable biomedical devices are highly potential in helping early disease detection and possible health threat. One of the significant physiological parameters that are measured by the sensors is that of body temperature for monitoring human activities [3]. Introduction of Body Sensor Network (BSN), which combines the biomedical field of engineering and wireless sensor network can be widely useful in biomedical to daily activity monitoring. The use of wearable body sensors would allow one to realize the importance of human body monitoring systems based on body sensor network [4]. The technology of biomedical implants and wearable devices have rapidly entered digital health in numerous medical fields and applications, which includes monitoring, recording, and tracking of vital signs of patients with the sole purpose of improving their quality of health. A number of these technologies have integrated well in today's lifestyle in the form of accessories such as armbands, glasses, and smartwatches [1].

Humans, by nature, produce an excess amount of heat of the metabolic rate that is necessary for maintaining the core body temperature at 37 °C in a neutral temperature environment. In most cases, an elevated body temperature is said to be fever; however, there exist circumstances where the elevated body temperature does not represent fever but rather hyperthermia. Hyperthermia can be introduced as an uncontrolled elevation of body temperature that exceeds the body's ability to lose heat. In contrast to infections in fever, hyperthermia does not involve pyrogenic molecules. Hyperthermia can be the result of exogenous heat exposure and endogenous heat production, which subsequently causes a high internal temperature. One of the common causes of hyperthermia syndromes is heatstroke. Moreover, central nervous system damage is also another cause of hyperthermia, such as hypothalamus injury and status epilepticus, to name a few. For instance, working and exercising in the hot environment can produce heat faster than a peripheral mechanism able to lose heat. It is stated that core body temperature more than 37.7 °C can be defined as having hyperthermia like that of fever symptom [2].

Measurement of skin temperature, amongst measurement of other vital signs, can provide relevant information about human physiology which includes a person's cardiovascular health, malignancy, and cognitive state. Traditional methods used in thermometry are paste-on temperature sensors, or sophisticated infrared digital cameras are highly effective for one-point measurement. Even though many vital signs can be picked up through wearable devices, detecting all relevant indicators by using several sensors is still challenging to be performed [5]. Hyperthermia during exercise elevates heart rate with the possibility of SV reduction due to ventricular filling time as a secondary effect. Cardiovascular drift is a phenomenon that can be characterized by increasing heart rate and reducing of SV, which correlates the interaction of core body temperature, SV, and heart rate. It is understood that the concept of cardiovascular drift maintains that the reduced number of SV is likely due to progressive increase of Cutaneous Blood Flow (CBF) as a body's core temperature increases [6]. Body's thermoregulatory system can adjust body temperature during exercise to provide higher blood flow to working muscles. In countering the heat produced, the body produces sweat in releasing excessive heat on the skin, which subsequently allows the body's core temperature to be readjusted to normal [7].

A study was conducted on the use of an AI algorithm and machine learning for early detection of kidney disease. The "Healium" pilot program was introduced with an aim to address the gap in the early detection of chronic kidney disease (CKD). The main goal of the pilot program was to develop a machine learning algorithm that is capable in detecting CKD in early stages with a limited set of data from a laboratory test, by cross validating the gold standard test and training data set for accuracy. The group has come up with a customized program and clinical parameters for CKD using machine learning to be integrated with the Hospital Electronic Records (HER). The initial set of data was gathered to train the AI algorithms, which includes data cleaning, data manipulation, feature selection, correlation detection from the data. Methods for data training used were Pearson's correlation, ANOVA, and Cramer's in finding the correlation and dependency between set variables. Best algorithm modelling was then selected for accurate CKD early detection. Regarding machine learning algorithms, Logistic Regression (LR), Support Vector Machine (SVM), and neural network were used. The study found that the LR method has been the most effective and accurate due to its high sensitivity [8].

In a study for early detection of heatstroke, a group of researchers designed a wearable heat stroke detection device. The device could detect early signs of stroke in a person by alerting the user through its notification system. Several physical sensors were used, which include heart rate and body temperature sensors to obtain medical parameters that can be utilized in determining heat stroke syndrome. To detect heatstroke for its early signs, a risk evaluation system was designed based on fuzzy theory. The study also found that for the people who live in the tropical and subtropical regions, it is somewhat inevitable to avoid exposure to hot temperatures and weather. As such, by having a wearable device such as the developed system to monitor risks continuously, it is possible that severe attack of heatstroke could be prevented at an early stage. The study also covered four categories of risk states for each of the clinical parameters to measure its overall risk level in an effective manner [9].

In this paper, a condition named 'Hyperthermia' is being studied in the context of early detection through the development of predictive machine learning algorithms of Logistic Regression (LR) and Random Forest (RF).

2   Materials and Method

Figure 1 shows the processes that are involved in the proposed system of wearable biomedical device for early hyperthermia detection and monitoring. The system begins with the process on a NodeMCU V3 microcontroller based on ESP8266. The NodeMCU will begin by establishing a WIFI connection to the local network to connect with the MQTT client using the MQTT protocol. The board will initiate almost instantly to read and measure all the sensors for both clinical parameters and non-clinical parameters. All the readings from these sensors are immediately sent to the Node-RED dashboard through the MQTT protocol locally. The Raspberry Pi will host the Node-RED that acts an intermediate process to store and display data to the medical professionals where real-time data of a patient can be monitored almost instantaneously.

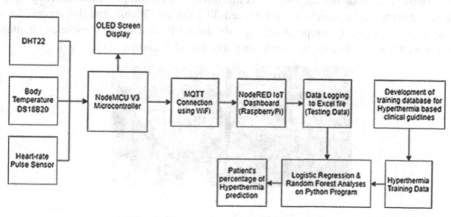

Fig. 1. Proposed system block diagram

The user or medical professional would then be required to import the stored data from the Raspberry Pi to Python software where the data can be analyzed. Once the data has been imported to the Python program, it would allow the user to run Logistic Regression or Random Forest methods for prediction. The result will then indicate the prediction of the hyperthermia together with its probability analysis.

2.1   The Wearable Device Prototype

The wearable device consists of Pulse Sensor for monitoring of heart rate, DS18B20 for measuring body temperature, and DHT22 for measuring of surrounding temperature and humidity as shown in Fig. 2. All the sensors are connected to NodeMCU microcontroller that in turn is connected to an OLED screen for display. The system is powered by a battery as an external power source, for the system to work wirelessly.

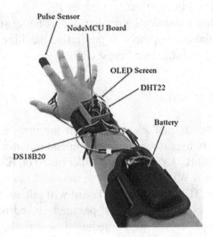

Fig. 2. Prototype of the proposed wearable device

Figure 3 shows the two available displays that can be seen from the OLED screen under two different conditions. The first condition is when readings are normal (Fig. 3(a)) where the body temperature does not exceed 37.7 degree Celsius, and the second condition is when the body temperature exceeds the set limit triggering the alert display system on the wearable and the monitoring dashboard as shown in Fig. 3(b).

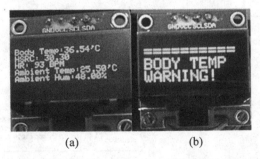

(a)   (b)

Fig. 3. OLED displaying (a) Normal Temperature (b) Abnormal Temperature

Figure 4 shows the IoT dashboard of Node-RED, where all the data from the wearable device are sent and displayed. The dashboard on Node-RED allows a medical professional to continuously monitor the progress and the trend of patient's parameters remotely. From the dashboard, body temperature, heartbeat, inter-beat interval, ambient temperature, and humidity, together with Heat Stroke Risk Coefficient (HSRC) are displayed. The dashboard is also equipped with an alert system, that triggers when a specific safety limit is surpassed as received from the wearable device.

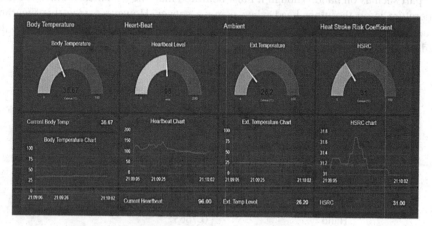

Fig. 4. IoT Node-RED dashboard for the developed system

Figure 5 shows the prediction program on python with Tkinter GUI which allows user to select desired excel file through window's file explorer. The program also allows user to select the type of analysis of machine learning prediction to be made between logistic regression and random forest.

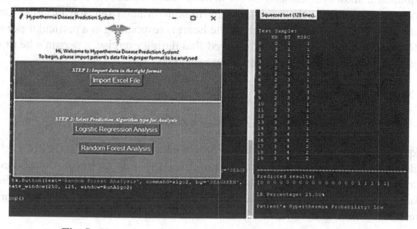

Fig. 5. Hyperthermia prediction on Python using LR and RF

2.2 Parameters and Calculations

Body Temperature
$$T_{core} = T_{skin} + \alpha \times (T_{skin} - T_{surrounding}) \tag{1}$$

Equation 1 shows the method to determine a person's core body temperature using a wearable sensor. Determination of body temperature using this method helps in obtaining the closest measurement of one's core body temperature by taking a reading on a specific body part such as on hand. Though it must be noted that, the best measurement of body temperature is on the ulnar head when using a sensor. However, since this wearable device ought to be worn on hand area when the sensor is located, the relevant α value based on Table 1 is therefore 0.7665 [10].

Table 1. α value of different body parts

Body Part	α
Rectal	0.0699
Torso	0.5067
Head	0.3094
Foot	2.1807
Hand	0.7665

Heart Rate

$$H_{max} = 206.3 - 0.711 \times age \tag{2}$$

Equation 2 shows the calculation for the maximum heart rate estimation based on age for every individual. Having known the maximum heart rate for an individual is exceptionally vital in understanding how the heart is responding at a particular point of time for hyperthermia analysis. It is believed that during exercise, a person's heart rate is between 60–90% of their maximum heart rate [11].

Heat Stroke Risk Coefficient

$$HSRC = T_{surrounding} + H_{relative} - 0.1 \tag{3}$$

Equation 3 shows the calculation for the Heat Stroke Risk Coefficient (HSRC), where the calculation helps to determine the risk factor for a person to catch heat stroke based on the surrounding temperature 'T' and humidity 'H'. By knowing HSRC, determination for hyperthermia can be made by considering the environmental factors of the surrounding at a certain point of time [9].

3 Results and Discussion

3.1 Machine Learning Performance Test

In logistic regression, as seen in Fig. 6, when the amount of training data decreases, accuracy also decreases along with precision, in contrast to recall that increases as training data decreases. Thus, it can be concluded that the rate of the correct prediction made by the classification model was reduced as lower training data was introduced which also gives a lower rate of relevant instances returns by the classification model. However, it was noticed that a higher rate of relevant instances was able to be identified by the classification model when lower training data was utilized. The logistic regression classification model has overall presented a reliable and high-quality prediction considering its high-performance results throughout the tests, which consequently proves its capability to perform valuable prediction.

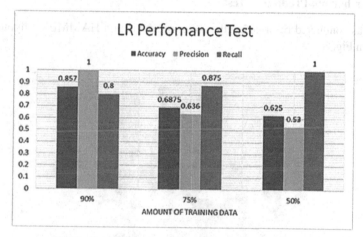

Fig. 6. Performance test for Logistic Regression (LR)

It was noticed that accuracy and precision values of random forest performance decrease when training data decreases as shown in Fig. 7. It was also observed that there was a dramatic drop for both accuracy and precision values between 90 percent and 75% difference but only a slight drop in both values between 75% and 50%. Meanwhile, the recall value was at the same value of 1 throughout the tests, which were highly impressive. The obtained results show that the classification model of random forest is highly capable of making a reasonably good prediction for the developed system through its high performance from the tests conducted.

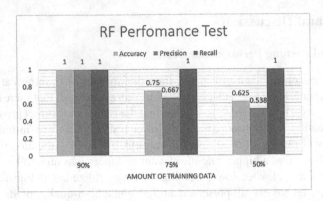

Fig. 7. Performance test for Random Forest (RF)

3.2 Hyperthermia Prediction Test

The test was conducted by wearing the wearable device on HAMMER Ellyptech CT3 as shown in Fig. 8.

Fig. 8. Wearing the wearable device on HAMMER Ellyptech CT3

Readings from the wearable device after the warm-up period were considered for the testing, with an interval of 10–12 s that corresponds to around five samples every minute for the whole duration of 30 min including that of the cooling period as shown in Table 2. Subsequently, amounting to around 150 samples for each test were conducted.

Table 2. Testing procedure for hyperthermia

5 min	15 min	15 min
Warm-up period on HAMMER Ellyptech CT3	Exercise on HAMMER Ellyptech CT3	Rest for cooling down period
Readings not recorded	Readings recorded	Readings recorded

Figure 9 shows the trend of the data that was obtained from the test conducted on a volunteer (participant 2). By referring to the graph, the body temperature of the participant varies between level 2 and 3 for more than half of the test duration, followed by a constant reading of level 2 towards the end of the test. The heart rate of the participant was also varying between level 1 and level 2 but returned to level 1 towards the end of the test.

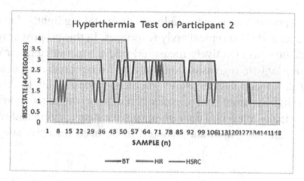

Fig. 9. Test data from non-hyperthermia patient

HSRC value was controlled in the test, which started at level 4 due to the surrounding factors of the gymnasium, which then dropped when air circulation is applied, and participant moved to a colder place for the cooling down period. Overall, the data has demonstrated an expected trend of normal body temperature regulatory response with low hyperthermia symptoms presented that is consistent with the prediction made by the system.

Figure 10 shows the trend of data that was developed for the imaginary volunteer (participant 4) with hyperthermia condition. The data was developed by using the same trend of HSRC, with elevated varying values on body temperature between level 2 and level 3 throughout the test. The heart rate of the participant was also maintained at level 3, with a delayed drop to level 2 towards the end of the test. The developed data was made to merely mimic the expected data that a person with hyperthermia would be having for the sole purpose of the system's testing. Based on the graph, the trend shows a consistent result to that of the prediction made by the two classification models.

The results of the volunteers showed that random forest has a higher rate of prediction in comparison to that of logistic regression, which appeared to be consistent to the performance test result for the two predictive machine learning.

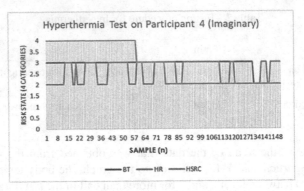

Fig. 10. Test data from hyperthermia patient

4 Conclusion

Hyperthermia is a condition that many individuals are taking lightly due to its common symptoms like fever and other typical body responses. In this proposed work, the developed wearable device has effectively measured relevant parameters for data gathering and analysis using logistic regression and random forest predictive machine learning techniques. The developed system allows medical professionals to efficiently obtain clinical and non-clinical parameters of patients remotely, where the monitoring process of patients is drastically alleviated through automatic data logging and real-time health monitoring. Thus, allowing the data gathered to be used for early-stage detection of hyperthermia.

References

1. Koydemir, H., Ozcan, A.: Wearable and implantable sensors for biomedical applications. Ann. Rev. Anal. Chem. **11**(1), 127–146 (2018)
2. Fauci, A., Harrison, T.: Harrison's Principles of Internal Medicine, 17 edn., pp. 117–118. McGraw-Hill Medical, New York (2008)
3. Mukhopadhyay, S.: Wearable sensors for human activity monitoring: a review. IEEE Sens. J. **15**(3), 1321–1330 (2015)
4. Zhao, J., Li, G.: Study on real-time wearable sport health device based on body sensor networks. Comput. Commun. **154**, 40–47 (2020)
5. Liu, Y., Wang, H., Zhao, W., Zhang, M., Qin, H., Xie, Y.: Flexible, stretchable sensors for wearable health monitoring: sensing mechanisms, materials, fabrication strategies and features. Sensors **18**(2), 645–649 (2018)
6. Trinity, et al.: Interaction of hyperthermia and heart rate on stroke volume during prolonged exercise. J. Appl. Physiol. **109**(3), 745–751 (2010)
7. Harris, G.C.: Identifying muscle fatigue and hyperthermia in sports activities using thermal imaging and facial recognition software (2019)
8. Jacob, B., Kumar, N., Huilgol, S., Vincent, L.: Sat-084 use of an AI algorithm and machine learning for screening and early detection of chronic kidney disease. Kidney Int. Rep. **5**(3), s38–s39 (2020)

9. Chen, S., Lin, S., Lan, C., Hsu, H.: Design and development of a wearable device for heat stroke detection. Sensors **18**(2), 17–21 (2017)
10. Gammel, J.S.: High-Precision Temperature Sensing for Core Temperature Monitoring in Wearable Electronics. Electrical Engineering News and Products, (2017)
11. Gulati, M.: Heart rate response to exercise stress testing in asymptomatic women: the St. James women take heart project (2010). https://pubmed.ncbi.nlm.nih.gov/20585008/

Intelligent Evaluation Framework of English Composition Based on Intelligent Algorithm

Lingling Wang[✉]

Jilin International Studies University, Changchun, Jilin 130117, China
eilunwenjiansuo@163.com

Abstract. The English composition intelligent evaluation system is a tool for automatic writing scoring using computer and natural language processing technology. At present, more and more practical English composition intelligent evaluation systems have been put into use, which can reduce a large number of teachers and evaluation agencies. Manual repetition of labor realizes the scale of composition correction. This paper aims to study the intelligent evaluation framework of English composition based on intelligent algorithm. This paper researches and integrates the features of word vector, paragraph vector, part-of-speech vector, and LDA. This paper researches and integrates the characteristics of word vector, paragraph vector, part-of-speech vector, and LDA, and uses the kNN semantic algorithm similar to the model to obtain the abstract tag label; The regression model of XGBoost calculates the evaluation scores of English compositions; and uses the summaries of 900 English students as samples to construct an intelligent composition evaluation system. Experiments show that the user satisfaction of the English composition intelligent evaluation framework constructed in this paper has reached 100%, and the mean square error is about 10, the error is small, which meets the needs of intelligent evaluation system.

Keywords: Intelligent algorithm · English composition · Intelligent evaluation · KNN algorithm

1 Introduction

English composition can reflect students' writing, thinking and analytical ability, and is an essential and important assessment content in various English examinations, such as standardized tests, senior high school entrance examinations, college entrance examinations, CET-46, TOEFL, IELTS, etc. At present, the evaluation of composition is mostly done manually, which requires a lot of teachers' time. Since teachers have to evaluate many compositions every day, visual fatigue is easy to manifest; subjective preferences, physical fatigue, and the mood of the scoring teacher will also affect the evaluation results. Therefore, the evaluation of composition has a certain degree of subjectivity, and it is difficult to adapt to fairness and justice [1, 2].

In the research on the intelligent evaluation framework of English composition based on intelligent algorithm, many scholars have studied it and achieved good results, for

N. Khare et al. (Eds.): MIND 2022, CCIS 1762, pp. 264–271, 2022.
https://doi.org/10.1007/978-3-031-24352-3_21

example: Yang Q summarized the domestic and foreign writing research, and came to the conclusion that reviewing the composition is better than not reviewing it. It can improve the writing ability of students, but the method of reviewing error correction or error marking can sometimes, sometimes not, improve the writing ability and modify its content. Composition can often improve the quality of composition, and correcting the wrong evaluation method may cause students to dare not use language boldly [3]. Yang D et al. pre-rank the article quality based on Text Rank, and then use the classifier to grade the article [4].

This paper researches and integrates features such as word vector, paragraph vector, part-of-speech vector and LDA, and uses the kNN semantic algorithm similar to the model to obtain the summary label label; uses the regression model based on XGBoost to calculate the evaluation score value of English composition; and uses 900 English students The summary is used as a sample to build an intelligent composition evaluation system.

2 Research on the Intelligent Evaluation Framework of English Composition Based on Intelligent Algorithm

2.1 The Advantages and Disadvantages of the Intelligent Evaluation Framework for English Composition

(1) Objective and immediate feedback on the writing effect

Evaluation framework can provide immediate feedback on the writing effect after students submit the composition, and there will be many very specific correction suggestions, such as spelling errors, capitalization errors, sentence structure confusion, sentence components missing, subject-verb inconsistency, Chinglish, articles, nouns In other aspects, especially listing many synonyms that can be replaced, etc., it is very helpful for the improvement of students' writing level. In the analysis of writing activities, spelling mistakes topped the list of mistakes. After talking with classmates, we found that students did not memorize words firmly and could not output them freely. Students often only memorize the meaning of words when they memorize them. The actual use of spoken language is largely ignored. Therefore, in the future teaching, we should focus on guiding students to memorize words in the context, at least in sentences, instead of just remembering the meanings simply listed in the word list, and strengthen the practice of single-sentence writing. The use of the evaluation framework can timely detect and avoid the occurrence of plagiarism by students. The evaluation framework can allow teachers to see signs of suspected machine translation and allow teachers to focus on these students [5, 6].

(2) Students have strong interest in writing and enhance their self-confidence

At each activity using the assessment framework, students were more motivated than ever. The reasons for this are as follows: Compared with the limited number of face-to-face corrections by teachers, the evaluation framework can provide immediate evaluation and correction of each student's composition, and students can strike while the iron is hot and make corrections immediately. During the sentence-by-sentence review process, the evaluation framework will provide a wealth of vocabulary expressions, word meaning analysis, etc. Many students are very interested in these vocabulary words, and have accumulated a large number of vocabulary by looking up dictionaries, asking classmates, and asking teachers [7].

Disadvantages of Intelligent Evaluation System for Composition.

1) Error analysis has errors

    In the process of using the evaluation framework, attentive teachers and students will find that the automatic online correction method of the evaluation framework will cause some wrong judgments when reading and analyzing the composition, or make judgments without analyzing the meaning of sentences A certain usage or expression is wrong.

2) Teachers do not make timely corrections and rely too much on the evaluation framework

    Framework can easily make teachers feel completely dependent on the evaluation framework and slack off.

2.2 Algorithm Selection

In this paper, XGBoost is used to construct the intelligent evaluation framework for English composition. Compared with the traditional GBDT method, XGBoost has been improved in both error approximation and numerical optimization. In recent years, XGBoost has been used in various machine learning-based applications and competitions. Has become one of the most popular methods. Suppose there are k trees to form the model [8, 9]:

$$\hat{y} = \sum_{k=1}^{K} f_k(x_i), f_k \in F \tag{1}$$

Solve the objective function for each parameter in the tree:

$$\text{Loss} = \sum_i l(\hat{y}, y_i) + \sum_k \Omega(f_k) = \sum_i (y_i - \hat{y})^2 + \sum_k \left(\gamma T + \frac{1}{2}\lambda\|w\|^2 \right) \tag{2}$$

Among them, $\Omega(f_k)$ consists of two parts: the parameter γ reflects the influence of the number of leaf nodes T on the error; the parameter λ reflects the influence of the leaf node weight won the error, and L2 regularization is used here to prevent the occurrence of too many leaf nodes. Phenomenon.

2.3 Writing Fluency and Discourse Fluency

The concept of fluency does not have a unified definition. In the field of literary writing and foreign language teaching, the definition of the concept of fluency is different. In the field of natural language processing, different AES systems have different methods and angles for judging fluency.

Writing fluency is an objective and active factor that restricts writing results. The smooth writing process is splendid and smooth, and the writing is not smooth, and the writing is exhausted. Especially when taking the test, within the specified time and scope, the thinking is also limited, and the mind cannot write it out, and the quality of the questioning is naturally not good. The definition of this fluency can be understood from this perceptual experience [10].

If these key elements of an essay were not included in the definition of fluency, students would assume that the faster the writing speed and the more words written per unit time, the smoother the essay. This is obviously inappropriate as a basic definition of fluency in foreign language teaching. In order to avoid these problems, considering that the real idea speed of students cannot be measured in computer writing, in the automatic composition scoring system, fluency is defined as a result-oriented quantity—discourse fluency. Combining word complexity, content and grammatical structure, discourse fluency can be intuitively understood as the readability and comprehensibility of the article. In the design and discussion of the AES system for English learners, Feller defines discourse fluency as a four-layer structure.

Such a definition is very meaningful for English teaching. First, discourse fluency is distinguished from the aspects that reflect the theme of the content of the article. As the definition of article readability and understandability, the most important thing is to link with the spelling, grammar and words of the article, which is also an important indicator to reflect the writing level of English learners. Spelling, diction and grammar errors are common among English learners and a distinct and analyzable feature. This is obviously different from native English speakers. Native speakers hardly need to think too much about grammar in writing at the same level. In contrast, the same expression content is unfamiliar with the language. The aspects to be considered at the time of writing will be completely different [11, 12].

3 Research and Design Experiment of Intelligent Evaluation Framework for English Composition Based on Intelligent Algorithm

3.1 Research Steps

This study takes the 2019 -level landscape college students of a university as the research object. Due to the limitation of class hours, there is no extra time to conduct individual composition coaching training for students, but to arrange composition exercises for students after each unit of teaching, and to explain after the exercises; the composition writing theme of each unit is basically the same as the theme of this unit. The explanations will be directly integrated into the classroom lectures. For the first time, freshmen take traditional paper exercises, and they will personally evaluate the test papers according to the four-level scoring standard. After the evaluation, they will select samples based on the scores. Among the 53 essays reviewed, 9 essays were selected. According to the composition score as the standard for segmenting, there were 3 people with a score of 5 to 7, 3 people with a score of 8 to 10, and 3 people with a score of 11 to 14. After the first assignment, it is transferred to the intelligent composition writing process. A total of 4 essays are arranged in 7 weeks, and the last assignment exercise is performed in the eighth week, which is reviewed by the teacher in person. The first and last writings are compared and researched, and the students' compositions and classroom performances transmitted to the online platform are used as the basis for analysis and research, and then the rules of students' writing changes are observed. Finally, the 9 students were interviewed orally, and the students' essays were further analyzed and discussed.

3.2   Experimental Design

The CET-4 exam draws 900 essays from college English essays with 150–200 words in the syllabus. To ensure the accuracy and authenticity of the original labels, each group must be scored individually by two teachers to obtain a grade point average for the set, combined with the comments of the two teachers to obtain an accurate description. Finally, the number of legends in the middle of each score was collected. Then, the superiority of the method in this paper is reflected from the difference of the mean square error of multiple scores of multiple scoring methods.

4   Experimental Analysis of Intelligent Evaluation Framework for English Composition Based on Intelligent Algorithm

4.1   The Feeling of Intelligent Evaluation of Composition

Table 1. Score and experience of intelligent composition evaluation framework

	Failed	Qualified	Good	Excellent
Composition score	1	4	3	1
Essay evaluation feelings	0	2	4	3

This paper aims at 9 college students who have used the intelligent composition evaluation system for a long time, and records their average scores in the intelligent composition evaluation system and the users' feelings about the use of the intelligent composition evaluation system, which are mainly divided into four categories: unqualified, qualified, good and excellent. The evaluation index and the experimental data are shown in Table 1.

As shown in Fig. 1, after the use of the intelligent composition evaluation framework, most of the students have passed the composition level, but in contrast, compared with the traditional manual correction and teaching part, the intelligent composition evaluation framework does not have Teaching, the improvement of students' writing level is small. However, the vast majority of students have a good experience in using the intelligent composition evaluation framework.

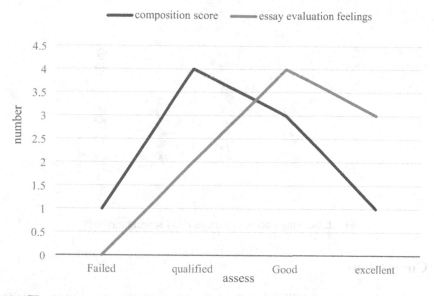

Fig. 1. Score and experience of intelligent composition evaluation framework

4.2 Scoring Effect

In this work, the 900 compositions are divided into 5 parts (ie, 180 in each part), of which 4 (ie 80%) are randomly selected as training samples, and the remaining 1 is used as test samples. Five rounds of cross-validation were used to train and test for five times, and each time the scoring index and the average of the five indexes were used as the evaluation results. The comparison between the evaluation results of the construction method in this paper and the previous evaluation methods is shown in Table 2.

Table 2. Scoring effects of various essay scoring methods

	The method of this paper	This article comprehensive vector + SVM	This article comprehensive vector + gbdt	LDA + XGBoost
Text1	10.39	18.12	12.91	21.93
Text2	10.42	19.13	12.45	21.45

As can be seen from Fig. 2, among many intelligent English composition evaluation frameworks, the mean square error of the algorithm constructed in this paper is the smallest among all methods. Moreover, after two different types of composition evaluation tests, the evaluation stability of the algorithm constructed in this paper is also high, which meets the needs of intelligent composition evaluation.

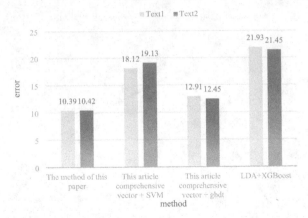

Fig. 2. Scoring effects of various essay scoring methods

5 Conclusions

The English composition intelligent evaluation system in this paper is an automatic composition evaluation system developed according to the characteristics of Chinese English learners. The system uses natural language processing technology to analyze and extract features of students' essays, and uses feature dimensions and scoring models to predict the scores of essays. This paper studies the discourse fluency evaluation technology in the English composition intelligent evaluation system. Through the method of writing error detection, the discourse fluency dimension is introduced into the system and the performance of the system is improved. The discourse fluency evaluation technology in this paper is designed and experimented completely according to the writing characteristics of Chinese English learners, and this technology is integrated into the composition scoring dimension, which has played a role in improving the scoring effect of the system.

References

1. Liu, L., Tsai, S.B.: Intelligent recognition and teaching of english fuzzy texts based on fuzzy computing and big data. Wirel. Commun. Mob. Comput. **2021**(1), 1–10 (2021)
2. Avsykevich, D., Yu, T., Shishkin, E.: Approach to formalization of the intelligent information control systems based on the topos theory. J. Phys.: Conf. Ser. **2131**(3), 032013 (2021)
3. Ou, G.: Automatic correction service system for english composition based on big data. J. Phys. Conf. Ser. **1852**(4), 042013 (2021)
4. Babson, A.: Imperfect english composition. Westview **35**(1), 20 (2019)
5. Besada, J.L., Cánovas, C.P.: Timelines in spectral composition: a cognitive approach to musical creativity. Organised Sound **25**(2), 142–155 (2020)
6. Saihanqiqige, H.E.: Application research of english scoring based on TF-IDF clustering algorithm. IOP Conf. Ser.: Mater. Sci. Eng. **750**(1), 012215 (2020)
7. White-Farnham, J.: Resisting 'Let's Eat Grandma': the rhetorical potential of grammar memes. Comput. Composit. **52**(JUNE), 210–221 (2019)
8. Lentschat, M., Buche, P., Dibie-Barthelemy, J., et al.: Food packaging permeability and composition dataset dedicated to text-mining. Data Brief **36**(4), 107135 (2021)

9. Eilitt, T., Haddington, P., Vatanen, A.: Children seeking the driver's attention in cars: position and composition of children's summons turns and children's rights to engage. J. Pragmat. **178**(3), 175–191 (2021)

10. Fedewa, M.V., Nickerson, B.S., Tinsley, G.M., et al.: Examining race-related error in two-compartment models of body composition assessment: a systematic review and meta-analysis. J. Clin. Densitom. **24**(1), 156–168 (2021)

11. Kokoszyński, D., Arpáová, H., Hrnar, C., et al.: Carcass characteristics, chemical composition, physicochemical properties, texture, and microstructure of meat from spent Pekin ducks. Poultry Sci. **99**(2), 1232–1240 (2020)

12. Iparraguirre, J.: Household composition and the dynamics of community-based social care in England. Ageing Soc. **40**(8), 1–16 (2019)

Multimedia English Teaching System Based on Computer Information Technology

Haixia Yin[✉], Lu Zhang, and Xiao Wang

Xi'an Fanyi University, Xi'an, Shaanxi, China
fiona_xxn@163.com

Abstract. With the rapid development of computer science education, multimedia-assisted teaching has become an important teaching tool in college teaching practice. Multimedia teaching integrates video teaching, image teaching, and text teaching, deeply triggers students' sensory system, provides students with a full range of teaching experience, changes the teaching mode that traditional teaching cannot stimulate students' passion for learning, and makes computer network teaching and independent learning more efficient and independent. In the context of the rapid development of computer information technology, this paper designs a multimedia English teaching system based on the powerful information processing functions of WEB, and the test results show that the system CPU usage rate is 62%, and the memory usage rate is 38%, the development reaction time is 2.27 s, the operation stability is 99%, all of which meet the operation standards, and avoid system failures during teaching and using.

Keywords: Computer information technology · Multimedia English teaching system · Traditional teaching mode · Performance test

1 Introduction

With the rapid development of information technology, traditional teaching models can no longer meet the needs of modern education. The development of multimedia technology provides excellent teaching support for information and intelligent education. With the rapid development of the Internet and multimedia, teachers need to make full use of multimedia technology for teaching, thereby enhancing the differentiation, diversity and interest of English teaching, and improving the quality and efficiency of English teaching.

A large number of scholars at home and abroad have carried out experimental researches on the design and realization of multimedia English teaching system based on computer information technology, and many researchers have achieved good research results. A scholar pointed out that the English-assisted teaching model based on computer information technology is the foundation of modern education. The introduction of multimedia technology into college English practical teaching has become the development direction of modern English teaching models. He believes that the combination of multimedia and English teaching can maximize the great functions of multimedia,

N. Khare et al. (Eds.): MIND 2022, CCIS 1762, pp. 272–279, 2022.
https://doi.org/10.1007/978-3-031-24352-3_22

thereby improving students' learning initiative and opening up a new teaching model for English teaching [1]. A scholar deeply discussed the transformation of multimedia English teaching mode, and believed that in order to improve the quality of English teaching, we should strengthen the production of English teaching courseware, improve teaching equipment, and improve the proficiency of teachers using multimedia for teaching, so as to give full play to the benefits of multimedia teaching. Teachers use multimedia teaching resources to improve the effect of English teaching, and students' English ability will also rise to a new level [2]. Although the multimedia English teaching method under the computer information technology has been recognized by the academic circles, the traditional teaching mode is generally adopted in the actual English classroom teaching in colleges and universities. It is hoped that colleges and universities can implement multimedia English teaching to promote the growth of students' learning ability.

This article first analyzes the advantages and defects of the multimedia English teaching model, and then builds a multimedia English teaching system based on the WEB architecture according to the design requirements of the multimedia English teaching system. In order to ensure the normal operation of the system, the performance of the system is tested and demonstrated, also, the user registration process of the system is implemented to ensure that users can log in to the system.

2 The Pros and Cons of Multimedia English Teaching and the Demand Analysis of Teaching System Design

2.1 Advantages and Disadvantages of Multimedia English Teaching

(1) Advantages
First of all, multimedia can combine English language images, texts, sounds, animations and videos to stimulate students' senses in all aspects of the English teaching process, and bring English learning content into life according to learning interests and needs. The environment of a variety of audio, image and text information can enhance students' hearing and vision, and present the teaching content in a more three-dimensional manner [3].

Secondly, multimedia teaching integrates interactive participation into English teaching process. Students have the opportunity to participate and express their views in English, which makes learning English more active. This teaching method creates a reflective and innovative learning environment for students, and promotes students to form a new cognitive structure. Teachers and students, as well as students and students, can communicate and interact through the computer network, so that teaching and learning activities are no longer limited to the classroom [4, 5].

(2) Disadvantages
Although the use of computer multimedia technology in English teaching has many advantages, everything is relative. First of all, multimedia has a great impact on traditional teaching. In terms of presentation methods, teaching materials presented through multimedia are displayed to students in the form of images, text and audio. The main learning task of students is to watch teaching videos so that they are lack of thinking and practice in acquiring new knowledge. Due to the fast presentation

speed, some students simply accept knowledge blindly and lack questioning and thinking; in addition, students do not have enough time for discussion and inter- action. If they are exposed to knowledge unilaterally, students may lose interest in learning and lack initiative. Improper handling of the new and old knowledge will make students think that knowledge transfer does not require thinking, which reduces the students' reflective power in the classroom [6].

Secondly, in the multimedia teaching environment, the amount of information disseminated is larger, and the teaching speed is faster than traditional teaching methods. According to the different levels of students' cognitive development, there is a certain limit to the degree of acceptance of knowledge in a certain period of time. If the teacher cannot grasp the amount of learning information in the English teaching process, once it is too large, the students cannot fully absorb all the learning content, which will ultimately affect the teaching effect [7].

Finally, for some inexperienced young teachers, when using multimedia tech- nology to make English courseware, only presenting the teaching content in text will make students visually fatigued when watching the courseware, and students will be distracted, which will lead to poor listening effects; on the contrary, if your courseware contains a large number of videos or animations, which will also distract students' attention and keep them mentally in good spirits when the animations are played. But once they are converted to text teaching, students will listen listlessly, and the important points in teaching content will be reversed, which does not meet expected teaching effect. Therefore, teachers need to devote more time and energy to elaborate multimedia course materials and prepare well before class so that they can appropriately use multimedia teaching resources in English teaching [8, 9].

2.2 System Requirement Analysis

(1) Functional requirements

Basic information management function: This functional module is to pave the way for multimedia core business management functions, and the educational administration system will open students' and teachers' information to the out- side world. The management authority of this functional module is mainly system administrators.

Multimedia database management function: The modules involved in the multi- media function are the core business modules of the system, which includes videos, audios, pictures, texts, tables, PowerPoints and so on. Because the classification of multimedia information is different, and the format of the information is also diverse, the multimedia information needs to be segmented and managed. The management authority of this part is mainly for teachers.

Personal management function: As some of the relevant resources and modules in the system are open to school teachers and students, some relevant information management functions will be provided for them during the system deployment. For example, teachers can upload teaching resources, students can download teaching videos, and so on. The management authority of this part is for teachers and students [10, 11].

(2) Performance requirements

Smooth English video playback: The video program must be guaranteed to be more than 20 frames per second. For videos with too large capacity, buffer technology and segmented downloads are used to achieve a good playback effect.

Good interactivity: The user can freely locate the playback node when playing the video. During the playback process, the computer can conveniently fast forward and rewind the on-demand resources, as well as play, pause, stop and other controlling operations. Users can order resources by resource classification, or search for target resources based on keywords. The system must support the simultaneous on-demand function of one resource by multiple users, without interfering with each other.

(3) Hardware requirements

Network environment requirements: This system has high requirements for network bandwidth, because the data volume of the video stream is very large, if the bandwidth is not enough, it will inevitably affect the playback quality of the teaching video. For example, to ensure that the resources of MPEG-1 format files can be played normally, the average bit rate should be 1.5Mbps.

Storage system requirements: Generally speaking, one minute of DAT video requires more than 10M storage space. For college English teaching, the multimedia video resources are rich and colorful. Therefore, the storage space of this system must be large enough to meet the current application needs of the school and ensure future development. For this reason, the disk array of this system must have more than 20T.

(4) Software requirements

Main application server: It is installed on the campus network management server, responsible for managing user information, data retention and resource download, and interconnecting the three aspects through resource management scheduling, providing user functions such as website access, custom video, and personal information maintenance.

Video cluster server: To meet the school's curriculum requirements and the storage and access needs of many teachers and students, the system must solve the streaming media problem. The system can manage and program all the resources of the network server, provide dynamic load balancing for various user requests, and ensure that the application main server responds efficiently.

3 The Design of Multimedia English Teaching System under Computer Information Technology

3.1 System Deployment Architecture Design

Figure 1 shows the deployment of a multimedia English teaching system based on the WEB architecture. The main servers of the system include a database server, a web server, and a video resource server. It is connected to a video projector through a campus network, and English videos can be placed on the projection screen.

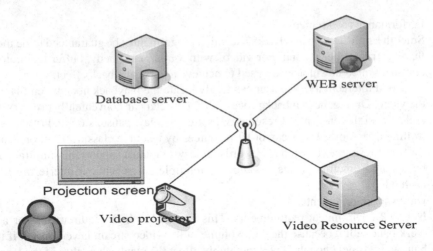

Fig. 1. System deployment architecture

3.2 System Structure Design

Figure 2 shows the overall structure of the multimedia English teaching system, which is composed of a basic information management subsystem, a multimedia database management subsystem, and a personal management subsystem. The basic information management subsystem includes English dictionary setting module, course management module, teacher information module and student information module; multimedia database management subsystem includes English video presentation module and English teaching resource retrieval module; personal information management subsystem includes view history module, my class schedule module, upload and download modules related to English teaching.

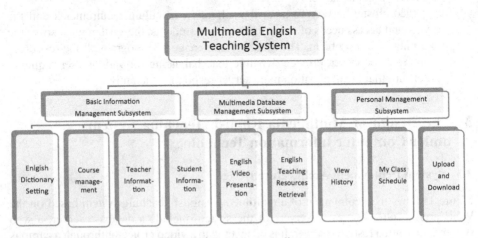

Fig. 2. System structure diagram

4   The Realization of Multimedia English Teaching System

4.1   System Operation Test

Table 1. System running test results

	Theoretical value	Actual value
CPU usage	$\leq 75\%$	62%
Memory usage	$\leq 50\%$	38%
Boot response time	$\leq 3s$	2.27s
Stability	≥ 93	99%

As shown in Table 1, the CPU usage, memory usage, boot response time and stability of the test system are running. When comparing the theoretical value and actual value of these test performances, if the actual value is not within the theoretical value range, the system needs to be improved continually. It can be seen from the data in the table that the theoretical value of CPU usage should not exceed 75%, and the actual value should be 62%; the theoretical value of memory usage should not exceed 50%, and the actual test value should be 38%; the system boot response time should not exceed 3 s, the actual value is 2.27 s; the system stability must exceed 93%, and the actual value reaches 99%. The performance of these four running tests all meet the theoretical requirements, so the normal operation of the system can be guaranteed.

4.2   Implementation of User Registration Module

As shown in Fig. 3, a user must register before using the system. When registering, the user first fills in relevant information, including user identity (such as student, teacher, administrator), user gender, user name, and account password. The system will determine whether the user name is available. If the user name is occupied, the user needs to reset the user name, and then the user needs to enter the same password twice. If the two password entries are inconsistent, the user needs to re-enter the same password. After the user information is registered, the system will store the information in the database, and the next time you log in, the system will compare the user information in the database to ensure that the user logs in normally.

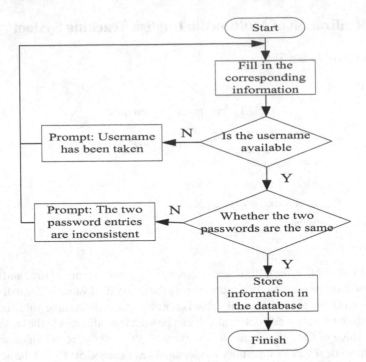

Fig. 3. User registration process

5 Conclusion

The development of computer information technology has changed people's life patterns and at the same time changed the teaching methods in the field of education. This paper uses advanced science and technology to design a multimedia English teaching system. After the design is successful, the performance of the system is tested. The test results show that multiple performances of the system meet the operating requirements, and prove that the system can be used normally. It is hoped that multimedia English teaching system can be introduced by colleges and universities to conduct English teaching activities, which can effectively improve students' English proficiency.

Acknowledgements. This work was supported by J21A08.

References

1. Geng, L., Zhao, Y., Xu, F.: Design and realization of student dormitory information management system based on C/S structure. C e Ca **42**(6), 2602–2606 (2017)
2. Jiang, F.: Design and realization of 3D simulation system for large-scale architectural landscape based on BIM technology. Revista de la Facultad de Ingenieria **32**(11), 619–625 (2017)
3. Sun, X., Zhang, L., Li, C.: Design and realization of Webgis-based tourism information system. C e Ca **42**(5), 2065–2069 (2017)

4. Liang, W.: Scene art design based on human-computer interaction and multimedia information system: an interactive perspective. Multimed. Tools App. **78**(4), 4767–4785 (2019)
5. Zheng, H., Perez, Z.: Design of multimedia engineering teaching system based on internet of things technology. Int. J. Continuing Eng. Educ. Life-long Learn. **29**(4), 293–305 (2019)
6. Hu, H.: Design and research of english self-study system based on computer network. Revista de la Facultad de Ingenieria **32**(4), 534–540 (2017)
7. Liu, Z.: On the design of college english precision teaching pattern based on the information technology. IOSR J. Res. Method Educ. (IOSRJRME) **07**(4), 26–29 (2017)
8. Ju, Y., Wan, H.: Analysis of physical education teaching mode based on computer multimedia and network system. Int. J. Multimed. Ubiquit. Eng. **12**(1), 311–322 (2017)
9. Liao, W.L., Lee, T., Jiang, W., et al.: Augmented reality teaching system based on cognitive theory of multimedia learning - an example system on four-agent soup. Appl. Sci. Manage. Res. **6**(1), 54–69 (2019)
10. Hung, H.T.: The integration of a student response system in flipped classrooms. Lang. Learn. Technol. **21**(1), 16–27 (2017)
11. Duan, C.: Design of online volleyball remote teaching system based on AR technology. AEJ - Alexandria Eng. J. **60**(5), 4299–4306 (2021)

Correlation Analysis of Central Bank Communication Behavior and Monetary Policy Independence Based on VR Technology and Machine Learning

Feng Gao[✉]

Hao Jing College of Shaanxi University of Science and Technology, Xi'an, Shaanxi, China
gaofeng_0062021@163.com

Abstract. Maintaining independence of monetary policy based on VR technology and machine learning is an effective guarantee for the central bank to flexibly use macroeconomic control measures to achieve domestic economic goals. In-depth exploration of the influence of the choice of the RMB exchange rate system on the independence of China's monetary policy has important practical significance for China to choose a suitable exchange rate system and enhance the central bank's macroeconomic control capabilities. This paper combs, analyzes and reviews the domestic and foreign research literature related to the development of machine learning theory and the application of adaptive learning in the research of optimal monetary policy. It points out the explanation of adaptive learning in inflation fluctuation and persistence, provides an explanation closer to the real economy for expectation management, and provides a new perspective for the research of the central bank's optimal monetary policy. The experimental analysis results show that this paper uses the hybrid Phillips curve to regress the price policy issued by the People's Bank of China, and shows that the residual ADF value after regression of each model is less than the ADF critical value-1.95 at the 5% significance level, indicating The impact of inflation expectations under adaptive learning on inflation is significantly higher than the expected price index of the People's Bank of China.

Keywords: Adaptive learning · Central bank communication behavior · Monetary policy independence · Correlation analysis

1 Introduction

Economic globalization has brought closer economic ties between countries, and has also made the communication behavior of central banks based on VR technology and machine learning increasingly important. From 2016 to the first half of 2018, China's domestic price index continued to rise, but the accelerating accumulation of double surplus in the balance of payments made the liquidity injected into the economy by monetary policy increased unabated. Although monetary policy has been under pressure since the second half of 2019 It has been eased, but as the world economy stabilizes, the loose monetary policies of countries in the crisis will definitely cause further flooding of global liquidity. Therefore, it is very meaningful to study the independence of monetary policy in advance and avoid it becoming a vassal of the open economy.

Monetary policy independence refers to whether the implementation of monetary policy can achieve the expected goals. It has always been a research topic that economists enjoy. Many economists have conducted research on this. For example, Tumala M M analyzed the communication strategy of the Central Bank of Nigeria (CBN) from 2004 to 2019 using text mining techniques. In terms of monetary policy sentiment, the average net score was found to be −10.5%, reflecting the level of policy uncertainty faced by the MPC during the sample period. The themes driving the language content of the bulletin are considered to be influenced by the Bank's policy objectives and the nature of economic shocks in each period [1]. Dittrich W H describes a new model of the communication process between the central bank and financial market participants, exploring in particular the barriers and resistance in the transmission of information from the sender to the receiver, since indirect communication can lead to distortion of information. Proper communication that takes into account these obstacles and the psychology of the receiver can significantly improve the efficiency of monetary policy [2]. Triand-hari R analyzes the risk-taking behavior of economic agents such as banks, households and firms in response to monetary policy and macroprudential choices in Indonesia. The results show that credit risk influences the deepening of credit procyclicality. In addition, the optimal policy response is analyzed using the loss function of the central bank in the presence of risk-taking [3].

This paper selects different return parameter values to represent different adaptive learning mechanisms to calculate the inflation expectations of the Chinese public, and obtain different regression results, so as to compare and analyze the corresponding economic interpretations. Based on the adaptive learning hypothesis, this paper compares the general analysis of the optimal monetary policy rules with the characteristics of the monetary policy in the special development stage of Chinese society in the transitional period, combined with the results of the empirical analysis, and draws the conclusion of China's optimal monetary policy under adaptive learning.

2 Correlation Between Central Bank Communication Behavior and Monetary Policy Independence Based on VR Technology and Machine Learning

2.1 Adaptive Learning Based on Machine Learning in Monetary Policy

The consideration and introduction of learning can change the evaluation of monetary policy [4, 5]. The initial research on adaptive learning of monetary policy focused on how to design monetary policy rules to make the economy converge towards REE in the long run [6, 7]. Subsequent research focused on the use of adaptive learning to analyze economic behavior in the short and medium term [8, 9].

(1) Adaptive learning and the persistence of inflation. Under normal circumstances, the reasons for the sustained period of inflation mainly include lagging inflation, costs

caused by various adjustments, etc. If the hypothesis of rational expectations is replaced with the hypothesis of adaptive learning, it can provide a new explanation for the causes of the sustained period of inflation. Either fixed-income learning (or permanent learning) and diminishing return learning can be classified as adaptive learning.

(2) Adaptive learning and optimal monetary policy. An important aspect of research on adaptive learning is to design reasonable monetary policy rules to guide the private sector in the economy to gradually converge in the long-term expectations of the future, that is, how to choose appropriate monetary policy rules to achieve the equilibrium solution of rational expectations, and ensure the stability of public inflation expectations. Adaptive expectation the future forecast value of the subject of adaptive expectation is only affected by historical experience. The adaptive expectation model is defined as follows:

$$p_t^* = p_{t-1}^* + \beta(p_{t-1} - p_{t-1}^*) \tag{1}$$

Among them, β is the non-negative adaptive expectation coefficient, and p_{t-1}^* is the price forecast in t-1 period. As the forecast error of the previous period, $(p_{t-1} - p_{t-1}^*)$ is used by economic entities to revise the current forecast p_t^*. The difference between the actual price of the previous period and the predicted price of the previous period will be used as feedback input into the forecast output of the next period [10, 11]. After formulating formula (1), another expression of adaptive expectation is obtained:

$$p_t^* = \beta p_{t-1} + (1 - \beta)p_{t-1}^* \tag{2}$$

The formula actually expresses the recurrence relationship between the current expected value and the previous forecast and actual value. According to the formula (2):

$$p_{t-1}^* = \beta p_{t-2}^* + (1 - \beta)p_{t-2}^* \tag{3}$$

After infinite iterations, the formula (2) can be expressed as:

$$p_t^* = \beta p_{t-1} + (1 - \beta)p_{t-1}^* = \beta p_{t-1} + (1 - \beta)\left[\beta p_{t-2}^* + (1 - \beta)p_{t-2}^*\right]$$

$$= \cdots = \sum_{i=1}^{\infty} \beta(1 - \beta)^{i-1} p_{t-1} \tag{4}$$

It can be seen from formula (4) that p_t^* is actually the weighted average of all historical price data.

2.2 Basic Objectives of Central Bank Policy Communication

(1) Maintain the independence of the central bank. In the next stage of monetary policy formulation and implementation, the central bank must not be completely free from the constraints of relevant government departments, be independent of the

government, and must not override government agencies [12, 13]. It should be guided by the national macroeconomic policy [14, 15]. In the current situation where the independence of the central bank is gradually increasing, the central bank should make full use of the tool of policy communication to better achieve macroeconomic goals, and effectively perform its duties under the supervision of the public, government and laws [16, 17].

(2) Improve the effectiveness of monetary policy. This is also one of the basic goals of conventional monetary policy. By coordinating with monetary policy through written documents or oral communication, the central bank can play the role of monetary policy more efficiently [18, 19].

2.3 The Theoretical Analysis Framework of China's Monetary Policy Independence

Although the reform of the renminbi exchange rate system is still on the way and the renminbi has not yet fully floated, it is very likely that the renminbi will implement a floating exchange rate system in the future [20, 21]. Here, still take China as an example for analysis. This article analyzes the de facto free floating exchange rate system, that is, the central bank does not use foreign exchange reserves to intervene in the foreign exchange market [22, 23].

When the Federal Reserve raised the federal funds rate, demand for US dollar assets rose, and China's capital outflow scale increased. If China's current account balance plus capital account balance still has a surplus, then the US dollar foreign exchange supply exceeds demand in the Chinese foreign exchange market, the US dollar depreciates relative to the RMB, and the RMB will have appreciation pressure [24, 25].

3 Experimental Research on Correlation Between Central Bank Communication Behavior and Monetary Policy Independence Based on VR Technology and Machine Learning

3.1 Goal System Under Adaptive Learning Based on Machine Learning

This article makes appropriate amendments to the economic model, combined with China's current monetary policy goals, and continues to analyze the optimal monetary policy rules under adaptive learning. This article analyzes the optimal monetary policy research under adaptive learning under the traditional monetary policy analysis framework.

(1) Aggregate demand curve, the curve is expressed as follows:

$$y_t = E_{t-1}y_t - \delta(i_t - E_{t-1}\pi_t) + d_t \tag{5}$$

Among them, y, is the current output gap, which is the difference between actual output and potential output. i is the nominal interest rate of the current period, $E_{t-1}\pi_t$ is the inflation expectation of period t formed by the main body based on the information of period t-1.

(2) As the aggregate supply curve, inflation is determined by the aggregate supply curve empirically tested in this article:

$$\pi_t = a\pi_{t-1} + \beta E_{t-1}\pi_t + \gamma y_t + \eta_t \tag{6}$$

π_t represents the current inflation rate, π_{t-1} is the inflation rate of the previous period and represents inflation inertia, $E_{t-1}\pi_t$ is the forecast made by the private entity on the inflation of period t based on the information of period t-1, y_t is the output gap in period t, the coefficients of inflation inertia and inflation expectation a, $\beta \in (0,1)$, the output gap weight $\gamma > 0$, and η is a series of uncorrelated shocks.

3.2 Selection of Variables

This article uses the Phillips curve to represent the alternating relationship between unemployment and inflation. When the inflation rate is high, the unemployment rate is low; when the inflation rate is low, the unemployment rate is high; unemployment and economic growth have an inverse correlation, that is, it shows from the side It further shows that there is a trade-off relationship between price stability and economic growth in the process of monetary policy implementation.

3.3 Research Methods and Data Collection

Although the government's intervention in economic discretion will bring difficulties to the test, this article regards the interest rate differential and the nominal effective exchange rate between China and the United States as shocks. When investigating the impact of China's central bank policy changes on the money supply, the causality test is used. When investigating the impact of exchange rate changes on the money supply, Granger is used to find the co-integration relationship to establish a vector error correction model.

4   Experimental Research Analysis of the Correlation Between Central Bank Communication Behavior and Monetary Policy Independence Based on VR Technology and Machine Learning

4.1   Estimation of Phillips Curve Under Adaptive Learning

In order to ensure the validity of the initial value of the iteration, the sample size is selected according to the ratio of 1:10, calculate the regression coefficient C_0 for the second quarter of 2016. Again, the inflation expectation sequence generated by the adaptive learning corresponding to different k values and the expected price index issued by the People's Bank of China are respectively regressed to the hybrid Phillips curve. The regression results are shown in Table 1:

It can be seen from the regression results in the above table that when the sample size is the same, at the 5% significance level, the residual ADF value of each model after regression is less than the ADF critical value -1.95 at the 5% significance level, so Each model has a co-integration relationship.

Table 1. The regression results of the expectations generated by adaptive learning and the People's Bank of China's expected price index

Regression coefficients	People's Bank of China expected price index	$K_t = 0.02$	$K_t = 0.1$	$K_t = 1/t$
Constant term	132.37	43.225	57.378	3.274
π_{t-1}	−0.127	0.176	0.154	0.283
y_t	−1.36	−0.985	−0.644	−0.842

4.2 Impulse Response Model

Since this article mainly explores the impact of shadow banking scale on the effectiveness of monetary policy, three representative impulse response diagrams are selected to describe the impact of SBV and RM2 on COE. Impulse response of SBV, RM2, COE are shown in Fig. 1.

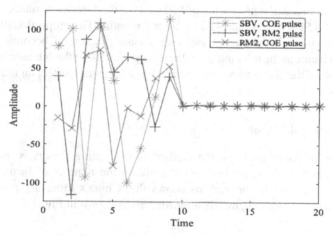

Fig. 1. Impulse response of SBV, RM2, COE

From the above volatility graphs, it can be seen that in the long run, SBV and RM2 have no long-term effect on COE, and SBV has no long-term effect on RM2; in the short and medium term, SBV and RM2 have more volatility on COE. The results show that the effect of the effectiveness of monetary policy is that the intermediary target plays a more important role.

4.3 Impulse Response Function and Variance Decomposition

In order to more clearly examine the degree of influence of various factors on the base currency, based on the error correction model, the variance decomposition of the forecast errors of different forecast periods of the base currency is carried out to examine the contribution of the variance explained by each variable.

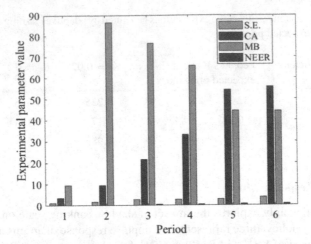

Fig. 2. Variance decomposition of base currency

As shown in Fig. 2, the proportion of MB itself in the forecast variance continues to decline, from 86.51% to less than 47.75% after 6 months. The proportion of the current account balance factor in the forecast variance gradually increased, becoming the largest variance ratio factor in the 6th month, and reaching 75.95% in the 6th month, indicating that the growth of the current account balance has a long-term effect on the issuance of base currency.

4.4 Factor Analysis Results

In the process of factor analysis, the method of estimating factors is the maximum likelihood method, and the method of determining the number of factors is Kaiser-Guttman. The result of factor analysis shows that China's monetary policy has two factors, and the factor loading matrix after rotation is shown in Fig. 3.

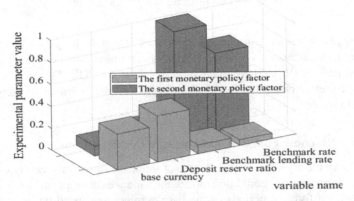

Fig. 3. China's monetary policy factor loading matrix

Note: If the estimated factor is more than one, rotate the factor loading matrix. The results shown in the article are the results obtained after rotation.

4.5 Overall Effect of Policy Communication on Market Exchange Rates

By obtaining the coefficients of the explanatory variables of the mean and variance equations of the GARCH model, the specific results are shown in Fig. 4. In order to test whether the results are robust, ARCH-LM test is performed on the regression results, and it is found that there is no ARCH effect in the residual series, indicating that the results are valid.

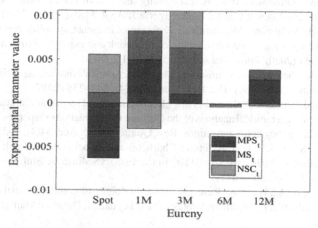

Fig. 4. The impact of central bank policy communication on market exchange rates

From the perspective of the mean equation, the central bank's policy communication has a positively significant impact on the spot exchange rate. It shows that the currency authorities will directly price the RMB exchange rate when communicating tighter policies, which is generally consistent with the actual situation. Policy communication has a significant impact on the medium and long-term exchange rate, but the coefficient of the exchange rate for each period is relatively small.

5 Conclusions

Through empirical research in this paper, the marketization of deposit and loan interest rates in my country has an impact on bank and credit risk through monetary policy. In addition, there is a significant positive correlation between the comprehensive indicators of interest rate marketization and the proxy variables of bank credit risk, indicating that the higher the overall interest rate marketization degree, the higher the bank credit risk. This article verifies that China's central bank's policy communication has played an important role in the operation of monetary policy and has a certain impact on financial market expectations and the fluctuations in the exchange rate of RMB against the euro.

However, the current use of policy communication by China's central bank is still in its infancy. There are still some problems in the operation of its monetary policy. For example, the adjustment of China's monetary policy at the stage of economic transition has caused more uncertainty and reduced the effectiveness of policy communication. At the same time, it has also produced a multi-purpose monetary policy to make policy communication credible. It is more difficult to increase the degree of currency, and even affect the transparency of China's monetary policy.

References

1. Tumala, M.M., Omotosho, B.S.: A text mining analysis of central bank monetary policy communication in Nigeria. Central Bank Nigeria J. Appl. Statist. **10**(2), 73–107 (2019)
2. Dittrich, W.H., Wohlmann, M.: Hurdles and obstacles in monetary policy communication. A model for the communication between the central bank and markets. Ekonomia XXI Wieku **2020**(23), 7–34 (2020). https://doi.org/10.15611/e21.2020.01
3. Triandhari, R., Safuan, S., Syamsudin, M., et al.: Banks' risk taking behavior and the optimization monetary policy. Eur. Res. Stud. J. **20**(4), 244–258 (2017)
4. Su, S., Ahmad, A.H., Wood, J., et al.: How effective is central bank communication in emerging economies? An empirical analysis of the Chinese money markets responses to the people's bank of China's policy communications. Rev. Quant. Financ. Acc. **54**(4), 1–25 (2019)
5. Ambade, B., Sethi, S.S., Giri, B., et al.: Characterization, behavior, and risk assessment of polycyclic aromatic hydrocarbons (PAHs) in the EstuarySediments. Bull. Environ. Contam. Toxicol. **108**(2), 243–252 (2021)
6. Zeng, W., Xu, H., Li, H., et al.: Research on methodology of correlation analysis of sci-tech literature based on deep learning technology in the big data. J. Database Manage. **29**(3), 67–88 (2018)
7. Zhou, L., Wu, H.: Impact study of central bank communication to money market benchmark interest rate. Open J. Soc. Sci. **04**(2), 69–78 (2016)
8. Cieslak, A., Schrimpf, A.: Non-monetary news in central bank communication. Working Paper Ser. **2018**(25032), 1–56 (2018)
9. Montes, G.C., Nicolay, R.T.F.: Does clarity of central bank communication affect credibility? Evid. Consider. Govern. Spec. Effects. Appl. Econ. **49**(31–33), 3163–3180 (2017)
10. Winkelmann, L.: Forward guidance and the predictability of monetary policy: a wavelet-based jump detection approach. J. Roy. Statal Soc. 65(FEB.PT.2), 299–314 (2016)
11. Dräger, L., Lamla, M.J., Pfajfar, D.: Are survey expectations theory-consistent? The role of central bank communication and news. Eur. Econ. Rev. **85**, 84–111 (2016). https://doi.org/10.1016/j.euroecorev.2016.01.010
12. Cieslak, A., Schrimpf, A.: Non-monetary News in central bank communication. J. Int. Econ. **118**(MAY), 293–315 (2019)
13. Jubinski, D., Tomljanovich, M.: Central Bank actions and words: the intraday effects of FOMC policy communications on individual equity volatility and returns. Financ. Rev. **52**(4), 701–724 (2017)
14. Garcia-Herrero, A., Girardin, E., Dos Santos, E.: Do as I Do, and also as I say: monetary policy impact on Brazil's financial markets. Economía **17**(2), 65–92 (2018)
15. Montes, G.C., Nicolay, R.T.D.F.: Central Bank's perception on inflation and inflation expectations of experts. J. Econ. Stud. **42**(6), 1142–1158 (2017)
16. Lombardi, D., Siklos, P.L., St, A.S.: Government bond yields at the effective lower bound: international evidence. Contemp. Econ. Policy **37**(1), 102–120 (2019)

17. Tillmann, P., Walter, A.: The effect of diverging communication: the case of the ECB and the Bundesbank. Econ. Lett. **176**(MAR), 68–74 (2019)
18. Baek, S., Lee, J., Park, I., et al.: Systematic analysis of oxide trap distribution of 4H-SiC DMOSFETs using TSCIS and its correlation with BTI and SILC behavior. Solid-State Electron. **140**(feb), 18–22 (2017)
19. Feroli, M., Greenlaw, D., Hooper, P., et al.: Language after Liftoff: fed communication away from the zero lower bound. Res. Econ. **71**(3), 452–490 (2017)
20. André, J.D., et al.: A correlation analysis of international newspaper coverage and international economic, communication, and demographic relationships. Ann. Int. Commun. Assoc. **1**(1), 307–317 (2017)
21. Zhou, R., Liu, S.: How situational cognition, communication behaviour and public trust of NPOs affect individual donation intention: the case of anti-COVID-19 in China. China Nonprofit. Rev. **13**(1&2), 1 (2021)
22. Alizadeh, S.M., Iraji, A., Tabasi, S., et al.: Estimation of dynamic properties of sandstones based on index properties using artificial neural network and multivariate linear regression methods. Acta Geophys. **70**(1), 225–242 (2022)
23. Cornand, C., M'Baye, C.K.: Does inflation targeting matter? An experimental investigation. Macroecon. Dyn. **22**(2), 362–401 (2018)
24. Di Bartolomeo, G., Di Pietro, M., Giannini, B.: Optimal monetary policy in a new Keynesian model with heterogeneous expectations. J. Econ. Dyn. Control. **73**(DEC), 373–387 (2016)
25. Moura Marins, J.T., Machado Vicente, J.V.: Do the central bank actions reduce interest rate volatility? Econ. Model. **65**(sep), 129–137 (2017)

Power Demand Data Analysis and Recovery for Management of Power Distribution Systems

Haisheng Hong[1]([✉]), Chende Xu[1], Zhe Liu[1], Yang Qin[1], Yuanyi Chen[2], and Yubin Wang[2]

[1] Guangzhou Power Supply Bureau of Guangdong Power Grid Co., Ltd., Guangzhou, China
honeyhycere@qq.com
[2] College of Electrical Engineering, Zhejiang University, Hangzhou, China

Abstract. Efficient anomaly detection and repair method is an important means to solve the problem of time series data quality. Current pair research on the quality of time series data mainly focuses on the lack of attribute value, data anomaly and data disorder, but the phenomenon of data loss is very common in the industry. This work presented a solution for power demand measurement analysis and recovery for the management of power distribution systems. The developed method and the algorithm are extensively evaluated and validated based on the simulation experiments for different test cases and the numerical results demonstrated that the proposed missing data recovery method can perform efficiently to recover the missing data for the improvement of data quality to enhance the operation of power distribution system operations. The solution can be further extended to different application domains to improve the data quality of advanced intelligent functionalities.

Keywords: Data analytics · Missing data recovery · Convolutional network · Data processing · Power distribution systems

1 Introduction

The power industry has developed rapidly in recent decades. With the continuous construction of an intelligent power system, a large volume of data is generated in the process of power production, marketing and service, and each business will accumulate a large amount of historical data. Managers spend a lot of time and energy analyzing and processing these data every day. In the face of huge data, the support of their operation and management methods for power production and decision-making is inevitably insufficient and weak. There are two main reasons for this problem: first, the traditional methods are not only inefficient but also the results are not representative, If effective data is extracted from huge data for processing, the result is that managers cannot make more comprehensive decisions; another reason is that the current management information system only pays attention to the processing links of business processes, which makes the dependence of enterprise production and decision-making on big data unsatisfied. As far as the power system is concerned, the future power industry production and management are closely related to power big data. Therefore, big data technology needs to be adopted in the power system to solve the problems caused by the growing data in various application domains and sectors.

In power systems, the main types of power system data are divided into the following four types:

(1) Basic data: this kind of data is mainly the data associated with transformers, generators and other power equipment. The Power Grid plans and manages the basic data according to the actual situation, and updates the data in the power system accordingly, to ensure that the decision-making made by the dispatching center is based on the new data.

(2) Real-time data: this kind of data is generated during the whole operation process of the power system. The huge amount of real-time data needs to be equipped with large storage space. The real-time data can show the operation of the power system.

(3) Daily management data: this kind of data mainly includes the data sorted by each department after the problems of the power system are handled. The daily management data is generated in the specified range. Based on establishing the sharing platform, it can feed back the operation status of power equipment in a real-time fashion, which is convenient for each department in the power grid to get the required data information and is conducive to the next work of all departments.

(4) External data: this kind of data is mainly generated from other networks connected with the power system. These networks mainly include the Internet of things, primary energy network, Internet and other networks. This kind of data has an important relationship with the operation and maintenance of the power system. For example, the weather and temperature change data can have an impact on the wind and solar power stations, making the power system dispatching change. Therefore, considering this external information in the data of the power system can help the dispatching department to make more comprehensive decisions.

In literature, many studies have been carried out to address the challenge. Many solutions have been developed and adopted in many application domains, e.g., Principal component analysis (PCA) and independent component analysis (ICA) [1]. Different types of machine learning methods, e.g., k-NN algorithm [2], random forest (RF) algorithm [3], support vector machine (SVM) [4] and artificial neural network (ANN) [5], were also studied and implemented. In addition, the deep learning based solutions are also receiving increasing attention, e.g., deep belief network (DBN) [6], sparse self-encoder (SAE) [7], sparse filtering [8], convolutional neural network (CNN) [9] and recursive neural network (RNN) [10], as well as variants and improvements based on the above basic model, which shows strong feature learning ability and satisfactory diagnosis results. Therefore, data restoration technology based on deep learning has become a research hotspot and has a very broad application prospect.

To sum up, it is a novel problem to detect and repair the dislocation of attribute values on the data stream. Anomaly detection can find the dislocation errors in the system in time, to help troubleshoot the problems in time and maintain the system's High availability to reduce the occurrence of problems; Exception repair can be performed when the error has occurred without changing the data value itself, the data is exchanged to obtain the original real data, to provide a reference for the follow-up Analysis and mining provide high-quality time series data.

2 Proposed Algorithmic Solution

This work designs a data enhancement algorithm to reconstruct the one-dimensional data into two-dimensional matrices, which are regarded as "generalized" images. After then we divide the detected missing mask into three grades and use the image processing techniques in the deep learning field to recover the missing data grade by grade.

2.1 Two-Dimensional Reconstruction

In this study, the electricity demand in the power distribution system generally varies over time and is characterized by multiple periodicities on different time scales. Thus, such periodical features need to be examined for demand data analysis.

It should be noted that the conventional estimation and interpolation methods have not been able to examine the useful information from the available data, as shown in Fig. 1. As a result, the repair accuracy of the missing segment is low, especially for the long continuous missing segment. The adaptive adjustment of the reliability ratio of directly adjacent data and indirectly adjacent data is important to improve the missing data recovery performance.

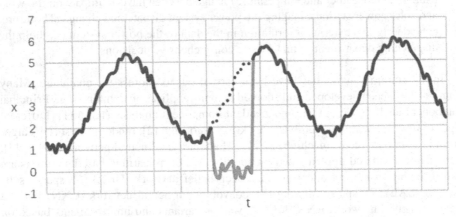

Fig. 1. Perceived range for the traditional interpretation methods

In addition, it should be noted that:

(1) The missing mask will be truncated and reconstructed as a matrix and divided into submatrices with the same shape as the data.

(2) Because the grayscale in the computer is usually 8 bits (the integer between 0 and 255), it likely to cause irreversible accuracy loss when converting the original data value into grayscale. Therefore, what we do indeed is just keep the data in the matrix, and use that in the following computation. Only when we want to virtualize the matrix, do we convert them into grayscale. That is also the reason we call these matrices "generalized" images.

When dealing with similar numerical conversion problems, some scholars suggest using RGB (24 bits) images to represent the actual value. One of the conversion methods used is shown in formula (1.1) to (1.2–1.4). Its basic idea is to use the 8 bits of R, G and B to represent the high, middle, and low bits independently of the actual value. By doing so, the advantage is that it can eliminate the problem of precision loss, and RGB images can hold more semantic information compared with grayscale images.

$$(R_i, G_i, B_i) = map(\hat{x}_l) \tag{1}$$

$$R_i = [\hat{x}_l \cdot 2^8] \tag{2}$$

$$G_i = [\hat{x}_l * 2^{16}]\%2^8 \tag{3}$$

$$B_i = [\hat{x}_l * 2^{16}]\%2^8 \tag{4}$$

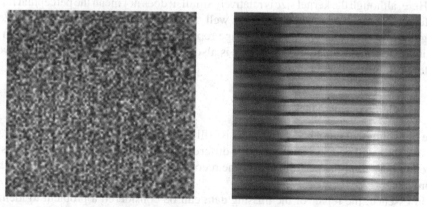

Fig. 2. Map comparison between RGB and grayscale

However, this map relationship between data values and RGB is an artificial design rather than a natural transfer. Because in the natural color spectrum, there is not such a carry relationship between R, G and B. To be more specific, two adjacent values such as 255 and 256 will be mapped as blue (0, 0, 255) and green (0, 1, 0) separately, which are far away from each other in the color spectrum. This could break the continuity in the original data, and result in semantic confusion, as shown in Fig. 2. For this reason, we would not use the RGB images as a virtualization approach in this work.

2.2 Pure Convolutional Autoencoder

This work adopted a two-dimensional image to represent the one-dimensional data and designed a novel network model for data recovery in the constructed image. In reality, the missing mask of the images can be known in advance through detection methods. This paper proposes a GAN framework that takes the data and the missing mask as inputs at the same time. Rather than taking the missing mask as an extra input on the first layer of the network, here we use the missing mask as a filter on the final output layer. Only the output on the missing area will remain, and then we add this to the input image to form a repaired image. Notice that the image is still a padding slice, so we would take the core area out as the final output of the network. The loss function is computed only on the core area and the variables of the loss function in PCAE are given in Table 1.

Table 1. Variables of loss functional in PCAE

Variables	Definition
θ	Parameters of PCAE
$PCAE(X \| \theta)$	PCAE recovery network
RMSE	Root mean square error
MAE	Mean absolute error

Here, although the kernel size is relatively small, it does not mean the perceptual range for feature vectors is in a small region as well. Since here the data in the "generalized" image is folded, a small area in this image represents a very wide range of data in its original one-dimensional structure. This is also the reason why the improved network could work for the "generalized" image.

2.3 Graded Missing Masks

Pure convolutional autoencoder (PCAE) is still a one-step repair method, where all the missing data will be recovered without a difference. To previous analysis, this one-step structure may limit the performance of the recovery. Here, we discuss a more powerful improvement.

In essence, the repair of the missing data can be considered a problem to identify the best estimation for the missing data based on the adjacent normal data. So, how to fully use the adjacent normal data or increase the number of the adjacent normal data is the key to solving this problem. It is required to reshape the one-dimensional data into two-dimensional "generalized" images increasing the number of available adjacent data. In the implementation, the mild missing data can be recovered using simple linear interpolation methods with high accuracy. Taking the Belgian load data as the test dataset, the experiment shows that for the discrete point missing data, only using the mean value of the adjacent data can realize the recovery error within 1.2%. The graded mask is illustrated in Fig. 3

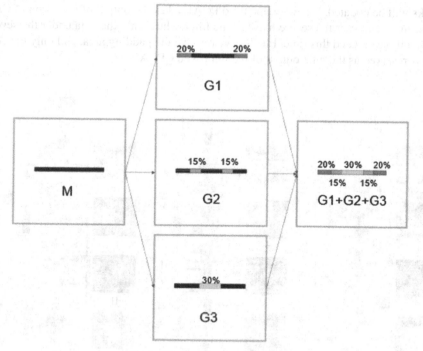

Fig. 3. Illustration of graded mask

It should be noted that the grading process here is operated on the missing mask, and we call the missing mask after grading a graded missing mask. And a potential phenomenon is that those moderate and severe missing in the core area might become mild and moderate missing after padding slice, which also reflects the improvement due to the padding slice algorithm.

2.4   Cascaded Pure Convolutional Autoencoder

Since the missing mask has been detected and divided into different grades in advance, we could transfer the grade idea to our model design. Here we use three cascaded PCAEs (CPCAE), instead of only one PCAE, to recover the corresponding three missing grades, as shown in Fig. 4. The first PCAE will only recover those mild missing data. The second PCAE will only recover the moderate missing data based on the output of the first PCAE, and so on for the third PCAE.

For the first PCAE, we take the mild, moderate and severe missing masks together as a filter acting on the output of the first PCAE. All the input normal data will keep unchanged in the output, while the first PCAE only updates the values of the mild, moderate and severe missing regions. The second PCAE will take the output of the first PCAE as its input, and use the mild and severe missing masks together as a filter on its output. Similarly, the normal data in the input will be kept, and the recovered data under the mild missing mask will be kept too, while the data under the moderate and severe masks will be updated. Likewise, the third PCAE takes the output of the second PCAE as the input and uses the severe mask as the filter. Thus, only the data under the severe mask will be updated this time. Finally, we remove the padding area, and only the core area is reserved as the final output of the improved CPCAE.

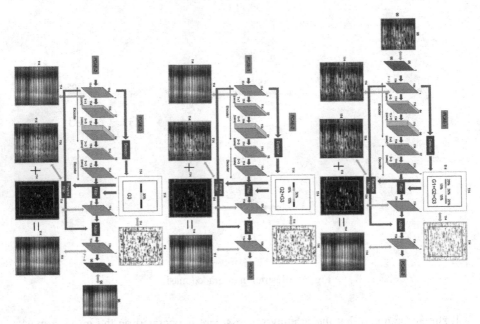

Fig. 4. The pipeline of CPCAE

3 Numerical Results and Analysis

Here, this work evaluates the CPCAE and the improved CPCAE models on different padding depths from 0 to 11, corresponding to the padding ratio from 0% to 23%. Here, during the model training process, the batch size and learning rate are set as 20 and 0.01, respectively. The training determinates until the loss function stops decreasing. The final result is shown in Table 2, where Mean Absolute Error (MAE) is used as a complementary index.

Even though the number of parameters in the CPCAE is the same as that in the improved CPCAE. The improved CPCAE model performs much better than the original CPCAE due to its more powerful deductive ability, while the padding depth can further decrease the recovery error. Also, it is worth noting that too deep padding depth may lead to performance degradation and the optimal choice of 9 is selected corresponding to the padding ratio of about 20% in this work.

Table 2. Recovery RMSE(MAE) for data normalized in (0.01,1)

Padding depth	CPCAE ($\times 10^{-2}$)	Improved CPCAE ($\times 10^{-2}$)
$p = 0$	4.15 (2.72)	3.15 (2.11)
$p = 7$	3.94 (2.61)	2.92 (2.01)
$p = 9$	3.79 (2.54)	2.86 (1.97)
$p = 11$	3.84 (2.56)	2.89 (1.99)

4 Conclusive Remarks

This work presented an algorithmic solution for missing data recovery that can perform efficiently to recover the missing data for the improvement of data quality to enhance the operation of power distribution system operations. In future research, we would further consider relative problems such as increasing the number of the grade levels to five or seven, and whether the CPCAE model can predict the load as well, instead of just repairing the historical missing data. In addition to the one-dimensional data, we are pretty interested in the extended application of the CPCAE model on the real image inpainting problem, which remains to be tested.

Acknowledgment. This work is supported by China Southern Power Grid science and technology project "Research on data collaborative application based on key elements of distribution network" 080043KK52200004 (GZHKJXM20200037).

References

1. Koldovský, Z., Kautský, V., Tichavský, P., Čmejla, J., Málek, J.: Dynamic independent component/vector analysis: time-variant linear mixtures separable by time-invariant beamformers. IEEE Trans. Signal Process. **69**, 2158–2173 (2021)
2. Abosamra, G., Oqaibi, H.: Using residual networks and cosine distance-based K-NN algorithm to recognize on-line signatures. IEEE Access **9**, 54962–54977 (2021)
3. Huang, Z., Chen, D.: A breast cancer diagnosis method based on VIM feature selection and hierarchical clustering random forest algorithm. IEEE Access **10**, 3284–3293 (2022)
4. Ertekin, S., Bottou, L., Giles, C.L.: Nonconvex online support vector machines. IEEE Trans. Pattern Anal. Mach. Intell. **33**(2), 368–381 (2011)
5. Yu, Y., Yu, D., Cheng, J.: A roller bearing fault diagnosis method based on EMD energy entropy and ANN. J. Vibr. Shock **294**(1), 269–277 (2006)
6. Shao, H., Jiang, H., Zhang, X., et al.: Rolling bearing fault diagnosis using an optimization deep belief network. Meas. Sci. Technol. **26**(11), 115002 (2015)
7. Sun, W., Shao, S., Zhao, R., et al.: A sparse auto-encoder-based deep neural network approach for induction motor faults classification. Measurement **89**, 171–178 (2016)
8. Lei, Y., Jia, F., Lin, J., et al.: An intelligent fault diagnosis method using unsupervised feature learning towards mechanical big data. IEEE Trans. Industr. Electron. **63**(5), 3137–3147 (2016)

9. Hoang, D.-T., Kang, H.-J.: Rolling element bearing fault diagnosis using convolutional neural network and vibration image. Cogn. Syst. Res. **53**, 42–50 (2019). https://doi.org/10.1016/j.cogsys.2018.03.002
10. Bruin, T., Verbert, K., Babuska, R.: Railway track circuit fault diagnosis using recurrent neural networks. IEEE Trans. Neural Netw. Learn. Syst. **28**(3), 523–533 (2017)

Optimization Design of Green Building Landscape Space Environment Based on LM-BP Algorithm

Xufeng Liu(✉), Li Chen, and Yong Chen

Architechture Designing Sichuan Highway Planning, Survey, Design and Research Institute Ltd., Sichuan 610000, China
liuxufeng987@126.com

Abstract. In recent years, with the rapid expansion of the scale of cities, the space of green ecological areas has been gradually eroded, and environmental problems have become increasingly serious. The purpose of this paper is to study the optimal design of green building landscape space environment based on LM-BP algorithm. Taking green ecological concepts and ideas as the introduction, starting from the general steps of architectural design, such as site selection, planning and design and other specific design process steps, it proposes architectural design strategies that combine ecological concepts and green technologies. The standard specification of indoor environment, use the trained LM-BP neural network prediction model to predict the water quality and air environmental pollutant parameter concentration data, conduct simulation, and analyze the prediction results, using MAPE, RMSE and TheilIC three evaluations The index evaluates the prediction effect of the model and evaluates the degree of water pollution. The experimental results show that the predicted deviation values are all close to 3%, and the current status of the indoor environment of green public buildings in the M area is obtained and the existing problems are optimized for the green building landscape space environment.

Keywords: LM-BP Algorithm · Green Building · Landscape Space · Environmental Optimization

1 Introduction

Humans have been exploring the relationship between themselves and the environment. The communication and interaction between humans and the environment affects the environment in which people live, and also affects human beings themselves [1, 2]. Improving people's perception of the environment itself and establishing a positive relationship between people and the environment are issues of environmental research, and this is where designers need to be careful. The construction of green building landscape requires new systems and approaches, and it is necessary to pay attention to the relationship between urban construction and environmental protection, environmental protection and management. In order to promote the sustainable development of cities,

N. Khare et al. (Eds.): MIND 2022, CCIS 1762, pp. 299–307, 2022.
https://doi.org/10.1007/978-3-031-24352-3_25

the concept of green urban infrastructure has been introduced [3, 4]. Green infrastructure provides a new way to build a complete green network by protecting and building green infrastructure.

Green infrastructure has multiple functions for urban development. Sekerin V D proposed the key points and methods for optimizing the ecological function of urban public space based on green infrastructure network. Taking the central urban area of Nanjing as an example, an empirical analysis is carried out. On the basis of identifying urban public space and green infrastructure, the land use suitability evaluation and classification are carried out on the public vitality and ecological sensitivity of these two types of infrastructure [5, 6]. The relationship between the two is studied and re-evaluated, and finally the optimization strategy of land use function is formed, in order to provide reference research ideas for the ecological planning of urban public space [7]. Gogoi B J redefines the concept of "green infrastructure", explains its connotation from the three scales of region, city and community, and selects three important measures of green roof, green street and rain garden to analyze its role and benefit, on this basis, summed up the advanced experience of the United States, the United Kingdom and other advanced experiences, combined with my country's actual situation, discussed the composition of the sponge city system from the perspective of "green infrastructure", and put forward relevant suggestions on how to scientifically formulate development strategies in my country, in order to provide my country's "green infrastructure". Provide reference for the construction of "sponge city" [8]. Using the LM-BP algorithm, it can analyze the existing urban ecological environment problems, ensure the effective coordination between urban ecological environment development and social economy, and help the country and society achieve more target economic and environmental benefits [9, 10].

This paper studies the concept, function, structure of urban green infrastructure and the tools and related theories of urban green infrastructure evaluation research. Many domestic and foreign practice cases are selected for analysis, and their respective characteristics and advantages are found. Predictive analysis using LM-BP algorithm. Establish two evaluation systems for regional water quality conditions and regional air quality, and use visual mapping to optimize the design of green infrastructure in combination with the results of index quantification. Put forward improvement strategies for the construction of green infrastructure in M area.

2 Research on the Optimization of Green Building Landscape Space Environment Based on LM-BP Algorithm

2.1 Optimization Principle

(1) The principle of landscape diversity
   For the construction of green infrastructure landscape, it is necessary to increase the richness of the landscape, increase the types of landscapes, increase the types of vegetation coverage, and increase the types of plants [11, 12].
(2) The principle of uniformity
   The green infrastructure construction in the region should maintain the uniformity of each region, and reduce the degree of fragmentation of the patches, so that the

green infrastructure patches are distributed in a balanced and orderly manner in the region, which is not only conducive to the stable development of the ecosystem in the region. It also increases residents' accessibility to green spaces.

(3) The principle of connection between man and nature

In addition to maintaining the sustainable and stable development of urban ecology, urban green infrastructure can also provide people with recreational places and increase opportunities for people to get close to nature. The construction of urban green infrastructure should strengthen the connection with people, serve people, and realize the coordinated development of people and nature, people and cities [13, 14].

2.2 Indoor Environment Standards for Green Public Buildings

(1) Acoustic environment

Noise can easily increase negative emotions such as anxiety, and continuous noise can disturb the coherence of people's thinking. Therefore, the purpose of controlling indoor noise is to create a good indoor acoustic environment for people. The propagation of sound in a building is mainly through the air and structure, so in addition to controlling the indoor noise level, the air sound and impact sound of the envelope are also important indicators of the acoustic environment [15].

(2) Air quality

Air quality reflects people's satisfaction with ambient air quality. Generally speaking, an environment with excessive pollutants not only degrades the air quality, but more importantly, endangers people's health. The concentration of pollutants is generally affected by both outdoor pollutants and indoor pollutants, such as particulate matter generated by outdoor fossil fuel combustion, and particulate matter re-suspended due to the operation of indoor printer equipment and personnel activities. In recent years, people's living standards have gradually improved, and the emphasis on air quality has also deepened. The four major types of air pollutants that affect human health are volatile organic compounds (VOCs), inhalable particulate matter, harmful gases and polycyclic aromatic hydrocarbons [16].

2.3 Green Ecological Building Design

(1) Building site selection and ecological security

The site selection of the project should avoid pollution sources and geological disasters, and keep away from dangerous sources.

If the building site is located between mountains, it is necessary to consider the possibility of natural disasters such as landslides, and take targeted countermeasures.

Buildings should maintain sufficient protective distance from gas stations, oil depots, toxic substance workshops, high-grade highways without sound insulation measures, etc.

The site selection of the building should pay attention to the site soil, and it is necessary to analyze and detect the toxic substances in the soil [17].

When designing the site, the premise is to conduct a relatively comprehensive environmental and economic assessment of the original conditions of the site, and then start planning and designing the site [18].

(2) Site water resources planning and design

In the design and planning of the space, the overall utilization of the site's water resources is an important content. The design should follow the principle of "adapting measures to local conditions". On the premise of meeting local water-saving requirements, through overall control analysis, the best and most systematic water resource utilization plan can be formulated, which can effectively improve the recycling rate of water resources.

When the building has a variety of complex functional requirements, it is necessary to conduct a comprehensive and unified inspection of the overall utilization of water resources and the site environment to find the most reasonable design scheme.

The determination of the water features and the volume and scale of water bodies in the site shall be judged according to the actual situation such as rainwater collection in the site. At the same time, the collected rainwater and building water can be used as non-drinking water sources in the site to avoid waste of water resources, as shown in Fig. 1.

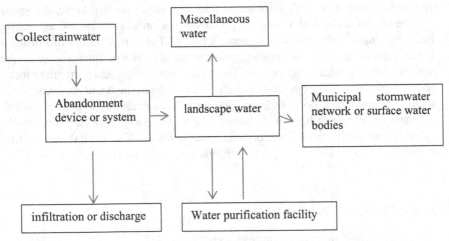

Fig. 1. Schematic diagram of rainwater collection on site

For the original water environment and ecological facilities of the site, they should be fully utilized and used as a measure for regulating and storing water resources on the site.

2.4 LM-BP Algorithm

The weights and thresholds in the traditional BP neural network are adjusted according to the gradient descent method, but the condition is that the objective function must be continuous and producible. Therefore, the training process will delay the convergence, and it is easy to fall into a local optimum. Therefore, this paper uses the Levenberg-Marquardt algorithm (referred to as the LM algorithm) to adjust the weights and thresholds. The LM algorithm uses the nonlinear least squares method to deduce the approximate form of the Hessian matrix, which can greatly reduce the amount of computation.

There are three stages of prediction using BP neural network: initialization stage, training stage and testing stage. The initialization phase needs to determine the network structure; the training phase mainly uses the determined network structure to train the model to obtain the optimal neural network model; the testing phase is used to evaluate the generalization ability of the final neural network model, that is, the prediction of the model ability.

3   Design and Research of Green Building Landscape Space Environment Optimization Based on LM-BP Algorithm

3.1 Structural Design

The regional water quality condition prediction takes temperature as input, and takes COD concentration, ammonia nitrogen concentration, total nitrogen concentration and total phosphorus concentration as output, so the number of nodes in the input layer is 3, and the number of nodes in the output layer is 1.

The regional air quality forecast is mainly based on the concentration of pollutants (SO2, NO2, CO, O3, PM2.5 and PM10) and meteorological (air pressure, temperature, relative humidity, wind speed and direction) data for the previous four days and the current five days. To predict the air quality index (AQI) of the next day, the number of nodes in the input layer of the BP neural network is 55, and the number of nodes in the output layer is 1.

3.2 LM-BP Neural Network Prediction Model

Denote ω as the vector composed of network weights and thresholds, $e(\omega)$ as the error vector, and the modified $\Delta\omega$ of the weight thresholds of each layer of the neural network is:

$$\Delta\omega = (J^T J + \mu I)^{-1} \cdot J^T e \tag{1}$$

Among them, J represents the Jacobian matrix, which is composed of the first-order derivative matrix of the network error to the weight threshold, and the expression is:

$$
J = \begin{bmatrix}
\dfrac{\partial e_1}{\partial \omega_1} & \dfrac{\partial e_1(\omega)}{\partial \omega_2} & \cdots & \dfrac{\partial e_1(\omega)}{\partial \omega_n} \\[2mm]
\dfrac{\partial e_2(\omega)}{\partial \omega_1} & \dfrac{\partial e_2(\omega)}{\partial \omega_2} & \cdots & \dfrac{\partial e_2(\omega)}{\partial \omega_n} \\[2mm]
\cdots & & & \\[1mm]
\dfrac{\partial e_m(\omega)}{\partial \omega_1} & \dfrac{\partial e_m(\omega)}{\partial \omega_2} & \cdots & \dfrac{\partial e_m(\omega)}{\partial \omega_n}
\end{bmatrix}
\tag{2}
$$

I represents the unit matrix; μ is a scalar that can be adjusted adaptively. When μ is large, the weight adjustment method is close to the gradient descent method, and when μ is small, the weight adjustment method is close to the Gauss-Newton method.

The specific selection range of the initialization value is mainly affected by the activation function. When it is a logistic function, an initialization value is generally selected in the interval $(0, 1)$; when the activation function is a tangent function, it is generally in the interval $(-1, 1)$.) to select the initialization value. Therefore, the initialization value of this paper is between the interval $(0, 1)$.

The weight threshold initialization of the BP neural network usually obtains the initialization value by generating random numbers. When the network structure of the BP neural network remains unchanged, the same training samples will be used, and different simulation results will be obtained. This paper chooses to randomly generate 10 groups of weight threshold random numbers between $(0, 1)$, and then determines the optimal weight threshold initialization value by comparing the errors of the validation set.

4   Design and Analysis of Green Building Landscape Space Environment Optimization Based on LM-BP Algorithm

4.1   Regional Water Quality Conditions

The calculation results of the prediction evaluation indexes of the four water quality parameters are shown in Table 1. It can be seen that for the four water quality parameters of COD, ammonia nitrogen, total nitrogen and total phosphorus, the value of the evaluation index MAPE is below 3%, as shown in Fig. 2. It shows that the deviation between the predicted value and the actual measured value is small, and the accuracy of the prediction results obtained by using the LM-BP neural network to predict the concentrations of the four water quality parameters is very high.

The local water pollution problem is extremely serious. Most of the surface water of M land is facing serious pollution, among which the most important pollution is nitrogen compound pollution and a large amount of organic pollution. With the continuous deepening of the urbanization construction process, the annual domestic sewage discharge continues to accumulate, and it remains high all the year round. It has not been effectively controlled, and eventually leads to a serious pollution level exceeding the standard, making the surface water in a long-term pollution state.

Table 1. Evaluation indicators for the concentration prediction of the four parameters

Predictive evaluation indicators	COD concentration prediction	Ammonia nitrogen concentration prediction	Total Nitrogen Concentration Prediction	Total Phosphorus Concentration Prediction
MAPE	2%	1%	0.8%	0.9%
RMSE	5%	3%	1.5%	3%
TheilIC	2.5%	0.9%	2.8%	3.1%

Rivers can be used as important connecting corridors in cities. The green belt along the river in the M area has problems of insufficient greening and broken corridors in many areas. Therefore, it is necessary to carry out continuous greening and landscape construction in the river waterfront area, form a connecting corridor with the water system as the direction, and combine it with the pedestrian system and recreational places to guide people's recreational activities to the waterfront area and play an important ecological role. Value and social value.

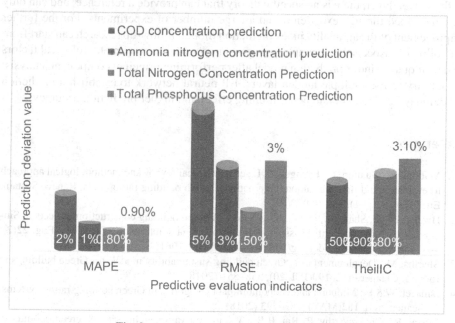

Fig. 2. Regional water quality prediction bias

4.2 Regional Air Quality

The air quality in the M area still needs to be improved. Since 2020, with the joint efforts of all regions in the M region, the air quality has been improved to a certain extent, but it is still often mildly polluted and moderately polluted, with occasional severe pollution, and the air quality ranking is lower than that of the whole country. The air quality situation still needs to continue to strive to improve.

The air quality in the M area is poor and the pollution is more serious. Protective green spaces and parks should be added around pollution sources. The construction of green infrastructure should combine the overall thinking of urban culture to create a targeted cultural resource system. It can be considered to build more historical green planting gardens of this type based on the local Zhao Wang culture, supplemented by other key historical cultures., expand the area and quantity of green space, and implement the related work of the shelter forest system on the basis of expanding the use area of urban roads.

5 Conclusions

Building a modern green space environment with a high level is an inevitable requirement to achieve sustainable urban development. Although the improved model proposed in this paper has achieved good prediction results, it still has some shortcomings. First of all, for the selection of the structure of the BP neural network and the number of nodes in the hidden layer, there is no specific theory that can provide a reference, and can only be determined through experience and a large number of experiments. For the further improvement of the air quality index prediction model, follow-up research can start from the following aspects. For example, we can consider adding more meteorological factors to the air quality index prediction model after performing principal component analysis; we can try to use multiple hidden layers. BP neural network to establish a prediction model may be able to obtain better training effect and higher prediction accuracy.

References

1. Mattoni, B., Guattari, C., Evangelisti, L., et al.: Critical review and methodological approach to evaluate the differences among international green building rating tools. Renew. Sustain. Ener. Rev. 82(pt.1), 950–960 (2018)
2. Hwang, B.-G., Shan, M., Phuah, S.L.: Safety in green building construction projects in Singapore: performance, critical issues, and improvement solutions. KSCE J. Civ. Eng. 22(2), 447–458 (2018). https://doi.org/10.1007/s12205-017-1961-3
3. Sharma, M.: Development of a 'Green building sustainability model' for Green buildings in India. J. Cleaner Prod. 190(JUL.20), 538–551 (2018)
4. Ismaeel, W.S.E.: Midpoint and endpoint impact categories in Green building rating systems. J. Cleaner Prod. 182(MAY), 783–793 (2018)
5. Janani, R., Chakravarthy, P., Raj, R.R.: A study on value engineering & green building in residential construction. Int. J. Civil Eng. Technol. 9(1), 900–907 (2018)
6. Darko, A., Chan, A.: Strategies to promote green building technologies adoption in developing countries: the case of Ghana. Build. Environ. 130(feb), 74–84 (2018)
7. Sekerin, V.D., Dudin, M.N., Gorokhova, A.E., et al.: Green building: technologies, prospects, investment attractiveness. Int. J. Civil Eng. Technol. 9(1), 657–666 (2018)
8. Gogoi, B.J.: Green building features and factors affecting the consumer choice for green building recommendation. Int. J. Civil Eng. Technol. 9(6), 127–136 (2018)

9. Vertal, M., Zozulak, M., Vaskova, A., et al.: Hygrothermal initial condition for simulation process of green building construction. Energy Build. **167**(MAY), 166–176 (2018)
10. Retno, D.P., Wibowo, M.A., Hatmoko, J.: Science mapping of sustainable green building operation and maintenance management research. Civil Eng. Architect. **9**(1), 150–165 (2021)
11. Cynthia, H.H., Wu, H.: Tourists' perceptions of green building design and their intention of staying in green hotel. Tour. Hosp. Res. **21**(1), 115–128 (2021)
12. Lwin, M., Panuwatwanich, K.: Identification and evaluation of green building assessment indicators for Myanmar. J. Green Build. **16**(2), 143–172 (2021)
13. Hamilton, E.M.: Green Building, Green Behavior? An analysis of building characteristics that support environmentally responsible behaviours. Environ. Behavior **53**(4), 409–450 (2021)
14. Oguntona, O.A., Aigbavboa, C.O., Thwala, W.D.: A scientometric analysis and visualization of green building research in Africa. J. Green Build. **16**(2), 83–86 (2021)
15. Gaikwad, R., Dod, R.D.: The analysis of obstacles in green building construction. Gradiva. **7**(7), 29–35 (2021)
16. Kurnaz, A.: Green building certificate systems as a greenwashing strategy in architecture. Int. J. Nat. Appl. Sci. **4**(1), 73–88 (2021)
17. Hidayat, F., Setiyono, B., Putranti, I.R., et al.: green building asset management toward the end of usefulness: a case of the relocation of Jakarta to New Jakarta. PalArch's J. Archaeol. Egypt/Egyptol. **17**(6), 10646–10659 (2020)
18. Omar, K., AlSwidi, A.K., Saleh, R.M., et al.: The effect of awareness, knowledge and cost on intention to adopt green building practices. Int. J. Environ. Sustain. Dev. **19**(1), 33–58 (2020)

Design of Computational Thinking Intelligent Training System Under Big Data Technology

Xin Wang[1,2] and Xiaoyong Bo[1,2(✉)]

[1] Electrical and Information Engineering College, Jilin Agricultural Science and Technology University, Jilin, China
boxiaoyong@jlnku.edu.cn
[2] Smart Agricultural Engineering Research Center of Jilin Province, Jilin, China

Abstract. As a new product of the computing era, computational thinking embodies the development process of learners' problem-solving thinking, and capturing its procedural data can provide a data basis for effective and accurate evaluation of computational thinking. To this end, this article takes the problem attributes of computational thinking as an opportunity, based on the learning behavior data generated in the problem-solving process, constructs a problem-solving model that promotes the development of computational thinking, and designs a teaching process and an intelligent training system based on this model. The effect evaluation results show that the problem-solving model can effectively promote the cultivation of students' computational thinking. The design of the intelligent training system and the capture of learning behavior data provide a reliable basis for learners to solve problems and are a double guarantee for the development of computational thinking.

Keywords: Computational thinking · Problem solving model · Instructional design · Computer courses

1 Introduction

At present, "the ability to use computers to solve problems in this professional field" has gradually become a core problem in the field of computer education [1]. Computational thinking, as the basic literacy and basic abilities necessary for learners in the 21st century [2], is closely related to the basic concepts and problem-solving skills of computational science [3]. In the "Declaration of Computer Teaching Reform", the Teaching Steering Committee of University Computer Courses of the Ministry of Education clearly pointed out that computational thinking should be regarded as the entry point for the reform of university computer courses, and further clarified the connection between computational thinking and computer courses [4]. In basic computer education, "Database principles and Applications" is an important part of its content. Effectively cultivating computational thinking through this course has become the first choice of many college teachers [5]. In view of the current database course teaching, there is still a problem that "Although learners have learned relevant knowledge, it is difficult for knowledge transfer to occur in the process of using knowledge to solve practical problems" [6], this research has studied the "Database Principles and Applications" course. A comprehensive analysis of the learners' learning behavior, learning effectiveness, and diagnostic reports found that one of the main reasons for the learners' poor problem-solving ability is that the design of the course content does not meet the learners' differentiated cognitive level and learning needs. Therefore, on the basis of considering the initial level of the learner's computer, this research combines the learner's learning behavior data to model the learner's problem-solving process in computer courses, and conduct teaching verification and analysis of the problem-solving model. In order to explore the effective ways of computer courses for improving learners' problem-solving ability and cultivating learners' computational thinking.

2 Problem Solving Model Construction and Data Source Analysis

2.1 Problem Solving Model Construction

Collecting and analyzing the multiple learning behavior data generated by the learner in the problem-solving process is conducive to clarifying the learner's knowledge mastery level and the achievement of the goal [7], and then judging the learner's computational thinking development level. Analyzing the inner relationship between computational thinking and problem solving, we can find that computational thinking is a thinking process involved in problem solving, and has problem solving properties [8]. Taking this as an opportunity, this research takes online learning and classroom learning as the contextual orientation, starting from the two dimensions of learners and teachers, and constructs a problem-solving model that promotes the cultivation of learners' computational thinking, as shown in Fig. 1.

The problem-solving model takes the learner's six steps of problem-solving (i.e. situation recognition → problem extraction → analysis of the cause of the problem → making and evaluating the solution → implementing the solution → explaining the problem solution) as the main line, and each step contains computational thinking the core content of training enables learners to develop computational thinking by gradually solving problems in real situations. The learner's problem-solving process starts with the problem scenario created by the teacher in advance. On the basis of identifying the scenario and abstracting the problem, the learner first analyzes, formulates and evaluates the problem solution by means of independent inquiry and cooperative learning. Then, use tools to test and iterate algorithms, implement and optimize solutions. Finally, sort out and reflect on the problem-solving process to achieve cognitive construction.

At the same time, the problem-solving model is supplemented by the adjustment and optimization of the teacher's teaching design. First, the intelligent training system automatically collects and analyzes learners' learning behavior data. Then, based on the visual output of the learning behavior data, the teacher judges whether the learners' computational thinking level has been improved. Finally, the teacher adjusts and optimizes the teaching design, and is targeted sexually guide learners to solve problems in all aspects.

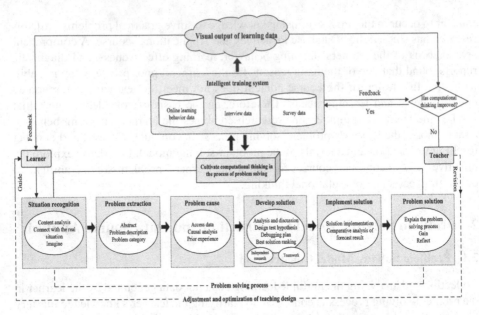

Fig. 1. Problem solving model

2.2 Data Source Analysis

Data source analysis is not only the basis for the construction of problem-solving models, but also the main basis for testing its scientificity and effectiveness. Clarifying data sources helps teachers accurately grasp the training standards of computational thinking, realize targeted guidance for learners' problem-solving process, and adjust and optimize instructional design, thereby enhancing learners' problem-solving abilities and ultimately promoting learners' computational thinking development of. Based on the analysis of the learner's problem-solving process, this research determines that there are two main data sources for the problem-solving model:

(1) Online learning behaviour data

Online learning behavior data mainly includes: ① Learning data refers to the online learning behavior data generated by learners when they study the materials provided by teachers, including log-in time and frequency, learning duration, browsing order of each module, etc. Integrating these data, you can discover the browsing path and the content of knowledge points in the learning process, search for the knowledge points and learning rules that learners have problems. ② Exercise question data refers to the learning behavior of learners when they test the questions provided by the teacher Data, including the content, frequency, duration, etc. Submitted by learners during daily experiment operations and testing. Using the captured data, the learner's knowledge mastery and the development process of problem-solving ideas can be visualized. ③ The study note data mainly includes the problems and new questions collected by the learners in the daily experimental operation test and the group test released by the teacher type, error-prone questions, the content collected by the learner in the process of learning knowledge points, and the notes made by the learner according to their own questioning situation and the level of understanding of the course content. Analyzing these data can obtain the focus and difficulty of learning that learners pay attention to. Compared with computer-generated information, online learning behavior data focuses more on learners' specific problems, and can reflect learners' knowledge and understanding of learning content.

(2) Interview data and questionnaire survey data

The objects of interviews and questionnaire surveys are learners and teachers, and strive to capture the relevant data of teachers and students to grasp the focus of the classroom learning process as a whole. In the whole research process, the interview data and questionnaire survey data mainly come from: ① At the beginning of the research, through interviews with teachers and questionnaire surveys of learners, the learning problems in the course of "Database Principles and Applications" were determined. ② Teaching In the process, through semi-structured interviews with the learners, the teaching progress, the important and difficult points of teaching, and the modification and presentation of the learning materials in the training system are determined. ③ The learners are measured three times of computational thinking level during the whole research process, so that teachers can make timely adjustments. Optimize the teaching design to ensure the scientificity and effectiveness of the teaching design of the "Database Principles and Applications" course.

3 Teaching Design Based on Problem-Solving Model in the Course of "Database Principles and Applications"

3.1 The Teaching Process of the Course "Database Principles and Applications"

This research takes the learning content of "SQL query sentences" in the course of "Database Principles and Applications" as an example to design teaching activities based on problem-solving models. The knowledge points of the learning content of "SQL query" involve simple query, conditional query, sorted query, multi-table query, sub-query, etc. Focusing on the entire teaching process of how to cultivate learners' computational thinking in the problem-solving training system. The teaching process designed for the "Database Principles and Applications" course mainly includes six steps: ① Create a situation and introduce an intelligent training system. Cultivating computational thinking first needs to provide a suitable problem context [9], so teachers need to set up a teaching context with an appropriate degree of difficulty according to the learner's previous knowledge level, and introduce the intelligent training system into the teaching link. ② Problem extraction, independent exploration. Learners can select and use relevant learning materials in the intelligent training system according to the actual needs of learning, provide relevant factual material evidence for hypotheses and reasoning in the problem solving process, and mainly examine the learners' ability to extract problem information in real situations. ③ Collaborative learning, split problems. The teacher organizes the learners to collaborate and communicate, and at the same time guide the learners to analyze the sub-problems contained in the problem and the inter-relation between the sub-problems and the sub-problems. ④ Formulate a plan to solve the problem. The teacher examines the learners' ability to decompose the problem and design the algorithm steps, and requires the learner to check the process of formulating the problem solution using the forward and backward methods, and apply the program to practice after the second adjustment [10]. ⑤ Ideas to solve the problem. Each group pays attention to the description of the process when reporting solutions to help learners connect with the original knowledge points and carry out knowledge transfer, thereby deepening the understanding and understanding of the nature of the problem. ⑥ Classroom evaluation, to complete the teaching goal of computational thinking training. The teacher comprehensively evaluates the learners based on the overall performance of the learners in the classroom, the procedural data of completing tasks, and the reported data.

3.2 Technical Realization of Intelligent Training System

The curriculum teaching for training learners' computational thinking relies on two major conditions: ① The problem-solving model provides directional and theoretical guidance for teaching design. ② The intelligent training system provides an equivalent support for teaching implementation and can promote learning in the teaching process. The learner solves the problem meaningfully, and then promotes the development of learners' higher-order thinking. Among them, the intelligent training system is the result of the efforts of experts in the computer field, teachers and researchers. Its functional structure design principle is centered on research problems and teaching design to improve the ability to capture learners' learning behavior data and difficult to achieve in conventional teaching. The pain point of personalized teaching and differentiated guidance is the goal, and its structure diagram is shown in Fig. 2.

According to the operation process, the intelligent training system is divided into a basic layer, a function layer, a data layer, and a feedback layer. Through the data storage and flow between layers, it promotes teachers to adjust teaching, intervene in learner learning, and learners to adjust learning independently. Ensure the cyclic operation of the entire system. Among them, the basic layer includes two data sources: a database and a question bank, which provide data support for the functional layer. The functional layer includes three functional modules: learning log, knowledge point learning, and evaluation, which are the key to the supporting role of the system. The data layer is accurate for learners through conventional display and knowledge map, the learning situation of individual learners and their classes is displayed. The feedback layer is the main front to promote the optimization of teaching. On the one hand, teachers can use learning behavior data to adjust teaching (such as the rhythm of teaching, methods, key and difficult points, etc.), intervention in learning (such as learning methods, materials and progress, etc.). On the other hand, learners can adjust learning based on learning results (such as learning strategies, focus and progress, etc.) to improve teaching and learning the results.

The realization of the intelligent training system based on the completion of the structural design mainly includes: ① The monitoring and dynamic analysis of learning during the problem-solving training process. Among them, monitoring is the real-time capture of various learning behavior data of learners, such as online operation data, submission content and the filling of learning logs, etc. While dynamic analysis is to integrate the collected monitoring data into the back-end database, and then analyze

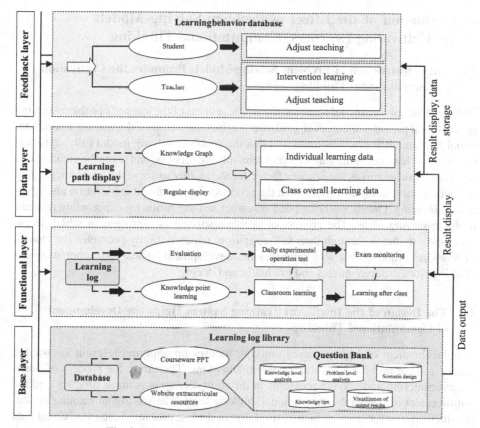

Fig. 2. Block diagram of the intelligent training system

the data. Perform efficient, comprehensive and dynamic analysis. The purpose of monitoring and dynamic analysis is to discover the potential information in the data, and make accurate judgments on the ways and methods of solving learning problems in a timely manner. It is the prerequisite for teachers to accurately teach and learners to learn efficiently. ② Realize the visual output of problem solving training results. Data visualization aims to convey information clearly and effectively with the help of graphical means. This requires that the form of graphics and visualization functions go hand in hand, and through intuitively conveying key dimensions and characteristic information, accurately grasp the deep meaning of the data. The objects of data visualization in this research mainly include effective data generated by learners in the process of learning assessment, behavioral data generated by learners in the process of learning, and process data of learning problems and problem solving.

4 Evaluation of the Effect of Problem-Solving Models for Cultivating Learners' Computational Thinking

4.1 The Construction of Problem-Solving Models Promotes the Cultivation of Computational Thinking

The problem-solving model relates to the whole process of the learner's problem-solving process, and provides theoretical guidance for the cultivation of the learner's computational thinking. It is not difficult to find that the problem-solving model fully considers the process elements of the learner's problem-solving process, and takes the creation of a real problem scenario as the primary factor for the learner to solve the problem, guiding learners to solve complex problems in the process of independent exploration and cooperative learning. Questions, reflect and construct self-cognition by expounding relevant problem-solving ideas. The process of problem-solving is a process in which learners constantly break through their self-cognition, which not only promotes the change of learners' thinking, but also promotes the development of learners' computational thinking from different angles and gradually and deeply.

4.2 The Design of the Intelligent Training System Helps the Development of Computational Thinking

The development of computational thinking focuses on applying relevant knowledge points to solve problems in actual problem situations. Therefore, the process of learners encountering and solving problems in different scenarios is more conducive to the improvement of learners' computational thinking level. The intelligent training system provides support for learners in the expression of diverse problem scenarios, visual data presentation, such as ① The system creates multiple problem scenarios for learners such as company hires employees and students choose courses. Learners can use the prompt information on the functional interface. Debugging information, expected results, to optimize the design of the problem solution. ② The contextual task arrangement is conducive to the learners to find problems in different scenarios, and to quickly diagnose and solve the problems. Based on this, it can be inferred that, on the one hand, the development of learners' computational thinking is affected by the individual learner's cognition of computer courses, and on the other hand, it relies on the diversified problem scenario expressions and data visualization provided by the intelligent training system for learners. Functional support to promote learners to independently explore and find the relationship between knowledge and problem-solving skills in different problem scenarios, and to realize the active construction and transfer of knowledge.

4.3 The Capture of Learning Behavior Data is Conducive to the Improvement of Computational Thinking

The intelligent training system provides learning behavior data such as the type, quantity, time, and accuracy of the questions, which not only points out the direction for the learners to review and consolidate the knowledge points, but also facilitates the learners to carry out targeted exercises on the relevant knowledge points, which can stimulate the learners the enthusiasm for problem-solving, and encourage learners to participate in the process of problem-solving. In addition, the learning behavior data captured by the system records the learners' learning process, learning effects, and the mastery of relevant knowledge and skills. It has the characteristics of pertinence, timeliness, and clarity, which can provide a basis for teachers to accurately carry out teaching evaluations, and It provides a reference for learners to debug and optimize problem-solving solutions, so it is conducive to the improvement of learners' computational thinking level.

5   Conclusion

In computer courses, improving the learners' problem-solving ability is the key to cultivating computational thinking. However, there is a general gap between theoretical knowledge and problem-solving in the course of course implementation. In response to this problem, this research is based on the problem-solving properties of computational thinking, constructs a problem-solving model that promotes the development of computational thinking, and designs a teaching process and an intelligent training system based on this model. Among them, the design of the intelligent training system realizes the effective communication of knowledge and problems in computer courses, the capture of learning behavior data, and the visual presentation of learning results. Through practical training, the learner's ability to use the knowledge learned to solve problems in different scenarios can be improved, and then their computational thinking level can be improved. The follow-up research will further carry out the teaching practice application of the problem-solving model in other disciplines, explore the transferability and scientific validity of the problem-solving model in different disciplines and the corresponding teaching design, as well as the accuracy and user experience of the intelligent training system. Iterative optimization is carried out to improve the operational validity and fault tolerance of this system, in order to provide reference for teachers to use problem-solving models and intelligent training systems in other disciplines to cultivate learners' computational thinking.

Acknowledgement. This work is financially supported by "Digital Agriculture" Emerging Cross Key Discipline of Jilin Province, Smart Agricultural Engineering Research Center of Jilin Province, Jilin Agricultural Science and Technology University Students' Innovative Training Program (No. 202111439007 and GJ202211439001), Higher Education Research Project of Jilin Higher Education Association (JGJX2022B45) and Research Project on Teaching Reform of Jilin Vocational Education and Adult Education (2022ZCY248).

References

1. Stella, M., Kapuza, A., Cramer, C., Uzzo, S., Latora, V.: Mapping computational thinking mindsets between educational levels with cognitive network science. J. Complex Netw. **9**(6), 1–13 (2021)
2. Cachero, C., Barra, P., Meliá, S., López, O.: Impact of programming exposure on the development of computational thinking capabilities: an empirical study. IEEE Access **8**, 72316–72325 (2020)

3. Eguíluz, A., Guenaga, M., Garaizar, P., Olivares-Rodríguez, C.: Exploring the progression of early programmers in a set of computational thinking challenges via clickstream analysis. IEEE Trans. Emerg. Top. Comput. **8**(1), 256–261 (2020)
4. Lin, P.H., Chen, S.Y.: Design and evaluation of a deep learning recommendation based augmented reality system for teaching programming and computational thinking. IEEE Access **8**, 45689–45699 (2020)
5. Moreno-LeÓn, J., Robles, G., RomÁn-GonzÁlez, M.: Towards data-driven learning paths to develop computational thinking with scratch. IEEE Trans. Emerg. Top. Comput. **8**(1), 193–205 (2020)
6. Cruz Castro, L.M., Magana, A.J., Douglas, K.A., Boutin, M.: Analyzing students' computational thinking practices in a first-year engineering course. IEEE Access **9**, 33041–33050 (2021)
7. Zapata-Cáceres, M., Martín-Barroso, E., Román-González, M.: Collaborative game-based environment and assessment tool for learning computational thinking in primary school: a case study. IEEE Trans. Learn. Technol. **14**(5), 576–589 (2021)
8. Csernoch, M., Biró, P., Máth, J.: Developing computational thinking skills with algorithm-driven spreadsheeting. IEEE Access **9**, 153943–153959 (2021)
9. Kazimoglu, C.: Enhancing confidence in using computational thinking skills via playing a serious game: a case study to increase motivation in learning computer programming. IEEE Access **8**, 221831–221851 (2020)
10. Torres-Torres, Y.D., Román-González, M., Pérez-González, J.C.: Unplugged teaching activities to promote computational thinking skills in primary and adults from a gender perspective. IEEE Revista Iberoamericana de Tecnologias del Aprendizaje **15**(3), 225–232 (2020)

Creative Graphic Design System Based on Multi-objective Firefly Algorithm

Huimin Qu$^{(\boxtimes)}$

Guangdong Dance and Drama College, Guangzhou, China
angelaq676@163.com

Abstract. Creative graphics is the basis of visual design. The development of creative graphics design system can provide convenience for the creation of high-level innovative talents, effectively promote the reform of graphic design, and provide a broad space for the direction of creative graphics design. Based on the historical origin and current development of cultural and creative graphic design, this paper applies the firefly algorithm to the cultural and creative graphic design system, simulates the flight of fireflies based on luminosity, photosensitivity, distance and other factors, constructs fireflies, and finds the best cluster center in each cluster through the foraging and courtship behavior of fireflies, which provides a new method for the research of cultural and creative graphic design system, At the same time, it also promotes the development of firefly algorithm.

Keywords: Multi-objective Firefly Algorithm · Cultural and creative graphic design · Design system · Cultural and creative design

1 Introduction

Firefly algorithm is based on the foraging behavior and mate selection habits of fireflies in the natural environment, and summarizes that fireflies attract each other according to their own luminous brightness [1]. Based on the biological characteristics of fireflies, a firefly algorithm is proposed. Firefly algorithm is based on evolutionary population, but there is no evolutionary operator. Each individual is compared to a small particle. Each particle moves freely in space. The range of moving distance is determined by the brightness and light intensity absorption coefficient of other adjacent individuals. Based on the traditional firefly algorithm, in order to improve stability, simplicity, efficiency and practicability, this algorithm optimizes the traditional firefly algorithm by using the physical physiological characteristics of the actual firefly, that is, the optimization process is only determined by the luminous characteristics of adjacent individuals. Within a certain planning range, the brighter the brightness of small particles, the stronger the attraction, The remaining small particles will move towards their position according to the relationship of attraction. Based on the above steps, the firefly can update its position again [2]. The firefly population can be regarded as the search solution space, but each feasible solution in the solution space corresponds to each firefly individual. Therefore, the solution process of the algorithm is like the change process between fireflies. There

N. Khare et al. (Eds.): MIND 2022, CCIS 1762, pp. 317–324, 2022.
https://doi.org/10.1007/978-3-031-24352-3_27

are two key points: fluorescence brightness and attraction. The higher the brightness, the better the target is. The closer the objective function is to the expected value, the more attractive it will be. Other people in the neighborhood are more willing to move closer to it. If the brightness is similar, the result will be that the position between fireflies will produce randomness [3].

2   Cultural and Creative Graphic Design

Cultural and creative products are a perfect handicraft combining culture and art. Similarly, the extraction of design elements of cultural and creative products should also be distinguished from general commodities, and the different feelings brought by their different cultural attributes must be considered. The design of cultural and creative graphics is rooted in different cultural attributes. Although the extraction of elements in some cultural and creative products is too narrow, there are many products with good creative ideas to spread culture [4]. Taking Taipei Palace Museum as an example, its cultural and creative product headrest takes the ancient lady's head shape as the creative element of the headrest, which not only has the ancient element shape, but also combines with the practical cultural and creative products. Cultural and creative products can not only fully reflect their historical and cultural heritage, but also fully foil and highlight their artistic creativity. Only when cultural and creative products are widely developed and elements are widely extracted from traditional graphics and patterns, can the development speed of cultural and creative products be improved.

2.1   Creative Graphic Design Traceability

At present, some cultural and creative graphic design methods at this stage are mainly designed with graphic elements that are well-known by the whole people and represent the Chinese nation, and all the souvenirs displayed in the shops around some museums are identical. In terms of the promotion of cultural and creative graphics, directly taking the appearance of unearthed cultural relics as the design element and giving it new functions is also a method to extract traditional graphic elements, Because people who are interested in culture naturally stop to watch, so as to achieve the function of spreading regional culture [5].

The generation of graphics can be traced back to the primitive graphic symbols such as totem patterns and cave murals in ancient times. Later, there were hieroglyphics. Chinese oracle bone inscriptions and ancient Egyptian inscriptions were ideographic graphics. Hieroglyphics were a new form formed on the basis of the original graphics [6]. In the 19th century, with the birth of photography, a large number of real images were used in all walks of life and became one of the forms of graphic expression. In the 20th century, with the development of computer technology, digital graphic design has become the mainstream. Graphics in English is graphic. Its definition refers to the picture mark produced by painting, writing, engraving, printing and other means. It is an illustrative picture image. It is different from the visual form of literature, words and language. It is a visual form that can be copied and widely spread through printing and various media to convey information, thoughts and ideas. Graphics convey information through symbols, metaphors, similes or fonts (graphics).

2.2 Importance of Graphic Design in Cultural and Creative Products

Graphics are the visual center of design works. Excellent design works accurately and clearly narrate the design theme with their own unique graphic language [7]. Cultural and creative products pay attention to the combination of product modeling and graphic design. Graphic design uses symbols, metaphors, analogies and other methods to pursue personalized and diversified styles, which has played an important role in promoting the design, production and sales of cultural and creative products. Types of graphic design in cultural and creative products.

(1) Font graphic text is a symbolic language used to record and convey information. With the advent of the era of graphics, the relationship between text and graphics plays an important role in design [8]. Graphic type is a type that expresses design intent with graphics. After artistic design, the text image can have scene and image. And increase influence, which is very important to improve the design of cultural and creative products.

(2) Traditional graphics. Traditional graphics are rooted in the traditional art origins of various dynasties, nationalities and regions in China. Taotie graphics on bronze ware in the Shang Dynasty, tadpole characters and plum blossom seal characters in the spring and autumn and Warring States periods, Phoenix shapes on lacquer ware in the Han Dynasty, Baoxiang patterns in the Tang Dynasty and later forms of gold characters, totems and national cultural graphics of various nationalities and regions, as well as Chinese painting, traditional custom painting, historical painting and calligraphy constitute China's traditional graphics system [9]. It is the mainstream trend of cultural and creative design to derive the traditional graphic elements and then apply them to the design of cultural and creative products. Through the application of traditional graphics in modern product design, it not only reflects the aesthetic feeling of the integration of tradition and modernity, but also highlights the characteristics of traditional culture.

(3) Hand drawn graphics. Hand drawn graphics, through the combination of media, elements and techniques, use the method of hand drawing and draw lessons from various artistic forms to design the graphic language. It has the characteristics of creativity and originality. Compared with hand-painted text graphics, hand-painted graphics are more intuitive, interesting and visual impact [10]. The application of hand-painted graphics in the design of cultural products has greatly improved both the characteristics of goods and the artistic value

3 Development Status of Cultural and Creative Graphic Design

Interactivity is one of the important characteristics of cultural and creative visual graphics. Based on the background of the digital age, compared with traditional media, digital media is closer to the people's life, and its feedback path and effect are more concrete. It imperceptibly urges cultural and creative visual designers to pay more attention to the new design thought path, and better understand the information interactivity and thought interactivity brought by digital technology, so that those who receive information, Turn into people who share information and people who extend information. Dynamics is also one of its important characteristics [1]. With the advent of the information age, digitization is progressing faster and faster, and its scope of dissemination and use is becoming wider and wider. Many people understand the information released, compiled and designed by cultural and creative visual designers through the dissemination of digital media, and spread the information through the dynamics of digital technology. Such as "the circle of friends of the official account", "micro-blog's forwarding button", "micro-blog hot search entry screen" and so on, this dynamic nature can well spread the creative and creative graphics of the text to the vision of more audience groups.

For the personalized characteristics of creative graphics, "effectiveness" is generally the key standard to be observed. Designers will relatively emphasize the daily aesthetic requirements of the audience, and then promote the daily aesthetic requirements of the audience through the graphic design of personalized speech, and obtain the corresponding resource progress information based on spirit and material. With the advent of the digital age, people's daily life cannot be separated from digital information gradually. Their living habits and attitudes have changed greatly, and the requirements for the accuracy and innovation of digital information are more detailed [11]. Pure "single language talk" cannot meet the people's life needs. Only by deepening emotional communication can the people's emotional needs be further met, so as to complete the emotional communication and common language between design works and people. Because of the "Popularization" of digital media, the works of cultural and creative visual creative graphic design also have a certain "Popularization", which can not only highlight the public's emotion, but also show the public's life. Compared with the previous design works, the works of cultural and creative visual creative graphic design are closer to the public opinion, so that the audience can naturally obtain information.

4   Technical Path Based on Multi-target Firefly Algorithm

4.1   Implementation Principle

Essentially, use the following three ideal rules: A. fireflies are gender neutral. Regardless of gender, one firefly will be attracted to other fireflies; B. The brightness of fireflies is determined by the size of the objective function. For the moopf problem, the value of the objective function is regarded as the brightness of the firefly. C. The attraction of fireflies is directly proportional to their brightness, and they all decrease with the increase of distance [12]. Therefore, for any two flashing fireflies, the brighter firefly will move to the brighter firefly, and if it is not brighter than a specific firefly, it will move randomly; In the simplest case, the brightness of the firefly at any specific position x can be selected as I (x), and I (x) is directly proportional to the objective function value f (x) of the problem. Assuming that there are NF fireflies with d-dimensional control variables, the position vector of firefly I can be expressed as UI = (ui1, ui2... Uid), which is also used as the solution of the problem. For any firefly individual J whose brightness is brighter than that of another firefly individual I, I will tend to move towards the location UJ of J in the way shown in formula (1), as one of many followers. In the practical operation of single objective minimization problem, the objective function value of firefly I is smaller and the judgment brightness is brighter.

$$_i^{new}u = {}_i^{old}u + \beta oexp\left(-\gamma r^2\right)\left({}_j^{old}u - {}_i^{old}u\right) + \alpha * \varepsilon \tag{1}$$

Among them, γ Is the light absorption coefficient, β 0 is the attraction when Rij = 0, α Is a randomization parameter, ξ I is a vector of random numbers with Gaussian or uniform distribution. It is important to point out that Eq. (1) varies in random steps in favor of brighter fireflies. The location of fireflies can be updated in sequence by comparing them one-to-one in each iteration cycle. The distance Rij between any two firefly individuals I and j at positions UI and UJ can be obtained using Cartesian coordinates or Euclidean distances as shown in Eq. (2) below.

$$r_{ij} = \|u_i - u_j\| = \sqrt{\sum_{K=1}^{D} (u_{i,K} - u_{j,K})^2} \tag{2}$$

where UI, K is the k-th dimension vector of the corresponding decision variable UI, and UI, K is the k-th dimension vector of the corresponding decision variable UI. For most optimization problems, β 0 can be set to 1, α You can set an expression that decreases with the number of iterations. The firefly algorithm is analyzed mathematically and can be described as follows.

Definition 1: the relative fluorescence brightness of fireflies is.

$$I = I_0 e^{-\gamma r} \tag{3}$$

Definition 2: attraction of fireflies β:

$$\beta = \beta_0 \in^{-\gamma r} \tag{4}$$

where: R – is the distance between two random fireflies, 0 – the degree of attraction at the light source (r = 0) – the light absorption coefficient.

Definition 3: distance between Fireflies: the relative distance between any two fireflies in the population is expressed by I and j, and their coordinate positions are expressed by IX and JX. They can be defined by an Euclidean or Cartesian distance respectively, as follows:

$$r_{ij} = \sqrt{\sum_{k=1}^{d} (x_{ik} - x_{jk})2} \tag{5}$$

After firefly I is attracted by firefly J, the position will move. The position will be updated in each iteration, according to the following formula:

$$x_j = x_i + \beta_0 e^{-\gamma r_{ij}} (\chi_i - \chi_j) + \alpha[rand - 0.5] \tag{6}$$

where: Xi – position of firefly in the last iteration. Rand0. 5 - auxiliary random parameters to avoid the algorithm falling into local optimization.

(1) Initialize the parameters of the model used in this paper. The firefly population size is 50 and the number of iterations is 50 $\alpha = 0.2$, $\beta = 0.9$, $\gamma = 1.0$, the maximum weight coefficient is 0.9 and the minimum is 0.4. The brightness of the firefly represents the value of the objective function. This paper refers to the minimum difference between the cultural and creative graphic design and the expected goal. The higher the brightness of fireflies, the smaller the objective function, and it is easier to attract the surrounding fireflies to move to this position, so as to make the firefly cluster close to the optimal solution;

(2) The fireflies began to attract each other, and the data in the corresponding control variable matrix began to change. On the basis of considering the inertia weight, the firefly algorithm is improved, so that the global optimization ability of the algorithm is strong at the beginning, and the local optimization of the algorithm begins to increase significantly as the solution tends to the optimal solution;

(3) Carry out power flow analysis on the data in the population of the new iteration, obtain the objective function corresponding to the individual in this iteration, and compare it with the excellent individuals retained before to obtain the global and local optimal solutions. If the termination conditions are met, go to step 5. If not, go to step 2;

(4) The Pareto solution set is obtained by this algorithm, and the fuzzy membership function method is used to select the comprehensive optimal solution from the solution set;

(5) According to the comprehensive optimal solution, output the reactive power optimization results, visualize the data, and end the calculation.

4.2 System Features

(1) Reduce the complexity of drawing process
The advantage of developing cultural and creative graphic design system is to accurately assist the creation of graphic and image files through multi-objective firefly algorithm. As shown in Fig. 1, the visual communication system designed with algorithmic graphics can reduce the manual work of designers. It also reduces design time and energy consumption. Compared with hand drawing, the design system becomes more accurate [11]. It can also enrich the lines and colors in the design process, so as to improve the choice of cartographers. It does not even require operators to have high basic art skills, making the design work easier and more convenient.

(2) Enrich the expression of graphic design
The use of cultural creative graphic design system realizes the innovation of communication methods. Due to the improvement of design efficiency, the interaction between cultural and creative graphic design system and audience has also become faster. Timely interaction is one of the advantages of digital art. It is also widely used in the early stage of design system, such as selecting the theme of cultural and creative products, absorbing elements and so on. The interactive function brings the innovation of the passive role of the audience to the traditional art process. The audience can participate in the process of artistic creation, which encourages the audience to make independent decisions to a certain extent and improves the enthusiasm of the audience to participate.

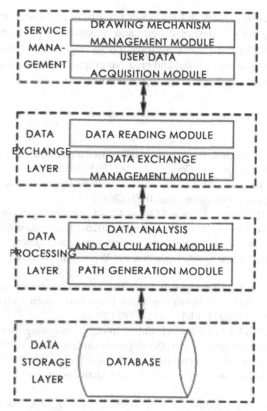

Fig. 1. Schematic diagram of cultural and creative graphic design system

5 Conclusion

The method of using multi-objective firefly algorithm in cultural and creative graphic design system is unique, which can fully show the advantages of this design method. It can not only effectively improve the visual communication effect, but also effectively show the value of computer graphic design. According to the visual information constructed by culture, the cultural and creative graphic design system extracts the image symbols for reconstruction, and brings art and culture into public life through the empowerment of cultural symbols. While meeting the deep spiritual and emotional needs of contemporary people, it also improves the value of products and integrates cultural resources to meet the requirements of sustainable development. In the process of globalization, study the value orientation under different cultural backgrounds and the cultural image symbols precipitated by different national customs, use innovative design methods to arouse visual identity, arouse cultural resonance and promote cross-cultural exchanges. Design research is carried out based on this, which provides more thinking paths for future design.

Based on the existing research results, through in-depth study of the relevant theoretical knowledge and framework of cultural and creative graphic design and firefly algorithm, this paper integrates and innovates the firefly algorithm with the traditional cultural and creative graphic design system, and makes appropriate enhancement measures for the shortcomings of the traditional firefly algorithm. Finally, the enhanced algorithm is re applied to the cultural and creative graphic design system to enhance the system design accuracy.

References

1. Taherkhani, M., Safabakhsh, R.: A novel stability-based adaptive inertia weight for particle swarm optimization. Appl. Soft Comput. **38**, 281–295 (2016)
2. Chen, J., Ye, F., Jiang, T.: Numerical analyses of three inertia-weight-improvement-based particle swarm optimization algorithms. IEEE (2017)
3. Peng, D., Zhao, H., Huang, L., et al.: Optimal load distribution in power plants based on dynamic inertia weight particle swarm algorithm 2016. Chin. Autom. Comput. Soc. (2016)
4. Han, Z., Li, Y., Liang, J.: Numerical Improvement for the mechanical performance of bikes based on an intelligent PSO-ABC algorithm and WSN technology. IEEE Access **6**, 32890–32898 (2018)
5. Darabi, A., Bagheri, M., Gharehpetian, G.B.: Highly accurate directional overcurrent coordination via combination of Rosen's gradient projection-complex method with GA-PSO ALGORITHM. IEEE Syst. J. **14**(1), 1171–1182 (2020)
6. George, S.: TRUTHFUL workflow scheduling in cloud computing using Hybrid PSOACO. In: 2015 International Conference on Developments of E-Systems Engineering
7. Yang, J., Yang, S., Ni, P.: A vector tabu search algorithm with enhanced searching ability for Pareto solutions and its application to multiobjective optimizations. IEEE Trans. Magn. **52**(3), 1–4 (2016)
8. Chiali, I., Debbat, F., Bendimerad, F.T.: Hybridization of tabu search and local search metaheuristic algorithms for multiuser detection of SDMA-OFDM system. IEEE (2017)
9. Wang, L., Zhang, X., Zhang, X.: Antenna array design by artificial bee colony algorithm with similarity induced search method. IEEE Trans. Mag. **55**(6), 1.47–4.47 (2019)
10. Wang, H., Wang, W., Xiao, S., et al.: Improving artificial Bee colony algorithm using a new neighborhood selection mechanism. Inf. Sci. **527**, 227–240 (2020)
11. Shen, J., Zhou, T., He, D., et al.: Block design-based key agreement for group data sharing in cloud computing. IEEE Trans. Dependable Secur. Comput. **16**(6), 996–1010 (2019)
12. Ghahramani, M.H., Zhou, M., Hon, C.T.: Toward cloud computing QoS architecture: analysis of cloud systems and cloud services. IEEE/CAA J. Automatica Sinica **4**(1), 6–18 (2017)

A Comprehensive Analysis of Lower Extremity Based Gait Cycle Disorders and Muscle Analysis

Sonu Kumar, Pranay Yadav, and Vijay Bhaskar Semwal$^{(\boxtimes)}$

Maulana Azad National Institute of Technology (MANIT), Bhopal, India
vsemwal@gmail.com, vsemwal@manit.ac.in

Abstract. This research focuses on muscle weakness in the lower extremity and related gait problems. Gait cycle disorder is an important issue in the human body. Due to gait disorder, human life suffers mentally as well as physically. In medical science, gait cycle cures are available in orthopaedic and physiotherapy. Most gait disorder cases are cured with the help of an orthopaedic surgeon, but the surgeon requires analysis of particular muscles. This research work proposed different muscle analysis-based gait cycle disorders. This proposed comprehensive analysis helps to diagnose different gait cycle problems. The analysis of various gait cycle problems necessitates the use of simulation tools, and this research article also discusses the various tools and software that aid in the justification of muscle injury. In a nutshell, this research work focuses on the analysis of the different gait cycle problems, symptoms and effected muscle analysis simulation tools.

Keywords: Gait Cycle · Calf muscle · Hamstring muscle · Gait disorders · Gait analysis and Ankle foot orthosis

1 Introduction

The human gait cycle is a complex process. Humans have been facing gait cycle disorders as well as gait-related problems for many years. There are different research organizations and scientists are focusing on remedies as well as proper solutions to gait cycle problems. The human stride is dependent on the sophisticated relationship of primary parts of the neurological system, the skeletal muscles, and the cardio-respiratory system [12]. Age, attitude, emotion, and sociocultural context all have a role in one's unique movement patterns [29]. Among senior citizens, the frequency at which they walk is an accurate indication of their overall health and longevity. Having healthy cognitive and executive function is essential for safe walking. Loss of autonomy, increased risk of falling and being injured, and a substantial decrease in quality of life are all direct results of gait problems [12]. Normal walking requires balance, motion, musculoskeletal stability, and neurological restraint abilities [31]. "Gait" refers to a person's walking style, manner, or pattern. An individual's gait style could differ [29]. The time it takes for the same limb to go from one heel strike to the next is called a gait cycle. Learn to recognize whether a person's gait is in a healthy range by observing them through

N. Khare et al. (Eds.): MIND 2022, CCIS 1762, pp. 325–336, 2022.
https://doi.org/10.1007/978-3-031-24352-3_28

the various phases of the gait cycle. Patients whose motion has been impaired may be evaluated but also helped through the use of gait analysis [26]. Gait analysis is the scientific study of how the lower extremities contribute to overall body function and movement [30]. There are different serious health issues that could arise from a loss of movement. Glitches in normal gait owing to pain, injury, paralysis, or tissue damage could cause additional musculoskeletal disorders (compensations). The gait disordered person also faces difficulties with mental problems such as depression and participation in activities including sports, exercise, rehabilitation, biometrics, and surveillance. The primary contribution of this research work is to concentrate on gait cycle disorders and gait-related problems and solutions using various muscle analysis tools. Also, discuss the comparison of different research work presented in the area of gait disorders. In the below, Fig. 1 shows the complex gait cycle process.

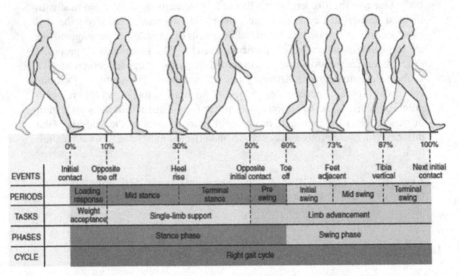

Fig. 1. Depicts the gait cycle in various stances [1].

In this above Sect. 1 discuss the introductory part of the proposed research work, and next the gait abnormality in Sect. 2. In Sect. 3, we discussed the comprehensive analysis of gait disorders by different researchers in the last decade. Section 4 discusses the different data sets used by the different researchers. In Sect. 5, we discussed the disorder's remedies, physiotherapy, and future aspects to solve the complexity of gait disorder are presented in this research work.

2 Gait Abnormality

A person is said to have an abnormal gait or a walking disorder if they are unable to stride in the typical manner. It's possible that fractures, pre-existing diseases, but also issues with the legs and feet are to blame for disorders [27]. Disorders of gait might have a neurological or a non-neurologic root cause, but they are a significant cause of disability, disease, and mortality in older people. Having an aberrant stride or walking abnormalities might be the consequence of problems with one or more of the systems that combine with one another to make walking possible [11]. On the basis of the symptoms shown or the outward appearance of an individual's walk, abnormal gait may be divided into five distinct kinds. They are as follows: **Spastic gait, Propulsive gait, steppage gait, waddling gait, scissors gait** [27].

2.1 Spastic Gait

When someone has a spastic gait, they stride with their limbs flailing. This kind of gait may also make a person seem incredibly inflexible [27]. Lesions anywhere along the corticospinal tract are the root cause of spastic gait, which may affect one or both sides of the body [11]. Spastic gait is common in patients with cerebral palsy or multiple sclerosis, characterized by a limping, rigid stance leg and a dragging, semi-circular swing limb [28]. In the below, Fig. 2 shows the spastic gait in which three figures, (a) describe the initial stage of the gait toe off, (b) shows the mid stance, and (c) shows the swing phase of abnormality. In this case of abnormality on one side of the leg, the knee and hip joints are not working properly.

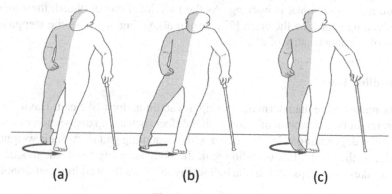

(a)   (b)   (c)

Fig. 2. Spastic gait

2.2 Scissors Gait

When walking with this kind of stride, the knees but also the thighs make a sequence that resembles scissors by either hitting each other or crossing in front of each other. It creates the appearance that the individual is squatting since the legs, hips, and pelvis all bend inward. The progression is gradual and also in baby stages. Patients diagnosed with spastic cerebral palsy are more likely to have this form of gait [28]. In most cases, a person whose legs bend inward will have a stride that is described as having the appearance of scissors. When moving with this kind, a human's legs would crossover and they could bone up against one another [27]. In Fig. 3, we describe the view of the disability walking pattern.

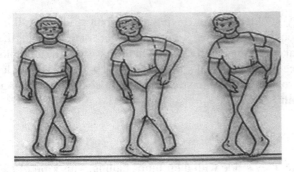

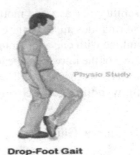

Fig. 3. Scissors gait   **Fig. 4.** Steppage gait

2.3 Steppage Gait

A variation of walking posture known as "high stepping," where the person walks with one foot elevated high, the other foot down (making it seem floppy), and the toes pointed downward, scratching the floor. This kind of gait may be caused by spinal issues (such as spinal stenosis or a disk herniation), as well as peroneal muscular atrophy, peroneal nerve damage [28]. A step page gait is characterized by the toes of the foot pointing downward as the individual is walking. As the individual moves ahead, their toes will make a scraping sound on the earth [27]. In the above Fig. 4 shows the steppage gait side view of the abnormality of diseases.

2.4 Waddling Gait

The trunk moves more than normal, creating a waddling, duck-like gait. Having a waddling gait might be a symptom of a congenital defect such as hip dislocation or progressive muscular degeneration [28]. A person with a waddling gait shifts their weight from side to side as they walk. In a waddling gait, the body is swung from side to side while the person takes little steps [27]. In the below, Fig. 5 shows the wadding gait disabilities.

2.5 Propulsive Gait

This People with Parkinson's disease often have this walk. This postural change was defined by a forward bending of the head, neck, and upper body. The norm is accelerated but also shortened strides [8, 9].When a person walks with their head and neck thrust forward, this is called a propulsive gait. One possible result is that the individual seems to be permanently hunched over [15, 16]. In the below Fig. 6, propulsive gait disabilities (Table 1).

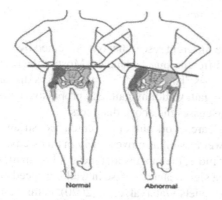

Fig. 5. Waddling gait

Fig. 6. Propulsive gait

Table 1. Physical signs of gait disorders

Physical Signs	Characterisation
Hemiparetic	Lengthening and circling around on one leg
Para paretic	Both legs are rigid, extended, adducted, as well as scissored
Sensory	Instability in gait during deprivation of visual feedback
Steppage	Dorsiflexor paralysis, foot drop, knee and hip bending, short stride length, and bilateral foot drop are all symptoms of this disorder
Cautious	The walk is wide-based, cautious, and sluggish; the walker reaches for support as if walking on ice; and the walker prefers the comfort of their own house to the open outdoors
Apraxia	Problems starting to walk; getting moving; feeling frozen; feet sticking to the ground; hesitating to turn; walking with a shuffling stride
Propulsive or retro pulsive	The patient looks to be having difficulty maintaining a neutral body position in which the patient's feet are above the level of the patient's center of gravity; this condition is known as festination
Ataxic	Symptoms of wide-based incoordination, including: staggering, disorientation, and movement fragmentation
Astasia	Initial Disturbance of Balance
Waddling	Having a wide base of support while walking; swaying; walking on the tips of one's toes; having lumbar lordosis; symmetric
Dystonic	Persistent foot or leg deformity; aberrant walking pattern; hip flexion that is too far forward
Chorea	A sluggish, wide-based, and erratic walk with a bunch of knee bending and leg lifting on the spur of the moment
Antalgic	A sluggish, wide-based, and erratic walk with a lot of knees bending and leg lifting on the spur of the moment
Vertiginous	Movement restrictions; limping; not putting weight on the injured limb
Psychogenic (hysterical)	Strange and devoid of normal stride; several subtypes; infrequent incidence of injury

3 Comprehensive Analysis

This comprehensive analysis discussed the different research work presented by various authors in the field of gait disorder using different muscle damage. Most of the research work focuses on gait disorder pattern analysis. There are different disorders discussed, such as spastic gait, scissors gait, steppage gait, waddling gait, and propulsive gait. The research presented in the below section discusses the above disorders.

N.F.J. Waterval, et al. (2021), in this research work author presented pedestrians with weaker plantar flexors are using more power as well as move slowly in this study. After a threshold of roughly 60% weakening or more, the models assume gait kinematics and kinetics change considerably, resulting in a significant decrease in walking speed and an increase in walking energy expenditure [1]. Niels Waterval, et al. (2020), in this research according to the author's findings, the biomechanical characteristics of the device should be aligned with the patient's limitations for beneficial results. In conventional orthotic treatment, patients often get ankle-foot orthotics that aren't tailored to their specific disability. Individuals whose ankle-foot fundamental building blocks with the stiffest ankle as well as footplates also benefited most significantly in terms of increased gait speed and efficiency [3]. Niels F J Waterval, et al. (2019), in this research According to this study, a person's walking energy cost may be reduced by customizing their shoe's hardness. A dorsal leaf spring ankle exoskeleton could help those with calf muscle weakness walk more normally (DLS-AFO). These AFOs store energy during stance then restore it at push-off, which lessens the amount of effort required to walk. The influence of the DLS-AFO on walking energy cost and gait biomechanics, as shown in simulation, was discovered to vary with the stiffness of the instrument and with patient characteristics [6]. Carmichael Fong, et al. (2019), The author of this study has provided a number of Their model switched to a calcaneal gait without crouching when its plantar flexors were too weak, and an equines gait when its plantar flexors were too tight. With us simulation models also revealed that a sole SOL (Soleus muscle) contracture or bilateral plantar flexor contracture resulted in a more crouched posture than a sole Gastrocnemius Muscle contracture, suggesting that equine walking style, rather than force from the GAS directly flexing the knee, is a major contributor to the observed crouch gait [5]. Niels F.J. Waterval, et al. (2018), This study demonstrated that individuals with unilateral flaccid calf muscular weakness adjust for a diminished ankle push-off by slowing their walking pace. Thus, energy is lost less during the opposite heel-strike, and no extra exertion is required at the lower limb joints as a result [10]. Hilde E. Ploeger, et al. (2017), The author of this study has provided a number of Predictions of gait patterns but also parameters were made using the Random Forest technique. In polio patients who suffered from calf muscle weakness, researchers found a wide range of gait patterns and disability characteristics. Despite sharing a similar impairment profile, not all polio survivors with calf muscle weakness walk in the same way. The gait pattern and individual gait characteristics could not be reliably predicted from a purely clinical evaluation. In conclusion, we advise that gait kinematics and kinetics be assessed alongside physical examination measures whenever orthoses are prescribed for polio survivors with calf muscle weakness [14]. Niels F J Waterval, et al. (2017), Researchers found that individuals with neuromuscular diseases and resulting calf muscle weakness almost invariably have an increase in their metabolic walking energy cost (EC), which may limit their ability to engage in everyday activities that requires walking. A spring-like ankle-foot orthosis (AFO) may be recommended to decrease walking EC. However, the amount by which EC can be reduced by using these AFOs depends on their stiffness, and it is not known which range of AFO stiffness would implementation details for calf muscle weakness. The purpose of the PROOF-AFO research is to evaluate the effects of stiffness-optimized AFOs to those of regular, non-optimized AFOs in decreasing walking EC, enhancing gait biomechanical, and increasing walking speed in patients with calf muscular weakness. The development of a model to determine the ideal AFO stiffness is a secondary objective [13]. Federica Menotti, et al. (2014), The author of this study showed that people with CMT1A had a different pattern of activity throughout the day than those without the disorder. Furthermore, in CMT1A individuals, stepping and sit-to-stand exercises linked with muscular strength. Practically, it seems that CMT1A patients might gain by exercising their lower limb muscles, especially their knee extensors. More research is needed to determine how best to enhance neuromuscular function in this population of individuals. [18]. Marjolein M. van der Krogt, et al. (2012) In this study, the author demonstrated how much muscular weakness in the lower extremities is tolerated before it becomes noticeable during normal walking. The hip and knee extensors seem to be the most resistant to the effects of weakening on gait, as they are able to walk with less than normal stability without experiencing an appreciable increase in muscular stress. When it comes to gait, however, weaknesses in the hip flexors, hip abductors, and plantar flexors are most noticeable [19]. made (Table 2).

Table 2. Comprehensive analysis of different research

Authors detail/Ref	Muscle	Data set
N.F.J. Waterval, et al./[1]	Hamstrings, Gluteus maximus, Gastrocnemius etc.	16 subjects with bilateral plantar flexor weakness
Niels Waterval, et al./[3]	Non-spastic calf muscle weakness	Thirty-four persons who used ankle-foot orthoses for non-spastic calf muscle weakness based on PROOF-AFO
Niels F J Waterval, et al./[6]	Calf muscle weakness	Thirty seven individuals with neuromuscular disorder and non spastic calf muscle were included
Carmichael F. Ong, et al./[5]	Soleus (SOL) or gastrocnemius (GAS)	Available in SimTK
Niels F.J. Waterval, et al./[10]	Calf muscle weakness	Ten healthy people participated in university hospital Rehabilitation department and patients who participated in the PROOF-AFO trail

(continued)

Table 2. (*continued*)

Authors detail/Ref	Muscle	Data set
Hilde E. Ploeger, et al./[14]	Calf muscle weakness	The database search revealed 87 polio patients with unilateral calf muscle weakness who had undergone a barefoot 3D gait analysis without using assistive devices
Niels F J Waterval, et al./[13]	Calf muscle weakness	37 patients with calf muscle weakness who already use an AFO will be recruited
Federica Menotti, et al./[18]	Gluteus maximum, gluteus medium, hamstring	Eight patients with CMT1A (three male and five female individuals) age range 20–48 years
Marjolein M. van der Krogt, et al./[19]	Lower limb muscle Hamstrings, Gluteus maximus, Gastrocnemius	Gait analysis data of six healthy adolescent subjects (three male, three female) were selected from abnormal paediatric dataset

4 Dataset

A disability data set is required for the analysis and simulation of gait disorders. In this section, we will discuss the different disability data sets which are presented by different research organizations. A data set is an important part of the gait disorder rehabilitation process. The data sets listed below are used in various standard research works.

A. ***PROOF-AFO:*** The purpose of the PROOF-AFO research is to evaluate the efficacy of stiffness-optimized ankle foot orthoses to that of regular, non-optimized AFOs in lowering walking energy cost, improving gait dynamics, significantly increasing walking speed in patients with calf muscular weakness. The development of a model to determine the ideal AFO stiffness is a secondary objective. The study procedures has been given the go light by the Academic Medical Centre's Medical Ethics Committee in Amsterdam. The trial registry of the Netherlands has been notified about the research (NTR 5170). Patients with calf muscle weakness are the focus of the PROOF-AFO trial, the first of its kind to compare stiffness-optimized AFOs to standard care AFOs [3]. Insight into what variables affect appropriate AFO stiffness in these patients [6] will also be gained from these findings. The findings, which will be shared with the scientific community at large through international peer-reviewed publications and at a scientific conference [13], are important for the future of orthotic therapy [13].

B. ***Hospital Rehabilitation Department:*** Ten healthy individuals were checked by the hospital's B. Rehabilitation department for the existence of calf muscle weakness in one leg, a diagnosis of a neuromuscular disorder, or nerve injury. That is, a rating of muscle strength based on the standards set by the Medical Research Council (MRC) [10].

C. **UILD Rehabilitation Centre:** The Laboratory of Molecular Genetics at the University of Illinois at Urbana-Institute Champaign's for Disability and Rehabilitation Research (UILD) studies the characterisation of neuromuscular illnesses, with an emphasis on facioscapulohumeral muscular dystrophy (FSH) [18]. The Laboratory has launched Telethon research partnerships with numerous Italian clinical and genetic facilities as part of the FSH initiative [20, 24]. Researchers in this lab are also interested in pinpointing the Mendelian and multifactorial causes of eye problems. Retinitis pigmentosa, age-related macular degeneration, Stargate disease, and Best's disease are the main illnesses studied [33].

5 Analysis Tool

In this section discuss the different software and analytical tools for the simulation of human gait disorders as well as disabilities of humans. Such as Opensim, MATLAB, Pythone etc.

A. **Open Sim:** OpenSim is an open-source software program that enables users to design models of musculoskeletal systems and produce dynamic simulations of movement [32]. The C. SimTK opensim related dataset includes data from OpenSim. Deliver intuitive, expandable software for studying the neuromuscular skeletal system in detail. The first public release of Opensim, version 1.0, was presented at the 2007 meeting of the American Society of Biomechanics [26]. OpenSim, created at Stanford University, is open source used mostly for biomechanical model building, modelling, as well as gait analysis [22]. This program is intended to help with the challenge of human movement simulation. Figure 7 depicts the OpenSim graphical user interface. OpenSim utilizes biomechanics, combining forward and inverse kinematics to determine the motion process. It could be used to simulate human contact and replicate human movement [4], as well as to measure human movement, quantify muscular strength, assess normal and abnormal gait, and more. First, designers must acquire the subject's kinematic parameters (the movement information using the motion capture device) for use in the OpenSim simulation study. Next, designers must choose the general model appropriate for the study item from the OpenSim model library.

B. **MaTLab:** For specific purposes, the gait phase detection technique is often implemented in a programming such as MATLAB. It's an interpretation language as well as interactive environment for numerical modelling, visualizations, but also coding. A technique to identify gait parameters has been created [21] by importing data from gait signals into MATLAB and performing the necessary mathematical computations. It is possible to identify the stage of the gait cycle with the aid of MATLAB. Decomposing a gait cycle into to the stance, swing phases and acquiring several other spatiotemporal movement patterns requires an algorithm that detects when the heel strikes the ground (i.e., initial contact; IC) and when the toes leave the ground (i.e., terminal contact; TC) during a gait cycle. Kinematics variables and angles may be computed in MATLAB for use in an image processing program [17].

C. **Python:** Biomechanics, the study of human movement, finds Python to be a powerful and user-friendly language [2]. The optimum programming language for data analysis is required for the study of locomotion. It comes with a wide variety of packages and toolkits, such as GaitPy and the Kinetics Toolkit [2, 7].

D. **Kinetics Toolkit:** Kinetics Toolkit is a Python package for general biomechanical study of human movement, and it's designed to be user-friendly for novice programmers. To use this toolkit, all you need is a passing familiarity with Python and Numpy. In maintaining with the way most people are presented to programmers, Kinetics Toolkit makes use of a procedural programming model in which processes are grouped as interrelated functions in different submodules. This is in addition to providing an entirely devoted category for containing and manipulating data (Time Series). Generic and extensible, Kinetics Toolkit is due in large part to the constrained and well-defined scope of each function. The documentation is well thought out, including in-depth guides and API references. Pandas Data frames (and hence CSV files, Excel files, etc.), JSON files, or C3D files are used as intermediate data containers with a focus on portability to other applications [2].

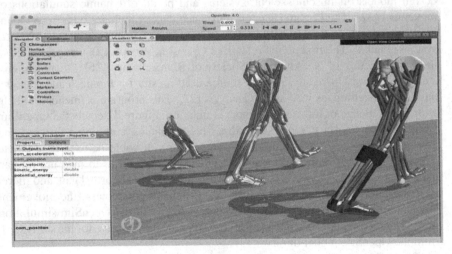

Fig. 7. GUI of opensim [32]

6 Conclusion

In this section, we discussed the common causes of gait disorder and conclusion of the research work. There is considerable etiologic diversity in gait disorders, because of the large number of anatomical systems involved in ambulation [25]. Disorders are heterogenous, and their causes are sometimes multifactor [25]. Gait disorders are common and often devastating companions of aging, leading to reductions in quality of life and increased mortality [23].

This research work focuses on gait disorders and other disabilities based on research. The primary goal of this study is to investigate the various muscle groups and. The primary goal of this study is to investigate the various muscle groups and issues related to disability. This software is preferred for analyzing human gait disability and its optimal solution to such problems is discussed. The presented work makes it simple to identify muscle weakness-related symptoms and problems in the lower extremity. A thorough analysis also compares the various research works presented by various researchers in the field of gait disorder analysis and rehabilitation. The presented research work aids in determining the best way to locate a rehabilitation disabled person. For the best rehabilitation process, it requires robust machine learning algorithms. The presented work helps to find the best method. In the future proposed an optimal method for the improvement of gait muscle prediction on the basis of disability analysis. In a nutshell, the proposed research work discusses the robust analysis of different methods, gait disorders, different disorder datasets, and simulation modelling tools.

Acknowledgement. Thanks to MANIT CSE department, and Prof. Dr. Nilay Khare to provide lab setup and other helps.

Funding Agency. This work was supported by the Ministry of Education, Government of India, through the project HEFA CSR under Grant SAN/CSR/08/2021-22.

Interest of Conflict. These is no conflict of interest.

References

1. Waterval, N.J., et al.: Validation of forward simulations to predict the effects of bilateral plantarflexor weakness on gait. Gait Posture **87**, 33–42 (2021)
2. Chénier, F.: Kinetics toolkit: an open-source Python package to facilitate research in biomechanics. J. Open Source Softw. **6**(66), 3714 (2021)
3. Waterval, N.F.J., Brehm, M.-A., Harlaar, J., Nollet, F.: Description of orthotic properties and effect evaluation of ankle-foot orthoses in non-spastic calf muscle weakness. J. Rehabil. Med. **52**(3), 1–10 (2020)
4. Yu, J., Zhang, S., Wang, A., Li, W.: Human gait analysis based on OpenSim. In: 2020 International Conference on Advanced Mechatronic Systems (ICAMechS), pp. 278–281. IEEE (2020)
5. Ong, C.F., Geijtenbeek, T., Hicks, J.L., Delp, S.L.: Predicting gait adaptations due to ankle plantarflexor muscle weakness and contracture using physics-based musculoskeletal simulations. PLoS Comput. Biol. **15**(10), e1006993 (2019)
6. Waterval, N.F.J., Nollet, F., Harlaar, J., Brehm, M.-A.: Modifying ankle foot orthosis stiffness in patients with calf muscle weakness: gait responses on group and individual level. J. Neuroeng. Rehabil. **16**(1), 1–9 (2019)
7. Czech, M.D., Patel, S.: GaitPy: an open-source python package for gait analysis using an accelerometer on the lower back. J. Open Source Softw. **4**(43), 1778 (2019)
8. Gujarathi, T., Bhole, K.: Gait analysis using IMU sensor. In: 2019 10th International Conference on Computing, Communication and Networking Technologies (ICCCNT), pp. 1–5. IEEE (2019)

9. Semwal, V.B., Gaud, N., Nandi, G.C.: Human gait state prediction using cellular automata and classification using ELM. In: Tanveer, M., Pachori, R.B. (eds.) Machine intelligence and signal analysis. AISC, vol. 748, pp. 135–145. Springer, Singapore (2019). https://doi.org/10. 1007/978-981-13-0923-6_12

10. Waterval, N.F.J., Brehm, M.-A., Ploeger, H.E., Nollet, F., Harlaar, J.: Compensations in lower limb joint work during walking in response to unilateral calf muscle weakness. Gait Posture **66**, 38–44 (2018)

11. Baker, J.M.: Gait disorders. Am. J. Med. **131**(6), 602–607 (2018)

12. Pirker, W., Katzenschlager, R.: Gait disorders in adults and the elderly. Wien. Klin. Wochenschr. **129**(3–4), 81–95 (2016). https://doi.org/10.1007/s00508-016-1096-4

13. Waterval, N.F.J., Nollet, F., Harlaar, J., Brehm, M.-A.: Precision orthotics: optimising ankle foot orthoses to improve gait in patients with neuromuscular diseases; protocol of the PROOF-AFO study, a prospective intervention study. BMJ Open **7**(2), e013342 (2017)

14. Ploeger, H.E., Bus, S.A., Nollet, F., Brehm, M.-A.: Gait patterns in association with underlying impairments in polio survivors with calf muscle weakness. Gait Posture **58**, 146–153 (2017)

15. Inoue, W., et al.: Are there different factors affecting walking speed and gait cycle variability between men and women in community-dwelling older adults? Aging Clin. Exp. Res. **29**(2), 215–221 (2016). https://doi.org/10.1007/s40520-016-0568-8

16. Jankovic, J.: Gait disorders. Neurol. Clin. **33**(1), 249–268 (2015)

17. Ashok, T.S.: Kinematic study of video gait analysis. In: 2015 International Conference on Industrial Instrumentation and Control (ICIC), pp. 1208–1213. IEEE (2015)

18. Menotti, F., Laudani, L., Damiani, A., Macaluso, A.: Amount and intensity of daily living activities in Charcot–Marie–Tooth 1A patients. Brain Behav. **4**(1), 14–20 (2014)

19. van der Krogt, M.M., Delp, S.L., Schwartz, M.H.: How robust is human gait to muscle weakness? Gait Posture **36**(1), 113–119 (2012)

20. Davoodi, R., Loeb, G.E.: MSMS software for VR simulations of neural prostheses and patient training and rehabilitation, pp. 156–162 (2011)

21. Remy, C.D., Buffinton, K., Siegwart, R.: A matlab framework for efficient gait creation. In: 2011 IEEE/RSJ International Conference on Intelligent Robots and Systems, pp. 190–196. IEEE (2011)

22. John, T., Guendelman, E., Thelen, D.G.: OpenSim: open-source software to create and analyze dynamic simulations of movement. IEEE Trans. Biomed. Eng. **54**(11), 1940–1950 (2007)

23. Snijders, A.H., Van De Warrenburg, B.P., Giladi, N., Bloem, B.R.: Neurological gait disorders in elderly people: clinical approach and classification. Lancet Neurol. **6**(1), 63–74 (2007)

24. Damsgaard, M., Rasmussen, J., Christensen, S.T., Surma, E., De Zee, M.: Analysis of musculoskeletal systems in the AnyBody Modeling System. Simul. Model. Pract. Theor. **14**(8), 1100–1111 (2006)

25. Sudarsky, L.: Gait disorders in the elderly. N. Engl. J. Med. **322**(20), 1441–1446 (1990)

26. https://en.wikipedia.org/wiki/Gait_analysis

27. https://www.medicalnewstoday.com/articles/320481

28. https://my.clevelandclinic.org/health/symptoms/21092-gait-disorders

29. https://study.com/learn/lesson/gait-definition-types-abnormality.html

30. https://www.walk-right.co.uk/biomechanics-gait-analysis

31. https://www.slideshare.net/AartiSareen/gait-analysis-16066737

32. https://simtk.org/projects/opensim

33. https://www.hsantalucia.it/en/molecular-genetics-laboratory-uildm

The Construction of English New Words Corpus Based on Decision Tree Algorithm

Hongxia Gao(✉)

Beihua University Teacher's College, Jilin 132013, Jilin, China
wangnannan1818@126.com

Abstract. An English word is a sound or a combination of sounds that we make with the vocal organs; words are representative, they represent some meaning, and they help humans communicate; words are part of the human language communication system. In short, words are the smallest and meaningful language units that humans can use independently. This paper aims to study the English neologism corpus based on decision tree algorithm. Aiming at the problems of low internal cohesion of words in the new word recognition algorithm of point mutual information and adjacency entropy, many high threshold invalid phrases and low threshold new phrases that exist in the single threshold setting of point mutual information, an improved multi-word point is proposed. A new word extraction algorithm for English of the year based on mutual information and adjacency entropy. In the preprocessing stage, according to the characteristics of English new words, it is further filtered, and the point mutual information is expanded into multi-word point mutual information, and the new words are extracted by setting double thresholds and adjacency entropy. In the recognition algorithm, this paper regards it as a classification problem to solve, analyzes English new words, and uses cosine similarity and path distance similarity to quantify word form and word meaning features. For phrase pairs containing acronyms, this paper An algorithm for identifying acronyms by rules is proposed, and a decision tree suitable for English new word recognition is constructed based on the features of word form and word meaning. Experiments show that the data of the algorithm in this paper is better than the traditional algorithm, the P value reaches 33.8%, and the accuracy rate is greatly improved. Compared with the word sense feature recognition algorithm, the method in this paper has a 4% improvement in accuracy.

Keywords: Decision Tree Algorithm · Synonym Identification · New Words · New Word Corpus

1 Introduction

The development of language is inseparable from the influence of the environment. With the rapid development of social economy, culture and politics, the more obvious manifestation of language development is the emergence of a large number of new words. The expressions of meaning are also gradually enriched. With the development of the era of big data and the emergence of massive new words, computers have gradually

N. Khare et al. (Eds.): MIND 2022, CCIS 1762, pp. 337–344, 2022.
https://doi.org/10.1007/978-3-031-24352-3_29

replaced manual work to solve related research problems in natural language processing. Language is not only a medium for human communication, but also a carrier of thoughts and feelings. Many data research work in natural language processing beyond the scope of manual processing is processed by computers, and real meaningful information is obtained through these data. The construction of corpus is an indispensable and important topic in the process of natural language processing. The study of English new words cannot be separated from the English new word corpus. Therefore, new word extraction and new word synonym recognition are the first problems to be solved in the construction of new word corpus [1, 2].

In the research on the construction of English neologism corpus based on decision tree algorithm, many scholars have studied it and achieved good results. For example, Huo C proposed the MBN-gram algorithm, which uses statistical feature mutual information and adjacency entropy to analyze new words. The word string is expanded and filtered, and finally, a dictionary is used to filter the included words to obtain a new word set. The experimental results show that its precision, recall and F value are significantly improved compared with traditional methods [3]. Using the formula formed by word frequency, word cohesion, word freedom, and three custom parameters combined with a small number of filtering rules, Su R proposes an unsupervised new word recognition method, which is identified from four large-scale corpora [4].

Aiming at the problems of low internal cohesion of words, many invalid phrases with high threshold, and unrecognized new phrases with low threshold, this paper proposes an English new word extraction algorithm based on improved multi-point mutual information and adjacency entropy. In the preprocessing stage, according to the characteristics of English new words, it is further filtered, and the point mutual information is expanded into multi-word point mutual information, and the new words are extracted by setting double thresholds and adjacency entropy. In the recognition algorithm, this paper regards it as a classification problem to solve, analyzes English new words, and uses cosine similarity and path distance similarity to quantify word form and word meaning features. For phrase pairs containing acronyms, this paper An algorithm for identifying acronyms by rules is proposed, and a decision tree suitable for English new word recognition is constructed based on the features of word form and word meaning.

2 Research on the Construction of English Neologism Corpus Based on Decision Tree Algorithm

2.1 Theories Related to New Word Extraction

(1) Probability Theory
To perform feature calculation on words, it is usually necessary to use the probability of the words appearing in the corpus. 1 represents an inevitable event, 0 represents an impossible event, and other possibilities are generally represented by real numbers between 0 and 1. In probability theory, the formula for calculating the frequency of word occurrence is as follows [5]:

$$P(w) = \frac{N(w)}{\sum_i N(w_i)} \tag{1}$$

Among them, N(w) represents the number of occurrences of the word w in the corpus, and N(w $_i$) represents the number of occurrences of any word in the corpus.

Usually, when analyzing the characteristics of words, the occurrence of other words will be considered. Therefore, the conditional probability of words needs to be calculated. The calculation formula is shown in (2) [6]:

$$P(A|B) = \frac{N(AB)}{N(B)} \qquad (2)$$

Among them, P(A | B) represents the probability of word A appearing when word B appears, N(AB) represents the number of times the phrase AB appears in the corpus, and N(B) represents the number of times the word B appears in the corpus.

(2) N-Gram Algorithm

The N-Gram algorithm was first applied to speech recognition of large-scale lexical corpus, and has now been widely used in many fields such as lexical analysis, part-of-speech tagging, and machine translation in natural language processing. In the preprocessing process of new word extraction, it is often used to segment the corpus, count the probability of words appearing in the corpus, and provide the required word set for subsequent research. The basic process of the N-Gram algorithm is: set a sliding window of length N to segment the corpus. After segmentation, each string of size N is called a gram, and the frequency of each gram is counted according to the set The threshold filters out the required candidate word set, that is, the gram table.

When the N-Gram algorithm is used to process large-scale corpus, it is necessary to consider the reasonable setting of the segmentation length N. If N is set large, the resulting segmented word set will have serious data sparseness and other problems; if N is set small, it will affect the later extraction effect. Therefore, the N-Gram algorithm is used to process the corpus in the new word extraction, and a sliding window with a suitable size should be set, that is, the size of the N value [7, 8].

2.2 Corpus Acquisition

Extracting new words is to identify correct words that have not been included in existing dictionaries in a certain amount of corpus. Therefore, the source and quality of the corpus are the first issues to be considered in new word extraction. Considering that web pages are usually real-time and retrospective, the dynamic update of traditional corpora is relatively slow, and cannot reach the update speed of network media reports. Therefore, this paper uses the timeliness and traceability of web texts to use web crawler technology to obtain English new words. Need corpus [9].

2.3 Corpus Preprocessing

In order to obtain a candidate word set suitable for the experiment, the corpus obtained by the python crawler needs to be preprocessed. The corpus preprocessing work includes the following:

(1) Filter the garbage string, and use the rule method to remove Chinese, url links, and invalid characters in the text corpus. As can be seen from the content of the previous

section, this paper uses the crawler technology to accurately locate and extract the corpus required for the experiment. However, due to some inherent characteristics of the website, for example, the body tag will contain some website description text, url links, and in the process of crawling some pages containing videos and pictures, the videos and pictures will be converted into garbled characters. Therefore, this paper first uses the rule filtering method to eliminate these garbage strings.

(2) According to the characteristics of English words, set the separator between words. Unlike Chinese writing, which has no obvious separator between words, English writing has the feature that words are separated by spaces. Therefore, a single space is selected as the separator between words to process the corpus. However, the downloaded corpus is often not separated by a regular space, so in order to facilitate post-processing, a regular method is used to solve the situation of line breaks and non-single spaces between other words.

(3) Use the N-Gram algorithm to segment the corpus and count the frequency of phrases. This paper uses the N-Gram algorithm to process the corpus as follows: First, set the sliding window size as: $1 \leq N \leq 5$, slide one unit each time, if the left and right length of the sentence is not enough N, end the division of the corpus until the end of the text; Secondly, the frequency of all grams is counted to form the corresponding vocabulary; finally, the vocabulary is filtered according to the set threshold, and finally the qualified gram vocabulary is formed [10, 11].

2.4 The Application of Decision Tree Algorithm in the Construction of English Neologism Corpus

The most important part of the decision tree algorithm is the construction of the decision tree. Many existing sample data are quite different from the real data. If the actual corpus is not considered, the classification of the constructed decision tree will be inaccurate. Therefore, combined with the characteristics of few Chinese English neologism synonym features and discrete sample data, and synthesizing the structure of decision nodes and branches in the decision tree model, an English neologism synonym recognition method based on a decision tree-like model is proposed. The order of feature nodes in the decision tree needs to be reasonably arranged, so the decision-making ability of these features needs to be evaluated, and the evaluation results are used as the basis for node position ranking. Therefore, it is a reasonable method to use class decision tree for synonym recognition of new words [12].

3   Research Design Experiment of English Neologism Corpus Construction Based on Decision Tree Algorithm

3.1   Experimental Data and Tools

In view of the need to include annual English new words and synonyms in the construction of the corpus, this paper selects all the English corpus of the New York Daily in 2017 from the obtained corpus as the experimental data for extracting new words. The 2937 phrases from 2012 to 2018 were extracted and manually sorted out by the algorithm in this paper, and the candidate phrases were combined into candidate phrase pairs. This paper randomly selected 100 pairs from them and used them to identify the synonyms of English neologisms.

This article uses the python language and its development platform to conduct experiments. Compared with other programming languages such as Java language and C language, Python language is closer to natural language logic, with simpler syntax and easier to build applications. In recent years, python has been widely used in big data mining and processing, because it has many built-in modules and third-party modules, which can be applied quickly and efficiently, and improve code maintainability. The modules mainly used in this article are Re module, Math module, Beautiful Soup module, Nltk module, etc.

3.2 Evaluation Indicators

In this paper, the accuracy, recall and F value of new word recognition are used to evaluate the experimental results. The calculation formula is as follows:

$$P = \frac{CN}{DN} \times 100\% \tag{3}$$

$$R = \frac{CN}{M} \times 100\% \tag{4}$$

$$F = \frac{2 \times P \times R}{DN} \times 100\% \tag{5}$$

Among them, CN represents the number of phrases correctly recognized by the algorithm, DN represents the number of phrases recognized by the algorithm, and M represents the total number of phrases in the corpus.

4 Experimental Analysis of English Neologism Corpus Construction Based on Decision Tree Algorithm

4.1 New Word Extraction Experiment

In this paper, a variety of traditional algorithms and the algorithm in this paper are used to carry out a comparison experiment of new word extraction, and the P value, R value and F value of each algorithm are recorded. The experimental results are shown in Table 1.

From the experimental results in Fig. 1, it can be seen that the algorithm proposed in this paper has a certain improvement in accuracy, recall and F value. This is because this paper found through later research that after the corpus was segmented, many invalid and partially overlapping phrases were generated. If the new word extraction based on the double-threshold multi-word mutual information and adjacency entropy algorithm is directly used, it will not only affect the later experiments. Resources will be wasted, and the extraction results may include these phrases that contain some of the same words as the new words into the new word queue. For this reason, this paper filters these invalid word strings in the preprocessing stage, so that the algorithm recognizes The number of invalid new words is reduced, thereby improving the accuracy.

Table 1. New word extraction experiment result table

	P	R	F
Single Threshold PMI + BE	27.0	14.2	18.6
Single threshold multi-word PMI + BE	29.1	15.0	19.8
Dual Threshold PMI + BE	29.5	15.1	20.0
Double Threshold Multiword PMI + BE	31.3	15.2	20.5
The algorithm in this paper	33.8	15.3	20.9

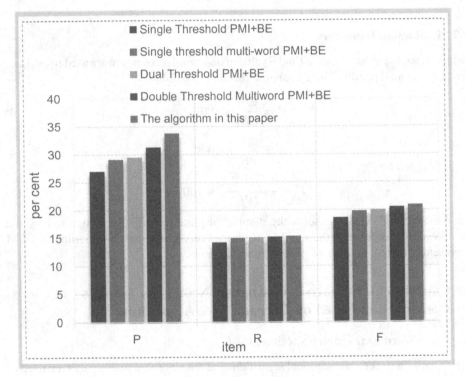

Fig. 1. New word extraction experiment result table

4.2 Decision Tree-Like Identification Results

In this paper, a class decision tree is constructed, which is arranged from top to bottom in the order of lexical similarity, morphological similarity, and acronym recognition to form a class decision tree that recognizes synonyms of English neologisms. In this paper, the following algorithms are compared and tested, including: word sense feature recognition synonym algorithm based on WordNet distance path, word shape feature recognition algorithm, the improved word shape feature recognition synonym algorithm proposed in this paper, and the synonym recognition algorithm proposed in this paper, The experimental results are shown in Table 2.

From the experimental results in Fig. 2, this paper proposes to improve the accuracy of the word shape feature algorithm. Although the improvement is not great compared with the common word shape recognition algorithm, the recall rate and F value are greatly improved, indicating that the acronym recognition the algorithm is beneficial to the identification of synonyms on the morphological features. At the same time, the recognition effect of the word sense feature recognition algorithm is obviously better than that of the word shape feature recognition algorithm. Analysis of the experimental data

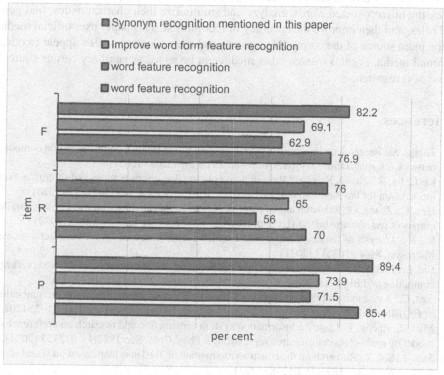

Fig. 2. Experimental results of synonym recognition

Table 2. Experimental results of synonym recognition

	P	R	F
Word feature recognition	85.4	70.0	76.9
Word feature recognition	71.5	56.0	62.9
Improve word form feature recognition	73.9	65.0	69.1
Synonym recognition mentioned in this paper	89.4	76.0	82.2

shows that the previous word shape restoration processing steps have greatly improved the calculation value of the path distance, which makes the word sense feature recognition algorithm in the accuracy rate and recall rate. And F-values were significantly improved.

5 Conclusions

There are very few corpora that can be used publicly at present. Based on the construction of the English neologism corpus, this paper completes the research on English neologisms and synonyms, which provides effective technical support for the later public use of the English neologism corpus. At the same time, it is hoped that we can further check the misrecognized words, analyze and summarize their characteristics, find general rules, and then improve the accuracy of recognition. This paper uses official media as the main source of the corpus. New words and their synonyms often appear in other informal media. For this reason, other media can be added as auxiliary corpus sources in the next research.

References

1. Zhang, X.: Research on the construction of subject group English corpus based on computer network informatization. J. Phys. Conf. Ser. **1915**(2), 022033 (2021)
2. Li, J., Jia, R., Zhang, K., et al.: Research on construction of crude set model of critical fault information for bus based on CAN-BUS Data. IEEE Access **8**, 14875–14892 (2020)
3. Huo, C., Zhang, G.: Research on the construction and application of Chinese-English parallel corpus of red tourism: taking Hebei province as a case. Creat. Educ. **13**(2), 5 (2022)
4. Su, R.: Analysis of language features of English corpus based on Java Web. Microprocess. Microsyst. **80**(4), 103611 (2021)
5. Liu, L., Tsai, S.B.: Intelligent recognition and teaching of English fuzzy texts based on fuzzy computing and Big Data. Wirel. Commun. Mob. Comput. **2021**(1), 1–10 (2021)
6. Yan, C.: A research proposal on applying Chinese phonetic system in teaching pronunciation of English words to older Chinese EFL adult learners. J. High. Educ. Res. **3**(1), 21–25 (2022)
7. Mao, Z., Zheng, T., Lian, Z.: Information system construction and research on preference of model by multi-class decision tree regression. J. Phys. Conf. Ser. **1982**(1), 012153 (2021)
8. Sun, T., Shi, X.: Research on the construction method of 3D dense map based on visual slam. J. Phys. Conf. Ser. **1871**(1), 012083 (2021)
9. Zhang, Q.: Research on the construction schedule and cost optimization of grid structure based on BIM and genetic algorithm. J. Phys. Conf. Ser. **1744**(2), 022065 (2021)
10. Wang, X.: Building a parallel corpus for English translation teaching based on computer-aided translation software. Comput. Aided Des. Appl. **18**(S4), 175–185 (2021)
11. Li, B.: Study on the intelligent selection model of fuzzy semantic optimal solution in the process of translation using English corpus. Wirel. Commun. Mob. Comput. **2020**(5), 1–7 (2020)
12. Wei, L.: Study on the application of cloud computing and speech recognition technology in English teaching. Clust. Comput. **22**(4), 9241–9249 (2018)

Data Analysis and Prediction of Electrochemical Properties of Carbon Nanomaterials Based on Machine Learning

Hui Wang$^{(\boxtimes)}$, Yanan Wang, and Shanmei Xiong

Nanchang Institute of Technology, Nanchang 330018, China
1776045319@qq.com

Abstract. Machine learning uses learning theory and modeling computations to learn and predict big data analytics, and these types of computations enable predictions or database decisions by modeling input data samples. It has been successful in several application areas such as computer vision, natural language processing, and biometrics. This paper aims to study the data analysis and prediction of the electrochemical properties of carbon nanomaterials based on machine learning. Taking a typical carbon nanomaterial - graphene as an example, in the analysis and prediction algorithm, the preparation method of graphene and the commonly used electrochemical analysis. On the basis of the method, graphene was prepared by hydrothermal method and chemical reduction method, and the electrochemical properties of graphene under different preparation methods were discussed. The test results show that the capacitance and rate characteristics of the H-RGO electrode are better than those of the T-RGO electrode.

Keywords: Machine Learning · Carbon Nanomaterials · Electrochemical Properties · Data Analysis and Prediction

1 Introduction

With the improvement of computer computing power, machine learning has once again become a research hotspot. Different from traditional algorithms, machine learning algorithms can iteratively learn data functions, allowing computers to detect raw data information [1, 2]. Machine learning discovers hidden data patterns by building models in the process, and then finds information of real interest in large and complex social data [3, 4].

In recent years, many researchers have carried out in-depth research on electrochemical sensors of carbon nanomaterials, and obtained good research results. Some researchers have used bismuth-modified carbon nanotubes to detect trace amounts of heavy metal ions such as lead, cadmium, and zinc in soil. The detection results by square anode stripper voltammetry showed that the bismuth-modified carbon nanotubes exhibited clear, reproducible and visible electron stripper signals on the cathode [5, 6]. In addition, some researchers also used multi-walled carbon nanotubes and chitosan-modified screen-printed electrodes to establish mercury electrodes for the determination

© The Author(s), under exclusive license to Springer Nature Switzerland AG 2022
N. Khare et al. (Eds.): MIND 2022, CCIS 1762, pp. 345–352, 2022.
https://doi.org/10.1007/978-3-031-24352-3_30

of colored heavy metal ions in solution. Compared with traditional mercury electrodes, screen-printed electrodes using multi-walled carbon nanotubes and chitosan modified materials can significantly reduce the cadmium concentration [7, 8]. Some researchers first re-arranged millions of ordered double-ultralong-wall multi-wall carbon nanotubes into a tower electrode composed of carbon nanotubes, and characterized it by SEM and TEM techniques. Its general electrochemical properties were investigated. Subsequently, using the carbon nanotube tower electrode as the main working electrode, the secondary wave voltammetry was used to measure the colored heavy metal ions, and the detection results also provided good sensitivity [9, 10]. Other researchers have begun to design disposable sensors that can be used to rapidly determine the content of metallic lead ions in food by depositing reduced oxide multilayer graphite crucible on the surface of screen-printed electrodes. The solar stripping anodic voltammetry was applied in the experiment, and the result was that the deposited graphene could enhance the activity of the screen-printed electrode on the initial surface, thereby significantly improving the electrochemical properties of the screen-printed electrode [11, 12]. Although the application of carbon nanomaterials has been well studied in electrochemistry, it still has certain drawbacks.

In this paper, on the basis of referring to a large number of relevant references, on the basis of theoretical prediction methods, experimental methods for the preparation of graphene, and conventional electrochemical analysis methods, the hydrothermal method and chemical reduction method are used for graphene. Prepared to study the electrochemical properties of graphene under various production modes.

2   Data Analysis and Prediction of Electrochemical Properties of Carbon Nanomaterials Based on Machine Learning

2.1   Prediction Class Algorithms

(1)   Collaborative Filtering Algorithm

Collaborative filtering algorithms are based on the intersection of features or individual predictions selected by others. By looking for people in the vast ocean of data who share the same traits or selection propensities as the target and surveying many of them, it is possible to predict their subject or predict his or her favorite propensities. The advantage of collaborative filtering is that it can filter some things that are difficult for machines to automatically predict, and can filter according to cumbersome and difficult to express concepts. The most important function is the ability to predict the user. The applicability of other algorithms cannot be compared. Other samples can be used to predict what an individual might not understand. Due to this feature, more and more collaborative filtering applications are available. As functionality continues to improve, so does the ability of predictive systems.

(2)   Logistic Regression (LR) and Regularization

Logistic regression is a classification algorithm whose output variable is always between 0 and 1. The prerequisites for a logistic regression model are:

$$h_\theta(X) = g^{\left(\theta^T X\right)} \tag{1}$$

X represents the eigenvector, and g represents the logistic function. It is a commonly used logistic function and also a sigmoid function. The formula is:

$$f(x) = \frac{1}{1 + e^{-x}} \tag{2}$$

Normalization is a method used to deal with algorithmic overfitting. During logistic regression, if the equation fits well to a specific training set and generalizes to other data, the predictions will be severely inconsistent. Therefore, the problem of overfitting should be solved by reducing the parameter size while preserving all features.

(3) Iterative Decision Tree Algorithm

Decision trees receive a predicted value at each node. Find the most effective branch condition, and finally pass through multiple branches to reach the final termination condition. There is also the problem of over-tuning, the solution is to split the decision tree into several trees and increase the weights of misclassifications in disguise. It also makes the database library more logical if it is not sorted correctly.

(4) Support Vector Machine Algorithm

It is a model for classification. The data points are put together in a two-dimensional space, and the different classification points are distributed in different regions. Because they are separated by a line, data with different characteristics are distributed on both sides of this line. This line is selected on the condition that it is the furthest from the data points on both sides at the same time. The way to find this line is the crux of the SVM algorithm. This solution also works in 3D and multidimensional spaces. Equivalent to finding a point in a multidimensional space that is farther away than all class data points.

2.2 Preparation of Graphene

(1) Mechanical Peeling Method

Graphene was initially isolated from highly oriented pyrolytic graphite by mechanical exfoliation. Mechanical exfoliation is a solid-phase method that separates graphene or graphene sheets from graphite crystals by mechanical force (friction, tension, etc.). The van der Waals interactions between two adjacent flakes in graphite crystals are weak and can be easily exfoliated by mechanical action. However, at the same time, graphene size is difficult to control, with poor reproducibility and low yield, which is not suitable for large-scale industrial production.

(2) Epitaxial Growth Method

The epitaxial growth method is also part of the solid phase method. By using SiC crystal as raw material and heating it to an ultra-high temperature above 1200 °C in an ultra-high vacuum environment, after the silicon atoms move and peel off from the substrate, the carbon atoms run and rearrange on the crystal surface. Thus, multi-layer graphene is produced. Graphene produced by epitaxial growth method can be widely used in the production of substrate materials such as 4H-SiC, 6H-SiC, β-SiC, etc. However, due to the heating of some carbon-containing metals in the maximum vacuum degree, graphene is produced on its surface. The thickness of the resulting graphene is determined by heating. Therefore, the epitaxial growth method provides high-quality graphene with higher carrier mobility, and due to the high temperature of the growth environment, harsh environmental conditions, the inert gas environment required by special manufacturing processes, and the inconsistent thickness of graphene, etc. defects and further suitable for mass production.

(3) Solvent Stripping Method

Solvent stripping is a simple liquid phase stripping method. The main principle is to use the ultrasonic cavitation effect of the low-strength graphene diffusion liquid to gradually exfoliate by breaking the van der Waals force inside the graphite layer dispersed in the solution to obtain a monolithic graphene material layer. Although the solvent exfoliation method can produce flawless high-quality graphene, it also faces a series of problems such as uncontrollable thickness of graphene sheets, tight integration with graphene in solution, and difficulty in subsequent cleaning and transportation.

(4) Redox Method

The method of reducing or oxidizing multilayer graphene is currently the most common and perfect method for producing graphene films. It can also reduce or oxidize graphene through a dispersive system, resulting in graphene. The toner oxidation method also introduces a variety of oxygen-filled functional groups on the surface and boundary of graphene, while reducing the van der Waals pressure between the toned graphene layers. On the one hand, the distance between the graphite crucibles is increased. On the other hand, due to the increased hydrophilicity of the multi-layer graphene, the multi-layer graphene is easier to diffuse into the solution, thus forming a uniform and stable dispersion system. This oxidation process is critical to the production of high-quality flat-top graphite crucibles. At present, the more common graphite oxidation technologies are used, mainly the Standenmeier method, the Brodie method, and the Hummers method. The Hummers method is the most widely used because of its simple operation and easy temperature control. However, in order to make the oxidation of graphene more sufficient, it is sometimes necessary to perform thermal expansion pretreatment on graphene.

2.3 Commonly Used Electrochemical Analysis Methods

(1) Cyclic voltammetry: one of the most widely used electrochemical analysis techniques. By controlling the potential of the working electrode, it scans one or more times in the form of a triangular wave at a certain scan rate over time. Using a well-selected low-potential scan range allows one to see distinct oxidation and reduction peaks so that the current-potential curve can be recorded. The shape of the curve, the reversibility of the cathodic reaction, the possibility of the generation of intermediary compounds, the

very limited amount of adsorption or the generation of new phases, and the effects on the electrochemical sensor activity in the cathode material at high pressure, the magnitude of the change in operating frequency, and the internal resistance In-depth research has been carried out on gender and so on. They can all be used to study cathodic reaction parameters, determine control processes and reaction mechanisms, and analyze chemical reactions that can be performed in a potential digitized scan range.

(2) Anode stripping voltammetry: At a certain potential, the measured metal ions in the solution are partially reduced to metals and concentrated on the surface of the working positive electrode, and then a reverse voltage is applied on the surface of the working cathode to make the working negative electrode react. The current is generated by the action of electrons, thus showing the melting peak of the current curve, and then the electrochemical sensor work is carried out according to the current-pressure curve of the melting process. Anode stripper voltammetry mainly involves two research processes: concentration process: after a constant current is applied to the working electrode, the detected element in the working solvent is ionized and reduced, so that it is re-aggregated on the working cathode. Dissolution process: The pressure of the working electrode is scanned from negative to positive. After concentration, the metal surface on the cathode is re-oxidized and dissolved in the solution. Anodic stripper voltammetry is also suitable for determining the concentration of metal ions in solution, because the dissolution peak potential is related to the type of analyte, and the peak current value is related to the concentration of the analyte, which has little advantage. Analytes, fast test speeds and expensive high performance. If other experimental variables are constant, the peak current is linearly related to the concentration of the analyte within a specific concentration range, so quantitative analysis can be performed. The main factors affecting the peak current are concentration time, stirring speed, concentration potential, electrode area, dissolution time, scanning time, scanning speed, etc. Therefore, it is necessary to strictly control the experimental conditions.

3 Experiment

3.1 Preparation of Graphene

Graphene can also be fabricated using hydrothermal and chemical reduction methods. Using graphite powder as the starting material, graphite oxide precursor (GO) was first produced according to the procedure given in Fig. 1, and then GO was sonicated and exfoliated in deionized water to form graphene oxide. Finally, we used hydrothermal and chemical methods to prepare graphene (RGO), respectively.

(1) Preparation of RGO by Hydrothermal Method

First weigh 0.05 g of the prepared GO solution and dissolve it in about 50 ml of deionized water. After ultrasonic treatment for about 60 min, a uniform GO diffusion solution is generated, which is then put into the PTFE coating and boiled in a thermal hydraulic pot Then put it in the water. Place the oven in a closed place, react at 180 °C for about 24 h, take a sample after natural cooling to room temperature, wash with deionized water, freeze-dry to obtain RGO, and the sample is marked as T-RGO.

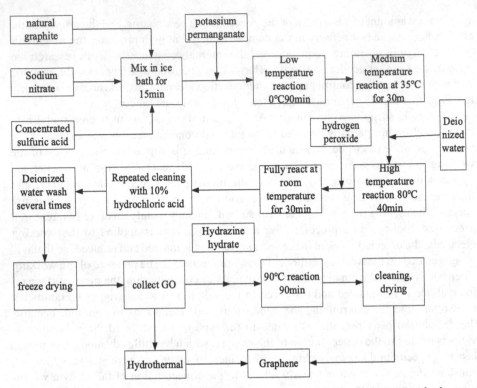

Fig. 1. Process flow diagram of preparation of GO and RGO by Hummers method

(2) Chemical Preparation of RGO

It is also possible to produce GO dispersions with a content of only 1 mgml^{-1} in a similar manner as described above. Put the solvent into a water bath at about 90 °C or a heating thermal hydraulic power, and slowly add about 5 ml of water and the reducing agent in HCl, the reaction is completed in about 90 min, after centrifugal washing with deionized water and freeze-drying. That is, an RGO solution labeled H-RGO is obtained.

3.2 Electrode Preparation and Electrochemical Performance Characterization

Electrochemical performance has also been tested on a 3-electrode system. 1 MKOH electrolyte is used at room temperature. A nickel foam coated with a chemically active substance was used as the working electrode, and the opposite sides of the negative and reference electrodes were used. Each is made of platinum sheets, with a high-voltage cortical electrode as the working electrode. Cyclic voltammetry (CV) measurements were performed on the then fabricated high-voltage functional electrodes using electrochemical workstation technology. CV voltages are measured in the −0.8–0 V range with scan speeds ranging from 5, 20, 50, 100, and 200 mV · s^{-1}.

4   Discussion

Table 1. Specific capacitance values of samples H-RGO and T-RGO at different scan rates

	5	20	50	100	200
H-RGO	82.7	71.5	60.0	43.6	27.4
T-RGO	75.6	51.8	26.8	16.0	8.6

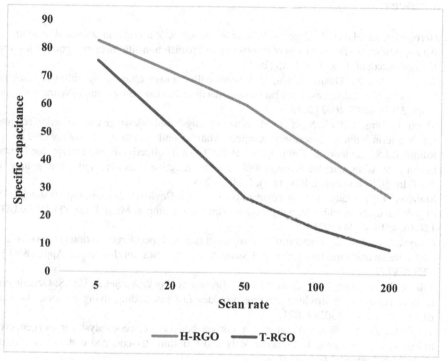

Fig. 2. Specific capacitance values of samples H-RGO and T-RGO at different scan rates

As can be seen from Table 1 and Fig. 2, as the scan speed increases from $5\ mV \cdot s^{-1}$ to $200\ mV \cdot s^{-1}$, the specific volumes of H-RGO and T-RGO electrodes decrease from 82.7 and 75.6 to 27.4 and 8.6, respectively, it can be seen that the H- The capacitance and velocity characteristics of RGO electrodes are higher than those of T-RGO electrodes.

5   Conclusions

From the above research, it is found that the capacitance efficiency of graphene can be significantly improved by changing the preparation conditions. The subsequent experimental research will further improve the oxidation degree of graphite oxide, improve the mechanism of graphene performance improvement, adjust its preparation conditions and select the appropriate dopant. Doping agents were modified to improve electrochemical performance.

Acknowledgements. Project name: Study on field effect transistor based on giant piezoresistive effect of carbon nano materials.

Jiangxi Province Department of Education Science and Technology Program key projects No: GJJ212518.

References

1. Hernández, J.F., Díaz, Z., Segovia, M.J., et al.: Machine learning and statistical techniques. An application to the prediction of insolvency in Spanish non-life insurance companies. Int. J. Digit. Account. Res. **5**(9), 1–45 (2020)
2. Wu, X., Yuan, X., Duan, C., Wu, J.: A novel collaborative filtering algorithm of machine learning by integrating restricted Boltzmann machine and trust information. Neural Comput. Appl. **31**(9), 4685–4692 (2018)
3. Moon, J., Jung, S., Park, S., et al.: Machine learning-based two-stage data selection scheme for long-term influenza forecasting. Comput. Mater. Continua **68**(3), 2945–2959 (2021)
4. Rahman, J.S., Gedeon, T., Caldwell, S., et al.: Towards effective music therapy for mental health care using machine learning tools: human affective reasoning and music genres. J. Artif. Intell. Soft Comput. Res. **11**(1), 5–20 (2021)
5. Mandru, D.B., Reddy, A.R.: A comparative study on Covid-19 cases in top 10 states/UTS of India in using machine learning models. Turkish J. Comput. Math. Educ. (TURCOMAT) **12**(10), 4514–4524 (2021)
6. Sharma, C., Singh, R.: A performance analysis of face and speech recognition in the video and audio stream using machine learning classification techniques. Int. J. Comput. Appl. **183**(13), 975–8887 (2021)
7. Saltepe, B., Bozkurt, E.U., Güngen, M.A., Ercüment Çiçek, A., Şeker, U.Ö.Ş: Genetic circuits combined with machine learning provides fast responding living sensors. Biosens. Bioelectron. **178**, 113028 (2021)
8. Yang, X., Zi, X., Wang, Y., et al.: A porous heterostructure catalyst for oxygen evolution: synergy between IrP2 nanocrystals and ultrathin P,N-codoped carbon nanosheets. Nanotechnology **32**(24), 245402 (2021)
9. Osman, S.M., Elhussein, A.M., Mahmoud, F.O., et al.: Obtained carbon nano-onions from underwater arc discharge without the complex purification procedures. Am. J. Nanosci. **7**(1), 23–27 (2021)
10. Gopalan, V., Vyas, R., Goswami, I., et al.: Tensile behaviour of sugarcane fibre/fly ash/carbon nano tubes reinforced epoxy composites. UPB Sci. Bull. Ser. D Mech. Eng. **83**(1), 181–192 (2021)
11. Hickey, D.R., Juhl, S., Biswas, A., et al.: Cryogenic transmission electron microscopy investigation of carbon nanothreads. Microsc. Microanal. **27**(S1), 684–685 (2021)
12. Shim, J.-J., Mohapatra, D., Dhakal, G.: Carbon Nano-Onions As a Candidate for Efficient Energy Storage and Conversion. ECS Meet. Abstracts **MA2021-01**(9), 499–499 (2021)

Next Generation Ultra-sensitive Surface Plasmon Resonance Biosensors

Arun Uniyal[1](✉), Sandeep Gotam[2], Tika Ram[2], Brajlata Chauhan[1], Ankit Jha[1], and Amrindra Pal[1]

[1] DIT University, Dehradun, Uttarakhand 248009, India
arunavenue@gmail.com
[2] Tula's Institute, Dehradun, Uttarakhand 248011, India

Abstract. This work gives the performance parameters computations using the conventional design of surface plasmon resonance biosensor, which uses Aluminium as the metal layer. The computed performance parameters are 135 deg/RIU for sensitivity, the detection accuracy of 0.571 deg^{-1}, full-width half maximum of 1.75 deg, and quality factor of 77.085 RIU^{-1}. The best things about SPR biosensors are that they respond quickly and can find multiple analytes simultaneously. It can be used to find biological analytes and study how biomolecules interact. SPR biosensors offer the advantages of real-time analysis, label-free sensing, small sample size, etc.

Keywords: Surface plasmon resonance · Sensitivity · Evanescent wave · Biosensors

1 Introduction

More than eight decades have passed since the first surface plasmon resonance (SPR) occurrences were detected in 1902 and the first gas sensing and biosensing concepts were introduced in 1983 [1]. SPR biosensors rely on the interaction of waves and electrons with the material being measured. The coherent oscillation of electrons at the boundary of metal-dielectric is meant by SPR [2]. This occurs when the metal is exposed to an incident wave on its surface. The dielectric constants will determine the propagation constant of a surface plasmon (SP), which shows the property of the structure's metal that supports the SP. Wood initially observed surface plasmons' phenomena in 1902 by utilizing a diffraction grating [3]. After that, in 1968, Kretschmann and Rather discovered that the attenuated total reflection method could be used to activate surface plasmons in a certain configuration [4]. SPR biosensors are frequently used in drug testing, food safety, disease diagnosis, pollution detection, environment monitoring, bioimaging, immunoassay, Bio-chemical sensing, telemedicine, [5–13], etc. More recently, some researchers proposed some numerical modelling-based results for the detection of COVID-19 (Coronavirus) early stage detection using SPR-based biosensors [14, 15]. So, by employing SPR biosensors, detecting various severe diseases at the initial stages is also possible, which is quite a breakthrough in the nano photonics field. SPR-based biosensors have

N. Khare et al. (Eds.): MIND 2022, CCIS 1762, pp. 353–361, 2022.
https://doi.org/10.1007/978-3-031-24352-3_31

been a potential biosensor among optical biosensors [16]. Taking advantage of the change in refractive index (RI) at the metal/heavily doped semiconductor/dielectric boundary determines the amount of an analyte. SPR is a real-world optical occurrence. Evanescent waves are electromagnetic waves steered through the boundary of two different media with unlike dielectric constants [10]. The electric field of an evanescent wave penetrates the adjacent medium and degrades rapidly away from the boundary. These waves are known as surface plasmon waves if one of the two substances is an electric dielectric and the other is metal. Internally reflected p-polarized wave can resonantly excite surface plasmon waves. When a large amount of planar, monochromatic, polarised wave strikes the glass-to-metal boundary in the incidence angle range, total internal reflection (TIR) results [17]. A resonance condition occurs when the wave vector of the evanescent wave and surface plasmon match [18].

The SP wave vector (SPWV) (β_{sp}) in the nanometal layer's surface is assumed using the equation [19]:

$$\beta sp = Re \left\{ \frac{2\pi}{\lambda} \sqrt{\frac{\varepsilon_m \varepsilon_d}{\varepsilon_m + \varepsilon_d}} \right\} \tag{1}$$

here λ = wavelength of the incident light; while ε_m us the real part value of metal and ε_d is the real part value of the medium's dielectric constant.

Similarly, the evanescent wave vector,

$$Kx = \frac{2\pi}{\lambda} \cdot n_p \cdot \theta \tag{2}$$

here, n_p = RI of the prism. The lowest reflected wave intensity emerges at a particular angle of incidence, called the resonance angle, indicating the resonant stimulation of SPs. This is because electronic absorption in the energy substantially reduces the intensity of the reflected wave. In combination with the RI of the metal surface samples, the resonance angle is different with the dielectric attached to the metal layer's surface or with the unlike quality of the same dielectric. Some major merits of SPR biosensors include real-time and rapid detection, label-free processes, and reliability with high sensitivity are preferred when utilizing SPR methods to analyse biomolecules at a cheaper price [20]. Apart from it, some demerits of SPR biosensors include low detection accuracy (DA), high full width, and smaller penetration depth.

There are some detection techniques employed for SPR-based biosensors. First is the angle interrogation approach in which a monochromatic wave source is needed to generate the surface plasmons by varying the incidence angle; second is the wavelength interrogation approach in which a polychromatic wave source is employed for SP generation by varying the incident wavelength. Other than these approaches, less useful intensity and phase interrogation approaches which show the highest sensitivity but call for several high-frequency circuits, are also not popular [3]. The angle and wavelength interrogation approaches are frequently employed in SPR biosensors.

The SPR biosensor system is currently divided into structures based on the coupling system. These types include prism couplers, waveguides, and grating couplers [21], as shown in Fig. 1.

In the grating-coupled arrangement, non-specular electromagnetic modes with varied phase speeds are produced by a periodically corrugated interface of a dielectric substance

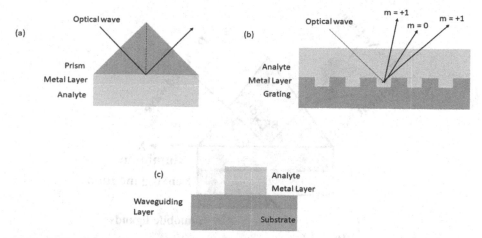

Fig. 1. Different coupling structures of SPR biosensors (a) Prism based, (b) grating-based, and (c) waveguide based

and a metal. In waveguide coupler, many researchers have studied SPR structure as a promising plasmons excitation method for improving the SPR biosensor's performance. For signal acquisition, wavelength interrogation is used in this coupling method.

The plasmon supporting material used in most SPR biosensor applications is gold or silver, with the ability of these materials to easily sustain plasmon modes at visible wave frequencies [22]. However, gold is typically favoured because of its resistance to oxidation and corrosion in various conditions [23]. The fundamental problem is that biomolecules don't adhere well to gold, which reduces the sensitivity of the traditional SPR biosensor. Other noble metals like Aluminium, nickel, and copper can be employed for SPR-based biosensor structures [24]. Although in the literature, highly sensitive sensors are available. As the conventional biosensor shows poor performance parameters, we can add other materials like 2D materials (such as graphene, black phosphorus, etc.) to enhance the performance parameters [25]. Nanoparticles, nanoholes, and metallic nano slits can increase adsorption. SPR biosensors evaluate interactions between protein-protein, protein-peptide, antigen-antibody, etc.

2   Proposed Design and Methodology

The prime parts of a prism based SPR biosensor are shown with the help of Fig. 2. It consists of an optical system which consists of the incident wave's propagation (optical) path made to fall on the prism surface with the source of a wave (He-Ne laser); the biosensor system senses the RI changes of the metal film due to biomolecular interaction between analyte and antibody interactions. Finally, the detection system (generally a photo detector with a computer system) detects the output reflected wave and observes the SPR peak. The whole setup of SPR biosensor must be placed over a rotary base [26].

The proposed biosensor design consists of three layers (Fig. 2). The first layer consists of BK7 prism, and the second layer is aluminum metal, followed by the sensing medium

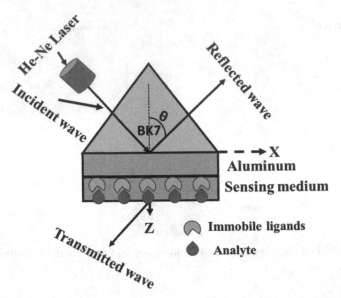

Fig. 2. Proposed Kretschmann configuration based conventional SPR biosensor

layer for biomolecular interactions. A TM polarized input wave of wavelength 633 nm emerges from the He-Ne laser source. The RI of the prism is 1.515 [24]. The Drude-Lorentz model evaluated the metal layer's RI (Aluminum). Its expression is [27]:

$$n_{Al} = \left(1 - \frac{\lambda^2 * \lambda_c}{\lambda_p^2(\lambda_c + \lambda * i)}\right)^{\frac{1}{2}} \tag{3}$$

where, λ_c, λ_p are collision and plasma wavelengths, respectively. Its typical values are 2.4511×10^{-5} m and 1.6826×10^{-7} m respectively. The thickness of the Aluminium layer $(d1) = 45$ nm is taken here. The RI of the sensing medium consists of water with $R.I. = 1.33$. With interaction between the immobile ligands and analyte, the RI in the sensing medium changes to $1.33 + \Delta n$. The Δn gives the alteration in sensing medium's R.I.

2.1 Reflectance and Performance Parameters Computation

An efficient transfer matrix method with no approximations is used here to compute the reflectance of the incident (p-polarized) wave [12]. The tangent fields at the first and last interfaces are related as follows:

$$\begin{bmatrix} S_1 \\ T_1 \end{bmatrix} = Z \begin{bmatrix} S_{N-1} \\ T_{N-1} \end{bmatrix} \tag{4}$$

where S_1 and T_1 are the electric and magnetic field components, respectively, at the first interface. S_{N-1} and T_{N-1} indicates the field components for the final boundary. The characteristic transfer matrix of the biosensor design is denoted by 'Z'. For TM mode, the transfer matrix is expressed as:

$$U = \prod_{k=2}^{n-1} U_k \tag{5}$$

The kth layer matrix,

$$U_k = [U_{11}U_{12}U_{21}U_{22}] = \left[cos\alpha_k \, (-isin\alpha_k)/q_k - iq_k sin\alpha_k \, cos\alpha_k \right] \tag{6}$$

Here α_k denotes the value of optical admittance. It is expressed by:

$$\alpha_k = d_k \Upsilon_0 \sqrt{\left(\epsilon_k - n^2 sin^2\theta \right)} \text{ and phase factor, } q_k = \sqrt{\left(\epsilon_k - n^2 sin^2\theta \right)}/\epsilon_k.$$

where θ = angle of incidence and Υ_0 = wave number in free space.

In case of N-layer SPR sensor, the reflectance is written as:

$$R_p = \left| \frac{(U_{11} + U_{12}q_n)q_1 - (U_{21} + U_{22}q_n)}{(U_{11} + U_{12}q_n)q_1 + (U_{21} + U_{22}q_n)} \right|^2 \tag{7}$$

The main parameters defining a biosensor's performance are sensitivity (S), detection accuracy (DA), the quality factor (QF), and full width half maximum (FWHM) [28].

The sensitivity parameter can be computed by knowing the alteration in the SPR angle $\Delta\theta$ SPR to the alteration in the sensing medium's RI (Δn SM) given by;

$$S = \Delta\theta_{SPR}/\Delta n_{SM} \tag{8}$$

It can be expressed in deg/RIU.

Next, the detection accuracy parameter can identify the biosensor's accuracy. It is expressed as:

$$DA = 1/FWHM \tag{9}$$

It can be expressed in deg^{-1}.

Another important SPR biosensor performance parameter is the quality factor (QF). It is the multiplication of the sensitivity with the detection accuracy of the SPR biosensor. They are mathematically expressed as:

$$QF = S * DA \tag{10}$$

It can be expressed in RIU^{-1}.

At last, the FWHM is the inverse of DA. It shows the incidence angle difference at half of the reflectance. Its expression is:

$$FWHM = 1/DA = \theta_b - \theta_a \tag{11}$$

It can be expressed in deg.

3 Results and Discussions

Figure 3 shows the reflectance plot with respect to the incident angle at RI of 1.33 and 1.34 of the sensing medium. It is to be noted that the dip in the SPR curve signifies the highest light absorption with minimum reflectance. Table 1 shows the computed values of performance parameters (S, DA, QF, and FWHM). The value of variation in resonance angle ($\Delta\theta_{SPR}$) = 1.35 deg.

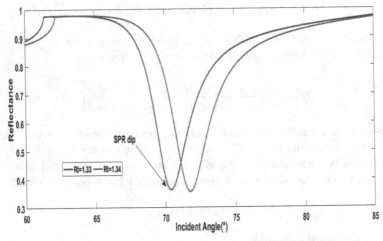

Fig. 3. SPR dips at RI = 1.33 and 1.34 for the conventional design (Prism/Al/ Sensing medium)

Table 1. Computed values for the conventional design

Proposed design	$S\left(\frac{deg}{RIU}\right)$	DA (deg^{-1})	QF (RIU^{-1})	FWHM (deg)
Prism/Al/sensing medium	135	0.571	77.085	1.75

The investigation performed here illustrates how RI affects the sensing medium. Table 2 summarizes the contrast between the current and other SPR-based works. This comparative analysis signifies our proposed work's advantages in enhancing performance parameters like S and QF. All the works considered here are prism based SPR biosensors.

Table 2. Performance enhancement of the SPR biosensor in terms of parameters (Summary) at 633 nm

Configuration	$S\left(\frac{deg}{RIU}\right)$	DA (deg^{-1})	QF (RIU^{-1})	Ref
Prism/Au/MoS$_2$/PBS solution	89.29	89.29	13.13	[29]
Prism/Ag/BaTiO$_3$/Ag/graphene	280	–	54	[30]
Prism/Ag/InP/BP	250.2	0.134	33.52	[28]
Prism/Chromium/ Au/ BP/ 2D Material	187	0.10	–	[31]
Prism/Cu/BaTiO$_3$/Cu/BP	378	0.3839	145.1	[32]
Prism/ Al	135	0.571	77.085	current

4 Conclusion

The conventional (Kretschmann configuration) SPR biosensor using BK7 prism and a metal layer of Al has been studied here. The thickness of Al is considered here as 45 nm. The sensitivity attained here for this conventional design is 135 deg/RIU with a DA of 0.571 deg^{-1}, QF of 77.085 RIU^{-1}, and FWHM of 1.75 deg. This ultrasensitive biosensor opens a gateway for various biochemical applications.

References

1. Damborský, P., Švitel, J., Katrlík, J.: Optical biosensors. Essays Biochem. **60**(1), 91–100 (2016). https://doi.org/10.1042/EBC20150010
2. Srivastava, S.K., Verma, R., Gupta, B.D.: Theoretical modeling of a self-referenced dual mode SPR sensor utilizing indium tin oxide film. Opt. Commun. **369**, 131–137 (2016). https://doi.org/10.1016/j.optcom.2016.02.035
3. Homola, J., Yee, S.S., Gauglitz, G.: Surface plasmon resonance sensors: review. Sensors Actuators, B Chem. **54**(1), 3–15 (1999). https://doi.org/10.1016/S0925-4005(98)00321-9
4. Kretschmann, E., Raether, H.: Notizen: radiative decay of non radiative surface plasmons excited by light. Zeitschrift für Naturforschung A **23**(12), 2135–2136 (1968). https://doi.org/10.1515/zna-1968-1247
5. Kaminski, T., Gunnarsson, A., Geschwindner, S.: Harnessing the versatility of optical biosensors for target-based small-molecule drug discovery. ACS Sensors **2**(1), 10–15 (2017). https://doi.org/10.1021/acssensors.6b00735
6. Neethirajan, S., Ragavan, V., Weng, X., Chand, R.: Biosensors for sustainable food engineering: challenges and perspectives. Biosensors **8**(1), 23 (2018). https://doi.org/10.3390/bios8010023
7. Masson, J.F.: Surface plasmon resonance clinical biosensors for medical diagnostics. ACS Sensors **2**(1), 16–30 (2017). https://doi.org/10.1021/acssensors.6b00763
8. Verbruggen, S.W.: TiO$_2$ photocatalysis for the degradation of pollutants in gas phase: from morphological design to plasmonic enhancement. J. Photochem. Photobiol. C Photochem. Rev. **24**, 64–82 (2015). https://doi.org/10.1016/j.jphotochemrev.2015.07.001
9. Uniyal, A., Chauhan, B., Pal, A., Srivastava, V.: InP and graphene employed surface plasmon resonance sensor for measurement of sucrose concentration: a numerical approach. Opt. Eng. **61**, 1–13 (2022). https://doi.org/10.1117/1.OE.61.5.057103

10. Homola, J.: Surface plasmon resonance sensors for detection of chemical and biological species. Chem. Rev. **108**(2), 462–493 (2008). https://doi.org/10.1021/cr068107d

11. Shankaran, D.R., Gobi, K.V., Miura, N.: Recent advancements in surface plasmon resonance immunosensors for detection of small molecules of biomedical, food and environmental interest. Sensors Actuators B Chem. **121**(1), 158–177 (2007). https://doi.org/10.1016/j.snb.2006.09.014

12. Azzouz, A., et al.: Advances in surface plasmon resonance–based biosensor technologies for cancer biomarker detection. Biosensors Bioelectron. **197**, 113767 (2022). https://doi.org/10.1016/j.bios.2021.113767

13. Hameed, M.F.O., Obayya, S.: *Computational photonic sensors*, June 2018

14. Moznuzzaman, M., Khan, I., Islam, M.R.: Nano-layered surface plasmon resonance-based highly sensitive biosensor for virus detection: a theoretical approach to detect SARS-CoV-2. AIP Adv. **11**(6), 065023 (2021). https://doi.org/10.1063/5.0046574

15. Behar, J.A., Liu, C., Halder, A., Datta, B., Lee, D., Lee, T.: Overview of surface plasmon resonance optical sensors for Covid-19 (SARS-CoV-2) detection. J. Phys. Conf. Ser. **20275**, 012009 (2021). https://doi.org/10.1088/1742-6596/2075/1/012009

16. Homola, J.: Present and future of surface plasmon resonance biosensors. Anal. Bioanal. Chem. **377**(3), 528–539 (2003). https://doi.org/10.1007/s00216-003-2101-0

17. Akib, T.B.A., et al.: Design and numerical analysis of a graphene-coated SPR biosensor for rapid detection of the novel coronavirus. Sensors **21**(10), 1–21 (2021). https://doi.org/10.3390/s21103491

18. Bijalwan, A., Rastogi, V.: Gold–aluminum-based surface plasmon resonance sensor with a high quality factor and figure of merit for the detection of hemoglobin. Appl. Opt. **57**(31), 9230–9237 (2018)

19. Prabowo, B., Purwidyantri, A., Liu, K.-C.: Surface plasmon resonance optical sensor: a review on light source technology. Biosensors **8**(3), 80 (2018). https://doi.org/10.3390/bios8030080

20. Singh, P.: SPR biosensors: historical perspectives and current challenges. Sensors Actuators B. Chem. **229**, 110–130 (2016). https://doi.org/10.1016/j.snb.2016.01.118

21. Yao, Y.: Surface plasmon resonance biosensors and its application. IEEE, pp. 1043–1046 (2007)

22. Karki, B., Uniyal, A., Chauhan, B., Pal, A.: Sensitivity enhancement of a graphene, zinc sulfide-based surface plasmon resonance biosensor with an Ag metal configuration in the visible region. J. Comput. Electron. (2022).https://doi.org/10.1007/s10825-022-01854-4

23. Karki, B., Trabelsi, Y., Uniyal, A., et al.: Zinc sulfide, silicon dioxide, and black phosphorus based ultra-sensitive surface plasmon biosensor. Opt. Quant. Electron. **54**, 107 (2022). https://doi.org/10.1007/s11082-021-03480-z

24. Singh, Y., Paswan, M.K., Raghuwanshi, S.K.: Sensitivity enhancement of SPR sensor with the black phosphorus and graphene with Bi-layer of gold for chemical sensing. Plasmonics **16**(5), 1781–1790 (2021). https://doi.org/10.1007/s11468-020-01315-3

25. AlaguVibisha, G., et al.: Sensitivity enhancement of surface plasmon resonance sensor using hybrid configuration of 2D materials over bimetallic layer of Cu–Ni. Opt. Commun. **463**, 125337 (2020). https://doi.org/10.1016/j.optcom.2020.125337

26. Kashyap, R., et al.: Enhanced biosensing activity of bimetallic surface plasmon resonance sensor. Photonics **6**(4), 108 (2019). https://doi.org/10.3390/photonics6040108

27. Xu, Y., Ang, Y.S., Wu, L., Ang, L.K.: High sensitivity surface plasmon resonance sensor based on two-dimensional MXene and transition metal dichalcogenide: a theoretical study. Nanomaterials **9**(2), 1–11 (2019). https://doi.org/10.3390/nano9020165

28. Karki, B., Uniyal, A., Sharma, T., Pal, A.: Indium phosphide and black phosphorus employed surface plasmon resonance sensor for formalin detection: numerical analysis. Opt. Eng. **61**, 1–14 (2022). https://doi.org/10.1117/1.OE.61.1.017101

29. Rahman, M.S., Anower, M.S., Hasan, M.R., Hossain, M.B., Haque, M.I.: Design and numerical analysis of highly sensitive Au-MoS2-graphene based hybrid surface plasmon resonance biosensor. Opt. Commun. **396**, 36–43 (2017). https://doi.org/10.1016/j.optcom.2017.03.035
30. Pal, A., Jha, A.: A theoretical analysis on sensitivity improvement of an SPR refractive index sensor with graphene and barium titanate nanosheets. Optik **231**, 166378 (2021). https://doi.org/10.1016/j.ijleo.2021.166378
31. Meshginqalam, B., Barvestani, J.: Performance enhancement of SPR biosensor based on phosphorene and transition metal dichalcogenides for sensing DNA hybridization. IEEE Sens. J. **18**(18), 7537–7543 (2018). https://doi.org/10.1109/JSEN.2018.2861829
32. Karki, B., Pal, A., Singh, Y., Sharma, S.: Sensitivity enhancement of surface plasmon resonance sensor using 2D material barium titanate and black phosphorus over the bimetallic layer of Au, Ag, and Cu. Opt. Commun. **508**, 2022 (2021). https://doi.org/10.1016/j.optcom.2021.127616

Author Index

Printed in the United States
by Baker & Taylor Publisher Services